Hi Caroline,

Thank you for your interest in my book & the lectures,

Fred

700 YEARS OF ART HISTORY:

Pre-Renaissance To Modernism

by
Frederick T. Dixon

700 Years of Art History: Pre-Renaissance To Modernism

by Frederick T. Dixon

Library of Congress Number: 2012923448
International Standard Book Number: 978-1-60126-367-4

Printed 2013 by

Masthof Press
219 Mill Road
Morgantown, PA 19543-9516

DEDICATED TO THE ONE PASSION IN MY LIFE GREATER THAN ART

MY LOVING WIFE, MARTHA, THE BEST ART PIECE OF ALL

CONTENTS

Veronese – *Monumental Feasts*
Tintoretto – *Bold Changes in Perspective*
El Greco – *Daring and Exaggerated Elegance in Religious Art*

INTRODUCTION

It was 36 years ago that my wife Martha and I were strolling along the upper east side of NYC. We came upon a street artist wearing jeans with holes in the knees. That was probably the required attire for someone in that end of the art business. Her name was Sandy Finkenberg. I will never forget her because she was the catalyst to the start of my interest in art.

Sandy was selling her watercolors of lions and other animals. As a child, my favorite African animal was the lion so I bought two of them. The price was $10 each and it cost me at least twice that amount to have them framed with a glass covering. It was our first "art" purchase except for a print we bought to decorate our apartment in New Jersey. That was Picasso's rendition of Don Quijote and Sancho Panza that we kept until the paper turned brown and the edges curled up. At any rate, with those purchases, my career as an art enthusiast was underway.

Several years later, I started touring the art galleries in NYC. How I made the transition to that level is still a mystery to me. Eventually, we made our first legitimate art purchase from a gallery on 57th street. It was an oil on canvas "still life" by an artist named James Ruby. Our art collection had started.

From then on we began to follow a steady routine of visiting art galleries, attending art expos (our favorite was the huge art expo held annually at the Javits Center in NYC) and finding struggling artists whose works we appreciated. Vacations in the U.S. and abroad were built around visiting art shows, galleries and prominent museums.

The end result of all this is that our home has taken on the appearance of a small museum. There are roughly 130 paintings and sculptures by artists from 25 countries. We have reached the point that just about the only space left to display more art is on the ceiling. By the way, the lion watercolors are still hanging. They may not attract much attention but they are a reminder to us of how it all started.

All of the works were purchased jointly by Martha and me. I can still remember the circumstances surrounding each piece that was purchased whether from a gallery, at an art expo or directly from an artist. The procedure was usually the same on each occasion. First, Martha and I jointly agreed that we would like to have the piece. Then I would negotiate the price. When we reached a dollar figure that was acceptable, Martha would give me a nod or dig her elbow into my side and the deal was done.

While on the art buying binge, I studied art history and both of us took courses at the Barnes Foundation in Merion, Pennsylvania which has one of the largest collections of Impressionistic and Post-Impressionistic art in the country. It has 181 Renoirs, more than anywhere in the world. Next was a docent training course for both of us at the Barnes. Time flies. Martha and I have been docents at the Barnes for the past nine years. We are the only husband and wife team there and always do our tours on the same day.

Where did all of this interest in art come from? I do not have a clue. I was raised in a blue-collar neighborhood in Philadelphia. No one in my family had any art background. In college I studied economics, not art history. Eventually, I earned a PhD in economics. I never visited a museum until years after I graduated from college. The origin of my interest in art is one of the biggest mysteries of my life.

As you might tell by my comments, art has become the passion of my life second only to my wife. She has been at my side throughout the art adventures. Without her support none of this would have happened. That is why this book is dedicated to her.

There are many great quotes by artists about their profession and by art lovers. Here are just a few. Picasso once said, "Art washes away from the soul the dust of everyday life." I think he was right and that is why I am so passionate about art. Albert Barnes, the founder of the Barnes Foundation said, "If you learn to appreciate art it will enrich your life." I repeat that quote for those on my docent tours in the hope that I can enrich their lives a tiny bit while we are together. Jasper Johns, the contemporary artist associated with the Pop Art movement said, "Art is much less important than life, but what a poor life without it."

In this book, I will try to share my enrichment and passion for art with the readers. Perhaps, by the end of the book, you will be a little more interested in art history. That is my goal. I have tried to write a book that anyone who barely knows what Italian Renaissance or Impressionistic art is about can appreciate and enjoy.

The commentary and visuals start with Byzantine mosaics in the 13th century and concludes with the Pop Art movement in the mid 20th century. Many of the most important artists of the periods covered are discussed. The images show their art and the prose explains their art. Each artist has their own style and their own unique way of seeing the subject matter and expressing it. I hope to convey this. You can catch a glimpse of the beauty of their art through the visuals. But visuals do not always speak for themselves when it comes to learning about art history. The prose will help do that for the reader.

The book discusses more than 60 artists and there are 250 images. Each artistic piece that is discussed is accompanied by a colored photograph. The commentary is straightforward. I have tried to avoid the overly sophisticated and flowery prose that occurs to often in art books. You will not need a dictionary at your side when reading this book to understand the descriptions. When terminology is used that is technical or may not be familiar to the average reader interested in art, it will be explained in the information boxes that appear in a number of chapters.

Many major art movements are covered. But, as you can tell by the book's size, this is not an encyclopedia of art history so there are voids. What is or is not included is a matter of the writer's expertise and interest. The book is best described as a highlights tour of seven hundred years of art.

One of the idiosyncratic aspects of this book is that, along with discussing major art movements over the past 700 years, separate chapters are devoted to Berthe Morisot and Mary Cassatt, Modigliani and Picasso. It may seem odd that equal space is not dedicated to other important art-

ists like, Leonardo, Michelangelo or Van Gogh. There are several reasons for this.

Berthe Morisot and Mary Cassatt are the only female artists discussed in the book. It seemed worthwhile to document their success in a male dominated field when there were clearly biases against professional women. Consequently, a chapter is dedicated to them. Modigliani's art has always held a special place with me because it is so different from anyone else in the modern era and his life was the most tragic. Picasso qualifies for special attention because his art dominated the 20th century and much of it was uniquely inspired by the women in his life. But the overwhelming reason for devoting so much space to these artists is that this writer has developed a particular attraction to their lives and their art in his studies of art history. Hopefully, this personal approach will contribute to the uniqueness of the book.

You do not need a master's degree in art history to understand this book. But this is not an art history book for dummies as many books on various subjects are titled today. It carefully lays out the development of art movements and the activities of the artists involved in great detail. Hopefully, by the end of the book, you will feel like you have that MA degree in art history that you did not need at the start. Most of all enjoy it!

ART BEFORE THE RENNAISSANCE

Everyone knows something about the Italian Renaissance. We are familiar with names like Michelangelo, Raphael and Leonardo and can recall seeing some of the great masterpieces of that era. But art did not start with the Renaissance. What preceded it?

Since one of the purposes of this book is to show how art changed over the centuries and how one movement impacted another, it is appropriate to step back and provide a glimpse of the Pre-Renaissance art. Then, when we get to the Renaissance, the reader will see how art styles changed dramatically.

The contributions made by artists over the past 150 years – the Impressionists, Cubists, Abstract Expressionists, etc. – have certainly been impressive. But when you see what was accomplished by artists in the Pre-Renaissance and Renaissance periods, you realize that the talent needed to create some of that art was truly mind boggling.

The innovations of the more contemporary artists have been unique but so were those of the early artists. It is just that we accept their innovations as commonplace today because they have been around so long. They did not just present the same biblical scenes over and over but the way they presented them and the methods they used changed significantly over time.

BYZANTINE MOSAICS

The Byzantine Empire and the art associated with it spanned approximately 1000 years from the 5th century to the fall of Constantinople in 1453. The period roughly corresponds with what is known as the Middle Ages. It is the art of the eastern Roman Empire or the Christian empire whose capital was Constantinople until it was conquered by the Turks and renamed Istanbul.

When Emperor Constantine moved the capital of the Roman Empire in 323, he named it Constantinople. The two parts of the Empire developed differently. The western Empire disintegrated in the 400s with the invasion of Germanic tribes. But the eastern section of the Byzantine Empire stayed in place for a thousand years.

The majority of the art in this period was created for the Eastern Orthodox Church. The church preferred a somber, reflective tone to the art. The figures appear flat, stiff and one dimensional. There are often lines around the figures to compartmentalize them. Sometimes they appear to be floating with large eyes. There was lavish color and solid gold backgrounds but almost no use of shadowing that would give them a more life-like appearance.

Frontal views are always the case. They have solemn looks often with staring eyes. Faces were usually long and narrow. In short, there was very little attempt toward realism in the depictions. Not only were the figures artificial but they sometimes looked like today's cartoons.

The art grew out of ancient Greece but it had its own distinguishing characteristics. The purpose of classical Greek art was the glorification of man while the purpose of Byzantine art was the glorification of God and Jesus. There were a number of consequences to this shift in emphasis. One was that the classical artistic tradition of depicting nude figures was banished. The classical emphasis on the human body was replaced with figures of God the Father, Jesus Christ, the Virgin Mary and the saints and martyrs that were part of the Christian tradition. These figures become almost the exclusive focus of Byzantine art. There was a complete loss of interest in realistic portraiture. Instead, ideal images of Christ, Mary and the saints became the norm.

Particular centers of Byzantine influence were Venice and Ravenna and a chief form of the art was mosaics. This is the decorative process of creating pictures and patterns on a surface by setting small colored pieces of glass, marble or other materials in a bed of cement or plaster. The result was shimmering masterpieces of gold or colored glass (a thin layer of gold leaf was put between two pieces of glass). This approach was used almost exclusively during the 1000 year span of the Byzantine Empire. By the time the Renaissance occurred mosaics had been replaced by fresco painting.

The mosaics were applied to domes and other surfaces of Byzantine churches. There was an established hierarchical order. The center of the dome would be reserved for Jesus as the ruler of the universe. The other religious personages would be presented in descending order of importance. The presentation was enhanced by stylized poses, gestures of the figures and the luminous shimmer of the gold background.

One of the best examples of Byzantine architecture is the Basilica of San Marco in Venice (fig. 1-1). It was nicknamed the "church of gold." It was originally built in

1-1. Basilica of San Marco, Venice.

1-2. Exterior mosaics of the Basilica of San Marco, Venice.

832. The body of Saint Mark is buried here after being transported from Alexandria, Egypt to Venice. The processional transfer of the body to the Basilica is commemorated in the series of exterior mosaics over the west entrance to the church (fig. 1-2). Note the use of gold even on the exterior. The widespread use of gold was an allusion to the luminosity of the Kingdom of Heaven.

The original church was built in the 9th century for Saint Mark but was destroyed by fire in 967. Reconstruction started and the main core was completed around 1070. Over the following centuries it was enhanced through alterations and elaborate adornments. It is a splendid example of centuries of work by some of the greatest Italian and European artists of the period.

Everywhere there are marble columns, sculptures and 4000 square meters of mosaics all presented according to a complex pictorial religious plan. It is all designed to let the viewer appreciate the varying effects of light on the mosaics at different times of the day.

Figure 1-3 shows why it is called "the church of gold." The 4000 meters of mosaics were developed over eight centuries but most during the 12th and 13th centuries. Venetian art had always been preoccupied with light from the glowing mosaics and later in painting. This is partly because the city is surrounded by light reflected on the water on which Venice seems to float. For centuries the Venetians continued to add to its treasures. But much of the interior marble, sculpture and columns were brought back from the Venetian sack of Rome in 1204 during the fourth Crusade.

Figure 1-4 provides a close-up view of the mosaics. It shows some of the characteristics that were referenced ear-

1-3. Interior mosaics of the Basilica of San Marco, Venice.

lier – flat surface, decorative color, lines around the figures to compartmentalize them. The figures are elongated and have a very artificial appearance.

The best place outside of Venice to see mosaics is in the town of Ravenna. It is on the east coast (on the Adriatic Sea) south of Venice. The greatest development of Christian mosaics occurred there during the second half of the

1-4. Mosaics from Ravenna, Italy.

6th century. The last examples occurred in the latter part of the 7th century.

Figure 1-5 is from Ravenna. It shows Herod's stepdaughter Salome celebrating with the head of John the Baptist. This is a gruesome subject but it doesn't come off that way here. She becomes almost sensuous with a colorful red costume. There is even a slit up the side of her dress. Note the dark lines around her body designed to make the figure stand out. It comes off almost like a cartoon. This is an often told story in Renaissance art and we will see an entirely different depiction later.

In general, the Byzantine artistic influence in Europe was in steep decline by the 14th century. This set the stage for a breakaway from the shackles of the Byzantine tradition first by Cimabue and then Giotto.

GIOTTO AND THE SCROVEGNI CHAPEL
A Forerunner to the Renaissance

When you talk about Giotto, you are talking about one of the great storytellers of art. But storytelling is only one of Giotto's many attributes. His innovations in artistic techniques had no precedent. They moved art out of the medieval period and paved the way for the transition to Renaissance art. He shows common people with emotion.

He uses light and dark to give his figures a more realistic appearance instead of the earlier cutout, lifeless type figures. Giotto adds nature and landscapes to his paintings to give them a more naturalistic look.

He can be considered the father of European painting because he breaks with the impersonal stylizations of Byzantine art and introduces new ideas of humanity, realism and even three-dimensional space. All of these contributions point the way to the innovations of the Renaissance a century later.

Giotto frescoed *Scenes from the Story of Isaac* and *Scenes from the Life of Saint Francis* in the Basilica at Assisi. But his monumental achievement was the frescos in the Scrovegni (or Arena) chapel in Padua. Outside, it is a simple building with pinkish brick. But not inside! The chapel results from the concept of purgatory developed by the Catholic Church. Purgatory can be considered a kind of halfway house where there was the opportunity for atonement before the final judgment. During medieval times it allowed the church to raise funds by working out financial arrangements with the heirs of wealthy deceased relatives whereby the time in purgatory of their dead loved ones could be reduced by the contribution of guilt money.

Scrovegni was a notorious usurer; lending money at exorbitant rates (today he would be called a loan shark). He was listed among the damned in Dante's <u>Divine Comedy</u> because his sins were so grievous. In 1302, his son Enrico set out to rescue his father's damned soul and perhaps the family's reputation by building a glorious chapel.

Inside the chapel, Giotto painted his greatest masterpiece from 1303 to 1305 (fig. 1-6). In the process he became the first of the great Italian painters active in Florence. Over time, he assumed the status of a legend. Depictions of the life of the Virgin Mary begin the series. Events in the life and ministry of Jesus circle the chapel. There are 37 scenes arranged around the lateral walls in three tiers. They start with the story of Joachim and Anna, the parents of Mary. The west wall is dominated by the *Final Judgment*.

The colors are still fresh and beautiful – lavenders, blues, rose and on and on. The deep blue sky provides an excellent background for the figures and settings. Garments hang naturally on the figures. They are often arranged in a way that we, as viewers, have a particular place. For example, he paints some figures from behind. We seem to be observing the event as part of the crowd in the painting.

The figures are not stylized or elongated like those in Byzantine art. They seem to move across the wall at a slow pace that suggests dignity and a solemn event. Men stand in lifelike positions and in groups. You get human looking figures that express human emotions. He sets a new standard for representational painting.

In short, the figures look real compared to those in earlier art. Of course, as you will see later and as art history progresses, they become much less real compared to those

1-5. Mosaic of Salome and Herod, Ravenna, Italy.

of Leonardo or Raphael 200 years later. His art is Pre-Re-naissance but it anticipates the Renaissance.

Giotto's characteristics are simplicity, emotion and narrative. Basically, he has the ability to communicate. As noted earlier, he is one of art's great storytellers making biblical events understandable, not only to the new patrons of art like Scrovegni, but to the masses who could not read. The strong emphasis on the narrative had the aim of informing the illiterate congregations of biblical events. Painting became the poor man's Bible.

Figure 1-7 is *The Lamentation Over The Death of Christ*. There is still the use of gold in the halos but the figures are more human. Most important is the introduction of signs of emotion. They appear in the grief of the angels (note their teary eyes) and the grief stricken embrace of Mary which is highlighted by a cliff that leads our eyes

down to the embrace. The barren landscape refers to the death of Christ. The women around Mary are deeply saddened and the men are filled with pity. Mary Magdalene at the left has her arms upraised in despair, another human reaction.

We seem to be witnessing this event as part of the crowd in the painting. It is as if we are forced to look over someone to see what is happening because a portion of Christ's body is obscured by a figure in the foreground.

Notice the scenery. There is a bare rocky landscape with a dead tree. It adds to the feeling of pain and suffering. There are sad eyes, partly opened mouths, open hands and clasped hands. Each character is different in its own way. We see people who could weep and show pity. Giotto's depiction of the human face and emotion sets his work apart. It begins a new epoch in art.

1-6. Interior of Scrovegni Chapel by Giotto, 1303-1305, fresco, Padua, Italy.

1-7. *Lamentation Over the Death of Christ* by Giotto, 1303-1305, fresco, Scrovegni Chapel, Padua, Italy.

In *The Betrayal of Christ* (fig. 1-8) Giotto expresses the dramatic religious story with understanding and simplicity. In the process, he makes the life of Christ understandable and human for the viewers. Where other artists might have had the figures grimace or gesticulate, Giotto merely uses a glance. The glance (or is it a stare) that passes between Christ and Judas as Judas kisses him is more dramatic than all the waving torches and spears of the arresting soldiers.

His *Final Judgment* (fig. 1-9) would reign as the supreme statement on this matter until Michelangelo gives us his impression of the subject in the Sistine Chapel nearly 250 years later. The details here are very impressive to say the least.

The focal point is Christ the judge. The gold background behind him suggests that Giotto is still adopting the Byzantines' use of gold. The other judges flanking him in a semicircle are the 12 apostles. Above Christ on each side are two groups of angelic choirs led by the flag bearing angels, Michael and Gabriel. The choirs are seated in rows as if they are in a theater.

Below Christ are the four fiery rivers of Hell where the damned are dragged into the abyss shoved down by gray devils. On the lower right is Lucifer tearing apart souls and devouring some. It is a scene of pain and indescribable suffering imposed on the lost souls.

On the left, in contrast to the ugliness and disorder of Hell, is the ascending crowd of the saved. They start with the common souls followed by the clergy. As depressing as his representation might seem, it is almost uplifting compared to the one Michelangelo gives us much later.

The Renaissance might have started right here in 1305 with Giotto's frescos in the Scrovegni Chapel but it was put on hold by the Black Death (or bubonic plague) that hit Europe in 1347. It unleashed an unprecedented rampage of death throughout Europe. It was one of the greatest disasters of European history killing 25% to 50% of the population. Many artists perished. One common belief at the time was that the plague was due to God's wrath caused by the sins of mankind. The church's power deteriorated because it was unable to control the plague.

1-8. *The Betrayal of Christ* by Giotto, 1303-1305, fresco, Scrovegni Chapel, Padua, Italy.

There was a great deal of despair and European culture turned morbid. The general mood became one of pessimism. Giotto's human element disappeared and was replaced by intense piety and art that emphasized guilt and the need to repent. Art regressed to the medieval style for the second half of the 14th century.

IMAGES

1-1. Basilica of San Marco, Venice.

1-2. Exterior mosaics of the Basilica of San Marco, Venice.

1-3. Interior mosaics of the Basilica of San Marco, Venice.

1-4. Mosaics from Ravenna, Italy.

1-5. Mosaic of Salome and Herod, Ravenna, Italy.

1-6. Interior of Scrovegni Chapel by Giotto, 1303-1305, fresco, Padua, Italy.

1-7. *Lamentation Over the Death of Christ* by Giotto, 1303-1305, fresco, Scrovegni Chapel, Padua, Italy.

1-8. *The Betrayal of Christ* by Giotto, 1303-1305, fresco, Scrovegni Chapel, Padua, Italy.

1-9. *Final Judgment* by Giotto, 1303-1305, fresco, Scrovegni Chapel, Padua, Italy.

1-9. *Final Judgment* by Giotto, 1303-1305, fresco, Scrovegni Chapel, Padua, Italy.

THE EARLY RENAISSANCE

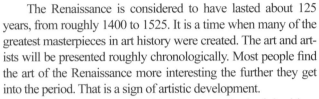

The Renaissance is considered to have lasted about 125 years, from roughly 1400 to 1525. It is a time when many of the greatest masterpieces in art history were created. The art and artists will be presented roughly chronologically. Most people find the art of the Renaissance more interesting the further they get into the period. That is a sign of artistic development.

Renaissance means "rebirth" or a revival of the ideas from classical Greek and Roman thinkers. It is called "the age of enlightenment." It affected all things that had to deal with intellectual inquiry - literature, philosophy, science, etc. Perhaps, most of all, it affected art. What occurred during this period was truly remarkable. There has been nothing like it since, certainly with regard to art.

A major driving force was the economic development that occurred in the 14th century. The prosperous class of merchants and bankers earned their wealth. They were unlike the inherited aristocracy that dominated society during the Middle Ages. As they attained their wealth through their own achievements, they developed an interest in art. Their patronage of the arts resulted in an unprecedented explosion of creativity known as the Renaissance.

The Renaissance starts in Italy and its birthplace was Florence. Since it represents a revival of the Greek and Roman cultures it was logical for it to have its roots in Italy because there was so much evidence of the Roman Empire throughout the region. In addition, much of the ancient Greek civilization was absorbed by the Romans. All of that classical past was concentrated in Italy waiting to be revived.

Why was Florence its birthplace? There is no clear cut answer to that question. Perhaps it was the role of the Medici family who devoted huge sums to commission works from some of the leading artists of the day. It might have been due to chance since some of the great names in art history like Botticelli, Leonardo, Michelangelo and Giotto were all born in Tuscany, near Florence.

When Giotto abandoned the highly stylized and formal medieval art for a more natural and simplified artistic approach, in effect, he became the earliest artist of the Early Renaissance. His successors went on to find more ways to improve their portrayal of the real world.

From time to time, there has been an inaccurate reference to the Low Renaissance and the High Renaissance. This is inappropriate because it implies that one period of art was inferior to the other. There is no such thing as the "Low Renaissance" but there is the Early Renaissance. The difference between the Early and High Renaissance is time and style. The Early Renaissance occurs from about 1400 to sometime after the middle of the 15th century. The High Renaissance then kicks in and it lasts into the 1520s ending with the sack of Rome in 1527.

The Early Renaissance is certainly important but it only begins to show the tendencies in style that would culminate with the High Renaissance artists. It is their work that epitomizes the Renaissance period and it is when some of the most famous artists in history rise to prominence.

GHIBERTI
The Gates of Paradise

Now let's fast forward to the beginning of the 15th century and the official start of the Renaissance. Also, we move from the Venice area to Florence. In a sense, Ghiberti brought to sculpture what Giotto brought to fresco painting but with some important innovations. Just as Giotto's frescos in the Scrovegni Chapel in Padua were the high point in Pre-Renaissance art, Ghiberti's second set of doors for the Baptistery of San Giovanni (St. John) in Florence was a high point in the art of the Early Renaissance.

Ghiberti achieved fame by combining his training as a goldsmith and knowledge of the science of optics. His melding of art and science resulted in the *Gates of Paradise* which was among the first works to apply a scientific approach to perspective and space.

He became famous when, at the age of 21, he won a competition among seven leading sculptors in 1401 for the first set of bronze doors on the north side of the baptistery of the cathedral in Florence. He won the competition with his version of *The Sacrifice of Isaac* (fig. 2-1) in bronze relief (i.e., a sculpture on a flat surface). The baptistery is possibly the oldest building in Florence dating to around 1059.

The entire scene is balanced in its parts and in keeping with the shape of the frame. There is a rock that extends diagonally from top to bottom splitting the scene into two distinct sections. On the left are two servants waiting with a donkey. On the right is Abraham about to sacrifice his son Isaac, in obedience to God's command. Above them an angel appears reaching out to prevent the terrible deed. The subject is very dramatic but Ghiberti handles it in an almost relaxed way.

2-1. *The Sacrifice of Isaac* by Ghiberti, 1401, bronze relief, Museo Nationale del Bargello, Florence.

There are multiple scenes of continuing narrative in each panel. For example, in *Scenes from the Life of Joseph the Patriarch* (fig. 2-5) the episodes are arranged in sequence. On the top right, the first scene shows Joseph being taken out of the well by his brothers and sold to the Ishmaelites (not shown in this image). Below it there is a large circular building where the harvest is being stored in Egypt's granaries to prepare for the great famine predicted by Joseph when he interpreted the pharaoh's dream. On the left, Joseph's cup is found in the bag of his brother Benjamin. Last, above this scene, Joseph forgives his brothers and embraces Benjamin.

Among the great technical advances is when Ghiberti employs the concept of one point linear perspective. It was initially discovered by Brunelleschi, a noted architect and sculptor who finished as the runner-up to Ghiberti in the original competition for the commission for the doors. In using this technique, he brings a new sense of space into sculpture. Linear perspective will be discussed when we get to the painter Masaccio next. Suffice to say that the technique makes the space in the panels where it is applied look almost real, as if the person viewing the panel could enter the scene.

There are other techniques used that contribute to the development of space and realism in the works. In all the panels, the sense of depth is enhanced by the use of gold over the surface of the reliefs. This provides the feeling of a golden atmosphere to the reliefs and it results from Ghiberti's early training as a goldsmith.

Another way he added to the illusion of space is by changing the size of the figures. For example, the figures in the foreground are thrust forward and they are larger than those in the background. As you move from the foreground to the background they diminish in size and height, receding from the foreground. Sometimes, the figures furthest in the background are barely raised from the surface of the relief.

It took Ghiberti 18 years (1403-1421) to complete the north doors (fig. 2-2). The original plan for the doors was to depict scenes from the Old Testament. However, the plan was changed to show scenes from the New Testament.

There are 28 panels with the 20 upper scenes taken from the life of Christ. The eight lower panels represent the four Evangelists and four Fathers of the Church. But this project was only the beginning for Ghiberti.

After he finished the north doors, he was commissioned to sculpt a second set of bronzes for the baptistery's third and last doors on the east side (fig. 2-3). He worked on this project for another 27 years (1425-1452). It represented his finest achievement. The design and subject are different. There are ten larger panels representing scenes from the Old Testament.

They start with the story of Adam and Eve. The nude figure of Eve in *The Creation of Adam and Eve* (fig. 2-4) is among the first sensuous female nudes in the Renaissance.

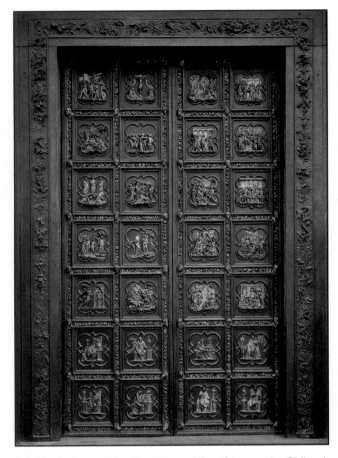

2-2. North doors of the Baptistery of San Giovanni by Ghiberti, 1403-1421, bronze relief, Museo dell'Opera del Duomo, Florence.

2-3. *Gates of Paridise* by Ghiberti, 1425-1452, bronze relief, Museo dell'Opera del Duomo, Florence.

Perfection is everywhere, in the expressions on the faces to the details of the garments. A new era in art dates from Ghiberti. His accomplishments in sculpture match those of his contemporary Masaccio in painting who turned a flat two-dimensional surface into one that looks three-dimensional (see fig. 2-7).

Ghiberti casts buildings, animals and people as if they had been frozen in time. Using sculpture he brought realism, emotion and drama to the stories of the Bible. No wonder when Michelangelo saw the second set of doors he referred to them as fit to be "The Gates of Paradise." That could well be the case. Michelangelo's description has held over the centuries.

MASACCIO

The Magic of Illusion

If the public were to vote on the most important artists in history, names like Michelangelo, Leonardo da Vinci and perhaps Picasso would probably head the list. The name Masaccio would not even get honorable mention.

Few have heard of the artist. Yet, given his accomplishments over such a short time, he deserves to be ranked with the very best.

Renaissance artists were great innovators. That is what the Renaissance was all about: change and innovation. Because Masaccio had a key role in introducing many of the innovations, he is often called "the father of Renaissance painting." He is the first great painter of the Renaissance, yet he lived to be only 27. Despite the shortness of his career, his accomplishments have astounded art historians.

In Florence, Masaccio could study the works of Giotto and he was influenced by him. You can see this in *The Crucifixion* (fig. 2-6). The figures are solid and, like Giotto, there is an emphasis on emotion. However, unlike Giotto, he uses both linear and atmospheric directional light and chiaroscuro, all of which will be discussed. As a result, his frescos are even more convincingly lifelike than those of his predecessor.

This piece is a great example of the use of emotion in his painting. It focuses on the intense agony of three

2-4. *The Creation of Adam and Eve* by Ghiberti, 1425-1452, bronze relief, Museo dell'Opera del Duomo, Florence.

2-5. *Scenes From the Life of Joseph* by Ghiberti, 1425-1452, bronze relief, Museo dell'Opera del Duomo, Florence.

figures. At the center is Mary Magdalene. We don't even see her face but we know she is feeling great anguish. She appears as if she is uttering a piercing scream with her arms flailing upward. The flaming red cloak adds to the feeling of despair. Her body is so powerfully expressive that this is considered one of the most poignant figures in the art of the Renaissance.

The Trinity, painted in 1428 (fig. 2-7), represents one of the great innovations in Renaissance art – linear perspective. It was Masaccio's crowning achievement. Unfortunately, a picture does not do it justice. You have to see it in person. The fresco is 22 feet high and is in Santa Maria Novella, one of the least dazzling of the Florentine churches.

PAINTING TECHNIQUES

This provides the opportunity to discuss briefly the material used in paintings like *The Crucifixion*. You probably assume it is oil on canvas but that technique did not come until later. At this point in time, paintings were done with tempera on panel. Tempera is water based in which ground colors are suspended in egg yolk. It was noted for its durability but it had to be applied fast in a precise manner because it dried very quickly.

Another popular painting technique was fresco. Wet plaster is applied to the wall and paint is applied on top of that. The advantage is that the paint becomes part of the wall, so the painting is extremely durable, almost permanent. The disadvantage is that it is very difficult to work with. You have to paint very quickly because the plaster sets overnight. You can only do one section each day. The next day, when you do another section, the challenge is to match the colors from the previous day in the next batch of plaster.

As already noted, the great technical achievement in this work is that Masaccio introduced the concept of linear perspective. Filippo Brunelleschi rediscovered it around 1420. It was rediscovered because the Greeks and Romans understood the concept but it was lost during the Middle Ages. It is a way of creating the illusion of space and depth on a flat, two-dimensional surface. Masaccio acquired knowledge of the principles of scientific perspective from Brunelleschi.

Nearly every Renaissance artist wanted to be able to use linear perspective because it was a way they could add to the new naturalism of the human figure in art. Florentine painters and sculptors became almost obsessed with it. But Masaccio was the first painter to utilize Brunelleschi's theories and *The Trinity* was the first painting where they

were clearly demonstrated. The powerful effect of the illusion created by an artist in his 20s is astonishing.

The effect of the artistic technique can be called *trompe l'oeil* which means in French deceiving the eye. There are diagonal lines (called orthogonals) receding into the painting. In this case, they are the ribs of the barrel vault. If you extend each of the orthogonals in the barrel vault down in a straight line they will all meet at one point near Christ's feet. This is called the vanishing point. It is usually near the center of the painting.

Because he painted *The Trinity* from a low vantage point, as if we are looking up at Christ, we can see the orthogonals in the barrel vaulted ceiling. Then we can visually trace them down to the vanishing point below. The result was that for the Florentines it was if they were looking into another room.

To develop the orthogonals, Masaccio stretched lines of string in the vault attached by nails in the wall. He stretched the taut string into the wet plaster. The lines lead to the vanishing point below. With close examination, one can still see the imprint of the string, preserved for nearly 600 years.

The lines in the ceiling are foreshortened. This helps to create the illusion of depth. It means the lines are not parallel. Foreshortening works in this manner. Imagine you are looking down a long straight road lined with trees. The two edges of the road will appear to move toward each other and the trees will look smaller the further away they are.

Masaccio would cover the wall with wet plaster each day but only using as much as he could finish in a day of painting. It is still possible to see the overlapping borders of plaster. There are 28, indicating it took only 28 days to complete the fresco, an amazing accomplishment.

Another important innovation by the early Renaissance painters and Masaccio was the use of modeling. That is, shadowing or contrasts of light and dark. It adds volume to the figures and makes them look more naturalistic. It is also another device to add depth. There is a significant amount of modeling in *The Trinity*.

An interesting part of the fresco is that God is standing, supporting Jesus on the cross. We can actually see part of his left foot. Masaccio presents God as a man, not a force or power or something abstract. In medieval art, God is often shown as an all-powerful image surrounded by angels and clouds. Here God looks like a man who can actually walk. It is a good example of the emphasis on humanism in Renaissance art.

Above Jesus' halo is the white dove of the Holy Spirit in downward flight with its wings open, the third part of the Trinity. Below Jesus are the Virgin Mary and John the Apostle. Mary is gazing out at us with a raised hand presenting the Trinity. On the lower level, and what seems to be outside the chapel, the donors of the painting kneel. It was not uncommon for an artist to include the donors in the piece during Renaissance times.

2-6. *The Crucifixion* by Masascio, 1426, panal, Gallerie Nationali de Capodimonte, Naples.

In the last part of the painting, below the altar, is a tomb holding a skeleton which represents Adam. It is a grim reminder that death awaits all of us and that our hope for redemption and life everlasting is through Christian belief. On the tomb above the skeleton are the words "I was what you are and what I am you shall be." The inscription reminds one of when priests say, "From ashes you came, to ashes you will return."

The significance of all this is that the painting shows the journey the human spirit must undertake to reach salvation. That is, rising from earthly life (represented by Adam) through prayer to salvation.

If *The Trinity* was not enough of an accomplishment, Masaccio also gave us what has been called the "Sistine Chapel" of the early Renaissance. In 1424, Masaccio and another artist named Masolino were commissioned by the wealthy Felice Brancacci to fresco the walls of the Brancacci Chapel in the church of Santa Maria del Carmine in Florence.

His work there would establish artistic direction for the rest of the Renaissance and beyond. Artists like Leonardo, Michelangelo, Botticelli, Raphael and most of the important artists of the Renaissance came to Brancacci Chapel to admire Masaccio's work. They studied his ideas about light, color, landscape, the human body and emotion. In short, you could say Masaccio invented Renaissance painting.

The painting began around 1425. However, Masaccio left the frescos unfinished in 1426 in order to respond to other commissions. They were finished in the 1480s by Filippino Lippi, the son of Fra Filippo Lippi who will be discussed later (the names are very confusing). It was probably the first time Masaccio painted in fresco since he started to fresco the Brancacci Chapel before *The Trinity*.

The majority of the scenes represent the life of Saint Peter. They start with the temptation and expulsion of Adam and Eve from the Garden of Eden. The overriding theme is salvation. It emphasizes scenes from Peter's life that are a response to the sins of Adam and Eve.

The Expulsion From the Garden of Eden (fig. 2-8) was done in four days. How do we know? Because restorers have identified four giornate (i.e. irregular sections of plaster) and each giornate of fresh plaster represents a day's work. To complete the fresco in such a short time is an example of the remarkable skill of the artist. Later, fig leafs were added in the 17th century because of the church's concern over explicit nudity. They were removed during restoration in the 1980s. This fresco and the *Tribute Money* are considered Masaccio's masterpieces in the chapel.

Masaccio is concerned with the psychology of humans that had been cast out of Paradise. For the first time Adam and Eve are depicted as real human beings. They show great despair and shame as they stumble blindly out of the Garden of Eden chased by a threatening angel.

Their bare feet tread through the dirt. The fresco is famous for its intensity of grief. It shows the emotional impact

2-7. *The Trinity* by Masascio, 1425-1428, fresco, Church of Santa Maria Novella, Florence.

of paradise lost in their twisted and constricted faces and bodies. Adam covers his face to express his shame and Eve covers up other areas of her body. You can almost hear Eve's piercing wail as she realizes all has been lost. No painter had told this story before with such starkness and emotional realness.

Masaccio's most innovative fresco in the chapel is the *Tribute Money* (fig. 2-9). It is an example of continuous narrative where the story of the tribute money (in the book of Matthew) is told in three separate scenes in the same fresco. This may seem odd to most viewers because we are not used to seeing an entire drama played out in one picture. But the approach adds to its uniqueness.

Christ is surrounded by the apostles. He tells Peter to get the money extracted from those wishing to enter the temple and pay it to the Roman tax collector who has his back to us. Peter follows the instructions of Jesus and is shown on the left taking a coin from the mouth of the fish he has caught in the lake. In the third scene on the right, Peter hands the money to the tax collector.

The scene has a solemn atmosphere to it. Christ is at the center. The apostles gathered around Jesus have a sort of majestic appearance. They remind you of a group of ancient philosophers.

What is remarkable about this fresco is the integration of figures, landscapes and architecture into one piece. There is an impressive wide range of colors in the garments of the figures. Rather than bathing the scene in flat, uniform light, Masaccio was the first artist of the era to use shadows and shade (chiaroscuro) as if they were coming from a single source of light. The casting of shadows on the ground gives a natural, realistic quality to the painting unknown in the art of the day.

Another technique that Masaccio applied in order to provide

2-8. *The Expulsion from the Garden of Eden* by Masascio, 1424-1427, fresco, Brancacci Chapel, Florence. Before and after restoration.

depth was atmospheric perspective. He does this by reducing Peter's size on the left and diminishing the size of the barren trees in the background. Also, notice how the mountains in the background fade from grayish green to grayish white. All of this helps to provide the illusion of depth.

Notice the halos. Rather than have the heads of the figures silhouetted against flat gold circles as was typical for that time, he shows the halo as a gold disk seemingly hovering in space above each head. This can also add to depth. Already, in the short time span of art history that has been covered in this book, we can see how artists were constantly striving to make the scenes they painted more realistic.

His frescos in the Brancacci Chapel became so well known and highly regarded that they became a gathering place for accomplished artists who came to view and sketch them, including Michelangelo. All of this was accomplished by a man that lived only to 27 and was a master artist for just six years.

FRA ANGELICO
Paintings to Inspire Meditation

In this case, I am not talking about the liqueur in a bottle shaped like a monk with a tie around the middle that

2-9. *Tribute Money* by Masaccio, 1424-1427, fresco, Brancacci Chapel, Florence.

some of us have tasted from time to time. I am discussing an artist born Guido di Pietro in 1395. He took his vows as a Dominican friar around 1418. The nickname Fra Angelico came into use after his death in 1455. The name recalls his spirituality as a man and in his art work. He became one of the most important painters in Florence after the death of Masaccio.

Fra Angelico is noted for his paintings of noble, holy figures and beautiful angels in human form with brilliantly colored robes. His paintings are permeated with the sincerest of religious feeling. Piety is everywhere.

All of these characteristics are evident in one of his most celebrated paintings *The Annunciation* (fig. 2-10). He painted this theme many times but this is considered to be his finest rendition. It was painted for the Convent of Santo Domenico near Florence for the purpose to inspire prayer.

The painting presents a solemn and peaceful atmosphere. There is a tranquility about it in the way the angel Gabriel and the youthful and modest Mary interact. Both figures are graceful and Mary accepts the news of her impending motherhood with composure. This is another example of human reaction. It is hard not to be captivated by how the artist paints her face showing such serenity and peacefulness.

The angel with outspread wings bows in reverence to Mary. His wings are brightly colored in gold. The radiant pink of the angel's robe contrasts with the blue of Mary's cloak. Royal blue is Mary's color. It indicates she is the "Queen of Heaven."

There are meticulous details in the piece. Barely visible in the upper left are the hands of God in source of the divine light that streams downward. The dove representing the Holy Spirit appears in the beam of light. God the Father looking down on the scene is shown as a relief sculpture

between the two arches. The entire piece is designed to be a representation of divine and spiritual beauty.

The drama of the painting is enhanced by the architectural details. Here Fra Angelico is influenced by Masaccio's use of architecture in some of his frescos. Also, like Masaccio, he understood linear perspective with the receding arches. Why are Adam and Eve driven from the garden on the left? It is symbolic. Their fall from grace leads to the atonement implicit in the Annunciation.

FRA FILIPPO LIPPI
Reluctant Friar But Gifted Artist

Unlike Fra Angelico, Lippi was a reluctant friar. He was famous for his unconventional life style. Perhaps no one was less fitted for religious life.

He was appointed chaplain to the nuns of Santa Margherita at Prato in 1456. Perhaps, partly rebelling against the discipline of the church, he had a scandalous love affair with the nun Lucrezia Buti. They eloped and she bore him a son, Filippino, who also became a famous painter. In 1461, influenced by Cosimo de'Medici one of the most powerful men in Florence who was a big supporter of Lippi's work, Pope Pius II released the couple from their vows and allowed them to marry.

The annunciation was a popular theme in Renaissance art but Lippi's version is much different from Fra Angelico's. Renaissance artists may have painted the same subject matter over and over, but they often did it in remarkably different styles.

Lippi was perhaps the greatest colorist of his time and it shows in his version of the *Annunciation* (fig. 2-11). He

2-10. *The Annunciation* by Fra Angelico, 1426, tempera on wood, Museo del Prado, Madrid.

was also fond of adding architectural accessories to his paintings. There are a number of architectural elements in this piece.

Both *Annunciations* shown here have lyrical aspects to them but in Lippi's there is a greater emphasis on elegance and decorative detail. There is the marble floor and columns, gold embroidered fabrics, inlaid furniture and Mary's royal blue cloak again. What makes this painting so different is that this is not the environment in which one would expect such a religious event to occur.

Another unusual aspect of this painting is the placement of the donors. As noted before, painting donors into a scene is not unusual in Renaissance art. But it is unusual for clients to be represented within the sacred scene. Remember, in Masaccio's *The Trinity* (see fig. 2-7) the clients appeared outside the scene.

DONATELLO
The Great Genius of Early Renaissance Sculpture

Fortunately, Donatello di Niccolo de Belto de Bardi's (1386-1466) name has been compressed to Donatello. He was one of the great geniuses of the early Renaissance. He participated in the competition to do the bronze reliefs for the doors of the Florence Baptistery of San Giovanni but lost to Ghiberti. From 1404 to 1407 he became a pupil of Ghiberti and was a member of his workshop on the doors.

His bronze relief, *The Feast of Herod* (fig. 2-12) for the Siena Baptistery illustrates the biblical story in Mark. John the Baptist antagonizes Herod and his wife by his criticism of Herod's marriage to the divorced wife of his brother. Herod arrests John. At a feast on Herod's birthday, Salome, the daughter of his second wife, dances for her step-father. Herod is so pleased that he offers her anything. She asks her mother, who tells her to request the head of John the Baptist. Both the spectators and Herod are horrified by the presentation of John the Baptist's head on a platter while the disinterested musicians play on.

In the relief sculpture, Donatello was able to create the impression of very deep space partly by varying the heights of the figures on the panel. Those in the foreground are presented in high relief while those in the background are shown in very low relief sometimes becoming almost invisible.

Donatello shows the presentation of the severed head of John the Baptist in the left foreground of the panel leaving the central part of the scene nearly empty. The result is that the eye is first led past the horrified spectators of the morbid scene back to the prison where the beheading took place and then back to the scene where John's head is presented.

The whole scene is a demonstration of how artists of that era began to focus on human reactions. In the relief, he is able to capture the extreme emotions of the spectators. It shows how Donatello stands out from artists at that time in his ability to capture human expressions and emotions.

Sometime between the mid 1440s and the next decade, Donatello was commissioned to do his most well known bronze piece *David* (fig. 2-13). This was pure sculpture. That is, it was not designed to compliment another architectural piece. It holds the distinction of being the first life size male nude sculpture of the Renaissance. Because of its uniqueness, there has been a great deal of speculation about what Donatello intended in doing this piece. Whatever the answer is, in *David* we are seeing the best of the artist.

The statue draws on the classical tradition of heroic nudity. There is no doubt about the artist's interest in

2-11. *The Annunciation With Two Kneeling Donors* by Fra Filippo Lippi, c. 1440-1445, tempera on panel, Galleria Nazionale d'Arte Antica, Rome.

2-12. *Feast of Herod* by Donatello, 1423-1427, bronze relief, Siena Cathedral Baptistery, Siena, Italy.

emphasizing the beauty of the human body. David is shown holding a stone in one hand and a long sword in the other. According to the biblical story, David killed the leader of the Philistines with a stone slung from a sling. But Donatello does not show the actual weapon unlike Michelangelo's *David* (see fig. 3-14). His foot is on Goliath's head. But you get the sense that he is resting, almost as if he no longer has any interest in warfare.

There are allusions to Greek mythology in the footwear and hat of David. The broad-rimmed low-crowned hat resembles the one worn by the Greek god Hermes, who served as a messenger for other gods.

As Donatello aged, his style underwent a noticeable change where his figures showed even greater emotion. An example of this is *Mary Magdalene* (fig. 2-14). This piece can shock you. It is unlike any Mary Magdalene you will ever see. Although the saint is usually represented as a young woman with great beauty, here she is shown as emaciated with hollow cheeks, a toothless mouth and sunken eyes. Gaunt and boney she has a vacant stare. Her body is clothed only in her own long hair. There is almost nothing left of her.

Donatello is showing her after the crucifixion. She is showing the effects of years of fasting and privation which she has subjected herself to. She is in a state of contrition, almost in a trance, perhaps absorbed by her vision of the hereafter. The physical deterioration from the years of self-denial represent a total rejection of the way the figure is normally presented. It is truly a masterpiece among the images of the Renaissance.

What is the message here from Donatello? Although he is able to show in great detail the extent of Mary Magdalene's physical decline, he is also able to convey a sense of trust in her somber expression. Despite all that has happened, her hands are nearly joined in prayer and this gives a feeling of dignity to the figure. She looks as if she is barely able to stand. Yet, despite the weakness and fatigue, she shows a strength and trust that comes from her profound faith. This is what Donatello is communicating. Religious subjects cannot be done any better than this. No artist of the era could have conveyed so much in a single sculpture.

2-13. *David* by Donatello, c. 1450, bronze, Museo Nazionale del Bargello, Florence.

PIERO DELLA FRANCESCA
The Mysterious Christ

Mysterious and solemn is one way to describe the fresco, *The Resurrection* (fig. 2-15) painted c. 1460. It was painted in Piero della Francesa's hometown of Sansepolcro, Tuscany. There is an aura about this painting, one that is haunting and mesmerizing as if from another world. There is no sign of emotion.

Jesus is at the center of the composition. He is shown at the moment of his resurrection, emerging from the tomb with one foot on the sarcophagus. The atmosphere is one of silent immobility. His eyes are disturbing. They seem to have an aura of the grave. The colors are new for this era. There is the soft green landscape, the pink of Christ's robe and his ivory flesh.

2-14. *Mary Magdalene* by Donatello, c. 1455, wood with gold highlights, Museo dell'Opera del Duomo, Florence.

There is a lot of symbolism here. Christ is a majestic and imposing sight. Behind him is a hilly landscape with the light of the dawn breaking through. To the left is a bleak, bear landscape with dead trees (winter) while to the right the trees are in bloom (spring). The passage from winter to spring suggests rebirth. It is probably an allusion to the renewal of nature and to Christ as a symbol of life triumphing over darkness.

The sleeping soldier in brown armor immediately on Christ's right is a self-portrait of the artist Piero della Francesa. The soldier's head leans against the pole of the banner carried by Christ. This represents his contact with God.

In his essay on *The Resurrection*, Aldous Huxley called this the world's best picture.

BOTTICELLI
Master of Lyrical Art and Allegory

Botticelli (1445-1510) was one of the most important painters of the Florentine art scene and one of the last before the center of art moves north and into the High Renaissance. At the age of 14 he apprenticed in the workshop of Filippo Lippi for eight or nine years. Although he spent most of his life in Florence where he created some of his most popular works under the sponsorship of the Medici family, he was summoned to Rome in 1481 to fresco the Sistine Chapel with *Scenes from the Lives of Moses and Christ*.

Perhaps his most highly complex allegorical piece was *Calumny* (fig. 2-16) painted in the 1490s. Calumny is the act of making false charges to ruin one's reputation. The first thing to notice about this painting is the architectural setting with numerous sculptures. Then there is the mysterious cast of characters. In this piece, as well as in the *Birth of Venus* and *Primavera*, Botticelli is giving us a respite from the religious art of the day.

King Midas with his donkey ears sits on a throne on the far right. He is surrounded by Suspicion and Ignorance who whisper in his ears. The innocent victim of the false charges is dragged before the king by Calumny. Behind her is Envy and Deceit who is plaiting her hair. Rancor is clinging to the arm of Calumny. On the far left stands naked Truth who is gazed upon by Repentance in the black cloak.

2-15. *The Resurrection* by Piero della Francesca, c. 1463-1465, fresco, Museo Civico Sansepolero, Tuscany.

Both Truth and the innocent victim are naked because they have nothing to hide.

Primavera (Spring) was painted c. 1482 (fig. 2-17). It is one of Botticelli's most celebrated paintings. It is also filled with complex allegory but this time much of it relates to Greek and Roman mythology. It is a large piece, 10 feet wide.

What Botticelli added to the art of the day was a new sophistication and sense of elegance and grace. This painting and the next one are examples of that. *Primavera* is like a slow moving dance. It is elegance, beauty and grace all wrapped up into one. The piece has been subject to a lot of speculation about its meaning. Here, we will concentrate on the characters.

This is a painting that should be read from right to left. At the far right is the discolored wind god Zephyr. He is the wind that ushers in spring. He carries off the nymph Chloris who is associated in mythology with spring and flowers. After capturing Chloris he marries her transforming her into Flora, the Roman goddess of flowers and fertil-

2-16. *Calumny* by Botticelli, c. 1490s, tempera on panel, Galleria degli Uffizi, Florence.

2-17. *Primavera* by Botticelli, c. 1482, tempera on panel, Galleria degli Uffizi, Florence.

ity. Now she is able to germinate flowers and you can see that she is already spouting flowers from her mouth.

The central figure is Venus, the goddess of love. She is framed by a bush of myrtle which is her sacred plant. But the foliage behind her head suggests a halo almost as if she is being equated with Mary, at least in mythological terms. Above Venus is her son a blindfolded Cupid with winged sandals. He shoots an arrow at the three dancing Graces: charm, beauty and creativity.

At the far left is Mercury the messenger god. He reaches upward with his wand to hold back the clouds so bad weather can never enter the garden. Everything will remain eternally perfect.

There are a number of sexual references in this piece. The garden has lush orange trees suggesting fertility. The presence of Cupid relates to romantic desire. Even Flora has sexual overtones. The whole scene is overseen by Venus who is the goddess of both earthly and heavenly love.

A few years later Botticelli painted *The Birth of Venus* (fig. 2-18). This is another large piece, 9 feet wide. Some of the same mythological figures from *Primavera* reappear here but in a less convoluted way.

Venus, who is born from the foam of the sea, floats to shore standing on a shell. She is driven by the breath of Zephyrus and Chloris clinging to each other. Both of these figures appeared in *Primavera*. She gracefully arranges her hands and hair to partially hide (or perhaps enhance) her sexuality. A devotee welcomes her with a garment embroidered with flowers. Venus has arrived at her earthly home. Yet, there is something strange here. She looks sad, almost as if she sees tragedy ahead.

Perhaps it is just part of the legend surrounding this painting but it has been suggested that it was painted at the request of a beautiful women Simonetta who was betrothed to Giuliano Medici. She told Botticelli, "I will be your lady Venus and you shall paint me rising from the waves." It is an interesting story and it may be just the type of hokum sometimes invented to arouse interest in a painting. But Botticelli's *Venus* needs no such embellishment.

In both paintings Venus, the goddess of love, has two natures. One has to do with her earthly relationship where she rules over human love. The other is heavenly where she rules over universal love or love under all conditions. In *Primavera* she seems to represent earthly love and marriage. Whatever the meaning of the two paintings, they represent the most tranquil and graceful phase of Botticelli's art and, for that matter, the art of the day.

2-18. *The Birth of Venus* by Botticelli, c. 1484-1486, tempera on panel, Galleria degli Uffizi, Florence.

IMAGES

2-1. *The Sacrifice of Isaac* by Ghiberti, 1401, bronze relief, Museo Nationale del Bargello, Florence.

2-2. North doors of the Baptistery of San Giovanni by Ghiberti, 1403-1421, bronze relief, Museo dell'Opera del Duomo, Florence.

2-3. *Gates of Paridise* by Ghiberti, 1425-1452, bronze relief, Museo dell'Opera del Duomo, Florence.

2-4. *The Creation of Adam and Eve* by Ghiberti, 1425-1452, bronze relief, Museo dell'Opera del Duomo, Florence.

2-5. *Scenes From the Life of Joseph* by Ghiberti, 1425-1452, bronze relief, Museo dell'Opera del Duomo, Florence.

2-6. *The Crucifixion* by Masascio, 1426, panal, Gallerie Nationali de Capodimonte, Naples.

2-7. *The Trinity* by Masascio, 1425-1428, fresco, Church of Santa Maria Novella, Florence.

2-8. *The Expulsion from the Garden of Eden* by Masascio, 1424-1427, fresco, Brancacci Chapel, Florence.

2-9. *Tribute Money* by Masascio, 1424-1427, fresco, Brancacci Chapel, Florence.

2-10. *The Annunciation* by Fra Angelico, 1426, tempera on wood, Museo del Prado, Madrid.

2-11. *The Annunciation With Two Kneeling Donors* by Fra Filippo Lippi, c. 1440-1445, tempera on panel, Galleria Nazionale d'Arte Antica, Rome.

2-12. *Feast of Herod* by Donatello, 1423-1427, bronze relief, Siena Cathedral Baptistery, Siena, Italy.

2-13. *David* by Donatello, c. 1450, bronze, Museo Nazionale del Bargello, Florence.

2-14. *Mary Magdalene* by Donatello, c. 1455, wood with gold highlights, Museo dell'Opera del Duomo, Florence.

2-15. *The Resurrection* by Piero della Francesca, c. 1463-1465, fresco, Museo Civico Sansepolero, Tuscany.

2-16. *Calumny* by Botticelli, c. 1490s, tempera on panel, Galleria degli Uffizi, Florence.

2-17. *Primavera* by Botticelli, c. 1482, tempera on panel, Galleria degli Uffizi, Florence.

2-18. *The Birth of Venus* by Botticelli, c. 1484-1486, tempera on panel, Galleria degli Uffizi, Florence.

THE HIGH RENAISSANCE

The period known as the High Renaissance roughly spans five decades from the second half of the 15th century to the sack of Rome in 1527. It is the period when the ideals of humanism in art reached their zenith. This is exemplified in the works of Leonardo such as his *Mona Lisa* which was a non-religious painting. Also, Michelangelo's *David* that was more human than it was a religious statue and Raphael's study of the greatest artists and thinkers in his *School of Athens*. Often, when the High Renaissance artists painted religious scenes or sculpted religious pieces they were glorifying Man as much as God.

It was a period when major new techniques in painting were mastered or some of the techniques already in place were enhanced. Oil on canvas became the preferred medium in painting replacing tempera. This allowed artists to achieve greater luminosity in their colors. Some of the new techniques included linear perspective, foreshortening, chiaroscuro, sfumato and atmospheric perspective. All of these helped to increase the realism of a piece.

Nevertheless, the masters of the High Renaissance were not preoccupied with simply creating realistic works of art. They had no interest in mere replication. Most of all they aspired to new heights of beauty in their art. They built on the foundations of their predecessors to create some of the most intricate and beautiful works of the Renaissance. They earned greater fame than their predecessors and they were in constant demand.

It was a period from which the phrase "Renaissance man" originates. Many artists accomplished amazing things in different areas. Michelangelo was the greatest sculptor and fresco painter of the era and made amazing contributions in architecture. Leonardo was a master oil painter but did few works. He had little time to paint because he was so busy designing new inventions.

Whereas the Early Renaissance was centered in Florence and largely paid for by the Medici family, the High Renaissance was centered in Rome and paid for by the exorbitant patronage of Popes who wanted to use art to heighten the glory of Rome. In the process, Pope Julius II (1503-13) and Pope Leo X (1513-21) secured the services of masters like Michelangelo, Raphael and Leonardo.

BELLINI
The Father of Venetian Painting in the High Renaissance

Our art history discussion started in Venice with the mosaics of the Byzantine period. Now, as the discussion turns to the High Renaissance, we are back in Venice. In the latter part of the 15th century Venice, which was once the center of Byzantine art, emerges as a major center of Renaissance painting.

As in real estate, location can mean a lot in art. Until now, for the most part, the discussion has centered on Florentine artists. There is a difference between the Florentines and the Venetians in art and a lot of it has to do with location. First, there was a different attitude toward life. The Venetians were more interested in enjoying life and delighting their senses. The Florentines were interested in intellectual pursuits. Because of its location with the shimmering water of the lagoon and constant changing light, color and light dominated Venetian paintings more than Florentine paintings. Venice becomes the city of color.

In general, Venetian artists embraced the oil medium on panel and canvas in their paintings. This made a difference. The advantage of oil is that color has a greater richness and glow to it. You can layer it on. That allows the painter to get more expressive colors. You get darker darks and lighter lights. The paintings become more realistic with a texture to them.

Bellini (1433-1516) brought to painting a new degree of realism. He was the first great Venetian master of the High Renaissance. He remained the leading figure in Venetian art during the late 15th century and the early years of the 16th century. From the 1490s onward, Bellini needed a number of assistants to complete the increasing number of commissions he received as his reputation grew. Venetian masters Giorgione and Titian, who will be discussed later, studied under him. In this regard, he became an influential bridge to the future of Renaissance painting in the 16th century.

Bellini revolutionized Venetian painting with his rich coloring and atmospheric landscapes. But he was also noted for his moving portraits of the Madonna and the Christ Child. His *Madonna with the Blessing Child* (fig. 3-1) is an example of this. The focus of the piece is on the eyes. There is a mournful Madonna. She is protectively clasping the Child with both hands. He is blessing us with his upraised hand but does not look at us. He is looking to the future and the Passion. The

3-1. *Madonna With The Blessing Child* by Bellini, 1460-1464, tempera on panel, Gallerie dell'Accademia, Venice.

death of Christ is represented by the black background. This is a deeply moving piece. It shows how paintings on this subject can vary from artist to artist.

In the *Pieta* (fig. 3-2), he presents a moving scene that is much different from Pieta's done by other artists either before or later. The term Pieta derives from the Italian word for pity. Most Pieta's show Mary mourning over the dead Christ who she supports on her lap (see fig. 3-13). This painting has also been titled *Dead Christ Supported by the Madonna and Saint John.* It is Bellini's masterpiece on the subject.

This Pieta is considered to be one of the most moving paintings in the history of art. The entire scene evokes sadness and pity. There is great emotion in the faces of Mary and Saint John. Then there is Mary's almost pathetic expression. Her grief is so profound that Saint John is forced to turn away. He cannot bear to look at the grieving mother clutching her dead son. The silent emotions are complimented by the masterly placement of the hands.

There is nothing more moving than a mother's sorrow for the loss of her only son and it shows here. The lifeless Christ is supported by the hands of Mary as she rests her chin on his shoulder. Notice the contrast in flesh tones as she presses close to Christ. There is a partial landscape behind them. Above it is the dawn of rebirth. Although it cannot be seen in this image, on the low wall on which Christ is held by the Madonna and Saint John there is an inscription that translates to: *When these swelling eyes evoke groans, this work by Giovanni Bellini could shed tears.* It sums up the painting.

3-2. *Pieta* by Bellini, c. 1460, tempera on panal, Pinacoteca di Brera, Milan.

3-3. *Wedding Chamber* by Mantegna, 1470-1474, fresco, Castel di San Giorgio, Mantua, Italy.

MANTEGNA
Daring Use of Perspective and Foreshortening

More than anything else, Mantegna (1431-1506) was known for his daring use of perspective in paintings like *Wedding Chamber* (fig. 3-3) and the illusion of depth in *Lamentation Over the Dead Christ* (fig. 3-4).

The Castello di San Giorgio was the residence of Ludovico Gonzaga who was the lord of Mantua. The *Wedding Chamber* was designed as a celebration of Gonzaga and his family. Mantegna undertook the demanding commission when he frescoed the illusory architecture on the ceiling. It looks like a porch with an open ceiling to the sky. There are prancing peacocks and cherubs leaning over and looking down from the railings. A plant is balanced precariously as if it could topple into the room.

As lively and joyous as the *Wedding Chamber* is, *The Dead Christ* is shocking and terrifying. Christ is laid out on a slab of stone. It is so terrifying because it provides the impression that Christ is in a morgue. In the upper right hand corner, barely visible, is a jar containing ointment that will be daubed on the body.

Everything in the painting conveys death. There is the pale bloodless body. Christ's hands and feet are pierced

with the holes made by the nails at the crucifixion. To the left is the weeping Mary flanked by two other mourners. Mantegna presents the scene at the eye level of the onlooker. This adds to the radical illusion of depth. The observer is made to feel like a part of the group of mourners.

It is a one-of-a-kind painting, brutal and gripping. This is a long way from the ideal body of Christ painted by most of the Renaissance artists. It may be hair raising but it also shows how the artists of the Renaissance could vary greatly in their depiction of Christ.

MESSINA
Creating A Mood

Antonello da Messina (1430-1479) was born in southern Italy but he was influenced by the art of Venice. Although he painted a number of important pieces, generally he is not considered to be among the top artists of the Renaissance. So, in a sense, including him in this book represents somewhat of a departure. It comes under the heading of "writers prerogative." It is hard not to be impressed by his exuberant color and the effects of the use of light and shade to create a mood.

This is certainly the case with *Our Lady of the Annunciation* (fig. 3-5). The Annunciation was a favorite topic of Renaissance artists. We have seen it before and will see it again. But Messina does it very differently. That is why this painting has been selected.

Mary is interrupted from her reading by the Angel of the Annunciation whose presence can only be imagined from outside the painting. The black background enhances the three-dimensionality of the space. Mary's right hand reaches out in our direction. Her face is calm.

As is usually the case with this subject matter, Mary is clothed in blue. Her oval face is framed by a blue cloak. The ruffled pages of the book and the subtle plays of light on her face, neck and hands add to the realism of the painting. There is no distortion here. This is art in its purest form.

SIGNORELLI
Monumental Frescos

If art enthusiasts were asked to select the most impressive monumental single frescos of the Renaissance names like Michelangelo's *Last Judgment* in the Sistine Chapel and Raphael's *School of Athens* in

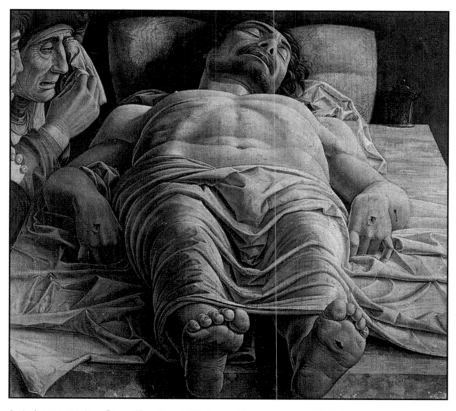

3-4. *Lamentation Over The Dead Christ* by Mantegna, c. 1480, tempera on canvas, Pinacoteca di Brera, Milan.

3-5. *Our Lady of the Annunciation* by Messina, 1476, oil on panel, Galleria Nazionale della Sicilia, Palermo, Italy.

3-6. *The Damned Consigned To Hell* by Signorelli, 1499-1502, fresco, Chapel of San Brizio, Orvieto Cathedral, Orvieto, Italy.

3-7. *The Resurrection of the Dead* by Signorelli, 1499-1502, fresco, Chapel of San Brizio, Orvieto Cathedral, Orvieto, Italy.

the pope's private library would probably top the list. But Signorelli's frescos should at least get honorable mention and, perhaps, be placed alongside those at the top.

Luca Signorelli (1441-1523) studied under Piero della Francesca. He had a penchant for the dramatic that is clearly evident in the two paintings that will be discussed. From 1499 to 1502, over a span of just three years, he painted an imposing series of monumental frescos in the chapel of San Brizio in the Orvieto Cathedral which is just north of Rome. The theme comes from the book of Revelations. Here you see the sights of the last days unfolding before your eyes. The focus is on subjects like the Preaching of the Anti-Christ, the End of the World and the Resurrection of the Bodies. They are beyond a doubt the most grandiose scenes on these subjects ever painted.

The Damned Consigned To Hell also known as *The Inferno* (fig. 3-6) is remarkable for its imaginative representation of the tortures of Hell inflicted by satanic fiends. Signorelli was highly skilled in painting the human body and it shows in both frescos discussed here.

There are no signs of organization as one would expect in Hell. There is a gigantic crunch of figures. Three archangels at the top are driving people down. Demons are in gray and the damned have skin tones. There are nose diving devils attacking everyone. Among the mass of humanity, a women is riding a demon down to Hell. Another demon is ripping a woman apart. The end of the world theme was popular around 1500 because it was the half millennium and that raised the possibility the end was at hand. Also, another plague hit in 1497 that killed about 10% of the population. It turned people morbid.

The Renaissance is associated with the introduction of the nude figure in art but it was gradual. The Church was wary about nudity with the exception of Adam and Eve. But in each of these paintings there is a mass of nudity which was very unusual. These nudes were astonishing at the time. Maybe it was the relative isolation of Orvieto and its distance from Florence that emboldened the artist. Nothing had been seen like it before.

In 1 Corinthians chapter 15, verses 51 to 53 appears one of Paul's most piercing messages:

Listen, I tell you a mystery. We will not all sleep, but we will all be changed. In a flash, in the twinkling of an eye, at the last trumpet. For the trumpet will sound, the dead will be raised imperishable, and we will be changed. For the perishable must clothe itself with the imperishable, and the mortal with immortality.

Every Sunday, when Christians affirm their faith they say, "I believe in the resurrection of the body" which, essentially, represents confirmation of the words of Paul. Signorelli's fresco *The Resurrection of the Dead* (fig. 3-7) represents his interpretation of the events laid out by Paul.

Here order is restored. Two giant trumpeting angels stand in the sky calling the saved from their tombs. The resurrected are pulling themselves out of the ground with great effort. They offer helping hands and gather to embrace one another as if this is a big reunion. Never before has there been such a self-help clinic in Renaissance art.

The rising and already risen are joined by a smaller number of skeletons. Some of those that have emerged already have new flesh and the skeletons are waiting to put theirs on. On the far right there is a group of skeletons laughing at a figure that is in the process of acquiring his new body of muscle. Some figures are posing as if showing off their new anatomy.

The white background sets off the bronze colored flesh and the shadows of the rising and already risen bodies. The blurriness in the middle of the fresco is decay. This is a different interpretation of the resurrection than ever before presented. Typically, the dead are in tombs whose lids have flipped off or there are opened graves. But Signorelli shows the bodies rising through the ground like worms.

The ground is like a kind of quicksand. It is soft enough for a body to pass through and then it closes behind. But in other areas it is hard enough to stand on. Interestingly, all the figures look about the same age, perhaps in their early 30s, regardless of their age at death. The reason is, at that time, the common belief was the resurrected would be about the same age as Christ at his death. There is the same massive nudity as in *The Damned Consigned To Hell*." Even if the church was suspicious about this much nudity, the muscular figures were admired and studied by Michelangelo. Perhaps he imitated them in his *Last Judgment* fresco in the Sistine Chapel.

Now we come to the most prominent artists of the Renaissance whose names are the most recognized. The works of these artists represent the high point of the High Renaissance. There was Leonardo, one of the greatest geniuses of all time. Raphael and Michelangelo, who not only created some of the greatest art masterpieces but also played a part in rebuilding Rome. Titian was the most prominent Venetian artist of the High Renaissance.

LEONARDO DA VINCI
The Great Genius

Leonardo (1452-1519) was not just one of the greatest painters of all time, he was truly the embodiment of the "Renaissance man" because of his interests and accomplishments outside of art. With his infinite curiosity and inventive imagination he was perhaps the most diversely talented person who ever lived.

3-8. *Ginevra de' Benci* by Leonardo da Vinci, c. 1474, oil on panel, National Gallery of Art, Washington, D.C.

THE MATTER OF LEONARDO'S NAME

Nicknames are common in Italian art. For example, Botticelli, Fra Angelico and Masaccio are nicknames and have no reference to the artist's full family name. Other artists are known simply by their first name as is the case with Michelangelo Buonarroti who became known as Michelangelo. It can become very confusing.

Be careful with the name Leonardo da Vinci. It means Leonardo from Vinci, his place of birth. You can shorten his name to Leonardo but you cannot call him da Vinci as is so often the case. Everyone will know who you are referring to but it is inappropriate because you will simply be calling him "from Vinci" or his place of birth. Call him Leonardo or Leonardo da Vinci but not da Vinci.

He was a painter, a specialist in anatomy, biologist, architect, scientist, mathematician, inventor and engineer. He studied optics and was even interested in bird watching because of his study of the basics of flight. He left hundreds of drawings accompanied by voluminous handwritten notes that run from right to left so that they are only legible in a mirror. This is another testimony to his range of experiments.

Perhaps only 15 of his paintings survive because his unquenchable quest to explore new ideas did not leave him time to paint. Also, constant and sometime disastrous experimentation with new painting techniques detracted from the volume of his output.

As an engineer his ideas were far ahead of their time. In effect, he anticipated the modern age. Although few of his designs were developed until centuries later, he conceptualized inventions such as the automobile, parachute, submarine and the helicopter. He did anatomical drawings of the inner head and blood vessels that conform to pictures now shown by X-ray.

His detailed knowledge of anatomy and how light can change in subtle ways were fundamental to his success as a painter. In addition, he had an interest in studying how emotions are shown by gestures and changes in facial expressions. All of these qualities were utilized in three of his most famous works *The Virgin on the Rocks*, *Mona Lisa* and the *Last Supper*, each of which will be discussed.

Leonardo was 22 when he was commissioned to paint the portrait of *Ginevra de Benci* (fig. 3-8). It is in the National Gallery of Art in Washington, D.C. It is the only painting by Leonardo in the U.S.

The portrait was done c. 1474 possibly to commemorate her marriage to Luigi di Bernardo Niccolini later that year. She would have been 16 at the time. The young lady looks sulky perhaps because she was not very happy about her forthcoming marriage. Behind her is a juniper bush which was a symbol of female virtue. This theme is carried over to the back of the painting where the words "Beauty Adorns Virtue" appear.

The bottom part of the panel was removed probably because of damage to the painting. This is where Ginevra's hands would have been. It is a great loss because no one painted hands as beautifully as Leonardo. We will see that in the *Mona Lisa* and *Lady With an Ermine*.

Ginevra has a marble complexion smoothed by Leonardo's own fingers. Her face is framed by undulating ringlets of hair. Behind her are spikes from the juniper bush that give the impression of a halo.

Perhaps most important are the exquisite skin tones and the use of sfumato which means smoky. There is a subtle blending of colors so there is no perceptible transition from one to the other. The graduation from light to dark is designed to make the light more beautiful gliding across her body. Leonardo did not create this effect but he became more skillful in its use than any other artist of the era. This piece shows the advantage of using oils. It helps the artist to get different tones: the smoky atmospheric look to the painting.

This is a study in temperament or perhaps lack of emotion. There is no doubt she is a beautiful young woman but then there is that austere look. There is no hint of a smile in

3-9. *Madonna of the Rocks* by Leonardo da Vinci, c. 1480s, oil on panel transferred to canvas, Louvre, Paris.

Gallery in London. The Louvre piece appears to be solely the work of Leonardo and dates from the 1480s. The London piece is thought to have been painted by his collaborators with perhaps some participation by Leonardo. It dates from shortly after 1500.

Both are large paintings, about 6 feet high and are painted in oil on panel although the Louvre piece was later transferred to canvas. Each is painted in a rocky setting, the source of their name. Such a background setting was unprecedented at the time. The extensive use of landscape represents another progression in Renaissance art. In the foreground, there is an edge to what seems to be a precipice perhaps suggesting the chasm that separates the viewer from the sacred figures and salvation.

There are some compositional differences in the two paintings. In the Louvre piece, the angel gazes in the direction of the viewer. In the London painting, the angel looks down. Also, in the Louvre piece the angel's hand is raised with the index finger pointed at John the Baptist. The London picture shows the angel with his right hand on his knee.

The figures are arranged in a triangular manner. Mary has her arm stretched out and her hand around the head of John the Baptist. Her other hand is above the head of Jesus in a blessing. John the Baptist is kneeling and gazing in admiration toward the Christ Child.

His hands are together in prayer. The Christ Child looks toward John the Baptist with his hand raised in a sign of benediction.

The scene is based on a popular story. Both John the Baptist who is under the protection of the angel Gabriel (at least as identified on the website of the Louvre) and the Holy Family are fleeing to the safety of Egypt to avoid Herod's massacre of innocents. They meet in the rocky desert of the Sinai.

Lady with an Ermine (fig. 3-10) is a portrait of 16 year old Cecilia Gallerani and her pet. It is a miraculous recreation of both of them. It was painted when she was the mistress of Lodivico Sforza, Duke of Milan. It is one of only four female portraits painted by the artist, three of which are shown in this book.

contrast to the *Mona Lisa*. She gazes out at us but her eyes do not connect to us. She seems indifferent. Why? What is she thinking? There is a mystery here that is hypnotic. Leonardo is giving us the essentials of the *Mona Lisa* more than a quarter century before he painted it.

Madonna on the Rocks (fig. 3-9) is a controversial piece because there are two paintings on the same subject that are quite similar. One is in the Louvre in Paris (which is pictured in this book) and the other is in the National

3-10. *Lady With an Ermine* by Leonardo da Vinci, c. 1490, oil on panel, Czartoryski Museum, Krakow, Poland.

Cecilia was the model used by Leonardo for a study of the angel in the *Madonna on the Rocks*. She became the mistress of the Duke in 1489 and bore him a son in 1491. Because of her rather ordinary dress worn for the portrait, she was probably not a noblewoman. Perhaps that is why the Duke did not marry Cecilia but chose to marry a girl from a nobler family.

This painting is particularly important because of the details in the way Cecilia is depicted. She is presented in a three-quarter profile portrait which was an innovation of Leonardo. There is great use of light and the expert use of sfumato as we saw in *Ginevra*. Cecilia emerges from a dark background with her gaze directed at the source of light to her left that comes from outside the painting. With her turn, Leonardo's preoccupation with the dynamics of movement comes through in this painting.

His expertise in anatomy and human form also is evident here. Leonardo was a great painter of hands and it shows in this portrait. Her outstretched hand is painted in marvelous detail. He paints every contour of each fingernail and each wrinkle around her knuckles.

Cecilia holds a white coated ermine (weasel). It is probably a winter scene because the coat of an ermine turns white in the winter. Another great part of this portrait is how she caresses the soft fur. It is expressive color. That is, the color immediately expresses or tells you it is fur.

There are a number of interpretations to the significance of Cecilia holding the ermine. They were

3-11. *The Last Supper* by Leonardo da Vinci, 1495-1498, tempera and oil on plaster, Refectory of Santa Maria della Grazie, Milan.

3-12. *Mona Lisa* by Leonardo da Vinci, c. 1503-1506, oil on panel, Louvre, Paris.

feet. As a departure from other paintings of the Last Supper, Leonardo places all the diners on one side of the table so that none of them have their backs to the viewer. He wanted everyone to see the emotional reaction of all the disciples. Often Judas was placed alone on the opposite side of the table. Or, halos are shown on Jesus and all the disciples except for Judas. Leonardo abandoned this approach. There are no halos not even on Jesus. Instead, there are windows behind Jesus with the light from the center one giving an impression of a halo.

The number 3 has importance in Christianity because it represents the Holy Trinity – Father, Son and Holy Spirit. In this painting there are several references to the number 3. The Apostles are seated in groups of three. There are three windows behind Jesus and three lunettes above the painting. Jesus' figure resembles the shape of a triangle.

The story of the painting is the emotional reaction of the disciples to Jesus telling them "one of you will betray me." They react with anger, shock, horror and disbelief. Typical of Leonardo, it is a study of emotions and gestures. To the right of Christ is the threesome: Peter, John and Judas. John appears as if he is about to faint. Peter is angry and is holding a knife pointing away from Christ.

The key figure is Judas. He is holding a small bag in his right hand probably signifying the silver given to him as payment for betraying Jesus. He is leaning back in the shadows as if he is trying to escape. He is the only one in the group that is drawing back from Christ. The other apostles lean forward. His left arm is extended with his hand over a dish. That is in reference to Matthew chapter 26 when Jesus says, "He that dippeth his hand with me in the dish, the same shall betray me."

Christ is the controlling figure. He shows calmness in contrast to the emotion of all the others. Leonardo was a keen observer of details and the reactions of humans. This piece vividly shows that.

The Last Supper is now only a pale shadow of the brilliant work it must have been when it was completed. That is because Leonardo wanted to experiment with a new technique.

Normally, a mural like this would be done as a fresco. Wet plaster would be applied to the wall and the painting done on the wet plaster. Then the paint becomes intermingled with the plaster. When it dries it is permanent. The problem is this type of painting is limited in its colors and cannot be retouched as the artist works. That was unappealing to Leonardo. Also, the slow pace one has to work at when doing a fresco was at odds with the spontaneity of his art.

Instead, Leonardo chose to take "artists license." He experimented by painting directly on the dry plaster of the dining room wall of the monastery with a mixture of tempera and

pets of the aristocracy and they used their white pelts to line garments. They were a symbol of purity because it was believed that an ermine would rather be captured by a hunter than soil its white fur by hiding in a dirty lair. Hence, there could be a dual reference here: to the purity of young Cecilia and the aristocratic status of her lover.

Perhaps the significance of the ermine in the portrait was more straightforward. Her lover had been installed in the Order of the Ermine in 1488 and used it as his personal emblem. Therefore, the ermine could simply call attention to that fact.

Whatever the significance of different aspects of the piece or how Leonardo painted it, *Lady with an Ermine* is a study in relaxed elegance. It is a captivating image of a young women and her pet. That is what makes it so impressive and why it is such an important work in all of art.

Leonardo painted *The Last Supper* (fig.3-11) on the refractory wall of the Convent of Santa Maria della Grazie in Milan from 1495 to 1498. It is a large painting 15 feet by 29

3-13. *Pieta* by Michelangelo, 1498-1500, marble, St. Peter's, Rome.

oil. This would allow him to use more colors and touch up portions if necessary. He thought he would get the same freedom and flexibility as if he were painting on wood panel.

Unfortunately, the experiment was a disaster. Humidity caused mold to form and the paint began to flake off the plaster not long after it was completed. Within 50 years after it was finished some of the figures were unrecognizable. A series of restorations resulted in large portions of the mural being repainted. Nevertheless, the masterpiece is in irreversible ruin.

If that were not enough, about 100 years after completion, a doorway was cut through a badly deteriorated part of the painting at the center near the base. It was later bricked up. This destroyed Christ's feet.

The *Mona Lisa* (fig. 3-12) was probably painted in the period 1503-1506. It is the most often looked at but least seen painting in the world. The throngs of people that surround it at the Louvre plus the protective shield make it almost impossible to see.

Mona is a contraction of ma-donna that means "my lady." The woman is Lisa Gherardini del Giocondo, the wife of a prominent merchant in Florence. She was 24. Unlike *Ginerva* (see fig. 3-8), Lisa has shifted her gaze boldly to the right so that she looks directly at us as if she is inviting us to return her gaze. This provides an almost flirtatious element to the painting.

It is her direct stare combined with the serenity of the painting that makes it so striking. Also, unlike *Ginerva*, there is no sulking here. In fact, it is the mystery of that bare hint of a smile that has captivated viewers. Then there are the relaxed hands that were a specialty of Leonardo.

Interestingly, the young woman is shown without any jewelry, not even a ring or a bracelet. This is in contrast with most portraits at that time where the norm was to adorn the sitter with elaborate decoration. But then Leonardo rarely followed traditions. Perhaps jewelry was excluded so that her eyes and hands and the subdued coloring would have no competition.

Behind her there is a vast landscape which reinforces the painting's mysterious atmosphere. The winding paths, the blurred outlines of the mountains and the dramatic contrasts of light and dark show Leonardo's expert use of aerial perspective (i.e. a method of providing depth in a painting by making objects look paler and hazier or less distinct in the distance).

Is she smiling or not? That question is one of the captivating mysteries of the *Mona Lisa*. It is why the painting is so haunting. Remember the lyric in the 1950s song by Nat King Cole, "the Mona Lisa strangeness in your smile." It is hard to tell if she is smiling because of the use of sfumato or the smoky blending of color around her mouth and eyes.

The most expressive parts of her face are the outer parts of her lips and eyes. Are they a result of a smile? Or, is the appearance of a smile the result of the shadows? This piece is one of the reasons why Leonardo is so closely associated with sfumato.

Leonardo worked for three years on the portrait and, in the end, kept it for himself. It was with him when he died in France 13 years later. He was court painter for the

French King Francis I. That is how the painting ended up in the Louvre.

MICHELANGELO
Sculptor, Painter, Architect and Poet

In the previous section Leonardo was introduced as "The Great Genius." He was also described as the "embodiment of the Renaissance man." But now we come to his contemporary, Michelangelo Buonarroti (1475-1564) who could also be considered the prototypical "Renaissance man."

Although Leonardo made more forays beyond the arts, Michelangelo's accomplishments in the disciplines that he took up were of the highest order ever. His output in each was prodigious. He was perhaps the greatest practitioner ever of the three visual arts of sculpture, painting and architecture. He was also a respected poet. His accomplishments in painting (even though he argued he was not a painter) and sculpture can be described as heroic and of awe inspiring grandeur.

Most people are aware of his accomplishments as a sculptor and his frescoing of the Sistine Chapel. But they do not know much about his architectural projects. In 1538 he started to design the layout of Piazza del Campidoglio in Rome. Even today centuries later, the Piazza closely resembles his plan.

In 1546, at the age of 71, Pope Paul III commissioned Michelangelo to complete St. Peter's Basilica, a project that was begun in 1506 but little progress had been made since 1514. Although the construction was not completed until after Michelangelo's death, the exterior contains more of his ideas than any other architect. The dome was not completed until 1590, 36 years after his death. Yet it retained Michelangelo's basic design.

This was an era of phenomenal men. When Michelangelo was frescoing the Sistine Chapel, only a few yards away Raphael was frescoing the Stanza della Segnatura in the Vatican with the *School of Athens* and the *Disputa* (see figures 3-19 and 3-18). Both of these monumental projects were completed only a few years after Leonardo painted the *Mona Lisa*. Where have all the great ones gone?

The personalities and appearances of the two great giants, Leonardo and Michelangelo could not have been further apart. Leonardo was tall and handsome. Michelangelo was short and homely. Leonardo was a loner and tended to remain aloof from the fray. Michelangelo plunged into things, headlong. He went about his art with a frenzy of passion. Leonardo preferred to sketch in his notebook.

A fiercely debated topic in Renaissance Italy was the question of the superiority of painting or sculpture. As might be expected, Leonardo insisted on the superiority of paintings as the best and most complete means of creating an illusion of the natural world. Michelangelo argued for

3-14. *David* by Michelangelo, 1501-1504, marble, Galleria dell Academia, Florence.

sculpture. You can be the judge. Michelangelo insisted he received his talents directly from God. Maybe so, because he studied with no significant sculptor and completed his first masterpiece, the *Pieta* (fig. 3-13) at 24.

Pieta means dead Christ on the Madonna's lap. It is hard to imagine that a block of marble personally chosen from the Carrara quarry, without shape, could be turned into such perfection. The details of the muscles, veins, the draperies and the expression on Mary's face are all so perfect. The dead Christ's head has fallen back and his right shoulder is raised by Mary's hand. His arm is hanging limply down. Then there is the colossal drapery on Mary.

There is a serenity and nobility here. But there is also the emotional impact that comes from the broken body of Christ laid on the massive ground swell of the Madonna's cloak. Of all the great paintings and sculptures of the Pieta (and there have been many) this one stands out from all the rest.

The youthfulness of Mary has always attracted attention and controversy almost since it was carved. Michelangelo explained he wanted to preserve Mary's flower of youth so that her virginity and eternal purity could always be demonstrated to the world.

Michelangelo's interpretation of the Pieta was different from those of other artists. He created a young, serene Mary instead of a grief stricken, older woman. But there is a lack of proportion in the piece because of the difficulty of depicting the young virgin with the lifeless body of her grown son cradled in her lap. In fact, if Mary were to stand up she would be more than six feet tall.

But the apparent inconsistencies of Mary's age and her size relative to Jesus are offset by the sweetness of her expression and the soft, ideal forms. Michelangelo meant for the piece to be seen up close and on the statue's own level so the viewer can look directly into Christ's face.

This is the only piece that Michelangelo ever signed. He was 23 when he got the commission in 1498. It was unveiled in St. Peter's for the Jubilee of 1500. He became incensed when he overheard people attributing the work to other artists so he added one more thing, his name going down Mary's sash. After this piece he was unknown no more.

Michelangelo's *David* (fig. 3-14) stands over 14 feet tall and was cut from an 18 foot marble block. Just as Mary is astonishingly young in the *Pieta, David* is more mature than the biblical child-hero. He fuses David and Hercules. In this regard, the powerful hero contradicts the description in the Bible where David is described as a small and slender youth.

Michelangelo broke away from other artist's representation of David. Traditionally, he was shown as the winner with the giant's head at his feet and a sword in his hand. Michelangelo places him in perfect contrapposto (see the discussion, What Is Contrapposto?) borrowing from the Greek representation of heroes. *David* seems to be gathering power immediately before the battle. No earlier Florentine artist had omitted Goliath altogether.

WHAT IS CONTRAPPOSTO?

It is a term that relates to the way a figure is standing. Specifically, it is when a figure stands with one leg supporting its full weight while the other leg is relaxed. The pose causes the figure's hips and shoulders to turn in opposite directions.

Despite the word being an Italian term, contrapposto was created by the ancient Greeks in order to give their statues more natural characteristics. It can give the figure a more dynamic or, alternatively, a relaxed appearance.

Contrapposto was rediscovered during the Renaissance and it became an important sculptural development. It can be used to express human temperament at a particular point in time. *David* is a perfect example of contrapposto in Renaissance sculpture.

David's gaze is entirely new. He stares into space as if he is preparing himself psychologically for the battle ahead. As in classical Greek antiquity, the male nude implies heroic or even divine qualities.

His weight is on the back leg as if he is recoiled prior to action. The tendons in his neck stand out. His face looks tense. *David* carries a slingshot over his shoulder but it is almost invisible. This suggests his victory is going to one of cleverness, not sheer force. Some of the proportions of *David* are not normal but there is a reason for this. He has an unusually large head. Also, his right hand is bigger than the left. This draws attention to the stone he is holding. The enlargements may also be due to the fact that *David* was intended to be placed on the Florence Cathedral roofline, not as easily visible if it were at ground level. Important parts of the statue were accentuated to make them visible from below. But that plan was changed after the statute was completed and it was placed at ground level in the Palazzo Vecchio.

As already noted, Michelangelo's *David* differs from other representations. Compare it with Donatello's (fig. 2-13). In the latter presentation, David is a triumphant hero with his foot on the head of the slain Goliath. But he is not looking down at the fallen enemy. Instead, he seems to be admiring his own powerful body as if his heroic triumph has made him aware of its beauty and strength.

The Papal Chapel was built within the Vatican between 1475 and 1480 by Pope Sixtus IV after whom it was named. The walls were frescoed between 1481 and 1483 with scenes from the lives of Moses and Jesus. Some of the leading artists of the day participated including Signorelli, Botticelli and Perugino. The ceiling was painted deep blue with gold dots to simulate the starry sky.

3-15. *Sistine Chapel* by Michelangelo, 1508-1512, fresco, Vatican.

3-16. *The Creation of Adam* by Michelangelo, 1508-1512, fresco, Vatican.

In 1508, Pope Julius II instructed Michelangelo to decorate the ceiling with scenes from the Bible prior to Moses. But Michelangelo protested because he had never completed a fresco and considered himself a sculptor, not a painter. But the Pope was adamant and his power forced Michelangelo reluctantly into the project. The result was the world's greatest fresco.

It was a Herculean task. He started in 1508 and he completed the project in 1512. He covered more than 5,700 square feet on the ceiling alone. Contrary to popular belief (and the 1965 movie Agony and Ecstasy staring Charlton Heston) he painted standing up, not lying down. He described his discomfort in an amusing sonnet (remember Michelangelo was also a poet). It is repeated below with some editorial liberties taken in the interest of readability. Note that at the end he states, "I'm not a painter."

"Here like a cat in a Lombardy sewer! Swelter and toil!
With my neck puffed out like a pigeon,
belly hanging like an empty sack,
head pointing at the ceiling,
and my brain fallen backwards in my head!
Breastbone bulging like a harpy's
and my face, from drips droplets,
patterned like a marble pavement.
Ribs are poking in my guts; the only way
to counterweight my shoulders is to stick
my butt out. Don't know where my feet are
they're just dancing to themselves!
In front I've saggd and stretched; behind,
my back is tauter than an archer's bow!
Giovanni, take up my cause, defend

both my dead painting and my reputation.
*I'm in a poor state and I'm not a painter."**

* From "Sistine Chapel ceiling" - Wikipedia free encyclopedia. p 2.

The original plan was for 12 large figures of the Apostles. But Michelangelo changed it. There are more than 300 figures on the ceiling. There are no architectural elements; they were painted by Michelangelo. He also painted 29 additional fields on the area of the vault that curves down toward the walls.

The theme on the *Sistine Chapel* (fig. 3-15) ceiling is: God made the world as a perfect creation and put humanity in it. But humanity fell in disgrace and was punished by death. The ceiling shows stories from the Bible prior to Moses. There are nine scenes from Genesis in three groups. The first group shows God creating the heavens and earth. The second group relates to Adam and Eve. The third group is scenes from Noah.

In the first scene, he shows God separating light from darkness. God is shown in all his majesty with arms outstretched. At the center is the creation of Eve preceded by the most famous scene in the group, the creation of Adam. The final scene records the drunkenness of Noah. The sequence on the ceiling has God's earliest acts of creation closest to the altar, followed by the imperfect acts of humanity and lastly God's destruction of all people except Noah. Michelangelo painted them in reverse order.

Why was the *Drunkenness of Noah* the subject of the last panel and painted first? This is where pure speculation comes in. Perhaps, disgusted with the painting conditions, stung by the critic who said a sculptor could not paint and

3-17. *Portrait of a Woman* by Raphael, c. 1515-16, oil on canvas, Galleria Palatina, Florence.

his neck is sunken within the shoulders. The left arm has to be supported by the left knee. His face is expressionless. Adam is not springing to life. Rather, you sense that life is just beginning to stir.

Most of the figures surrounding God are angels but there is one that draws particular attention. She is beneath the sheltering arm of God. It is as if she is being protected. She looks out perhaps a little apprehensively. Who is she? One suggestion is that she is the Virgin Mary. Another one is that she is Eve. But how could that be? Remember that Eve was created after Adam from his left rib. One speculation is that God is holding her in reserve for Adam. God's vision of the future was already in place before he created Adam.

Michelangelo died in 1564 at the age of 89, the year Shakespeare was born. He died in Rome but the people of Florence smuggled his body out and carried it home.

RAPHAEL
Grandeur, Harmony and Serenity

Raphael (1483-1520) was by far the shortest lived of the masters of the High Renaissance. He lived to only 37 while Leonardo died at 67, Titian 86 and Michelangelo 89. As we will see, like Leonardo, he was a great portrait painter. But he is best known for his majestic frescos in the Stanza della Segnatura in the Vatican.

The excellence of his work lay in the special characteristics, the beauty and majesty of his figures. Raphael was most attracted to the style of Leonardo particularly in his portraits. He adopted Leonardo's use of sfumato and his characteristic pyramid shaped compositions. But most people compare his frescos with those of Michelangelo because they spent years working in close proximity to one another. Michelangelo frescoed in the Sistine Chapel and Raphael in the Stanza della Segnatura.

Michelangelo was the brilliant egocentric genius. Raphael was the more ideally balanced painter. Their styles and energy were different. Michelangelo's frescos are representative of his colossal creative imagination. Raphael's are the embodiment of ancient Greek and Roman magnificence and harmony.

Raphael painted *Portrait of a Woman* (fig. 3-17) around 1515. The subject is alleged to be his longtime lover. Women with the same features appear in other paintings by the artist. Regardless of whom Raphael paints, there is always the same amount of incredible detail.

Like Leonardo, Raphael was a superb portrait painter. Her lovely face is framed by the veil. There is intensity in her gaze. Notice the detail of her fingers, something borrowed from Leonardo. There are other aspects of the painting that show the influence of Leonardo. One is the

forced to begin a project he did not want to undertake, a man with the temperament of Michelangelo might have seen the subject of drunkenness as a logical starting point. In that way he could show what he thought of the entire situation. Fortunately, as he worked his temper began to cool. True or not, at least it makes a good story.

The Creation of Adam (fig. 3-16) is one of the most recognized images in the history of art. Perhaps only Leonardo's *Mona Lisa* can rival it in terms of reproductions on posters, T shirts, etc. Nothing like it had ever been painted before.

God is wrapped in a swirling cloak while Adam is nude. Adam's left arm is extended in a pose mirroring God's right arm. Both have powerful bodies. This is a reminder that God created man in his image. The two outstretched hands show the passing of life from the Creator to his creation. This is what everyone focuses on and remembers.

Compare God's life giving hand with Adam's. Look at the difference between the two index fingers, thumbs and the two wrists. Adam's look limp. These may be the two most expressive hands in the history of art and they are within an inch of each other.

Notice the listlessness in Adam's outstretched leg and the weakness in his right arm. His head looks heavy and

3-18. *Disputa* by Raphael, 1509-1510, fresco, Stanza della Segnatura, Vatican.

pyramid shape of the composition. Another is the use of sfumato, the smoky graduation from light to dark that gives an atmospheric look to the painting.

There is perfection in the silken sleeve. That is why it is also known as "the portrait of a sleeve." This is excellence in portraiture. It is as good as it gets. Portraits are not done any better 500 years later.

As impressive as Raphael's portraits are, his greatest achievement was his intellectual history paintings, not about events but about intellectual and philosophical ideas. From 1509 to 1510 he painted frescos in what was then known as the Stanza della Segnatura, now known as the Stanza di Raffaello. It was the private papal library. The *Disputa* (fig. 3-18) was completed first followed by the *School of Athens* (fig. 3-19). The subject of each is Truth.

Disputa depicts the disputing over the true presence of Christ in the communion bread. The scene spans heaven and earth. At the top is God the Father seated above Christ who is surrounded by the Virgin Mary and John the Baptist. Various biblical figures like Adam and Moses are also represented.

Below, flanking an altar with a vessel containing the consecrated bread representing the body of Christ, is a group of theologians and others. They are debating the miraculous change of the bread and wine into the body and blood of Christ in the communion. Among them is Pope Julius II who authorized the frescos, Pope Sixtus IV who is dressed in gold and behind him Dante in red and wearing a laurel wreath that symbolizes his greatness as a writer.

Continuing on the theme of Truth, Raphael painted another fresco the *School of Athens* on the opposite wall. It is considered Raphael's masterpiece and one of the most famous paintings of the High Renaissance. It is the perfect personification of the ancient Greek and Roman spirit of the High Renaissance.

Nearly every important Greek philosopher is represented. Many of the figures have the faces of Raphael's friends and colleagues. In the center, under the arch and on the left, is Plato. He has the face of Leonardo and is pointing to the heavens as the ultimate source of philosophy. Aristotle, his student, is on the right with his hand outstretched and palm down. He is emphasiz-

3-19. *School of Athens* by Raphael, 1509-1510, fresco, Stanza della Segnatura, Vatican.

ing the importance of getting empirical knowledge from observing the world. There is a dignity in both figures, each providing an intellectual presence. Both are holding their books in their left hand which provide the details of their philosophies.

Some of the other figures represented are Heraclitus, a pre-Socratic philosopher, with the face of Michelangelo. He is the solitary figure with a beard looking as though he is in deep thought and, appropriately leaning on a block of marble and sketching. Socrates, with a beard and brownish robe and hands outstretched, is on the upper left. The figure lying on the steps is Diogenes, a Greek philosopher and beggar who made a virtue out of extreme poverty. He is shown with a beggar's cup. On the far right in the background wearing a black cap is Raphael.

This fresco is another example of the concept of linear perspective or creating the illusion of three dimensional space on a flat surface (see Masaccio's *The Trinity* fig. 2-7). But this is an even grander achievement because it is a much wider space with a large number of figures.

OIL ON CANVAS

Fresco was the favorite method of painting early in the Renaissance. But, gradually, tempera on panel began to take over. Finally, the Venetian artists began to utilize the technique of painting with oils on canvas.

One advantage is that canvas paintings are much less costly than frescos and less time consuming. Of course, in most cases they are smaller than frescos so there is less grandeur. Oil on canvas provided greater flexibility. They can be painted anywhere and hung anywhere. Oils dry slowly so errors could be corrected and changes made easily by scraping the paint off the canvas. Most important, there is greater radiance, depth and luminosity in the color pigments suspended in oil.

3-20. *The Tempest* by Giorgione, c. 1505-1510, oil on canvas, Gallerie dell'Accademia, Venice.

3-21. *Portrait of an Old Woman* by Giorgione, c. 1508, oil on canvas, Gallerie dell'Accademia, Venice.

A group of diagonal lines or orthogonals, if extended, converge at Plato's left hand which is the vanishing point near the center of the picture. For example, there are four diagonals that can be traced from the very top of the columns on each side of Plato and Aristotle. There is a diagonal from the side of the short column at the left of the painting. A diagonal can be traced from the right side of Diogenes' body. Finally, there is a diagonal from the bottom edge on the left side of the marble block on which Michelangelo leans.

What Raphael has accomplished is that he has orchestrated beautifully spaced frescos with a great variety of human figures. Many of the figures express intellectual activity displaying a wide range of poses and gestures unlike anything in earlier art. Both frescos are designed to present an ongoing dialogue in basic beliefs.

GIORGIONE
The Enigmatic Artist

Giorgione (c. 1477-1510) was an artist surrounded by mystery. Little is known about his life. What is known is that he died of the plague in his early 30s. Almost every aspect of his work is debated including the attribution and interpretation of his paintings. It is impossible to separate much of his work from his imitators.

Scholars can identify perhaps only half a dozen works painted entirely by Giorgione. In addition, the meaning of his small body of work is usually perplexing. All of this makes him one of the most mysterious figures in the history of art.

We know that Giorgione was a pioneer in the use of oil on canvas and a master of creating mood and mystery in his works. Despite the difficulty in interpreting the meaning of some of his paintings there is a poetic quality to them. Because the Venetian school of Renaissance painting is about color and mood, Giorgione can be considered one of the founders of Venetian art.

Giorgione was closely associated with Titian. He hired Titian as an assistant and, for three years until Giorgione's death, their careers were closely linked. Both were pupils of Bellini. Since none of Giorgione's paintings were signed it is very difficult to differentiate Titian's early works from those of Giorgione.

The Tempest (fig. 3-20) is Giorgione's most important painting. It is also one of the most puzzling paintings in the history of art because of the uncertainty over the allegory. Despite an endless number of guesses at its interpretation, the work still remains an enigma. No one has provided an entirely convincing interpretation.

3-22. *Sleeping Venus* by Giorgione, 1510, oil on canvas, Gemaldegaline Alte Meister, Dresden.

At the right of the painting is a partially nude woman nursing her child. On the left and on the other side of the stream is a man who appears to have stopped to look at her. But our attention is drawn away from the two figures to the threatening bolt of lightening that splits the sky.

The colors are impressive. They shade into one another through gradual shifts in tone. This occurs in the sky and in the forefront of the painting where there is a transition from the brown earth to the green grass. The questions seem endless. Why did Giorgione include the two figures? Why is one fully clothed and the other partially nude? Why aren't they shown together instead of separated by a stream? What happens next?

Perhaps the man is a soldier who is there to protect the young woman. Perhaps Giorgione has painted a metaphor by including the fragile baby as a symbol of the defenselessness of humans against all powerful nature as exemplified by the lightening bolt. Whatever the interpretation of this painting, all of the elements seem to be placed without any logical relation to one another. But that may be the ultimate appeal of the work.

Portrait of an Old Woman (fig. 3-21) has also been called *COL TEMPO*. Although Giorgione was a great portrait artist this is an unusual portrait for him or, for that matter, any Renaissance artist. It is another mysterious piece that cements his reputation as an enigmatic artist.

This is a beautifully painted portrait of an old woman who points to herself while a paper unfurls from somewhere behind her hand with the words in Roman script "COL TEMPO." They mean "with time." The implication being that, with the passing of time, you too will look like I am.

The format of the piece is like many Renaissance portraits. Her body is painted against a black background. Typically, the model would be a particular person who commissioned the portrait. But this does not look like a woman who would have her portrait painted for herself. She looks poor and disheveled. Her skin is weathered and her mouth is open with some teeth missing.

This is not a portrait, at least in the traditional sense. It was not painted to depict a particular person but it was painted to illustrate a point. It tells us that with time I have become and you will also become old. But we don't need to be told that. We all know that is inevitable. So the caption "COL TEMPO" may be designed to divert our attention away from the old woman and back to what once was and to the inevitable loss of youthful beauty.

Sleeping Venus (fig. 3-22) is a landmark work because it is the first example since Greek and Roman times of a full nude being the subject of a painting. In terms of a nude figure, Botticelli's *The Birth of Venus* (see fig. 2-18) is the closest precedent to this painting. Giorgione's piece marked a revolution in art because it served as an inspiration to artists painting reclin-

3-23. *The Pastoral Concert* by Titian, 1510, oil on canvas, Louvre, Paris.

ing nudes for centuries to come. In that regard, some art experts consider it as one of the starting points in modern art.

The piece was painted in 1510, the year Giorgione died. It is an example of the difficulty in determining which paintings can be attributed to him. In this case, the landscape and sky are considered to have been completed by Titian after Giorgione's death. It serves as another link connecting the two artists.

Sleeping Venus is often compared to Titian's *Venus of Urbino* (see fig. 3-25) which will be discussed in the next section along with a comparison of the two pieces. The linkages go even further in that both Venuses led directly to Manet's *Olympia* (see fig. 6-14) painted more than 350 years later.

There are sensual aspects to the painting as suggested by Venus's raised arm and the placement of her left hand. Her sensuality is augmented in that Giorgione places her body across the entire width of the painting and by the red velvet and white satin drapery on which her creamy body rests.

The painting has some of the typical qualities of Greek sculpture such as the idealized long, graceful body. The use of landscape to frame a nude was innovative. The contours of her upper body and the folds in the cloth match the slopes of the hills in the background. Giorgione's *Sleeping Venus* has a dreamy, romantic aspect to it that is enhanced by the use of delicate shades of color to depict light.

TITIAN
Undisputed Master of Venetian Painting

Early in his career, Titian (c. 1488-1576) entered the workshop of Bellini and then worked as an assistant to Giorgione. At that time his work showed a likeness to Giorgione's and he actually completed some of his paintings after his death. After Giorgione died in 1510 and Bellini in 1516, Titian was made the official painter to the Republic of Venice. For the next 60 years he ruled as the undisputed master of Venetian painting.

his becoming the most accomplished artist of the time.

You could almost argue that the golden, hazy sunlight is the subject of *The Pastoral Concert* (fig. 3-23). But that is not the case. The subject is not clear and there has been a great deal of speculation over Titian's intent in the piece.

The mysterious painting portrays two fully clothed men and two almost naked women. There is a shepherd tending his herd in the background. One of the men looks like a musician wearing rich, red silks. The two men seem to be in conversation and are ignoring the women. One of the women plays a pipe while the other pours water into a well. She seems oblivious to the fact that her white drapery is sliding down to the ground enhancing her sensuality.

The subject could be a symbolic reference to poetry and music. The women may not be real but only exist in the imagination of the men adding to the mood of innocence associated with music and poetry. Whatever the meaning, such a poetic painting was new in the history of art.

Originally, it was thought that *The Pastoral Concert* was a Giorgione-Titian collaboration. But later the work was credited to Titian. It is another piece that has been imitated by other masters. In 1863, after seeing it at the Louvre, Manet used the piece as an inspiration for his *Le Dejeuner sur l'Herbe* or The Luncheon on the Grass (see fig. 6-13).

The Assumption of the Virgin (fig. 3-24) brought many of the aspects of High Renaissance art to Venice. Nothing like it had been seen before by Venetians. On August 15 of every year the Assumption of Mary is celebrated by the Catholic Church. It commemorates the rising of Mary to heaven. Titian's painting relates to that event.

The majesty of the scene, the color and colossal size of the 23 foot high painting plus the drama of Mary rising up to her maker were all new to Venetians. The event unfolds on three levels. At the bottom are the Apostles who have their hands raised toward the sky, except for Peter whose arms are folded. There is a mixture of awe and wonder among them. In the middle level, Mary is standing on an illuminated cloud surrounded by a swarm of winged cherubs. She is wrapped in a red robe and blue cloak. At the top level are God the Father and an angel carrying the Holy Crown of Glory to honor Mary. The golden brown color of the background may represent a tribute to

3-24. *The Assumption of the Virgin* by Titian, 1516-1518, oil on panel, Basilica di Santa Maria Gloriosa del Frari, Venice.

Titian was a master of color and light often achieving a dramatic effect. Through the use of these means he defined Venetian art. He was the most versatile painter of the era. He was a true magician of portraiture but he could easily move adeptly into religious and mythological subjects, simple and allegorical themes and the use of landscape backgrounds. All of this adaptability translated into

3-25. *The Venus of Urbino* by Titian, c. 1538, oil on canvas, Uffizi, Florence.

3-26. *Penitent Magdalene* by Titian, c. 1565, oil on canvas, Hermitage Museum, Saint Petersburg, Russia.

the tradition of Venetian mosaics. Early on in his career, Titian was trained in mosaics.

Mary's upward movement toward God is amplified in her arm gestures, the flow of her drapery and the direction of her gaze. Her eyes are focused on God. Titian uses unnatural light to provide a supernatural aura. The light at the top seems to come from within the painting. It casts no shadow. It is the glow of heavenly light.

There is a lot of movement here. The Virgin seems to swirl upward toward the airborne God who is also in motion. The Assumption was traditionally painted in a more static manner with Mary carried passively to heaven. Red is used to direct the viewer's eye both to Mary and to God. In Christian symbolism, when worn by the virgin, red is the emblem of lifeblood. Two Apostles at the bottom along with the Virgin's red dress create a triangle of red that points up to God who is also partially clad in red.

There is a distinction between the ascension of Jesus and the assumption of Mary. Jesus rises up under his own power. But the assumption means that someone else is helping to raise Mary up to heaven.

The *Venus of Urbino* (figure 3-25) is a patently erotic painting. It is one of the sexiest paintings ever. Although it is titled Venus, she has only one

ment" by Pope Paul III. It was felt this was a more suitable subject for the 1530s given the turmoil created by the Counter-Reformation. It would serve as a reminder to all that, ultimately, they would be judged for their deeds.

When completed, unlike the frescos on the Sistine Chapel ceiling, the *Last Judgment* was subject to a great deal of controversy. The overall structure of the piece was a departure from previous works on the same subject. Typically, there would be three horizontal planes depicting heaven, earth and hell. But in Michelangelo's version, everything is swirling around. Christ is at the center. There is a whirl of bodies around him. Traditionally, the saved were neatly separated from the damned. In this case, there is a swarm of rising and falling figures.

The biggest dispute was over the nudity of some of the figures. One critic closely associated with the pope called the fresco "indecent" and "disgraceful." This led to a decision in 1564 shortly after Michelangelo died to have breeches painted over the private parts of figures considered obscene. Over the next two centuries more were added but some were removed during the restoration in 1994.

The project started nearly a decade after the seven month sack of Rome that rendered the city desolate and effectively ended the High Renaissance. Because of the shift in confidence, nothing could be in greater contrast between the *Last Judgment* and the frescos done on the ceiling 25 years earlier. The weight of pessimism is felt in every detail.

For the most part, the painting conforms to the basics of the new Mannerist artistic style. The fresco is a far cry from the beauty and balance of the High Renaissance. There is a crowd of desperate and tormented figures many with unusual poses, exaggerated gestures and expressions. All in all, the painting comes off strange and unsettling. All of this is characteristic of Mannerism.

At the center is Christ the judge with his left arm compelling the damned to the underworld and his right arm lifting the saved to heaven. But Christ the judge looks powerful and vengeful, not the normal image we would expect to see from a usually compassionate Christ. A shrinking Mary sits next to him. She looks shy and turns away perhaps as a gesture of resignation because she cannot intervene in the decision. This is another departure. Traditionally, Mary would sit enthroned beside Christ and equal in size to him. On the left, the powerfully built figure gazing over at Christ is John the Baptist.

The two large figures below Christ on the left and right are Paul and Peter who holds the golden key to heaven. Peter's face is a portrait of Pope Paul III. All around Christ is the continuing swirl of frantic bodies. Above Mary and Jesus are two lunettes filled with symbols from the Passion such as the cross and crown of thorns.

At the lower center, angels are sounding trumpets to awaken the dead. The archangel Michael reads from a book of souls to be saved. The large book on the right contains a list of the damned destined for hell. The book on the left is much smaller. It contains the names of the saved. At the bottom left the saved are rising up from their graves but with great effort. They do not look much different from the damned on the right. It looks like a titanic struggle for anyone to get into heaven.

At the bottom right is Charon with an oar raised up. His devils are forcing the damned toward Minos, the judge of the underground. Charon is the boatman from Greek and Roman mythology who ferried the damned to hell. He is featured in Dante's <u>Divine Comedy</u> that was an inspiration to Michelangelo for the fresco.

Minos, who is also from Greek mythology, has the face of Biagio da Cesena who was highly critical of the fresco and stated it was not work fit for a papal chapel. He is portrayed with donkey ears and his naked body is covered by a coiled snake. The serpent is biting at his genitals. Cardinal Biagio complained to the Pope about his representation in the fresco but the pontiff explained he had no jurisdiction over hell and the portrait should remain. With this portrayal, Michelangelo gained his pound of flesh on his most vehement critic.

To the right of Christ's feet is Saint Bartholomew who was martyred by being skinned alive. Here the artist himself is presented in a terrifying way. Saint Bartholomew holds the knife of his martyrdom in his right hand and his own flayed skin in the left. The face of Michelangelo is on the skin. This may have been Michelangelo's attempt to show his personal involvement in the agonizing representation of judgment day given all the tension and conflict that was occurring within the Catholic Church.

On the lower right, just above those being ferried to the underworld, there is a single figure. He has one eye starring is stark horror while the other is covered with his hand as demons drag him into hell. Compare this image of despair and damnation with the optimism on the ceiling of the Sistine Chapel and *The Creation of Adam* (see fig. 3-16) where a potential life is about to be fused with life's force from God. It is an example of how much things changed in 25 years.

The human detail in the *Last Judgment* is mind boggling!

PARMIGIANINO
Elegant Mannerism

Thank goodness for nicknames. Girolamo Francesco Maria Mazzola is commonly known as Parmigianino which means "the little one from Parma." He was one of the first artists to develop an elegant and sophisticated version of Mannerism.

Although the *Last Judgment* has Manneristic aspects, a full-fledged example of Mannerism is shown in Parmigianino's *Madonna With The Long Neck* (fig. 4-2). In this

4-2. *Madonna With The Long Neck* by Parmigianino, c. 1535-1540, oil on panel, Uffizi, Florence.

piece he set out to create an unorthodox painting. He wanted to show that when earlier artists like Leonardo and Raphael strove to achieve harmony and exceptional realism in their art that was not the only approach one could take. He deliberately tried to create something different and unexpected. Parmigianino succeeded on all accounts and this became his most famous and representational painting.

The Madonna portrayed is not even close to normal human proportions. She sits on a high pedestal. Her elongated neck, exceptionally long fingers, narrow shoulders and massive legs are all very prominent. In effect, her body shape resembles the vase being held by an angle on her right. She is about twice the size of the angels next to her. Even the baby Jesus is extremely large. He lies precariously on Mary's lap as if he could tumble off. One arm dangles down giving the mother and child the appearance of the Pieta.

Yet, there are aspects of the painting designed to make the Madonna elegant and sophisticated. The colors are

vivid. She appears relaxed. There is her ivory complexion and her hair is curled and decorated with pearls. Her robes are luxurious. Of course, these types of adornments are not typical for Madonna but they represent another departure consistent with Mannerism.

Parmigianino develops unusual special effects. Instead of distributing the figures evenly across the panel, the angels adoring the Christ child are gathered claustrophobically next to Mary. The disproportional presentation continues to the right. The architecture looks strange with a long column that leads nowhere. But perhaps that is in reference to some medieval hymns that compared Mary's neck to a great ivory tower. Next to the tower in the lower right hand corner of the painting is the prophet Saint Jerome holding a scroll. He is reduced in size so that he barely reaches the Madonna's knee.

VERONESE
Monumental Feasts

Paolo Veronese (1528-88) was a member of the Venetian school of painters along with Titian and Tintoretto. He became the dominate artist after the death of Titian. He was perhaps the greatest decorative artist of his generation. Rather than paint traditional religious scenes such as incidents from the Passion or the life of the Virgin Mary he had a penchant for depicting scenes of biblical feasts. But as much as he was interested in interpreting the event that was laid out in the Bible, he also paid tribute to the grandeur of life in Venice at the time.

Magnificent architecture including marble columns and lavish costumes of silk and satin would be featured in the paintings. Unlike the works of other artists at that time, you do not come away with deeply pious feelings after viewing Veronese's paintings. Rather, you are impressed by the grandeur.

There are many styles of Mannerism and Veronese's is much different from Parmigianino's. His massive *Feast in the House of Levi* (fig. 4-3) is an example. It is a work of great theatrical sweep. It incorporates the drama and color of the Mannerist's style but on a much larger scale. The figures have lavish costumes and there is a great diversity of poses. Figures are crowded into three separate spaces framed by huge, elegant arches. The architectural backdrop recalls sets used in the theater. In fact, at first glance the subject of the painting seems to be the architecture with the figures being secondary.

The painting is one of the largest canvases of the 16th century measuring 18 x 42 feet. The commission from the Dominican order of SS. Giovanni Paolo was to paint the last supper for their dining hall. Instead, Veronese painted a huge banquet scene unlike the episode described in the Bible. Needless to say, it was also unlike anything that had been done before on this subject matter.

4-3. *Feast at the House of Levi* by Veronese, 1573, oil on canvas, Louvre, Paris.

4-4. *The Wedding at Cana* by Veronese, 1562-1563, oil on canvas, Louvre, Paris.

Christ is at the center with a halo above his head. But church officials were shocked by the rest of the presentation. Their criticism was that the work did not show the proper respect for such a sacred subject. The Inquisition of 1542 had given new papal authority. The church had the job of investigating departures from doctrine, including those in art.

Veronese was called to account for his painting. He was asked to explain why he included such details as a man picking his teeth, dwarfs, scruffy dogs, a parrot on a buffoon's wrist and drunken Germans. His response was, "It is large and it seemed to me, it could hold many figures." Not surprisingly, his defense fell on unsympathetic ears. He was ordered to make changes but he made only one. He changed the name from "The Last Supper" to *Feast in the House of Levi*. He justified this by saying it was still a biblical scene. The new source was Luke 5:29, "Then Levi held a great banquet for Jesus in his house and a large crowd of tax collectors and others were eating with him."

Veronese's *The Wedding at Cana* (fig. 4-4) is another painting that has great theatrical sweep. Pictures in an art book can help inspire one's appreciation for art. Perhaps they will encourage readers to travel and see some of the works in person. That is one of the purposes of this book. But in many cases there is no substitute for seeing the art first hand. *The Wedding at Cana* is a perfect example of that (as is *Feast in the House of Levi*).

The first thing to consider is the detail of the more than 130 figures in the painting. Second, there is the lavish color. Finally, it is impossible to appreciate the work in a picture because it is 30 feet wide. Some of the figures in the foreground are actually life-size. This gives you some idea of the scale of the painting. There is great use of foreshortening. The figures become smaller in the center behind the railing giving a sense of depth to the work.

The theme of the painting comes from John chapter two. It tells the story of the first miracle performed by Jesus, the making of wine from water in Cana, Galilee. While attending a wedding with his disciples, Jesus commanded servants to fill jugs with water and then he turned the water into wine. On the lower right there is a man pouring wine from a large jug. Next to him is a man standing and studying the wine in a glass. On the far left is a seated man being offered wine by a dark skinned boy.

In addition to the crunch of people in the work, the architectural elements are impressive. The crowd of figures in the foreground is flanked by two sets of stairs that lead to a terrace that is framed by huge Roman colonnades. In the background is a brilliant blue sky. All of this shows the decorative and narrative genius of the artist.

At the table, Jesus is seated with Mary. Both have halos. Jesus looks straight ahead impassively at the viewer. Seated prominently in the front are three musicians. On the left in a white robe is Veronese on viola. Tintoretto is in the center on violin and on the right, dressed in red, is Titian on base. In the front of the musicians is an hourglass. All of these details are a showcase for the artist. They are also designed to show there are everyday pleasures to enjoy such as music but there is a reminder of mortality in the hourglass.

Above Jesus, on the balcony, are men butchering meat. On the left more meat is being brought in. Art historians have suggested that the meat is lamb. If that is the case, since Jesus is the sacrificed "Lamb of God" than the butchered lamb is symbolic of his future sacrifice. This is confirmed by Jesus being seated directly under the blade held by the man doing the cutting.

Like the *Feast at the House of Levi* this is a monumental painting with an incredible amount of detail. You can see it at the Louvre in Paris.

TINTORETTO
Bold Changes In Perspective

Jacopo Robusti (1592-94) was nicknamed Tintoretto because he was the son of a dyer (tintore in Italian). Like Veronese, he was part of the Venetian school of artists that used light and color to create vivid paintings pulsating with energy. His predilection was to paint miraculous events with strong emotional content. Sometimes they were done with almost theatrical extravagance. Although neither Veronese or Tintoretto could be considered pure Mannerists, both incorporated Mannerist devices into their works. Tintoretto relied on the bold use of perspective. There is a lot going on in his paintings, almost as if the canvas is too small to hold everything. His *Last Supper* is a great example of that.

The *Last Supper* (fig. 4-5), which was one of his last works before he died, epitomizes the Mannerist influence. The composition is unbalanced and complex. Tintoretto's depiction of the subject is much different from other artists. He takes Jesus and the table out of the middle of the room where they are usually situated. The painting emphasizes motion and unusual lighting effects.

If one were to assert that Mannerists chose to rely on unusual perspectives and the use of color and light to obtain a dramatic effect in their paintings, then you would have to accept that the *Last Supper* shows the influence of Mannerism. The composition is, at the very least, daring and perhaps even bizarre. There is no sense of symmetry. As the table shoots back into the darkened room there is a strange use of foreshortening. The figures diminish in size to an unusual extent at the back end of the table adding the illusion of depth to the room. The figure of Christ is the focal point of the work but it is unusually small and not at the center of the composition. Yet, despite all of this, Tintoretto never loses touch with providing a basic realism to the piece.

4-5. *Last Supper* by Tintoretto, 1590-1594, oil on canvas, Basilica di San Giorgio Maggiore, Venice.

One way to show how artistic styles evolved from the Renaissance to Post-Renaissance periods is to compare Leonardo's *Last Supper* (see fig. 3-11) with Tintoretto's interpretation of the subject. Leonardo's work emphasizes the realism that artist's of that era favored. It focuses on Christ at the center with the apostles strung out on each side of him with mathematical precision in groups of three that gives a symmetrical appearance to the painting. The space is relatively closed and the view is straight ahead. The figures react in individual ways to Jesus' statement.

In Tintoretto's painting, the view is from the corner with the table, apostles and Christ all pushed to the left side of the room. The setting has a more "earthy atmosphere," perhaps that of a Venetian inn. For drama, Leonardo relies on the expressions and gestures of the apostles. With Tintoretto that is almost completely missing. The drama comes from the interplay between light and darkness in the room.

One source of light is supernatural. It is the halos around the heads of the apostles and the glow emanating from Christ himself. That glow is the way to identify Christ. In Leonardo's work Christ is identified because he is at the center of the table and is the controlling figure.

The other source of light is from the single oil lamp. Transparent angels seem to swarm out of the lamp and around the ceiling of the room. All of this adds to the dramatic and emotional impact of the event. It is an action filled scene that comes off as almost eerie. Those elements do not exist in Leonardo's work. There is nothing eerie about it.

There is another difference in the interpretation of the two paintings that has religious significance. Leonardo's emphasized personal betrayal and the humanity of Christ as well as the human element of the disciples. Tintoretto emphasizes the Holy Communion as Jesus offers the bread and wine.

During the High Renaissance time of Leonardo, the focus was on realism, harmony and order in paintings. With Tintoretto and some of his contemporaries in the Post- Renaissance era there was a search for new expressive methods in art.

EL GRECO
Daring and Exaggerated Elegance In Religious Art

Domenikos Theotokopoulos (1541-1614) was born in Crete which, at the time, was part of the Republic of Venice. This is another example of why we can appreciate nicknames. He became know as El Greco, which means the Greek, because his name was too difficult to pronounce.

4-6. *The Burial of the Count of Orgaz* by El Greco, 1586, oil on canvas, Santo Tome, Toledo, Spain.

Some people think of El Greco as a Spanish painter and Spain does claim him. But, technically he wasn't because he was not born in Spain. He traveled extensively. First he went to Venice which was a logical choice since Crete was a possession of Venice. But he did not achieve success there so he moved to Rome in 1570 and then back to Venice. In 1577 he settled in Toledo, Spain where he finally achieved great artistic success. He lived and painted there for the next 37 years until his death in 1614. It is where he produced his best known works. That is why he is considered a Spanish artist.

One way you can describe El Greco's style is that of an exaggerated Mannerist. But he was also influenced by his early training in the Byzantine tradition. That shows up in his unusual and sometimes troubling representation of conventional religious images.

His paintings can be recognized immediately because of his distinctive style. There is a mystical quality to his works and a sense of turbulence. Often, there is nothing resembling a realistic depiction of human form which is a complete departure from the High Renaissance style. Figures are twisted, exceptionally elongated and look tortured. The composition is crowded and presented on a flat surface. The illusion of depth mastered during the Renaissance is missing. Figures can assume flame-like shapes. But all of this was done to enhance the emotional effect of the painting and, in that regard, it was very effective.

Because El Greco's art is reminiscent of the Byzantine era and of Mannerism, in that regard, it belonged to the past. Nevertheless, he has been called the most modern of the old masters because he relied on his imagination rather than imitating the real world. He had an influence on more modern painters like Cezanne and Picasso.

After centuries of near obscurity, it was not until the early 20th century that the almost forgotten artist was rediscovered. His dramatic and highly emotional style

4-7. *The Opening of the Fifth Seal* by El Greco, 1608-1614, oil on canvas, The Metropolitan Museum of Art, New York.

began to be appreciated. He began to be perceived as a precursor to Cubism and Expressionism. But his contemporaries reacted to his paintings with puzzlement. Because painters found his work incomprehensible he had no important followers. Words like "strange," "bizarre," "odd" and even "queer" crept into the dialogue about his paintings. But in the final analysis, El Greco's works came to be described as an "exaggeration of elegance."

The *Burial of the Count de Orgaz* (fig. 4-6) is generally considered El Greco's greatest masterpiece. His Mannerist method is clearly expressed in this painting. The space is extremely crowded and the figures are brought into the foreground in such a way to eliminate any sense of depth. There is no ground, no sky and no sense of distance. This is a sharp departure from Renaissance art where perspective was always recognized. Nevertheless, there is an enormous amount of spiritual energy.

The painting was inspired by a popular local legend at the start of the 14th century. When Don Gonzalo Ruiz died in the town of Orgaz he left a sum of money to the church of Santo Tome which was El Greco's parish church. After his death he became known as the Count of Orgaz. According to legend, at the time of his burial, Saint Stephen and Saint Augustine descended from heaven and buried him with their own hands. The painting is divided into two zones: heaven above and earth below. The scene of the miracle is depicted the lower part of the painting. Saints Augustine and Stephen, in golden vestments, bend over the body of Count Orgaz who is clad in decorative armor.

The count's soul can be seen ascending to Christ. There are swirling, icy looking clouds and they have parted to receive the count. The figures are elongated and distorted. But below, the figures look normal. Christ is clad in white. He is the peak of the triangle formed by Mary and John the Baptist. They are surrounded by apostles and martyrs. The colors are vibrant. Mary's blue and red robe is contrasted against the background of subtle grays. The use of gray (as well as black) can be symbolic of mourning in Christian works.

At the time, it was the custom for eminent men of the town to assist in the burial of the noble-born count. In fact, it was stipulated in El Greco's contract that their portraits appear in the painting. Life-like portraits of the most eminent men in Toledo at the time are shown in the earthly part of the work. In fact, they are so realistic that it demonstrates El Greco was among the great portrait painters.

El Greco may have reached his ultimate in his many attempts to depict emotional responses to religious events with *The Opening of the Fifth Seal* (fig. 4-7). It represents his fantastic interpretation of the Vision of Saint John the Evangelist as described in the book of Revelations.

Revelations 6:9-11:

"When he opened the fifth seal, I saw under the altar the souls of those who had been slain for the word of God and for the testimony which they held. And they cried with a loud voice saying, 'How long, O Lord, holy and true, until You judge and avenge our blood on those who dwell on the earth?' And a white robe was given to each of them; and it was said to them that they should rest a little while longer, until both the number of their fellow servants and their brethren, who would be killed as they were, was completed."

This was one of El Greco's last paintings. He started it in 1614 and it was left uncompleted. It is one of his most mysterious pieces. The left side is dominated by the figure of Saint John, his hands raised imploringly to heaven. To the right are the souls of the persecuted martyrs crying out to God for justice to be imposed on their persecutors on earth. One group of naked souls receives the white robes of salvation. The figures rising from the ground represent an image of the Last Judgment. Typical of El Greco, there are distortions, emotion, spiritual energy and a dramatic quality that comes from the work that still resonates today.

DID EL GRECO INFLUENCE PICASSO?

It has been suggested by art scholars that *The Opening of the Fifth Seal* served as an inspiration for some of Picasso's early works and, in particular, *Les Demoiselles d' Avignon* (see fig. 11-6). It is likely that Picasso studied El Greco's work either before or while painting *Les Demoiselles*.

There are certainly reasons for believing there is a connection between the two paintings. Picasso had an obsession with "borrowing from" other artists. The Mannerist and elongated forms of El Greco reappear in *Les Demoiselles*. The figures in each have disjointed poses. Both paintings have stylistic similarities and uncertain meanings.

You can judge for yourself. *Les Demoiselles d'Avigon* will be discussed in detail in chapter 11.

With El Greco we have come to the end of another phase of art history which this writer has called the Post-Renaissance era. By the early part of the 17th century another art movement was taking hold. It is called Baroque. It dominated the art scene in the 17th and 18th centuries.

IMAGES

4-1. *Last Judgment* by Michelangelo, 1536-1541, fresco, Sistine Chapel, Rome.

4-2. *Madonna With The Long Neck* by Parmigianino, c. 1535-1540, oil on panel, Uffizi, Florence.

4-3. *Feast at the House of Levi* by Veronese, 1573, oil on canvas, Louvre, Paris.

4-4. *The Wedding at Cana* by Veronese, 1562-1563, oil on canvas, Louvre, Paris.

4-5. *Last Supper* by Tintoretto, 1590-1594, oil on canvas, Basilica di San Giorgio Maggiore, Venice.

4-6. *The Burial of the Count of Orgaz* by El Greco, 1586, oil on canvas, Santo Tome, Toledo, Spain.

4-7. *The Opening of the Fifth Seal* by El Greco, 1608-1614, oil on canvas, The Metropolitan Museum of Art, New York.

BAROQUE ART

Baroque was the dominant style of European art between Mannerism and Rococo. It was not a "one type fits all" art movement. There were many styles in many places. It was born in Italy at the end of 16th century and spread throughout Europe ending its run in the late 1700s when it gradually gave way to the more decorative Rococo style. For the most part, Baroque art reflected the religious tensions of the age.

In response to the Protestant Reformation of the early 16th century, the Roman Catholic Church, as set forth in the Council of Trent, embarked on a program of religious renewal known as the Counter-Reformation. The Church used art to encourage piety among the faithful and to persuade those that had left the Church to return. It favored magnificent displays that were doctrinally correct, visually appealing and capable of generating strong emotional responses from the common people.

Among the favorite subject matters were the depiction of miracles, the suffering of the saints and paintings that documented well known Bible stories. The goal was to inspire the largest possible number of the illiterate masses. Prominent representatives of this type of Baroque art were Rubens and Bernini.

Given that the Catholic Church wanted to reaffirm the emotional depth of the faith and to enhance the power and influence of the Church, a sense of melodrama emerged in the art. The aim was to evoke a deep emotional response from the viewers. In many areas, Baroque became art of exaggeration. It features strong contrasts of light and shadows to enhance dramatic effects. There was an emphasis on grandeur and sumptuous color that could dazzle the viewer. Another characteristic of Baroque art was a strong sense of movement like swirling upward spirals. In short, it featured a kind of artistic sensationalism.

Two hallmarks of Baroque art were greater realism and the use of a revolutionary technique where figures emerge out of a dark background illuminated by a spotlight effect that increased drama in the painting. Caravaggio was a practitioner of both styles and that is why he is considered part of the Baroque movement even though he died when it was just getting underway.

Although Rome was the artistic capital of Europe in the 17th century, Baroque art spread outwards and underwent modifications as it migrated to other countries. In some areas it was toned down to fit more conservative tastes. In others it was enthusiastically received and reached its zenith of grandeur and exuberance. Rubens, from Flanders, was one artist that pushed it to its elaborate heights.

By comparison, Baroque art in the Protestant areas had far less religious content. For example, in Holland, Baroque made only slight inroads. Instead, genre paintings by artists like Vermeer became popular. They were aimed at the prosperous bourgeoise households. Baroque did not take root in England and, in France, its role was generally tied to the monarchy (e.g. Louis XIV and his palace at Versailles) rather than the church.

CARAVAGGIO
High Drama Through The Use Of Light

Considered a revolutionary, Caravaggio (1571-1610) changed the course of European art. He became known for his use of chiaroscuro or the application of contrasting light and dark colors and shadows. He also championed a new, more life-like style of figurative painting.

He approached his art in a different way. He worked at great speed and preferred to paint directly on canvas. Most of the skilled artists of that day worked from drawings and they criticized Caravaggio for not idealizing his figures. He used female models. Unfortunately, to the disdain of the Catholic Church, they were often prostitutes who he painted as well-known female religious figures.

In modern times, Caravaggio could have been a top notch Hollywood film director through the high drama of his subject matter. His use of a spotlight effect gives the shock-and-awe spectacle of a modern movie set. In the Post-Renaissance era he brought realism to a new level and then heightened it with his bold, theatrical use of tenebrism. What emerged was realism as had never been seen before.

Michelangelo Merisi was called "Caravaggio" after the small town where he was raised. He rose to prominence in 1600 when he received his first public commissions for the *Martyrdom of Saint Matthew* and *The Calling of Saint Matthew* both for the same church in Rome. His radical realism and emotional intensity coupled with the use of tenebrism in his paintings made him an immediate success with some collectors. But he did not handle life very well. He was a man of turbulent character frequently getting into brawls

5-1. *Penitent Magdalene* by Caravaggio, c. 1594-1595, oil on canvas, Doria Pamphilj Gallery, Rome.

and run-ins with the law. Because of his violent temperament he became known as an "accursed painter" and an "evil genius."

In 1606, he reached the point-of-no-return. He was condemned to death by default when he killed a man during a heated argument over a game of pallacorda which was the equivalent of tennis at the time. From that point on, over the last four years of his life, he was a man on the run.

He fled Rome to places like Malta and Naples. He died in 1610 just short of his 39th birthday while trying to reach Rome by boat having heard rumors of a papal pardon. There has always been a great deal of conjecture over the cause of his death. Perhaps it was during another brawl or perhaps he died from injuries from a previous brawl. No one knows for sure.

Caravaggio was known as a great innovator who introduced an unprecedented degree of realism, drama and a new level of emotional intensity into art. He brought figures out of the dark into the light. Often this took place in a closed space with a beam of light coming from a single source above and outside the painting to heighten the contrast of light and dark.

CHIAROSCURO AND TENEBRISM

Do not confuse them. There is a difference. Both techniques involve using contrasting areas of light and dark. But tenebrism is used exclusively to get a dramatic effect. Some areas of the painting are completely black. Other areas are strongly illuminated, usually from a single source of light that comes from someplace outside the painting. Essentially, you get a spotlight effect that can be used to focus attention on a face, a single figure or group of figures in the painting. It allows the artist to draw the viewer's attention to a particular part of the painting.

Chiaroscuro, on the other hand, involves the use of smaller amounts of shadow to help shape human figures. It may be used to highlight the muscles or curves of a body. It is not used to focus attention on particular areas of the canvas for dramatic effect as is the case with tenebrism. Both techniques can be applied together on the same canvas.

Chiaroscuro has been used throughout much of art history. Tenebrism is most often seen in connection with works painted during the Mannerism and Baroque periods. For example, the dramatic lighting effect in Tintoretto's *Last Supper* is a form of tenebrism. Other artists that can be associated with tenebrism are Rembrandt and El Greco.

5-2. *Calling of Saint Matthew* by Caravaggio, 1599-1600, oil on canvas, Contarelli Chapel, San Luigi dei Francesi, Rome.

Despite such innovations, the reactions to his art were often mixed. Some felt his powerful and sometimes brutal realism was unsuited for the dignity of a religious subject. Some clients were shocked by his approach because, to a certain extent, he mocked classical religious tradition by depicting figures in a manner far different from the usual idealized style. Religious figures looked like real people with natural flaws and defects instead of idealized creations. But this departure from the standard classical idealism of artists like Michelangelo was very controversial. His unusual interpretation of biblical events often led to the disapproval of the Catholic Church. In short, his art was considered unacceptable to some.

Nevertheless, the impact on artists that followed him was profound. His powerful use of light and shadow had a strong influence on artists for hundreds of years. Some historians believe that Caravaggio represents the beginning of modern painting because he was driven by many of the modern themes in art such as death, torture and psychology.

Typical of Caravaggio, his *Penitent Magdalene* (fig. 5-1) represents a departure from the standard paintings of that subject matter during the era. He places her in contemporary clothing, perhaps in reference to her former life as a courtesan. She sits in silent remorse in a humble position, close to the ground on a very low chair. The light of salvation shines down on the repented sinner. A single tear drop runs down one cheek at the side of her nose. It is a uniquely sensitive piece of repentance.

Beside her she leaves behind a pile of jewelry that represents the adornments of her dissolute life. In contrast to that, there is a bottle of liquid. This is in reference to the ointment which she used to wash Christ's feet with her long hair.

As already noted, Caravaggio was known to use prostitutes as models for his paintings. Historians have speculated that was the case here and she is the same person featured in his *Death of the Virgin* (see fig. 5-5).

The *Calling of Saint Matthew* (fig. 5-2) is a good example of many of the aspects of Caravaggio's art discussed above. He begins to perfect the use of light that would be-

5-3. *Supper at Emmaus* by Caravaggio, 1601, oil on canvas, National Gallery, London.

come his celebrated hallmark. There is a dark background with a beam of light penetrating the closed space. The sinner Levi, who is a tax collector, oversees the counting out of coins for the boy at the far left. The money on the table is a symbol of greed.

Jesus stands behind the cloaked Peter and is mostly hidden in the darkness. He points his right hand toward Levi, calling him to join his apostles. Peter repeats the gesture. Matthew (i.e. Levi), showing surprise, responds by pointing to himself as if to say: "Who? Me?" The conversion has begun. As he fixes his eyes on Christ it is as if he has already said, "Yes, I will follow you." But notice that this is accomplished with none of the typical adornments such as flying angels or parting clouds.

The composition is not balanced in the way one would expect. Neither of the protagonists is at the center. Jesus is at the far right and Matthew is on the left. At the center are two young boys dressed in modern aristocratic garb. They do not play an important role in the drama that is unfolding.

Since Matthew and the two well dressed young men look towards Christ, it is a sign of repentance and their hope that they will be saved. But the old bespectacled man and the young man next to him continue to look down counting

the coins. They don't answer Jesus' call and are doomed to damnation.

The stream of light has multiple purposes. It shows off the costumes and features of the figures at the table. It also has religious significance in that it is the Light of God and shows the way to salvation even for sinners. Finally, the light makes the outstretched hand of Jesus clearly visible. It recalls God reaching out to give life to Adam in Michelangelo's *Creation of Adam* (see fig. 3-16) on the ceiling of the Sistine Chapel. Now it is Jesus reaching out to Levi to begin a new life as a disciple.

Supper at Emmaus (fig. 5-3) depicts the climax of the story that appears in Luke 24: 13-30. Two of Jesus' disciples were walking to Emmaus after the crucifixion when the resurrected Jesus joins them. But they do not recognize him. At supper that evening in Emmaus, Christ is shown at the moment of blessing the bread thus revealing his identity to the disciples.

As usual, Caravaggio's innovative treatment of the subject has a powerful impact. Typical of the artist, there is no pomp and ceremony. The figures look ordinary. The divine becomes part of the everyday world. He shows the life-sized figures frozen in a moment of time like a snap-

5-4. Madonna of the Pilgrims by Caravaggio, 1604, oil and canvas, Church of Saint Agostino, Rome.

in disbelief, one flailing his arms and the other pushing his chair back and starting to stand.

Christ is shown with no beard because in Mark 16:12 Jesus is said to have "appeared in a different form to the two of them while they were walking in the country." To reflect that, Caravaggio shows him beardless in contrast to the bearded Christ in the *Calling of Saint Matthew*" (see fig.5-2).

The figures are far from the idealized images seen in Renaissance paintings. The innkeeper standing next to Christ is unaware of the significance of his blessing gesture. The disciples have rough hands, evidence of a life of hard work. Caravaggio even adds a hole to the right sleeve of the disciple who pushes his chair back. Their faces are wrinkled with age. The innkeeper has his sleeves rolled up ready to go to work. These are real people.

The entire painting is designed to draw us into the scene. The outstretched right arm of Christ not only serves to bless the bread but it invites us to join the table. There is even space for us at the table.

Great emphasis is given to the still life on the table. Its elements have symbolic meaning. The bread and wine refer to the Holy Communion. The grapes refer back to the wine which is a symbol of the blood of Christ. The apples relate to Adam and the fall of man. This is no ordinary table, it is an altar. Notice the basket of fruit that teeters precariously on the edge of the table perhaps reflecting the perilous nature of the journey, past and future.

Madonna of the Pilgrims (fig. 5-4) concerns the story of Mary's flight to Egypt from Palestine after

shot. Christ has raised his hand to bless the food. The disciples instantly become aware of who he is. His breaking of the bread reminds them of his broken body at the crucifixion and the supper they shared the night before. They react

being warned Herod was seeking to kill the Christ child. It demonstrates the contradictions in Caravaggio's art compared to the traditional approach of presenting the story. It is also an example of why his art created so much controversy.

5-5. *Death of the Virgin* by Caravaggio, 1604-1606, oil on canvas, Louvre, Paris.

Caravaggio abandoned the traditional image of the Virgin's flight where she is transported miraculously by angels. Instead, he portrays her on the threshold of a humble dwelling which has crumbling plasterwork as a reference to her poverty. She is lovingly presenting Jesus to the devoted pilgrims who have come to adore the Christ child and honor her. There is the delicate way she stands tip-toe which is the only hint of her flying.

Her beauty and cleanliness contrast with the common features of the two pilgrims. Symbolically, they represent all of humanity, a man and a woman like Adam and Eve. In the foreground is the peasant's dirty feet. It is an example of the heighten realism of Caravaggio's paintings and, in this case, an attempt to honor the poor and the humble. They are also a symbol of faithfulness and obedience.

Because of the peasant's feet, the painting became known as the "Madonna of the Dirty Feet." Some religious leaders were outraged by this presentation and considered Caravaggio's work as lacking in "decorum." Critics said it was too realistic.

Death of the Virgin (fig. 5-5) was one of Caravaggio's masterpieces but, at the time, the swollen appearance of the Virgin was considered outrageous. The painting was commissioned for the Carmelite church of Santa Maria della Scala in Trastevere, Rome. But when the friars saw it they were alarmed because her hair was undone, her blouse partially open, her feet bear and body swollen. She is clad in a simple red dress, arm hanging down. There is no sign of spiritual rebirth or salvation. This is not what the church wanted.

The only indication of the holiness of the Virgin is the thread-like halo. Except for that, Caravaggio completely abandons the images traditionally used to testify to the divine nature of the subject. Typically, in paintings of that era, Mary is shown in a healthy body assumed into heaven surrounded by angles and being greeted by God (see Rubens fig. 5-10 or Titian fig. 3-24). Instead, Caravaggio is totally rejecting the elegance of the High Renaissance and giving us something that is down to earth, perhaps even ugly.

The painting was rejected as being unworthy of the church. Adding to the shocking circumstances surrounding the work was the rumor that the model was a dead prostitute dragged from the River Tiber. But due to the recommendation of Peter Paul Rubens, who praised it as one of Caravaggio's best works, the painting was bought by the Duke of Mantua. It was later bought by Charles I of England and, after he was executed, sold to Louis XIV. That is

5-6. *Beheading of Saint John the Baptist* by Caravaggio, 1608, oil on canvas, Oratory of Saint John's Cathedral, Malta.

how it ended up in the Louvre in Paris.

The figures are nearly life-sized. They stand under the theatrical drape of a blood-red cloth that heightens the scene's dramatic effect. Mary's right hand falls across her swollen abdomen. Perhaps here Caravaggio is alluding to Mary being "full of grace," always pregnant with Divine Grace. The disciples are grouped around the corpse. Light coming from the upper left picks out the bald heads and then falls on the upper part of the Virgin's body.

The followers seem struck dumb with their sorrow. Grief is not highlighted by facial expressions but by the hiding of faces. At the front, Mary Magdalene stoops forward burying her head in her lap. There is no suggestion here that their sorrow will be soon turned into joy and Mary will be assumed into heaven.

The *Beheading of Saint John the Baptist* (fig 5-6) is as graphic as it gets in art. The spotlight effect bounces off the executioner's and John the Baptist's bodies. Just as viewers may gasp when they see this painting, you get the sense that John the Baptist has let out his last gasp.

We are witnessing the culmination point of the ex-

5-7. *David With the Head of Goliath* by Caravaggio, 1610, oil on canvas, Borghese Gallery, Rome.

ecution. The fatal wound has already been inflicted. Now the executioner, almost passively, is in the process of severing his head with a short dagger. This is a heart rendering scene. The effect is so powerful it leaves the viewer speechless.

The beheading takes place outside a prison and two convicts witness the scene from the window of their cell. Salome, who requested the head of John the Baptist to fulfill her mother's wishes, impassively holds out the tray on which the head is to be placed as the prison guard's gesture commands. The only person in the scene that shows any emotion is the old woman who has a horrified pose.

The gruesomeness is compounded by Caravaggio's signature in the red pool of blood that flows from the neck of

the saint. Fortunately, it is not clearly visible in the picture. It is so powerful that it is hard to look at the painting without shivering. This is the only painting that Caravaggio signed. That may be a reflection of his personal situation. It is a grim reminder that Caravaggio himself was under a death sentence. This painting is super realism perhaps carried to an extreme.

David With the Head of Goliath (fig. 5-7) was Caravaggio's swan-song. It may not have been his last painting but it was done in 1610 not long before his death. It was painted in Naples just before he started his trek back to Rome, hopefully to receive a papal pardon. But his coup de grace came on the way back.

This painting is another great example of his extensive use of tenebrism. David emerges from a dense black

5-8. *The Descent from the Cross* by Rubens, 1612-1614, oil on panel, Cathedral of Our Lady, Antwerp, Belgium.

There is a sorrowful look on David's face. It could even be interpreted as a look of pity. In the middle of the giant's forehead is a bloody stain where David's stone struck its fatal blow. The implication here is this would be Caravaggio's fate if his application for mercy was not granted.

RUBENS

A Flemish Painter Synonymous With Baroque Art

Peter Paul Rubens (1577-1640) was a master of grandiose paintings. He was influenced by the radiant color and majestic forms of Titian as well as the intense realism of Caravaggio.

Rubens was a devout Catholic. That is reflected in his infusion of the emotional objectives of the Counter-Reformation into his art. His style contrasts sharply with the more secular paintings of the Dutch master Rembrandt. His paintings have all the ideal aspects of Baroque art such as monumental size, lush color, extravagant composition, contrasts of light, movement and a diagonal flow. Often, there is so much activity that it seems about to overflow the edges of the canvas.

Rubens excelled at undertaking commissions that involved very large scale paintings. He wrote, "The large size of a picture gives us painters

background carrying the head of Goliath. The spotlight illuminates part of David's body and the head of Goliath. The decapitated head is a self-portrait. This is not the first time Caravaggio appears in one of his paintings. He painted his own head on the platter held by Salome in *Salome With The Head of John the Baptist*. Perhaps these paintings represented his tragic farewell. In identifying with the head of Goliath, Caravaggio is admitting his own guilt. He sent this painting to Cardinal Scipione Borghese in Rome who was the pope's nephew and had the power to grant pardons.

more courage to represent our ideas with the utmost freedom and semblance of reality ... I confess myself to be, by natural instinct, better fitted to execute works of the largest size."

He was extremely prolific and able to complete many large-scale paintings because he had one of the largest workshops in that era. Some of his apprentices like Van Dyke became famous in their own right.

His style was famous throughout Europe. In addition to his highly charged religious works sponsored by the Catholic Church, he was a painter of kings and queens.

Maria de Medici, then Queen of France, commissioned him to do a large number of paintings celebrating the life of her and her late husband Henry IV. They are among his best works and are hung in one vast hall of the Louvre in Paris. One is depicted below.

One of the best examples of religious Baroque art is Ruben's dramatic presentation *The Descent from the Cross* (fig. 5-8). It exudes emotion and struggle. He painted the huge piece that is nearly 14 x 11 feet after he returned to Flanders from Italy where he studied the works of Michelangelo, Caravaggio and others. The influence of Caravaggio is most evident in the work. It manifests itself in the use of chiaroscuro and in the heightened drama that comes from the spotlight effect on Christ's pale body (i.e. tenebrism).

This is the second of two enormous altarpieces that Rubens did for the Cathedral of Our Lady in Antwerp, Belgium. *The Elevation of the Cross* was executed two years earlier. Both are triptychs. If this piece were shown in its entirety it would present the Visitation, the Descent from the Cross and the Presentation of Jesus at the Temple.

The two side panels look unrelated to the theme of the center panel. But there is a hidden pictorial message in them. Saint Christopher is the patron saint of Antwerp. When Rubens was asked to paint the triptych it was requested that he do portraits of Saint Christopher. But Rubens knew this could get him in trouble with the authorities of the Counter Reformation because only scenes of the life of Christ could be shown in restored Catholic churches.

The significance of the name Christopher is "he who carries Christ." The central panel shows Saint John in red carrying the body of Christ. This makes him "Christopher." In the left panel Mary is visiting her cousin Elizabeth and Mary is pregnant. Therefore, she is carrying Christ which makes her "Christopher." In the right panel Simon is offering the new born Christ child to God in the temple. Thus, he is carrying the baby Jesus and that makes him "Christopher."

In paintings like the central panel of *The Descent from the Cross*, Rubens is able to evoke an almost unrestrained amount of pity and compassion. At times, it is as if he is trying to intimidate the viewer with the stunning effects in his works. But these paintings were very appealing to the Catholic Church because Rubens was unrivaled at the time in creating devout and very emotional images of Christ and that was exactly what the church wanted.

The degree of detail in the central panel is amazing. The use of diagonals is a prominent part of Ruben's work. As Jesus is lowered from the cross his body hangs in a line going from the lower left to the upper right. He is lifeless in a white shroud that also follows the long diagonal across the painting. The pale body of Jesus and the white cloth are highlighted by the spotlight effect of tenebrism.

There are nine figures. One of the workers at the top right holds the shroud in his teeth. Saint John, with one foot on the ladder, supports the body of Christ. Among the most poignant parts of the work is how Christ's foot rests on the shoulder of the beautiful Mary Magdalene brushing against her golden hair. Above her the Virgin Mary extends her arm toward her son. There is a gruesome part of the scene that, fortunately, is barely visible in this image. At the lower right there is a basin where the crown of thorns and the nails from the Crucifixion lie in thickened blood.

In 1600, Marie de' Medici became the second wife of Henry IV of France when she married him by proxy. Her uncle Ferdinando I de' Medici paid a large sum of money to Henry IV to seal the marriage thus buying her the Queenship of France. A year later she gave birth to the future King Louis XIII. Henry was assassinated when Louis was nine years old and Marie became Regent.

In 1621, she set about decorating the Luxembourg Palace and commissioned Rubens to paint two large series depicting the lives of herself and her late husband Henry IV. The first series of 21 paintings depicts the life of Marie. Three other canvases are portraits of the Queen and her parents. The cycle of paintings dedicated to the life of her husband were never completed.

Many of the paintings were designed to immortalize Marie's life by showing her struggles and triumphs. This was a daunting challenge for Rubens since Marie, in reality, had never accomplished very much. Her life could be measured by her marriage, the births of her children as well as the political problems with her son after he became king. There were no triumphant victories or scenes of vanquished foes that could be depicted.

Rubens had to stretch his considerable imagination to the limit in order to paint such a large number of extravagant depictions of rather mundane events. He had to rely on his impressive knowledge of classical literature. In almost all the paintings the Queen is surrounded by allegorical figures as well as those from ancient mythology. In this way, Rubens was able to glorify the Queen and present her as the embodiment of virtuous royalty.

The cycle's second painting *The Birth of the Princess* (fig. 5-9) shows Marie's birth in 1573. It has many of the trademarks of the Flemish Baroque artist already noted – extravagant presentation, lush color, a diagonal upward flow and so much swirling activity that it seems about to overflow the canvas.

There is much in the way of symbols and allegory in the painting. The river god in the lower right is an allusion to the Arno River that flows through Florence, her city of birth. The cornucopia above the baby's head is a harbinger of Marie's future fortune and glory. The lion is a symbol of power. The halo above the infant's head does not have the same significance as the imagery in Christian religious paintings. Here it is an indication she and her future reign are divinely empowered.

The Assumption of the Virgin (fig. 5-10) is even more dramatic than the previous painting. It clearly shows how Rubens was a master of color. Blue is the keynote color

5-9. *Birth of the Princess* by Rubens, 1622-1625, oil on canvas, Louvre, Paris.

here. As is often the case, the Virgin wears a royal blue cloak signifying she is the Queen of Heaven. There is swirling motion with enough activity that it also almost overflows the canvas, repeating his trademark in the previous painting.

It is interesting to compare this painting with the one done by Titian on the same subject (see fig. 3-24) painted in 1516-18. Titian highlights the color red and his piece is larger (i.e. 23 feet high compared to nearly 17 feet high for the Ruben's work). Both feature swirling upward motion.

In 1611, the cathedral in Antwerp announced a competition for an altarpiece. Rubens was awarded the commission and he completed the painting in 1626. Thus, 15 years elapsed between the start and conclusion of the project. Part of the delay was because the cathedral needed time to complete the majestic marble frame for the piece.

A tangle of baby angels lifts Mary's body upward toward the burst of divine light. Gathered around are the apostles, some watching in awe with their arms raised and others reaching to touch her discarded shroud. Rubens is able to create different postures and emotions for each of the apostles watching the event. Among the three women at the lower center of the painting, one is probably Mary Magdalene.

As is often the case, there is a spiritual message here. The multitude of angels surrounding the Virgin conveys the message that the idea of heaven is beyond the scope of the human mind.

5-10. *Assumption of the Virgin Mary* by Rubens, 1626, oil on panel, Cathedral of Our Lady, Antwerp, Belgium.

REMBRANDT

The Dutch Version Of Baroque Painting

Partly because he was Dutch, Rembrandt van Rijn's (1606-1669) art was the antithesis of the Baroque style of Rubens. He excelled in painting portraits of his contemporaries and self-portraits where he presented himself without vanity. Because Rembrandt was an avid reader of the Bible and due to his skill in representing emotion and his attention to detail, he was also an accomplished painter of biblical stories.

He was a very successful artist in his day and, therefore, had a large workshop. Because many of his pupils were able to imitate his style, it has been difficult for scholars to define with complete accuracy his body of work. Consequently, over the years, many paintings that had been attributed to him were assigned to other artists or listed as "in the style of Rembrandt."

Despite his success, his personal life was marked by tragedies and financial difficulties. His wife and several of

5-11. *Night Watch* by Rembrandt, 1642, oil on canvas, Rijksmuseum, Amsterdam.

his children died. He made bad business deals and spent more than he could afford. Rembrandt had to file for bankruptcy on two occasions.

Rembrandt became an accomplished printmaker. He was the first artist to popularize etching as a major form of art. Because of the great demand for his works and because etchings were much less expensive than original paintings and could be produced in large numbers, Rembrandt was able to service a very active market for his etchings and, later, drypoints.

The Netherlands is a protestant country and, in the 17th century, it was experiencing substantial economic improvement. The popularity of art was on the rise, not just among the aristocrats but among the working class people who were interested in decorating their homes.

There was a great deal of artistic freedom in The Netherlands at the time. Without the church patronage that occurred in Catholic countries, artists had to focus on capturing the interest of the public. What the public wanted were paintings of happy, Dutch mothers with their children, their homes and the life around them. In short, the subjects painted by artists were different from those of painters in Italy, France and Spain. It was like painting living history.

Consequently, artists like Rembrandt and, to an even greater extent, Vermeer were more renowned for their genre scenes rather than religious art. Rembrandt became known as the "Shakespeare of Holland."

For the most part, it was the same with the religious subjects that were painted. The point of view of the Church of Rome was not of interest to the people. But the Bible was read and studied and it was from its pages that artists drew the scenes to paint, usually more simply than the majestic and dazzling styles encouraged by the Catholic Church during the Counter-Reformation.

The most notable of Rembrandt's group portraits and his most famous painting is *Night Watch* (fig. 5-11).

The official title of the work is *The Militia Company of Captain Frans Banning Cocq* (*Night Watch* is a less accurate description but a more appealing title). It was to be a group portrait commissioned by a company of Dutch citizens sworn to defend Amsterdam against foreign invaders. Although the painting is dripping in patriotism, in reality, the militia had nothing to march against in that day unless it was off to a parade to celebrate a holiday or particular event.

It became his most innovative painting transforming what was supposed to be a traditional Dutch portrait into a dazzling scene of light, color and motion. What should have been a commonplace group portrait became a larger, more complex example of pictorial splendor.

Each of the 18 guardsmen expected that their faces would be clearly recognizable. After all, that is what portraiture is all about. But given that *Night Watch* is a colossal piece measuring approximately 13 x 16 feet in its original size, Rembrandt added 16 additional figures to give more animation to the tumultuous scene. He ends up painting a dynamic composition that reinvents group portraiture. He departed from convention in that he did not paint a static, formal scene of individuals lined up showing their clearly recognizable faces. Instead, he painted an action scene that shows the militia readying itself to embark on a mission.

The captain and his lieutenant stride out of the shadows into the light. Rembrandt was heavily influenced by Caravaggio and it shows in this piece. The spotlight effect leads the viewer's eye to the three most important figures in the crowd: the two men in the front and the young girl.

The illusion of forward motion is enhanced by the spotlight effect and by shading (i.e. chiaroscuro). Also, the zigzag pattern of the figures leads our eye in and out of the depth of the picture providing a sense of motion. Color helps to define space. The yellow of the lieutenant's uniform is picked up in the figure of the young girl running through another beam of light. The captain's red sash rhymes with the red uniform of the guard loading his musket on the left and the guard to the rear on the right.

The young girl appears to be the company's mascot. She carries a chicken that is meant to represent a defeated adversary. The color yellow is associated with victory.

Night Watch is not a nighttime scene. The title was attached to the painting during the 19th century because a dense layer of grime and dark varnish covered the canvas. Rembrandt's highly personal style where he used bold, rough strokes, thick paint applied with a palette knife and areas where he rubbed the paint lightly with his fingers (scumbling) can disturb the structure of the painting or, at least, give a less coherent look when viewed close-up. Rembrandt preferred that his works be viewed from a slight distance so the space would help fuse his strokes and colors giving the painting a more unified appearance.

Unfortunately, over time, dealers and collectors applied liberal applications of varnish that would not only protect the painting but give it greater coherence. But this darkened the work. Add in the buildup of grime over the years and you get what looks like a night scene. However, once it was cleaned in the 1940s and the varnish removed the painting brightened substantially. It was found that the scene occurred in broad day light.

Rembrandt may have been best known for his portraits but he was no secondary painter when it came to depicting scenes from the Bible. This is clear in his first *Supper at Emmaus* (fig. 5-12). He revisited the subject 20 years later with another superb rendition.

Rembrandt was fascinated with biblical themes and his favorite subject to paint was Jesus. He took a distinctive approach and painted innovative images of Christ. That is the case in this piece. Although Christ is shown entirely in silhouette, the work has the type of graphic realism for which Rembrandt was known.

The painting is linked to Luke 24:31. It shows the exact moment when the two pilgrims realize during supper that the person who has been accompanying them on their journey to Emmaus is their deceased master Jesus and not just a passer-by. One of the pilgrims falls to his knees and the other recoils in shock.

Rembrandt resurrects Caravaggio's use of light with an amazing intensity. The feature of this painting is the figure of Christ but it is almost erased by the burst of blinding light from an unknown source. The suggestion is that it has been released from heaven. Thus, Christ is presented as the Light of the World, the one who removes darkness and enables mankind to see that God is with us. It was this type of spirituality in his art that set Rembrandt apart from his Dutch contemporaries.

The story of Samson in the Old Testament fascinated the artist and he painted it a number of times in the 1630s. In the *Blinding of Samson* (fig. 5-13) he collapses the narrative in Judges 16: 19-21 into its most brutal part, the climax of the story. The biblical passage reads:

> *"Having put him to sleep on her lap, she called a man to shave off the seven braids of his hair, and so began to subdue him. Then she called, 'Samson, the Philistines are upon you.' He awoke from his sleep and thought, 'I'll go out as before and shake myself free.' But he did not know that the Lord had left him. Philistines seized him, gouged out his eyes and took him down to Gaza."*

In this work, perhaps more than any other, Rembrandt uses the Baroque style to appeal to those who were interested in sensationalism. It is his most gruesome and violent piece. Samson has been overwhelmed by the Philistines. One of them holds him down locking Samson in his grip. Another is shackling him and a third is plunging a sword

5-12. *The Supper at Emmaus* by Rembrandt, 1628, oil on panel, Musee Jacquemart-Andre, Paris.

5-13. Blinding of Samson by Rembrandt, 1636, oil on canvas, Stadelsches, Kunstinstitut, Frankfurt, Germany.

into his eye. The soldier standing in front silhouetted against the bright light pouring into the tent has his weapon ready to plunge into Samson if he is able to free himself before the hideous deed is completed.

Samson's right leg convulsing in pain points in the direction of the opening in the tent. There is Delilah fleeing the scene holding Samson's locks and the shears. Seen in a half haze, she has a look of terror despite her triumph.

Rembrandt is using chiaroscuro to very effectively enhance the emotion of the scene. Surely he must have had a feeling of great accomplishment when the piece was finished realizing he had even surpassed the dramatic effects of the Flemish master Rubens in his *Capture of Samson* in 1610.

Rembrandt was noted for painting historical and religious works but his portraits also earned him a great deal of notoriety. He especially liked to paint self-portraits. They form an intimate biography of the artist largely because he reproduced himself without vanity and with the utmost detail. *Self Portrait with Beret and Turned-Up Collar* (fig. 5-14) was one of his most successful portraits.

The background is a solid dark space. There is a dramatic light that bathes his entire face setting off a sense of solemnness in the portrait. Rembrandt was a master of painting eyes and it shows here. A recurring quality throughout his career is that everything appears natural and he accomplishes that in this piece.

He sits wearing a fur cloak and a beret with his hands clasped in his lap. The light that illuminates his face hollows out his cheek. It shows the blemishes on his face. The high collar hides part of his jowls although some loose flesh is still visible. This is a portrait that unflatteringly shows a man that is aging and the effects of life's experiences.

5-14. *Self Portrait with Beret and Turned-Up Collar* by Rembrandt, 1659, oil on canvas, National Gallery of Art, Washington, D.C.

VERMEER

Master of Genre Painting

Jan Vermeer (1632-1675) specialized at painting intimate scenes of ordinary people in everyday life. In short, he painted genre scenes.

Genuine Vermeer's are extremely rare. Less than 40 works can be attributed to him. That is because of his extraordinary precision as a painter and because he sold only to local patrons on commission. Due to the rareness of his works they became obscure after his death. He was almost unknown outside of his hometown of Delft. It was not until after the mid 19th century that his works became highly valued.

His forte was painting meticulous domestic interiors with a limited number of figures, usually women. The principal person would be engaged in an everyday activity such as reading or writing a letter, playing a musical instrument or even something as mundane as pouring out milk. The atmosphere would be one of peacefulness and serenity. The paintings showed a side of Dutch life of moderately well off but not wealthy people in the 17th century. He was a master at depicting the way light illuminates objects, often flowing in from a window on the left.

A splendid example of these characteristics of his artistic style is *Woman Holding a Balance* (fig. 5-15). It is an interior scene where the light flows from a window accentuating the woman's hand and face. It washes across the wall revealing a painting of the Last Judgment. The light highlights the gold and pearl jewelry that spills out of the open jewelry box and the balance that she holds in her hand. It also falls onto what looks to be the woman's ample belly that is further emphasized by the yellow streak on her clothing.

This raises the first question of many about the painting. Is the woman pregnant? To contemporary viewers it looks obvious that she is. But there are reasons for believing that is not the case. Art historians point out that pregnancy was not a common subject in the art of that day. In fact, there are few depictions of women in maternity clothes. More likely, the short jacket and thickly padded skirt reflect the style of dress at that time.

It was not uncommon for Vermeer to include allegory in his works with a number of hints and symbols. That appears to be the case here. This is one of his most interesting and mysterious paintings due to the amount of symbols and the numerous possible interpretations.

The two most important elements of the painting are the picture-within-the-picture aspect and the balance. The painting of the Last Judgment in the background shows when it is decided which souls will go to Heaven and which will go to Hell. It represents the final eternal judgment.

There is a feeling of stillness in *The Balance* almost as if the woman is meditating. The balance she is holding may be connected to the idea of judgment. A balance, typically, symbolizes justice and final judgment. Vermeer may want the viewer to see the link between the picture in the background and the balance.

The balance in the woman's hand is empty, so she is contemplating balancing. The suggestion is that it is the woman's responsibility to weigh and balance her actions. She should be focusing on the treasures of Heaven rather than those on Earth. One should conduct one's life with restraint and balanced judgment. This type of message appears in other paintings by Vermeer.

The Girl with a Pearl Earring (fig.5-16) has been called the "Dutch Mona Lisa." It is almost like a photograph, captivating in its use of light. The woman comes out of the dark into the light. It is an extremely popular painting as witnessed by the fact that a novel published in 1999 inspired a film in 2003. Both carried the name of the work. It is an unusual piece for Vermeer since many of his paintings focused on activities in a Delft household.

Her large eyes connect with ours. Vermeer records everything about her: the creamy whiteness of her skin, the light falling on her half-opened suggestive lips and even the nostril in the shadow. Her head is tilted to allow the light

5-15. *Woman Holding a Balance* by Vermeer, 1664, oil on canvas, National Gallery of Art, Washington, D.C.

to fall across her face. Out of the shadow on the side of her face a pearl earring glows. It is the focal point of the painting. In the 17th century, pearls were an important status symbol and they appear frequently in Vermeer's paintings.

She looks directly at the viewer. Despite her striking presence, the girl retains an air of mystery. Her costume and exotic headdress are not part of the fashion of that day. Perhaps she is representing an allegorical or biblical figure. We don't know. It is another one of the mysteries of Vermeer's paintings.

The Art of Painting (fig. 5-17) looks like another colorful, attractive 17th century interior piece. But it is much more than that. It is replete with allegory much like *Woman Holding a Balance*. In fact, it is also known as *The Allegory of Painting*. In this case, the symbols relate to history and fame. In addition, Vermeer applied his knowledge of the rules of linear perspective to give the appearance of depth to the scene and to emphasize the paintings important components.

This is the largest and most complex of Vermeer's works. The images represent much more than an artist at his easel and his model. The artist is thought to be a self-portrait of Vermeer. But the focal point is his model Clio, the muse of history in Greek mythology. The artist is dressed in an elegant costume which places him above the social level usually associated with tradesman. Clio wears a crown of laurel which denotes honor, glory and eternal life. In one hand she holds a trumpet which stands for fame. In the other she holds a thick folder which she uses to write history.

By placing the muse of history in the center of the piece, Vermeer is emphasizing the importance of history to the artist. Another reference to history is the large map hanging on the back wall. It draws attention to the recent history of The Netherlands. A prominent crease runs through the center of the map dividing it just as recent political changes divided the land into two distinct entities.

In front of the map hangs a golden chandelier with the sunlight reflecting off its polished surface. At the top is a double-headed eagle, the imperial symbol of the Austrian Habsburg dynasty, former rulers of Holland.

There had always been questions about the artist's place in society. Should he be considered simply as a craftsman on a par with goldsmiths and carpenters? Or, should he be considered a creative genius much like a writer or philosopher?

By including the map and chandelier in the scene, Vermeer may have been indicating that the artist can bring fame to his city or country. By depicting the artist from the rear, he may be emphasizing that artists often experience relative anonymity during their lifetime. Too often fame comes to them after death. Nevertheless, the artist can still bring fame and glory to his homeland.

5-16. *Girl With a Pearl Earring* by Vermeer, c. 1667, oil on canvas, Mauritshuis, The Hague.

BERNINI
Defines Baroque Art In Sculpture

Gianlorenzo Bernini (1598-1680) was by far the most important sculptor of the Baroque period. His art represented a breakthrough that takes us from the

5-17. *The Art of Painting* by Vermeer, 1666-1668, oil on canvas, Kunsthistorisches Museum, Vienna.

Renaissance to the Baroque style. He has often been credited with inventing Baroque art.

Bernini can be listed alongside of Michelangelo in his all-around competence. He was also a painter and his architectural accomplishments were unmatched during that era. They included religious and secular buildings and designs for plazas and fountains like the "Fountain of the Four Rivers" in Rome. He was responsible for what seemed to be an endless number of jaw-dropping sculpture works.

Arguably, Caravaggio was the greatest Baroque painter. He combined intense theatrical light with unmatched realism and in-your-face subject matter to achieve extreme emotional responses from his paintings. Bernini does the same in creating astounding sculptures that push the limit of stone to unprecedented levels of intensity.

Whatever the form of his creations they included the decorative dynamism of Baroque. His inexhaustible imagination allowed him to become the most brilliant interpreter of Baroque spirituality in sculpture. His figures are full of emotional energy. They capture a fleeting moment that generates a dynamic effect that bursts before the viewer.

If Baroque art targets the senses by using realism and great technical skill, and it does, than Bernini was a master. He used qualities like movement, theatricality and elaborate presentations to generate the energy and forcefulness that made Baroque the appealing art form that captured the spirit of the Counter-Reformation.

In *The Rape of Proserpina* (fig. 5-18) Bernini crafted a marble piece of explosive energy. He was only 23 years old when it was completed. Actually, although called The Rape, Proserpina is not being raped. The term here is being used to mean abduction.

According to legend, Pluto the Roman god of the underworld is struck by the sight of Proserpina the daughter of Jupiter and Ceres. He wants to marry her and take her with him to Hades to be the Queen of the Underworld. But the only way he can do this is to steal her away. Bernini captures the moment of the abduction.

5-18. *The Rape of Proserpina* by Bernini, 1621-1622, marble, Galleria Borghese, Rome.

We see Proserpina desperately trying to escape Pluto's grasp as he carries her to Hades. Pluto holds her up in his arms as though he is triumphantly showing her as his trophy. Bernini develops a twisting pose of the two figures that is reminiscent of Mannerism.

Between the legs of Pluto's aggressive stride we can make out part of Cerberus, the three headed dog with a snake tail. This is the guard dog of the underworld that allows the dead to enter but never allows them to leave. Cerberus is barking trying to drown out the cries of Proserpina.

Proserpina is crying and praying for her release. To a certain extent, her prayer is answered. Her mother Ceres strikes a deal that Proserpina will remain in the underworld for half a year and then return to the surface for the other half. This is the ancient Roman origin of the spring and winter cycles.

Figure 5-19 shows the exquisite detail of Plato's hand pressing into Proserpina's flesh. Pluto's tight grasp on her thigh is an amazing feature of the piece. The dimpling produced in marble is an example of the artist's genius. Bernini makes the surface of the marble sculpture appear to be as soft as the human body. This is just one example of the sumptuous realism of the piece.

Figure 5-20 shows how Bernini carved the marble tears that fall from Proserpina's life-like eyes. He depicts her open lips as though she is crying out for help. This is a horror struck face.

Apollo and Daphne (fig. 5-21) demonstrates again how proficient Bernini was in capturing a dynamic effect of a fleeting moment in sculpture. The mythological story surrounding the two figures goes as follows: Eros, the Greek god of erotic love, wounds Apollo with a golden arrow that induces him to fall madly in love at the sight of Daphne, a water nymph sworn to perpetual virginity. When he sees her, he is filled with desire and relentlessly chases her. Daphne flees and implores her father, the river god, to destroy her beauty and repel Apollo's advances by transforming her into a laurel tree.

Bernini's sculpture captures Daphne's moment of transformation as the infatuated Apollo catches up to her and touches her just as she turns her head to look at him. Her skin turns to bark, her hair to leaves and her arms to branches. Yet, her beauty remains even in this form and Apollo still loves her.

There is an enormous amount of motion here as you see her changing. Apollo is in motion with the billowing piece of drapery lifted off his back by the wind. It is as if he is jumping into the air to grab her. As Apollo puts his hand on her waist, he touches only bark. He senses something is wrong. He gazes directly into Daphne's face. His eyes have sadness about them as he realizes what is occurring and his face shows a sense of loss.

Bernini forces the viewer to move around the sculpture. The rear view is the capturing moment. That causes the viewer to walk to the front to see Daphne's transformation. What occurs here is the opposite of what other artists try to accomplish with marble sculptures. Almost always, the task is to take a natural material like marble and give it the appearance of flesh. Here, Bernini takes the look of flesh and turns it into natural materials like bark and branches.

The life-sized piece was carved for Cardinal Borghese. Bernini began it when he was only 24. One has to wonder why a sculpture based on a pagan myth would appear in the Cardinal's villa. That is explained by a moral verse engraved in Latin in the base by Cardinal Barberini who later became Pope Urban VIII. "Those

5-19. Detail of Pluto's hand pressing into Proserpina's flesh.

5-20. Detail of Proserpina's face.

5-21. *Apollo and Daphne* by Bernini, 1622-1625, marble, Galleria Borghese, Rome.

who love to pursue fleeting forms of pleasure, in the end find only leaves and bitter berries in their hands."

Twenty years later Bernini did a sculpture with a completely different subject matter. *The Ecstasy of Saint Teresa* (fig. 5-22 and fig. 5-23) is about a mystical religious experience.

Bernini was at his best when he could merge architecture with sculpture. He accomplished that magnificently in *The Ecstasy of Saint Teresa*. Saint Teresa was a nun who was canonized because of her spiritual visions.

An important goal of Bernini's art is to involve the viewer. He goes to great ends to accomplish this by creating a complete theatrical scene. This is not a sculpture in the conventional sense. It is a framed pictorial scene that includes the worshipers in what is a combination of sculpture, architecture and a religious drama. It is a very early example of installation art. All of the pomp and ceremony of the church is brought out here. It is typically Baroque in that it describes an intense religious experience.

As you enter the Cornaro Chapel, *The Ecstasy of Saint Teresa* is in front of you. On either side, on the walls, is what look like theatre boxes. In the boxes are seated posthumous representations of members of the Cornaro family many of them Cardinals. They seemingly observe the scene from their boxes.

Saint Teresa is positioned on a floating cloud while an angel holds a golden arrow and smiles down on her. He has already plunged the arrow into her heart and has withdrawn it. The nun is shown in a transcendental state, enraptured with her lips parted. Both figures appear to be rising toward heaven. Her garments are chiseled in a way that they look disheveled, perhaps a sign of the turbulence within her.

Bernini tries to reproduce her experience of religious ecstasy as she described it:

"The pain was so great, that it made me moan; and yet so surprising was the sweetness of this excessive pain, that I could not wish to be rid of it. The soul is satisfied now with nothing less than God."

The figure of the angel also comes from her account when she describes him as young and beautiful. The group is illuminated by an array of gilded bronze rays designed to represent golden celestial light. The entire setting is a representation of the ideals of Baroque art.

Bernini is trying to show how Saint Teresa has been transformed to a state of awareness with God. In the process, he is showing the power and ecstasy of the Christian faith as never had been demonstrated before. The way he depicts her heart-stopping surrender to God as

5-22. *Ecstasy of Saint Teresa* by Bernini, 1644, marble, Cornaro Chapel, Santa Maria della Vittoria, Rome.

a forewarning of the intensity of happiness that Heaven provides represents the culmination of Counter-Reformation art.

VELAZQUEZ
Court Painter and Master Portraitist

Diego Velazquez (1599-1660), like so many painters, was influenced by Caravaggio's realism and tenebrism. He spent the majority of his life painting portraiture. He painted scores of portraits of the Spanish royal family in his 37 year service in the court of King Philip IV. There were essentially only two patrons of art in Spain at the time – the church and the art-loving king and his court. Velazquez was supported by the crown.

In The Surrender of Breda (fig. 5-24) Velazquez makes an important statement about humane conduct amidst the horrors of war. In June 1625, after a four month siege when the provisions of the fortress at Breda had run out, the Dutch governor Justin Nassau petitioned for an honorable surrender, ending the siege.

Velazquez shows General Ambrogi Spinola, the leader of the Spanish troops, after he has dismounted from his xhorse to meet the Dutch commander on equal footing. There is none of the usual celebration that accompanies victory. Instead, Spinola places his hand on the Dutchman's shoulder, offering the consolation of one soldier to another.

Rather than focusing on the battle itself, the theme of the painting is respect and harmony. Literally, at the center of the work is the key to the fortress presented to

5-23. *Ecstasy of Saint Teresa* by Bernini, detail.

5-24. *The Surrender at Breda* by Velezquez, 1634-1635, oil on canvas, Museo del Prado, Madrid, Spain.

Spinola by Nassau as he bows to his conqueror. The exchange seems very gracious. Unlike other paintings of conflicts, there is no evidence of joy in victory. Rather, there is an extraordinary sense of respect and dignity on the part of both generals.

The two armies stand on a hilltop overlooking a valley where Breda burns in the distance. The victors are holding their lances upright providing the painting with its popular name *The Lances*. The defeated Dutch gather with their banners drooping. In addition to everything else, Velazquez demonstrates his mastery of gesture, portraiture and landscape all in one painting. In the background, The Netherlands stretches out painted in greens, blues and silvery light.

Complex compositions were a specialty of Velazquez and *Las Meninas* or *Maids of Honor* (fig. 5-25) was his magnum opus. Indeed, it was by far his most complex and mysterious composition. Consequently, it has become one

of the most widely analyzed works of art. It raises questions about illusion and reality and the relationship between the viewer and the figures in the painting.

Until this piece, Velazquez's portraits of the royal family were straightforward. But that changed here. The painting depicts Velazquez's studio in the palace of King Philip IV. Excluding the two images in the mirror at the back of the room, there are nine figures in the painting. It is a huge piece measuring roughly 10½ x 9 feet.

Princess Margarita, the eldest daughter of the new queen, is in the forefront surrounded by her entourage of two maids of honor, a chaperone and bodyguard at the right rear, a dwarf and a dog. At the rear, in a doorway, is the queen's chamberlain. He is shown in silhouette. Velazquez is on the left standing before a large canvas.

Standing outside the pictorial space, where we as the viewers are positioned, are the king and queen. Velazquez is looking outwardly at them. In the background there is

5-25. *Las Meninas* (The Maids of Honor) by Velezquez, 1656, oil on canvas, Museo del Prado, Madrid.

a mirror that reflects their upper bodies. A number of the people in the room look outward. In effect, we become part of the composition. We are looking at a picture in which the painter is looking at us. We take on the role of both the king and queen and the observed and observer.

Who is the true subject of the painting? At first glance, it would appear to be five-year old Margarita, the royal daughter. She is near the center of the painting bathed in light that comes from a window on the right. She is also receiving a great deal of attention from the maids of honor. Or, it could be the king and queen who, although not clearly visible in the painting, are the focus of Velazquez's attention. Given the size of the reflection of the king and queen in the mirror and the perfect cropping of the royal couple within the frame of the mirror, we are probably seeing a reflection of the king and queen in the painting, not what Velazquez sees in front of him.

Most likely, Velazquez is the subject. His unusual special arrangement of the scene has the intent of making himself, the artist, the most important figure in the painting. This is his only self-portrait and, in it, the artist placed himself among royalty. He shows that he is an official of the court, worthy of the acceptance of the royal family. He is also making a personal statement. Throughout his life, he had sought respect and acclaim for himself and his profession. Here he is pointing to the high status of both the artist and his art. In the presence of divinely ordained monarchs, Velazquez exalts in his artistry.

IMAGES

5-1. *Penitent Magdalene* by Caravaggio, c. 1594-1595, oil on canvas, Doria Pamphilj Gallery, Rome.

5-2. *Calling of Saint Matthew* by Caravaggio, 1599-1600, oil on canvas, Contarelli Chapel, San Luigi dei Francesi, Rome.

5-3. *Supper at Emmaus* by Caravaggio, 1601, oil on canvas, National Gallery, London.

5-4. *Madonna of the Pilgrims* by Caravaggio, 1604, oil and canvas, Church of Saint Agostino, Rome.

5-5. *Death of the Virgin* by Caravaggio, 1604-1606, oil on canvas, Louvre, Paris.

5-6. *Beheading of Saint John the Baptist* by Caravaggio, 1608, oil on canvas, Oratory of Saint John's Cathedral, Malta.

5-7. *David With the Head of Goliath* by Caravaggio, 1610, oil on canvas, Borghese Gallery, Rome.

5-8. *The Descent from the Cross* by Rubens, 1612-1614, oil on panel, Cathedral of Our Lady, Antwerp, Belgium.

5-9. *Birth of the Princess* by Rubens, 1622-1625, oil on canvas, Louvre, Paris.

5-10. *Assumption of the Virgin Mary* by Rubens, 1626, oil on panel, Cathedral of Our Lady, Antwerp, Belgium.

5-11. *Night Watch* by Rembrandt, 1642, oil on canvas, Rijksmuseum, Amsterdam.

5-12. *The Supper at Emmaus* by Rembrandt, 1628, oil on panel, Musee Jacquemart-Andre, Paris.

5-13. *Blinding of Samson* by Rembrandt, 1636, oil on canvas, Stadelsches, Kunstinstitut, Frankfurt, Germany.

5-14. *Self Portrait with Beret and Turned-Up Collar* by Rembrandt, 1659, oil on canvas, National Gallery of Art, Washington, D.C.

5-15. *Woman Holding a Balance* by Vermeer, 1664, oil on canvas, National Gallery of Art, Washington, D.C.

5-16. *Girl With a Pearl Earring* by Vermeer, c. 1667, oil on canvas, Mauritshuis, The Hague.

5-17. *The Art of Painting* by Vermeer, 1666-1668, oil on canvas, Kunsthistorisches Museum, Vienna.

5-18. *The Rape of Proserpina* by Bernini, 1621-1622, marble, Galleria Borghese, Rome.

5-19. Detail of Pluto's hand pressing into Proserpina's flesh.

5-20. Detail of Proserpina's face.

5-21. *Apollo and Daphne* by Bernini, 1622-1625, marble, Galleria Borghese, Rome.

5-22. *Ecstasy of Saint Teresa* by Bernini, 1644, marble, Cornaro Chapel, Santa Maria della Vittoria, Rome.

5-23. *Ecstasy of Saint Teresa* by Bernini, detail.

5-24. *The Surrender at Breda* by Velezquez, 1634-1635, oil on canvas, Museo del Prado, Madrid, Spain.

5-25. *Las Meninas (The Maids of Honor)* by Velezquez, 1656, oil on canvas, Museo del Prado, Madrid.

ART OF THE PRE-IMPRESSIONISTS

6

One of the important objectives of this book is to show how art history progresses. Each new generation produces artists that challenge the art of the day. They see it, they want to challenge it, change it and create something new. That is what drives the avant-garde artists. Perhaps there is no better example of this process than what occurred from the 19th century on. The speed at which new art movements break onto the scene to challenge the existing ones seems to accelerate.

DAVID

Glorifying the French Revolution and Napoleon

A good place to start the discussion of the process of art movements and counter movements is with Jacques-Louis David (1748-1825). He was the preeminent painter of the time. In the 17th century, the French Rococo style became a prominent part of the art and decorating scene of Europe. It was characterized by pastel colors, dainty figures and a lighthearted mood. In contrast to that, David produced a number of under-decorated, anti-Rococo paintings that glorified the French Revolution.

David's work came to epitomize the late 18th century reaction against what its critics described as the excessively decorative, frivolous Rococo style. He became deeply involved in the French revolutionary scene even to the extent of voting for the execution of Louis XVI. This led to what is generally considered to be his most important work, the *Death of Marat* (fig. 6-1). The painting was done with unvarnished realism.

In 1793, one of the new leaders of the French state and who was active in the Reign of Terror when thousands were executed was assassinated. His name was Jean-Paul Marat. He was soaking in his bathtub to treat a chronic disfiguring skin disease. The assassin, Charlotte Corday gained access to his apartment through a clever subterfuge of providing him with a list of those that opposed the revolution and should be executed.

In the painting, David combines Caravaggio's realism with an image that is reminiscent of Michelangelo's *Pieta*. Marat appears as if he his taking his last breath. His head

6-1. *Death of Marat* by David, 1793, oil on canvas, Musees Royaux des Beaux-Arts de Belgique, Brussels.

weighs heavily on his shoulder. The elongated right arm hangs down, recalling Christ in the Pieta. In fact, although David's intent was to paint Marat as a martyr of the revolution, the style reminds one of the paintings of Christian martyrs with his body bathed in a soft, glowing light.

David surrounds the victim with a number of details. There is the assassin's knife left on the floor. Marat is still holding the death petition that he was asked to sign. The light is designed to illuminate the victim's features and the assassin's petition. The rest of the painting is mostly in the shadows. The composition has a nearly supernatural aura. Although David was an atheist, he presents an almost religious scene as if the holy light is bathing the Christian martyr. Perhaps he is trying to provide a symbol of the new religion, the Revolution. The painting did become his most famous image of the French Revolution.

When Napoleon came to power in 1799, David was immediately impressed by him. The Emperor, in turn, realized the potential of the great painter as a propagandist to champion his imperial regime. He became the court painter and, essentially, his artistic task was the glorification of Napoleon.

Napoleon crossed the St. Bernard Pass in the Alps in May, 1780 to surprise the Austrian army and win victory. David did five similar versions of *Napoleon Crossing the Alps* (fig. 6-2). The aim in each was to flatter the emperor. He reminds viewers of the other two generals who accomplished the feat – Charlemagne and Hannibal – by etching the names of all three in the rock at the lower left of the painting.

Each piece is an example of art of exaggeration. His idealized presentation shows the hero wearing a pristine uniform. Napoleon crossed the Alps mounted on a mule led by a guide. But here he is shown calmly astride a rearing horse, exalting us to follow him. His windblown cloak follows the extension of his arm, suggesting that Napoleon directs the wind as well as his troops.

The Coronation of Napoleon (fig. 6-3) is another scene of French nationalism painted by David. Napoleon threw himself a spectacular coronation ceremony at Notre-Dame Cathedral in 1808 and hired David to commemorate it. Napoleon understood the craft of shaping his public image. The painting is a superb piece of political propaganda if in its size alone. It is nearly 20 x 30 feet.

Napoleon is actually crowning his first wife Josephine. At first David intended to depict Napoleon lowering the laurel wreath on his own head. But then he decided to focus on Josephine's crowning in order to make Napoleon appear more generous and less self-serving. In addition, this was also a way to highlight the future of Napoleon's Empire. After all, Josephine would at least theoretically bear Napoleon's heir.

Behind Napoleon stand the religious figures that would normally perform the coronation's duties and rituals. But Napoleon placed the crown on his own head signifying his absolute rule and almost god like

6-2. *Napoleon Crossing the Alps* by David, 1801, oil on canvas, Chateau de Malmaison Rueil-Malmaison, Paris.

6-3. *The Coronation of Napoleon* by David, 1807, oil on canvas, Louvre, Paris.

claim to power. Now Josephine receives her crown from the king again indicating his authority.

It was never Napoleon's intention to accept the Pope as his overlord. David depicts the Pope as submissive to Napoleon. Pope Pius VII is lifting his hand in a half-hearted blessing gesture. David has lowered his chair so that Napoleon appears relatively larger. The Emperor's back is symbolically turned towards the Pope and he sits no higher than Napoleon.

INGRES
Line Is Everything

Like David, Jean Auguste Dominique Ingres (1780-1867) aspired to be a great history painter. After all, why not, since history paintings were considered to be the most important theme to undertake by the French art leaders. That was because of the intellectual demands they made on the artist. Next in the pecking order of importance were genre paintings. At the bottom of the list were portraits and landscapes. But for Ingres, his portraits turned out to be recognized as his greatest achievements. His figures were classically influenced, but rather than harkening back to ancient times, he was inspired by the precise drawing of the Renaissance master Raphael.

INGRES VERSUS THE IMPRESSIONISTS

Delacroix, who will be discussed next, was Ingres greatest adversary because of his emphasis on the use of color. He has been considered a precursor of Impressionism. Given those connections, it is not hard to speculate on what Ingres would have thought about the Impressionists.

Although Impressionism was not even on the horizon at this point in time, Ingres' work would not have inspired them and vice versa. In many respects, Ingres was the antithesis of Impressionism. Color, light and visible brushstrokes were all important parts of the repertoire of the Impressionists. These were not artistic techniques that Ingres wanted to stress.

The painting *Napoleon Crossing the Alps* is much different from Impressionism not only in the clearly defined lines (the Impressionists did not stress drawing) but in the subject matter. Impressionists did not paint portraits of great historical Frenchmen. This is not to suggest that Impressionist works and those of some of the artists that can be connected to them in style like Delacroix are better or worse than the works of Ingres and painters like him. They are just different.

His paintings of contemporary history were less successful. He was not interested in painting battle scenes that were a favored topic of that era. Although portraits were most successful for him, he felt that they robbed from him the time he could have spent painting historical pieces. He complained that portraits were a waste of time.

Ingres' style changed very little over his long career. He painted a limited number of subjects, returning to the same theme again and again. According to Ingres, art is all about drawing. Color was no more than an accessory to drawing. Line determines the design, form, composition and feeling of the work. He saw it as seven-eights of what makes up a painting.

In this regard, he was at the opposite end of the artistic spectrum from his life-long adversary from the Romantic school, Delacroix, who put a strong emphasis on color. As a criticism of Delacroix's works Ingres once said that, "Color pleases the eye but line pleases the mind."

Ingres did not have many painters of the era who emulated his style. His legacy is the impact he had on later generations. Given his emphasis on drawing, Degas was influenced by his works. Among 20th century painters, Picasso and Matisse acknowledged a debt to him. The Cubists, in particular, admired him for his modification of form (see the commentary below on the *Grand Odalisque*). Some historians feel his novel distortions make him a precursor to modern art. Yet, it is those characteristics that were so admired by future generations of artists that exposed him to a significant amount of criticism during his career.

6-4. *Napoleon Crowned* by Ingres, 1806, oil on canvas, Musee de L'Armee, Hotel des Invalides, Paris.

Napoleon Crowned (fig 6-4) shows Ingres' emphasis on drawing. In this regard, he was a perfectionist to the point of obsession. Napoleon is painted in the costume he wore for his coronation. Given his disposition, it is unlikely that Napoleon would have sat for such a portrait. That makes the details in the painting even more impressive.

There is an unusual intensity of detail in the depiction of the garments and accessories. Napoleon wears a golden laurel wreath on his head. He has white shoes that are em-

6-5. *Grande Odalisque* by Ingres, 1814, oil on canvas, Louvre, Paris.

broidered in gold and his feet rest on a cushion. In his right hand he holds the scepter of Charlemagne and in his left hand that of justice. The details go on and on.

Ingres was a student of David and it shows in this painting. It is reminiscent of David's *Napoleon Crossing the Alps*. But some critics were not impressed. They said the subject looked "too finished." To them the figure resembles a living statue. It is an example of the criticism that Ingres' works were often subject to.

Ingres' historical paintings were less successful than his emotionally charged portraits of female nudes. *Grand Odalisque* (fig. 6-5) is his most important nude although it was subject to wide criticism at the time. It was painted in 1814 for Napoleon's sister Queen Caroline Murat.

The subject matter is a concubine who is there for the pleasure of an Oriental sultan, as a member of his harem. As in the previous painting by Ingres, there is a marvelous amount of detail as the nude is set in a sumptuous interior. The trappings are there to accentuate the eroticism of the work. There is the peacock fan, pearls and the turban. The crumpled sheets, the cool blue of the couch and curtain decorated with red flowers are all there to heighten the sexuality of her porcelain skin.

The odalisque levels a cool gaze at her master as she turns her naked body away from him. This makes her simultaneously erotic and aloof. The elongated curves of her body are designed to add to her sensuality. But something looks wrong here!

Ingres was noted for his flawless realism in portraits but, anatomically, there are noticeable distortions here.

The elongation of the woman's back makes it look like she has too many vertebrae. The rotation of her pelvis is too extreme. Her left arm appears shorter than the right. The undersides of her feet are smooth.

The critics were appalled and Ingres was attacked for his distortions. The critics believed the elongations were errors on his part or perhaps he was simply acting as a rebel against the accepted style of form.

The explanations for the distortions have even reached a psychological level. The lengthening of the spine places the woman's head further away from her pelvis. This impression is enhanced by the right arm that is stretched down her body being longer than her left arm that is partially hidden. Given those details, now the psychological explanation of the painting comes into play. It has been suggested that Ingres is trying to show in physical terms that there is a gulf between the woman's feelings as expressed in her resigned gaze and her role in the harem to satisfy the carnal pleasures of the sultan. This is symbolized by her deliberately lengthened spine that separates her head from her pelvis. In this regard, the painting becomes a study of the complex emotions of the odalisque.

This writer believes the psychological explanation for the distortions is much too complex to accept. It simply shows the extremes that some critics will go to in analyzing an unusual painting. It is also likely that the elongations were not errors on the part of Ingres given his unparalleled ability to render a physical likeness. More likely, in his attempt at sensual perfection, he deliberately overempha-

WHAT IS ROMANTICISM IN ART?

Romanticism is one of those concepts that is not what it seems to be. It is hard to define because the artists of the Romantic Movement did not have one style. Each of the artists seemed to adopt their own style.

First, it is necessary to discuss what Romanticism isn't. It has nothing to do with the modern interpretation of the word. Today, it is synonymous with love. It can conjure up images of two people wistfully gazing into each other's eyes over a candle lit dinner. But in this case, Romanticism does not refer to romance at all.

In the 19th century, it was a movement that placed greater emphasis on emotional reactions such as awe or horror. Imagination and spontaneity became desirable characteristics of an artistic piece. This was at the opposite end of the spectrum from realism and classical works. Classical is calm, orderly and serene. An example would be the *Venus de Milo*. Romantic art of the time is something with great energy perhaps even wild. It was at the other end of the art spectrum from painters like David and Ingres.

Romanticism meant being an individual and standing up for the rights of other individuals. For example, the most famous Romantic novels of the era were *The Hunchback of Notre Dame*, *Les Miserables* both by Victor Hugo and *Frankenstein*. Each of these books represents a protest against man's inhumanity to their fellow man. In order to drive this point home, each author directed the inhumanity against outcasts: an ex-convict, a hunchback and a man made monster.

Romanticism was a revolt against the art of the day. It was synonymous with freedom of expression. Artists took their emotions and imagination to whole new levels. While neoclassicism or the art of the day followed a set of rules, Romantic art did not adhere to any rules. There was a greater use of strong colors and the artists tended to use whatever brushstrokes they thought best to execute the painting. Expressive poses and gestures were common in some compositions. The two paintings by Delacroix discussed in this book are good examples of many of the features of Romanticism.

sized the long flowing lines of the nude taking liberties with anatomical realism.

There is a precedent for this approach. It is a throwback to the Mannerist art style of the Post-Renaissance period that emphasized elongated forms. Parmigianino's *Madonna With The Long Neck* (see fig. 4-2) became famous because of these characteristics. Looking ahead to the 20th century we will see it again with Modigliani.

Grand Odalisque had a significant influence on painters that came generations later. There is an interesting lineage going forward and even backward. Ingres must have looked at Titian's *Venus of Urbino* (see fig. 3-25) for inspiration. But the difference in his piece is that it is not done in a classical setting. The tradition of reclining nudes goes back to Giorgione and Titian. But Ingres painted a living woman and set the scene in the distant world of the Orient. Giorgione used an allegory of the mythological goddess Venus.

Looking ahead, Manet's *Olympia* (see fig. 6-14) was patterned after *Grand Odalisque*. Picasso was influenced by the lines of Ingres' nudes. The nude in Ingres' *Venus Anadyomene* assumes a pose much like one of the central figures in Picasso's *Les Demoiselles d'Avignon*. The lineage also extends to Matisse's own odalisques. Artists do not paint in a vacuum. The longer art history progresses, the more there is to study, copy and be inspired by.

DELACROIX
The Romanticist

Eugene Delacroix (1798-1863) was a leader of the French Romantic movement described in the section entitled "What Is Romanticism In Art?" The shocking and emotional nature of some of his art confirms that Delacroix drew inspiration from Michelangelo and his *The Last Judgment* (see fig. 4-1) in the Sistine Chapel. Delacroix painted images of dread such as in *The Massacre at Chios* (fig. 6-6). His tragic vision approached that of *The Last Judgment* hence the premise he rediscovered the spirit of Michelangelo. He has been called the last of the great Renaissance artists because, in addition to the inspiration from Michelangelo, his use of color shows the influence of the Venetian artists.

His position on color was opposite that of his adversary Ingres. While Ingres believed drawing was the most important part of painting, Delacroix thought color was one of the founding principles of painting. He said color gives the appearance of life to a work. He used color and movement to depict conflict and the fate of individuals. The classicalists like Ingres focused on ideal form in their drawing. They criticized Delacroix for what they perceived as a lack of draftsmanship.

Delacroix had the ability to unite allegory with history as exemplified in the two paintings discussed here. His legacy was far reaching. His color and brushstrokes inspired Matisse as well as the Impressionists. The Impressionists came to see him as the great liberator. His passion for the exotic influenced the Post-Impressionists such as Symbolists like Gauguin. He was a model for them because of his independence from the critics and because of his enthusiasm for experimentation.

Greece had been under Turkish occupation since the 15th century. But a liberation movement by the Greek people started at the beginning of the 19th century. There was a big uprising in 1821 and Ottoman forces responded by massacring Greeks throughout the country. One of the massacres occurred in April 1822 on the peaceful island of Chios which had a population of about 100,000. Nearly 98,000 Greeks were killed or sold into slavery in North Africa. Thus, the inspiration for Delacroix's *Massacre at Chios* was born.

The event resonated with Delacroix because of his inclination toward painting historical events as well as victims and anti-heroes. Delacroix denounced the genocide as a crime against humanity. The work presents a scene of savage violence and utter hopelessness. Although painted in an entirely different style, the subject matter is reminiscent of Picasso's reaction to the bombing of the Spanish town of Guernica in 1937 by German war planes. Picasso was an admirer of Delacroix.

The work is more than 12 feet tall which, in itself, makes it unique. Also, paintings of this type of ruin usually contained some sort of heroic figure. But there is no heroism here to offset the terror and suffering. There is nothing to suggest hope for the crushed victims.

The scene is painted against a desolate landscape racked with fire that seems to stretch endlessly into the distance. It adds to the hopelessness of the group of prisoners waiting to be executed.

The composition is arranged in two human pyramids. The one on the left culminates with the wounded man wearing a red fez. The pyramid on the right culminates with the mounted attacker. The pyramids are separated by two Greek soldiers in the background and a man and a woman embracing as if they are preparing to die together. Neither of the two men on the left appear able to defend themselves. In fact, the man in front seems near death. His vacant stare adds to the aura of despair. Most poignant are the two figures on the lower right. An infant is clutching its dead mother's breast. After a painting like this, 19th century art could never be the same.

Nevertheless, many critics were not impressed with this work. There is no glorious event here, only disaster. One critic labeled it "a massacre of art." The child clutching its dead mother's breast was condemned as being unfit for art.

6-6. *Massacre at Chios* by Delacroix, 1824, oil on canvas, Louvre, Paris.

6-7. *Liberty Leading the People* by Delacroix, 1830, oil on canvas, Louvre, Paris.

Unlike *Massacre at Chios, Liberty Leading the People* (fig. 6-7) is a glorious event filled with heroism. This is Delacroix's best known work. At first glance it looks like a political poster but it is much more than that. It focuses on the determination and commitment of the working class to overthrow the reigning monarch Charles X who was the brother of beheaded Louis XVI. Charles was restored to the throne after the fall of Napoleon.

Marianne is the personification of freedom. She is the combination of a goddess like figure and a robust woman of the people. She climbs a mound of corpses that are a kind of pedestal for her. The painting is an unforgettable image of Parisians taking up arms marching forward carrying the tricolor banner that represents liberty, equality and fraternity. Marianne's figure inspired the Statute of Liberty that was given to the U.S. by France 50 years later.

Again, the composition is triangular. The man on the left in the top hat and Marianne on the right form the two peaks of the triangles. The figures lying dead in the foreground represent the horizontal base. On the left there are two figures representing different social and economic positions. The man in the top hat is a member of the middle class. The man next to him carrying a sword is a laborer. On the right there is a boy holding pistols. The message is that the revolution unites these classes and includes all ages.

In the foreground are two dead bodies. The one on the left wears a long nightshirt that is pulled up to his waist. Presumably, he has been shot and dragged to the street from his bedroom. Here, Delacroix is alluding to the hated practice of royal troops who spread terror by murdering suspected revolutionary sympathizers in their beds and dragging their bodies into the street as a warning. The entire composition is made even more visually dramatic by the use of primary colors: reds, blues and yellows against the areas of brown and gray.

Why did Delacroix expose Marianne's breasts? Not because he wanted to add sexuality to the painting. Marianne represents democracy which was born in ancient Greece. Delacroix reminds us of that by making Marianne comparable to ancient nude sculpture with the partial use of nudity.

COURBET
Depicts Social Realism

Gustave Courbet (1819-77) was inspired by the revolutionary events of 1848. It immediately focused his attention on ordinary and poor people. He believed art should represent real life. He did not want to paint figures with classical poses. He was interested in presenting the facts of daily life, the way it really was for the common people. This was a major departure from French art at the time.

History paintings, even though they were considered most rigorous in terms of subject matter by the critics, did not interest Courbet. He focused on realism but his approach was different from the realistic artists like David and Ingres. Often Courbet made bold social commentary in his work. If not that, his paintings focused on ordinary people such as the rural bourgeoisie and peasants. He was convinced that artists should only paint things they had experienced or saw in their own lifetime.

In contrast to earlier realists, Courbet's realism did not focus on line and the structure of the painting. For him, the artist's mission was to pursue the truth and, in the process, help ease social imbalances. He addressed the working conditions of the poor. Because of that he became a very controversial painter. His subject matter, such as the harshness of life for the poor, was deemed vulgar by the critics. This was a long way from the idealized pictures of the lives and emotions of the aristocrats.

Eventually, the public became more interested in the new Realism and that art style gained in popularity. Daumier and Millet were among the other prominent artists that became part of the movement. They served as a bridge between the Romantic Movement led by Delacroix and both the Barbizon School and the Impressionists.

The Stone Breakers (fig. 6-8), at first glance, looks like a boring piece. It depicts two haggard men laboring to produce gravel that will be used in building roads. That is not exactly a stimulating subject matter. It is easy to see why it was scandalized and attacked by the critics.

Not only was it considered crude but it was also labeled as socialistic because most critics knew Courbet's position on social issues. In a letter that Courbet wrote, he described the discouraging message of the painting. "Alas, in labor such as this one's life begins this way and it ends in the same way."

6-8. *Stone Breakers* by Courbet, 1849, oil on canvas, destroyed during WWII bombing.

6-9. *A Burial at Ornans* by Courbet, 1849, oil on canvas, Musee d'Orsay, Paris.

Such fatalism raised the wrath of the critics. He was accused of raising a "cult of ugliness." The piece was in direct contrast of the favored concepts of beauty and the ideal. Such an unpleasant and trivial subject presented on a grand scale (the painting was 5'5" x 8'6") was unacceptable.

There is not a hint of glamour here. The painting expresses feelings of hardship and exhaustion. Courbet shows sympathy for the workers and disgust for the upper class. His realism is much like that of Caravaggio in his early 17th century paintings. Courbet violates the rules of proper art of the day by setting every detail of the worker's wretched state before the viewer. He referred to the painting as a depiction of "injustice." Nevertheless, it is not an obvious piece of political propaganda.

A short time later, Courbet went even further at least in size. *A Burial at Ornans* (fig. 6-9) was a giant painting 10 x 21 feet. It contains over 40 life-size people. The subject again focused on ordinary people. It is probably Courbet's most famous work.

In September 1848, Courbet attended the funeral of his great uncle in the village of Ornans. The next year, he transferred that experience into a realistic reenactment on canvas. He used the townspeople who had actually attended the burial as models. This was innovative because models were typically hired from the outside to portray the lives of people in paintings. Other than in portraits, people rarely represented themselves.

The work drew both praise and denunciations from the critics. At the very least, a painting of life-sized ordinary people was controversial. To sophisticated Parisians, it was acceptable to

THE PENDULUM OF ART MOVEMENTS SWINGS IN THE 19TH CENTURY

Art movements swung like a pendulum in the 19th century, never stopping in one place for very long. That has been the history of art movements but it seemed more pronounced in the 19th century.

At the start of the 19th century, there was a return to Classicism or the neo-Classic movement. Traditional art techniques in the use of line, proportion and balance were applied to portray subjects sometimes recalling Greek and Roman themes. Even more modern subjects had the traditional techniques applied to them.

Next, the pendulum swung the other way to the Romanticism led by Delacroix. The movement focused on more emotional art styles to tell stories in paintings. For a time, Romanticism changed people's ideas of what art should look like.

That approach eventually lost some of its appeal and artists returned to a more realistic style of painting. But instead of going back to the Classical themes, everyday life activities such as people working in the fields or attending funerals provided the inspiration for art.

Finally, the pendulum swung to the last major art movement of the 19th century, Impressionism. Rather than concentrating on providing realistic presentations of the subject matter, Impressionists focused on using quick, visible brushstrokes to paint their ever changing impression of what they were seeing. Light became extremely important to these painters.

In the 19th century, art movements swung back and forth between a focus on techniques, emotion in paintings and how to present an image. The groundbreaking movements did not end here. As you will see, the art pendulum continued to swing in the 20th century.

paint rural people in small genre scenes but it was unacceptable to include them in such a huge piece. Paintings on giant scales were reserved for subjects like heroic history scenes, images of the lives of royalty or religious works. Devoting such a large amount of space to a mundane event like a funeral attended by rural people was objectionable. Plenty of inspirational death scenes had been painted over the years but they were usually views of battlefields.

The realism of the piece was enhanced by Courbet adding human touches. An altar boy gazes up at a poll bearer. A young girl next to the priest looks into the distance. Grief-stricken women clutch handkerchiefs to their faces. These details were designed to add dignity to the scene and to the lives of ordinary people. But the critics thought that grieving figures dressed in black were vulgar and ugly.

Instead of following conventional compositional standards by arranging the figures in a pyramid that would show a hierarchy of importance, Courbet lined them up in a row across the picture. He thought this arrangement was more democratic.

There was also the deliberate choice of the title of the painting. It refers to the location of the burial and not the person. This was considered a radical departure from tradition. Usually, the dead individual was honored in the title not the town. But Courbet was undeterred by the objections. He described his new Realism as the "burial of Romanticism."

In the final analysis, after numerous denunciations, the public began to respect the dignity of the painting as well as his other works. They began to desire paintings that they thought were more real and ones that they could relate to in their own lives. It turns out that *A Burial at Ornans* did begin the process of burying Romanticism. Art historians have come to view Courbet's stubborn independence and determination in achieving artistic freedom as an inspiration to future generations of innovators such as the Impressionists.

COROT
A Leader of the Barbizon School

By the time the 19th century got underway, a major change was beginning to take place in the art world. For centuries the major sources of art patronage had been the church and nobility as in the Renaissance. But, as the power of the church and crown declined, so did their influence on art. In their place, the capitalistic bourgeoisie or middle class became the major patrons. With this came an important change in the subject matter of art.

Courbet and his documentation of the lives of the common people is an example of what was taking place. The art world was dominated by large annual exhibitions run by national academies such as the French Academy (see the explanatory comments on the French Academy and Salons in the information box) and their role became increasingly controversial. Art criticism proliferated helping to make or break careers.

Parisian life began to change. Between 1831 and 1851 the city's population doubled. There were massive renovations led

6-10. *Souvenir de Mortefontaine* by Corot, 1864, oil on canvas, Louvre, Paris.

by Georges-Eugene Haussmann that transferred Paris into a modern, crowded, noisy, fast-pace metropolitan center. The result was that artistic images of peaceful country life served as a counterbalance to a more hectic pace of life. Those images were the staple of the Barbizon painters and they became increasingly popular with critics and collectors. Landscape painting may have started out as being considered second class citizens to history painting but, over time, it became history in the making.

Jean-Baptiste Camille Corot (1796-1875) was a leading member of the Barbizon School of landscape painting. The group was named after the village of Barbizon near the Fontainbleau forest that was about 35 miles southeast of Paris where the artists gathered. Their emphasis was almost entirely on landscape paintings.

They painted "en plein air" or out of doors like the Impressionists and drew their inspiration from nature. Unlike the artists that preceded them, there was no drama in their art, no story being told. They were different from earlier landscape painters. Those artists might make some sketches outdoors but then they would return to their studio to begin the painting. In many respects, Barbizon artists were the forerunners of Impressionism and had the most influence on them. Some call them the first Impressionists. One appropriate quote was, "The road to Impressionism goes straight through the forest of Fontainbleau."

Nevertheless, there were differences between the Barbizon painters and the Impressionists. They painted color as it was supposed to be before it was changed by light or shade. Grass was supposed to be green so they painted it green. Impressionists painted the color they saw, not what it was supposed to be. They painted a mixture of color. Also, they had an aversion to striking color in contrast to the up-and-coming Impressionists who embraced vivid hues.

There were other differences. The brushstrokes of the Barbizon painters were usually controlled. Works were carefully painted. Impressionists used rougher, more vivid brushstrokes because they painted quickly. Their paintings were lighter because they concentrated on light and its effects on the surroundings. When Impressionists painted shadows they used purple or blue, not black or gray like the Barbizon artists.

6-11. *Woman with a Pearl* by Corot, c. 1868, oil on canvas, Louvre, Paris.

simple, unhurried rural existence. It is a scene of rustic beauty that shows the foundations of Impressionism. Monet, one of the leading Impressionists, was aware of the linkage. He was quoted as saying, "There is only one master: Corot. We are nothing compared to him, nothing."

In this work, Corot is not painting a scene from life. The title *Souvenir* translates into recollections. This suggests he is painting memories of earlier visits to the village. Corot visited the area many times to study the reflections of light on the water.

Although Corot would have an important impact on the Impressionistic movement that would evolve shortly, there were differences. His colors were more restrained. Impressionist's favored bolder, more vibrant colors. Corot's paintings tend to be dominated by light browns, grays and dark greens. These were colors that were forbidden by the Impressionists. There was never anything daring about the colors of the Barbizon painters like Corot. In contrast, Impressionists often experimented with vivid colors. That is one reason why their work became so appealing. Nevertheless, a number of Impressionist followers called themselves pupils of Corot. These included Camille Pissarro whose art will be discussed in the next chapter and Berthe Morisot who will be discussed along with Mary Cassatt in chapter 8.

As impressive as Corot's landscape paintings are, he is also considered a master of portraiture and *Woman with a Pearl* (fig 6-11) is an example of that. In fact, Degas said he was a better portrait painter than a landscape artist.

The model is the 16 year old daughter of a fabrics dealer who was a friend of Corot. She is clad in Italian made clothing that the artist had brought back with him from his travels abroad. As is the case with his landscapes, the color in the painting is restrained.

The realism of the piece is enhanced by the expert use of shadows. There is a shadow at the center of the lower lip and one that caresses the model under her chin. Comparisons have been made between this piece and Leonardo's *Mona Lisa* (see fig. 3-12) particular-

Corot's images of rural landscapes had a soft, dreamy atmosphere. That effect was captured in his masterpiece *Souvenir de Montefontaine* (fig. 6-10). There is a misty play of light over the lake that adds to the tranquility of the scene. Corot's careful attention to the play of light provides an image of the sunlight bouncing off the glass like water of the lake making it look shimmery. Reflections of the hills and trees from the other side of the lake are visible in the water. He gives you the contrast of a bare tree and one covered with lush foliage.

This is no ordinary landscape painting. It has a soothing almost poetic effect. When he includes figures as in this piece, he invites us to identify with them and to share their

6-12. *The Gleaners* by Millet, 1857, oil on canvas, Musee d'Orsay, Paris.

WHAT WERE THE FRENCH ACADEMY AND THE PARIS SALONS?

The French Academy was founded in 1648 under King Louis XIV. In 1795, there were a series of mergers with other groups to form the Academie de Beaux-Arts (French Academy of Fine Arts). The French Academy had the power to decide the "official" art for France. They determined what was good and bad art.

The French Academy oversaw the training of artists as well as the artistic standards and, to a large extent, what was painted. It sponsored one official exhibition each year to which artists could submit their works for approval. It was called the Salon. To achieve any hope of success, artists would have to exhibit their work in the annual Salon. Acceptance or rejection could make or break a career.

The increasingly conservative juries were not receptive to the Impressionist painters or to any avant-garde art for that matter. The Salon opposed shifts away from the traditional styles of art some of which dated from the Renaissance. The mid-19th century was probably the high point of the Salon's influence on European art.

In 1863, the Salon jury turned away an unusually high number of submitted paintings. This caused an uproar among the rejected artists, many of whom had been accepted at previous exhibitions. In response, Napoleon III instituted the Salon des Refuses for a selection of works that had been rejected. Essentially, this represented the birth of the avant-garde. Nevertheless, a decade later the Impressionists broke away from the Salons and began to hold their own independent exhibitions in 1874.

With the institution of the Salon des Refuses (exhibition of refusals) and artists beginning to organize their own shows, the exclusivity of the official Salon began to be undermined. Today, the Paris Salon is merely one of a number of art shows. But for many decades the Salon was the only major art show in France and it exerted massive influence on the career of artists and the type of art that could be shown.

ly in the direct gaze and the placement and detail of her hands. Another painting that is considered similar is Vermeer's *Girl With a Pearl Earring* (see fig. 5-16) given the rather exotic attire of both models. But unlike Vermeer's piece there is some controversy over the title of this painting. It is an odd title given that the young woman is not wearing a pearl but what hangs on her forehead is a leaf.

MILLET
A Different Approach to Barbizon Landscape Painting

Jean-Francois Millet (1814-75) had a different approach to landscape painting. He was a committed realist and that shows in his painting *The Gleaners* (fig. 6-12). He took the landscape idea and extended it to figures. He was an innovator because he added the world of peasants and their rural labor to his landscapes. In fact, Millet's works are closer to genre painting (i.e., intimate scenes of ordinary people in everyday life) than landscape art.

All his life, he painted farm laborers with blunt realism and quiet dignity. In *The Gleaners* he depicts three women stooping in the fields to glean grain from the harvest. This was regarded as one of the lowest jobs in the rural society. It required hours of backbreaking work to gather enough wheat to produce a single loaf of bread.

By focusing on the brutal hunching of backs, Millet portrays the women as heroic figures. The light illuminates their shoulders as they labor in the fields. This is different from the past when servants were shown in paintings as subservient to a king or someone who was part of the aristocracy.

In 1857 when Corot submitted this painting to the Paris Salon, he got an unenthusiastic reception. By putting the focus on the misery of peasant workers, people misread his intentions. They thought he was trying to rekindle the revolutionary passion of 1848. Some saw the painting as political propaganda. That he was trying to awaken the oblivious peasants to the fact that this will be the way they will live for the rest of their lives.

Although Corot was an adamant supporter of the working class, there were no political intentions to his work. He painted poor people because he knew and loved them, not because he considered them downtrodden. In this regard, he differed from Courbet who painted poor people not because he loved them but because they were downtrodden.

Millet was an avid reader of the Bible. He saw in scenes like this the fate of humanity, condemned since the expulsion of Adam and Eve from the Garden of Eden, to earn their food through hard labor. He was a fatalist much like Courbet showed himself to be in his work *The Stone Breakers* (see fig. 6-8).

MANET
His Avant-Garde Art Brings Us to the Edge of Impressionism

Do not get Manet (1832-83) confused with Monet. Their names are spelled and pronounced alike but, as we will see, they are worlds apart in art styles. Monet is about impressions. That is why he is grouped with the Impressionists. As his career progresses he concentrates more and more on his own visual sensations. As he dissolves into abstraction he defines a path to modernity. Manet is about ideas. His art is more intellectual. He concentrates on the human situation. But his two masterpieces changed the course of art. So both artists are responsible for the start of modernism.

Manet is hard to pigeonhole. Was he a Realist or an Impressionist? Many people believe he was an Impressionist because of his close association with the group. But association is not enough to establish one as part of a movement.

His painting style was different from the Impressionists. He was not interested in capturing light and its effects on the surroundings. His brushstrokes were more refined. He painted some outdoor pieces but he believed serious work could only occur in the studio. He was probably the most Parisian artist who ever lived, rarely leaving the city. In contrast, the Impressionists lived in the country or would journey to it from the city to paint. He was an expert in the use of black and got a luminous effect from it. But that was a color the Impressionists avoided. For example, Renoir once said, "It is a hue I have banned from my palette."

Manet did not exhibit with the Impressionists. Nevertheless, he became like a spiritual leader of the group. They rallied around him and were inspired by his art. He broke away from the prevailing art scene and that was something they were trying to do. So they learned from him. Like the Impressionists he tried to capture the moment in his paintings and that was something they respected.

Manet is a good example of how art history progresses. He challenged the past and the present. In the process he created a new art form. The Impressionists respected his innovations and his paintings that were a radical departure form the art of the day. He opened the door to Impressionism and a new way of art.

Two of his paintings represent turning points in art history. Both will be discussed immediately below. They generated so much controversy that they served as an inspiration for the younger artists that would create Impressionism. Although debased by the critics and the public at the time, today the two paintings are considered watershed works of art.

Manet produced the most radical paintings of the time. They were so shocking that they opened a debate over morality in art. Because of his innovations some historians see him as the start of the modern art movement. That is hard to disagree with.

6-13. *Le Dejeuner sur l'Herbe* by Manet, 1863, oil on canvas, Musee d'Orsay, Paris.

Unlike the Impressionists who broke away from the traditional art scene and started their own exhibits, Manet continued to put great emphasis on acceptance by the Salon. Despite the debasing of some of his works by the critics, he believed that success as an artist could only occur through recognition at the Salon. Consequently, he refused to show at any of the Impressionist exhibits. In staying with the Salon, in effect, Manet tried to bring about a revolution in art from within the system. The Impressionists, by breaking away from the Salon and organizing their own exhibits, tried to bring about a revolution from outside the system.

His painting style was criticized for its lack of perspective or the lack of attention to providing the illusion of depth. His brushstrokes were considered haphazard, at least in comparison with the meticulous style of many of the Salon painters. But, it is not just talent with a paintbrush that makes an artist important; it is having that talent and complimenting it with a visionary mind. Manet had both.

He experimented with a new, clever sense of reality. He wanted to be rebellious yet adored. That is a difficult combination to achieve. He did not come close to reaching that goal with the first two paintings discussed. In fact, rather than achieving respect, they made him the most notorious painter in France in the 1860s. That was not something Manet aspired to.

Le Dejeuner sur l'Herbe (The Luncheon on the Grass) (fig. 6-13) was one of the thousands of paintings that the Salon jury rejected in 1863. It is not surprising that the work was rejected since originality was despised by the Salon jury and this was certainly an original painting in terms of subject matter. But it was exhibited in the Salon des Refuses the same year. Viewers were scandalized. It was the painting that drew the most criticism and helped propel Manet to the role of "bad boy" of French art.

Manet depicts a female nude and two fully dressed men in the foreground. There is a scantily dressed female bather in the background. The models were all closely associated with Manet. That added to the negative reaction to the painting. The men were Manet's brother and future brother-law. The seated nude has Victorine Meurent's face. She was his favorite model. But Manet substituted the plumper body of his wife Suzanne Leenhoff for Meurent's thinner body. The public did not warm to her cold stare that she fixes on the viewer. The fact that Meurent was reputed to be a prostitute did not help matters.

There was nothing surprising about painting a nude woman. Nudity was a popular theme in art. The shocking aspect was that she was with two fully clothed men. But what the critics missed or refused to accept was that the painting was inspired by works of Renaissance masters. His piece represented a bold reworking of Titian's *Pastoral Concert* (see fig. 3-23) and perhaps Giorgione's *The Tempest* (see fig. 3-20) both showing nude women with fully clothed men in a country setting. Another precedent was Marcantonio Raimondi's engraving *Judgment at Paris* c. 1515 after a drawing by Raphael.

Manet's piece would have been more readily accepted if he had depicted the female as a nymph or mythological being. But this was a modern Parisian woman. His approach was too bold to accept the painting as a tribute to Europe's artistic heritage dating back to the Renaissance. One critic described it as "...a young man's practical joke."

Interestingly, Thomas Couture painted his gigantic Romans in the Decadence of the Empire that hangs in the d'Orsay just 16 years before. It is one of the best known and most influential paintings of the second half of the 19th century and he never received the type of harsh criticism that was directed at Manet. Yet, it incorporates much more licentious behavior than anything Manet ever imagined in his art work. The reason is that Couture's figures were taken from antiquity and Manet's were not.

It was not only the subject matter that bothered the critics, it was Manet's painting technique. There is no subtle graduation in colors. Instead, there are harsh contrasts. The lighting looked unnatural. It cast no shadows. The critics claimed the pictorial treatment was inept. There is no sense of depth to the background scene where the bather seems to float above the other figures. The three figures in the forefront stand out from their background. They appear as if they are seated before a painted backdrop. But all of this is testimony to Manet's reluctance to conform to the art conventions of the day and to emphasize a new artistic freedom.

Because of the uproar over *Le Dejeuner*, Manet chose to wait two years to submit *Olympia* (fig. 6-14). The wait did not help. The uproar was even greater. The public and

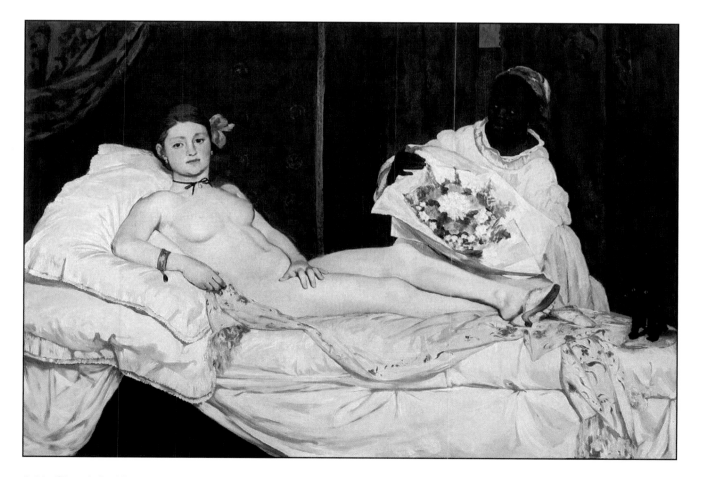

6-14. *Olympia* by Manet, 1863, oil on canvas, Musee d'Orsay, Paris.

critics saw both pieces as vulgar and ridiculous. The open sexuality in the two pieces was shocking. Instead of being adored as Manet hoped he would, the paintings made him the world's first "shock artist."

In both paintings, we as the viewer become voyeurs. In *Le Dejeuner* it is as if we are being invited into the picnic by the woman. In *Olympia* she is looking at us almost as if she is casually saying "next" as her next customer. Her gaze makes us feel uncomfortable. Picasso uses the same technique in *Les Demoiselles* (see fig. 11-6).

The 19 year old model was the same in both pieces. The public was outraged by her gaze, particularly in *Olympia*. Is that a look of indifference? It really doesn't matter because she is there for sex and she regards the viewer with a look that seems part invitation, part dare and part indifference. She overturns the centuries old tradition of a passive nude. The public and critics could not deal with all that.

Notice the tilt of her head. She could not hold it in that position comfortably for any length of time. It is as if a customer has just entered the room and she notices. The servant is presenting her with flowers from him. It all highlights the sense of casualness and thus the immorality of the piece.

Just as *Le Dejeuner* was inspired by Renaissance paintings the same holds true with *Olympia*. It was based on Titian's *Venus of Urbino* (see fig. 3-25). But, in this case, Manet's painting became the antithesis of Titian's.

The nude figure in *Venus of Urbino* is softly curvaceous. Manet's figure is angular. Titian's nude looks lovingly or perhaps flirtatiously at the spectator and shows affection with roses in her hand. Manet's appears coldly indifferent to the viewer. There is a black cat in *Olympia* that arches its back at us as if annoyed by our presence (or the presence of the customer). Contrast this with the sleeping dog in the Titian. We get the sense that Olympia is in a position of power and in command of the situation. We are

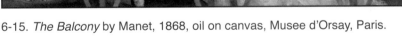

6-15. *The Balcony* by Manet, 1868, oil on canvas, Musee d'Orsay, Paris.

the submissive ones.

In this one painting, Manet overturns the entire tradition of the accommodating female nude. He relocates the *Venus of Urbino* to the brothel. Manet redefines what art can be. *Olympia* doesn't look beautiful in the idealized way of Titian's nude. The painting asks the question: Must nudity in art be beautiful? No wonder the painting was misunderstood and vilified.

If all of this were not enough, the controversy was heightened by *Olympia* wearing some small decorative items. She has an orchid in her ear, a bracelet, a ribbon around her neck and the slipper on the right foot has

6-16. Majas on a Balcony by Goya, 1814, oil on canvas, Metropolitan Museum of Art, New York.

a mockery of the relaxed, shielding hand of the woman in Titian's *Venus of Urbino*.

Even though Olympia became a public scandal at the time, it was championed by the art avant-garde both then and later. They recognized that Manet was addressing art history and inviting the viewer to compare his paintings with those that inspired them. He was emphasizing his own radical innovations.

The Balcony (fig. 6-15) is a painting that was inspired by Goya's *The Majas at the Balcony*. Here, Berthe Morisot makes her first appearance in Manet's art. Her haunting beauty is obvious and her dark eyes captivate you. She would become his muse and close companion, sitting for 11 portraits (their relationship will be discussed in some detail in Chapter 8). In fact, all the models in *The Balcony* are friends of the artist. The man is painter Antoine Guillemet and the woman the musician Fanny Claus.

There is a contrast between the sitting dark haired beauty and the two other figures. Her face has been painted with greater precision. The faces of the other two look bland and unfinished almost as if they have been pasted on. Berthe's eyes are the only ones that look distinctly focused, perhaps too focused. Manet gives her a consciousness, at least more so than the others. Perhaps these details are because he was attracted to her and he anticipated that a close connection was in the offing. Or, perhaps, he was simply painting what he saw.

dropped off carelessly. All of this accentuates her sexuality and how comfortable she is with her lifestyle.

There are contradictions in the painting. *Olympia* is thin which is counter to the prevailing view at that time that thin women were not considered attractive. Her hand rests over her leg shielding the private area of her body. But this reference to female modesty is ironic given that any other allusion to modesty is completely absent. It becomes

The painting tells no story, no anecdote. The figures are frozen as if in a photo. It is really a study in color. Manet was famous for his use of black. The black background from which the figures seem to emerge provides a sharp contrast to the white dresses. The figures are framed in green shutters and railings. It all resembles a theatre scene.

There is a distinguished looking man with a high winged collar, a wide purple tie and black suit. He looks

6-17. *Luncheon in the Studio* by Manet, oil on canvas, 1868, Neue Pinakothek, Munich.

into the distance and holds his hands up as if startled by something he had just seen. Standing in front of him is a woman putting on fawn colored gloves. The placement of her hands is designed to compliment the hands of the man. The green umbrella she is holding is at the angle of a violin because the model is a famous violinist. The slightly absurd bouquet of flowers on her hat echoes her round face.

Berthe Morisot is wearing a fancy dress. She holds a red fan that forms a V with the umbrella. The V is designed to frame the man. In contrast to the other woman, Berthe is bareheaded with wild curls on her forehead and jet black hair flowing down her shoulders. She looks almost gypsy like compared to the other woman.

Despite all the details, as usual, the critics were unimpressed. There were sarcastic reactions like "close the shutters" and "Manet lowered himself to the point of being in competition with the painters of the building trade." But Manet was taking liberties with tradition again and freeing himself from the academic constraints laid down by the French Academy.

Like so many of Manet's paintings there are oddities about this piece that instill a somewhat unsettling quality. Perhaps that is what bothered the critics so much. There is the total lack of any interaction between the figures. Why are they so disengaged from each other? What is the tiny dog doing in the scene? It is almost lost in the folds of Berthe's dress as it seems to be struggling to stand up. It would seem to be better placed on her lap. In the background hardly visible in this image is the mysterious Leon who is the focal point of Manet's painting done the same year, *Luncheon in the Studio* (see fig. 6-17). It has been speculated that he is the illegitimate son of Manet. Why is he there? Why is he hidden? Then there is the unusual green of the balcony and the shutters that seem to distract us from the figures.

As already noted, Morisot comes across as a beautiful woman but mainly from a distance. Close up, her lovely eyes look almost dull and glazed over as she stares off into the distance. This is not the romantic figure that we will see later. Morisot judged herself as being "more strange than ugly" in the piece. Why did Manet paint her this way?

6-18. *A Bar at the Folies-Bergere* by Manet, 1882, oil on canvas, Courtauld Institute Art Gallery, London

What the critics missed as they had in the past with Manet's *Le Dejeuner sur l'Herbe* and *Olympia* was its reference to a classic painting. In this case were its Goyaesque aspects. That is, it was inspired by the work of another famous artist, the masterpiece *Majas on a Balcony* by the Spanish painter Francisco Goya (fig. 6-16). Manet would have seen that piece during a trip to Spain in 1865 just three years before he painted *The Balcony*.

There are similarities. The women in *Majas* are well dressed and from the upper class. They are also frozen as if in a photo and black is the dominant color. Their dresses are in sharp contrast to the black background and the two dark figures in the rear. But one striking difference is that the Goya piece seems more sinister.

Luncheon in the Studio (fig. 6-17) is shown as an example of Manet's use of luminous black. It is one thing that separated him from the Impressionists. They rarely used black. As already noted, Renoir once said, "It is a hue I have banished from my palette." The velvet jacket on the young man is an example of that luminosity. Matisse was enchanted by this piece. Decades later he would describe the jacket as "pure black."

The young man has been identified as 16-year old Leon Leenhoff, the son of Suzanne Leenhoff before her 1863 marriage to Manet. But it has also been speculated he could be the son of Manet. If that were the case, then the two figures in the background could symbolically represent Suzanne and Manet. Leon's yellow tie, pants and straw hat connect with the lemon in the still-life on the table. There are also oysters and a knife handle jutting off the table.

There is a black cat on the chair that is probably a reference to the popular poet Baudelaire who died the previous year and was identified with cats. He was known as "the poet of cats." Also, Manet had used a cat in previous paintings. Remember the one that appears in his famous *Olympia*.

This painting was exhibited at the 1869 Paris Salon along with *The Balcony*. Both pieces were criticized. A quote by the critic Jules-Antoine Castagnary reflects not only the hostility toward Manet's work but also the rigid expectations of what a painting should look like in that period. For that reason, it is worth repeating in part. Remember, this was before the turbulence that the Impressionists brought to the art world.

"True, he is well painted, brushed by a vigorous hand; but where is he? In the dining room? In that case, having his back to the table, he has the wall between him and us, and his position no longer makes sense...Like the personages in a play, it's necessary that every figure in a painting is in its proper plane, fulfills its role, and thereby contributes to the expression of the general idea. Nothing arbitrary and nothing superfluous, that is the law of all artistic composition."

In the last years of his life, Manet painted a number of café scenes. *A Bar at the Folies Bergere* (fig. 6-18) is Manet's most enigmatic painting. Art historians still debate its meaning. It is his last great painting completed about one year before his tragic death at the age of 51. He was at the height of his career.

Lively scenes like the *Folies* were never painted from real life. This piece was painted in his studio. The model posed behind a table filled with bottles and food. He certainly was not copying life directly. He interpreted what he saw.

At first glance, the piece looks like nothing more than a realistic view of Parisian night life at a famous night club in the late 19th century. But it is much more than that. Standing in front of a mirror that is behind the barmaid we see a reflection of what she sees directly ahead. We are not just observers of the painting. We become participants in it.

The room is filled with details of people enjoying the entertainment. In the upper left hand corner, there is a pair of green shoes that belong to a trapeze artist that is performing for the crowd. To the left of center, there is a woman with binoculars perhaps watching the show or surveying other patrons.

Directly in front of the viewer there is a marvelous still-life of tangerines, flowers and champagne bottles that Cezanne would have appreciated. They are there to highlight the pleasures for which the Folies Bergere was famous. But the barmaid's expression refutes these associations with pleasure. She does not smile at the customer but looks self-absorbed, even depressed.

This is where Manet's composition presents a visual puzzle that has perplexed art historians. He plays with the rules of perspective. The barmaid's own reflection is not directly behind her as it should be. Instead, it is at a right angle to where she is standing. It is as if the mirror has been placed on a slant. There is no reflection of the customer who, supposedly, stands directly in front of her. The bottles are not reflected accurately.

These placements were criticized at the time as mistakes by Manet. But, in effect, they show there is a double reality in the painting. There is a depiction of Paris night life and something else. But what is the something else?

The painting appears to be about loneliness. The barmaid has a forlorn expression as if she is there to dispense pleasure but receives none herself. But the reflection of her and the customer in the top hat to the right tell a different story. She bends toward him and their gazes meet. Perhaps Manet wants to contrast a longing for companionship reflected in the mirror with the disappointing reality of an ordinary or even dull existence that directly confronts her.

It has been speculated that there could be a less innocent meaning to the painting. Perhaps Manet, the painter of modern life in Paris, introduced a morality aspect into the work. It was not uncommon for women of ill-repute to frequent night clubs like the Folies. Nor was it uncommon for the servers to be available to the male patrons. It was one of the appeals of the clubs. The man in the reflection could be a potential client with whom she is conducting business. But looked at directly, her withdrawn, sad expression shows how she feels about her life style.

The critics did not get it. They thought the subject of a bar scene was beneath the dignity of art. Whatever the exact meaning of the painting, it is much different from the Impressionist's optimistic view of modern life. This painting provides a more pessimistic one. Nevertheless, it is capturing the moment and that is what the Impressionists do. It is an example of why Manet was an inspiration to them.

Recognition for Manet came very late in his life, perhaps too late. That seemed to be the case for a number of the painters in his circle like Sisley and Cezanne. A friend had been appointed Minister of Fine Arts. He suggested that Manet be awarded the Legion of Honor medal. At first the President of the Republic was opposed to the idea but eventually he signed the decree. It came in 1882 but Manet was far from ecstatic over the honor. He was bitter over the years of neglect and felt the gesture by the state was too belated.

Eventually, recognition and rewards became frequent. In 1889, he was honored as one of the great painters of the 19th century. George Clemenceau, the Premier of France, had *Olympia* hung in the Louvre in 1907, more than forty years after the public scandal over the painting. Even then, after all the revolutionary changes that had occurred in the art world, there were still those that remained shocked by *Olympia*.

By 1880, Manet's health began to take a serious turn for the worse. The syphilis he had contracted as a young man began to spread. Gangrene affected his left leg and it had to be amputated. Complications developed and, after much suffering, Manet died in March 1883.

With the death of their spiritual leader, Impressionism as a group movement came to an end. Monet, Cezanne and Pissarro all moved to different areas in France. The group spirit that once existed died along with Manet. Meetings were rare. From that point on, Impressionism would be represented by individual painters each with a different style.

IMAGES

6-1. *Death of Marat* by David, 1793, oil on canvas, Musees Royaux des Beaux-Arts de Belgique, Brussels.

6-2. *Napoleon Crossing the Alps* by David, 1801, oil on canvas, Chateau de Malmaison Rueil-Malmaison, Paris.

6-3. *The Coronation of Napoleon* by David, 1807, oil on canvas, Louvre, Paris.

6-4. *Napoleon Crowned* by Ingres, 1806, oil on canvas, Musee de L'Armee, Hotel des Invalides, Paris.

6-5. *Grande Odalisque* by Ingres, 1814, oil on canvas, Louvre, Paris.

6-6. *Massacre at Chios* by Delacroix, 1824, oil on canvas, Louvre, Paris.

6-7. *Liberty Leading the People* by Delacroix, 1830, oil on canvas, Louvre, Paris.

6-8. *Stone Breakers* by Courbet, 1849, oil on canvas, destroyed during WWII bombing.

6-9. *A Burial at Ornans* by Courbet, 1849, oil on canvas, Musee d'Orsay, Paris.

6-10. *Souvenir de Mortefontaine* by Corot, 1864, oil on canvas, Louvre, Paris.

6-11. *Woman with a Pearl* by Corot, c. 1868, oil on canvas, Louvre, Paris.

6-12. *The Gleaners* by Millet, 1857, oil on canvas, Musee d'Orsay, Paris.

6-13. *Le Dejeuner sur l'Herbe* by Manet, 1863, oil on canvas, Musee d'Orsay, Paris.

6-14. *Olympia* by Manet, 1863, oil on canvas, Musee d'Orsay, Paris.

6-15. *The Balcony* by Manet, 1868, oil on canvas, Musee d'Orsay, Paris.

6-16. *Majas on a Balcony* by Goya, 1814, oil on canvas, Metropolitan Museum of Art, New York.

6-17. *Luncheon in the Studio* by Manet, oil on canvas, 1868, Neue Pinakothek, Munich.

6-18. *A Bar at the Folies-Bergere* by Manet, 1882, oil on canvas, Courtauld Institute Art Gallery, London.

IMPRESSIONISM

7

Like the Barbizon artists, one of the favorite subjects for Impressionists was landscapes. But they did not concentrate on the unchanging aspects of a landscape. They captured moments. That is, fleeting impressions of what they saw and those impressions were always changing. Their objective was to paint what the eye sees, not what the head knows. In other words, don't paint what you expect to see. To do this they had to paint on location, en plein air.

There were many influences on Impressionism. The Impressionists built on the styles and techniques established before them. Delacroix's visible brushstrokes and color combinations had a big impact. The same can be said about Courbet's realism, the landscapes of Corot and the other Barbizon painters as well as Manet's paintings that focused on modern subjects. But instead of the themes of working class people and rural life depicted by artists like Courbet and the Barbizon school, the pure Impressionists were devoted to the study of leisure by the upper middle class.

Everything about their work seemed to represent a rejection of the principles and practices set down in the teachings of the French Academy. They violated nearly all the rules of academic painting. For the Academy, line and drawing should be stressed. For the Impressionists, color took precedence over line. The Academy favored the use of muted sometimes somber colors like brown, gray and dark green. The Impressionist's avoided black and favored brilliant, luminous colors. Shadows were painted in blue and violet, not black or gray.

Originality was despised by the Academy and they favored historical paintings. The Impressionists embraced originality. For them, historical themes were out and nature was in. The Academy wanted artists to capture the details of carefully painted images in their works done in the studio with suppressed brushstrokes. The Impressionists painted en plein air, trying to capture momentary effects with short visible brushstrokes. Historical subjects, religious themes and portraits were highly valued by the Academy. Landscapes, the staple of most Impressionists, were at the bottom of the pecking order in terms of importance to the French Academy. Given all these differences in the approach to art, it is no wonder that the early Impressionist paintings were routinely rejected by the Salon.

Because of rejection after rejection of most of their works by the Salon, in 1874 a group of artists banded together and formed an independent society to exhibit their works. The intention behind their association was simple: they needed to sell their works. Many of the exhibitors have become household names to art lovers. They included Cezanne, Morisot, Sisley, Monet, Renoir, Degas and Pissarro. It is hard to believe now but many of them lost money in the early exhibitions.

Manet did not exhibit with the group. Despite repeated rejections he was steadfast in his belief that the only course of success was through the Salon. Nevertheless, through his close association with the artists he thoroughly understood the Impressionists and what they were trying to accomplish. He said, "One doesn't paint a landscape, the sea or a figure, one paints their impression of the effects of the time of day on a landscape, the sea or a figure."

Even though a group of artists exhibited together, the preferred subject of their paintings was diverse. Manet, who preceded the group but had a major impact on it, chose enigmatic themes and Renaissance master paintings recreated in a novel way. Some of his works were noted for the scandal they created. Sisley and Pissarro focused on landscapes and the effects of changes in light. Degas painted the ballet, horse races and ordinary people often as if they were photos in which he was capturing an accidental image. Renoir used bright color to get vibrant images of women, social gatherings, children and landscapes. Monet was interested in painting the same subject at different times of the day to capture the effects of light. The subject matter of his works really becomes light.

One way to conclude the introductory discussion on Impressionism is to try to answer a number of questions frequently asked about the movement. Some of the answers provided here have already been covered in the discussion above but the information is worth repeating.

WHY IS IMPRESSIONISM SO DIFFERENT AND IMPORTANT?

It is different because it challenged the art of the day on almost every front. The brushstrokes were very visible, rough almost crude compared to the fine lines of other artists. Subject matter changes with the Impressionists. Often they painted out of doors surrounded by nature, so landscapes become important. In observing nature closely, they rejected the roles of emotion and imagination in their art.

It is one thing that separates them from artists who immediately followed in their foot steps like Van Gogh and Gauguin.

There is more informality in their works. For example, when they painted portraits they became more informal with less posing and more casual postures. They painted genre scenes, that is, intimate scenes of ordinary people in everyday life. In the process, they elevated common people and their activities to a level in the art world and on canvas that had not been seen before.

Impressionists were different because they tried to capture light and its effects on the surroundings. They often captured fleeting moments like you might do with photography. Finally, it is different because of the way they used color. Instead of mixing colors on the palate, they often put colors beside each other and let the eye mix them. In the process, they got more vibrant color combinations. If they wanted to produce the effect of green, they put yellow and blue beside each other which produced a more brilliant effect than if they mixed them together. They had no rules but used their senses to get the right combination.

Impressionism is important because it represented a pivotal turning point in art history. They broke away from the previous, more academic styles of painting to such an extent that they paved the way for many groundbreaking art developments in the 20th century. In short, their style changed people's expectations of what a painting should look like and, in the process, opened the way for modernism.

WHAT MAKES IMPRESSIONISM SO APPEALING?

Intuitively, most people can answer this question. It is pretty and easy to show off. It seduces the eye and makes people feel good about themselves. There are bright colors and serenity in their works. Their style is easy to recognize and there is an attraction to the era that they document.

The public's view on Impressionism has changed drastically over the decades. Initially, the French saw their work as vulgar and ridiculous. Now, it is seen as serene and beautiful. It provides a fundamental definition of beauty. Gradually their works gained a degree of public acceptance and support with the French in the late 19th century. In fact, Impressionism gained favor with the public before the critics began to accept it with any degree of enthusiasm. Renoir achieved success in the 1880s. Monet was secure financially in the early 1880s and Pissarro by the early 1890s.

Impressionism is appealing to the rich and commands astronomical prices at auctions partly because of the "feel good" factors. More importantly, it has appeal because of the prestige of owning an Impressionistic work and because it has been a very good investment. That is always appealing.

There is also the opportunity for smugness of hindsight. These are painters who were not understood when they started. The Impressionist's contemporaries could not understand what they were about. Their works were rejected as being beneath the standards of what qualified as good art. But now, it is art that is easy for us to understand just how important it is. With the benefit of hindsight, we can feel wiser than the art critics of an earlier era. People did not understand artists like the Impressionists or Van Gogh, but we do. That makes us seem special.

WHAT WERE SOME OF THE TECHNICAL CHANGES THAT CONTRIBUTED TO THE GROWTH OF IMPRESSIONISM?

There were several during the 19th century. First in importance was paint in tubes. They provided artists with a great deal more flexibility than mixing paints in their studio. It allowed them to become plein air painters. Renoir told his son, "It was these tubes of paint, which were so easy to carry around that enabled us to paint entirely from nature. Without these tubes of paint there would have been no Cezanne, no Monet, no Sisley or no Pissarro, no such thing as Impressionism as the journalists were to call it."

Second, there was photography. While photography grew in importance and began to challenge the appeal of realistic paintings, the Impressionists were the first to offer a subjective alternative to a photograph. They could do something better than a photo. They could express their perception of nature rather than showing an exact image of it created mechanically. Also, they could provide vivid color which a photo could not do at that time.

Third, there was the development of railroad systems. They opened the countryside to the city based artists to paint. Also, railroad fortunes provided new wealth that added to the demand for Impressionistic works.

HOW DID IMPRESSIONISM GET ITS NAME?

As you already know, the art world in Paris in the 19th century was dominated by the French Academy. Every year they would conduct a giant art show called the Salon. It was the cultural event of the year. Artists would send their works to the Salon jury and hope to be selected. Thousands of works were shown but thousands were also rejected.

The entire success of a painter depended on being accepted to the Salon because there were no private galleries to speak of. In short, everything began and ended with the Salon. Without acceptance there could be no awards and no awards often meant there were no commissions for the artist to do other works.

Originality was considered unacceptable by the French Academy. It preferred finished images that mirrored reality. Color should be conservative and brushstrokes surpassed. What a change from the Italian Renaissance. In Paris in the 19th century, new ideas were suppressed. In Florence, Venice and Rome in the 15th and 16th centuries they were encouraged.

In response to consistent rejections by the Salon, the Impressionists started their own exhibitions in 1874 and held eight over a 12 year span from 1874 to 1886. In the first exhibition, Monet showed a painting called *Impression Sunrise* (fig. 7-1). It had all the characteristics that offended the Academy and broke with the style of what was considered acceptable art.

A critic, Louis Leroy wrote a scathing review of the exhibition in the newspaper *Le Charivari*. Using the title of Monet's painting as an example, he derisively titled the article "The Exhibition of the Impressionists." The name stuck with the group and the word Impressionism was born. Leroy took particular aim at Monet's *Impression Sunrise* by declaring the painting was, at most, a sketch and could hardly be termed a finished work. He stated, "Wallpaper in its embryonic state is more finished than that seascape."

The members of the group that Leroy was attacking were not upset when labeled Impressionists because they felt it really was their impressions that they were trying to capture in their works. But the name did nothing to help the painters. It simply reinforced the view that their art was casual, sloppy and unfinished. In fact, each of their first three exhibitions lost money.

Jules Castagnary, in his review in the newspaper *Le Siecle* in 1874 offered a more favorable opinion on why he regarded Pissarro, Sisley, Morisot, Renoir and Degas as Impressionists: "They are Impressionists in the sense that they reproduce not the landscape but the sensory perceptions it evokes."

HOW DID THE FRENCH REACT TO IMPRESSIONISM?

You already know the answer to that question. But here are some quotes. In 1876, a critic Emile Porcheron wrote in Le Soleil, "An Impressionist, having neither the

7-1. *Impression Sunrise* by Monet, 1872, oil on canvas, Musee Marmotten Monet, Paris.

7-2. *Garden of Pontoise* by Pissarro, 1877, oil on canvas, private collection.

talent or the necessary training to achieve anything reasonable, contents himself with banging the drum for his school of painting and offering the public canvases whose value is scarcely greater than their frames."

Two other reactions show the hostility toward women artists in particular. "Five or six lunatics, one of whom is a woman, and a group of unfortunates deranged by ambition." Lastly, "There is also a woman in the group as is the case with all famous gangs." Parisian publications ran cartoons of pregnant ladies being barred from early Impressionist exhibitions for fear that the shock of what they would see might precipitate childbirth.

WHO WERE THE IMPRESSIONISTS?

That is not an easy question to answer. Just because you were part of their inner circle or exhibited with them does not qualify the painter as an Impressionist. It is a matter of style. For example, Degas called himself a realist and believed drawing was more important than color. He belittled the practice of painting outdoors. Yet, he is usually grouped with the Impressionists because of his loyalty to the artists and because he often exhibited with them. He will be discussed in this chapter as part of the Impressionistic movement.

Cezanne was an Impressionist for five years and also exhibited with them. But, for the most part, his style represents a departure from Impression. He will be discussed in Chapter 8 on Post-Impressionism. Pissarro, Sisley, Monet and Berthe Morisot are probably the "purest" Impressionists. Each pursued spontaneity, color and light throughout their career.

PISSARRO
The Quintessential Impressionist

Camille Pissarro (1830-1903) can be considered as the quintessential Impressionist because he was totally committed to the movement. He was the only one of the group to show in all eight of their exhibitions. He worked alongside of some of the most important artists of the day including Cezanne, Monet, Degas and Seurat. He had a particularly close association with Cezanne and Monet. One critic said that Pissarro was "basically the first Impressionist."

He was born on the Caribbean island of St. Thomas in the West Indies. He lived there for 12 years. That probably worked against him in his efforts to exhibit at the Paris Salon because he never became a French citizen. Hence, he was sometimes treated as an outsider.

Pissarro was heavily influenced by the Barbizon painter Corot, who tutored him. It was Corot who inspired him to paint outdoors. But there was a difference in their approach. Corot would start outdoors but complete his painting back in the studio. There he could revise his initial perceptions.

Pissarro would start and finish his painting outdoors. He painted what he saw in the true Impressionistic style. His colors were brighter than Corot's and he applied the paint more thickly with dabs and short brushstrokes.

In the 1880s, Pissarro began to explore a new method of painting. He met Georges Seurat and Paul Signac. They had adopted a new "scientific" approach to painting called Pointalism. Instead of using brushstrokes, they would apply small dots of paint next to each other. This was intended to create the illusion of blended colors and shading. As you can imagine, it was a very time consuming technique.

For the most part, the new approach was rejected by the Impressionists. Some decided against exhibiting with Seurat. Only Pissarro, the most open minded of the group, aggressively defended him from the attacks of some of the others.

Pissarro tried his hand at Pointalism from 1886 to 1888. This was an example of his willingness to experiment. He was the only artist that went from Impressionism to that Post-Impressionistic style also sometimes referred to as Neo-Impressionism. However, Pissarro did not stick with it. He found it too laborious and he was unable to paint quickly responding to his true sensations. He returned to his earlier love of the pure Impressionistic style.

The Garden at Pontoise (fig. 7-2) is one of Pissarro's prettiest landscapes. Pontoise is a city northwest of Paris. He loved to paint landscapes there. In this painting Pissarro's love of nature shines through. It shows a beautiful garden, full of greenery and multicolored flowers. The weather looks perfect. The sky is blue with some occasional white clouds.

Pissarro once gave this advice on painting. "Work at the same time on sky, water, branches, ground, keeping everything going on an equal basis... Don't be afraid of putting on color... Paint generously and unhesitatingly, for it is best not to lose the first impression." It looks like he did all of those things in this painting.

What makes the painting more interesting than most landscapes is the inclusion of a woman wearing a lacy white dress seated on a park bench facing the viewer. She is holding a parasol and looking at a young girl dressed in a red frock. The girl is surrounded by her toys and is playing a toy horn. The lady must be enjoying the lush garden and, hopefully, the serenade.

In *Boulevard Montmartre, Afternoon Sunlight* (fig. 7-3), Pissarro shows his diversity by going to the other end of the spectrum in terms of subject matter. Rather than a lush garden, he paints a crowded street in the Montmartre section of Paris.

Early in 1897, Pissarro began an artistic series of the intersections of Boulevards Montmartre, Haussmann and des Italiens with the rue de Richelieu and Drouot. He painted 16 separate views providing ever changing perspectives of the time of day, weather and season.

He needed a view from above the street so he rented a room at the Hotel de Russie at the corner of Boulevard des Ita-

7-3. *Boulevard Montmartre, Afternoon Sunlight* by Pissarro, 1897, oil on canvas, Hermitage, St. Petersburg, Russia.

liens and rue Drouot. He was looking down the new streets of Paris developed during Baron Haussmann's reconstructions in the 1860s. The painting shows the hustle and bustle of city life. There is a scatter of people and a mixture of dresses, hats and carriages all moving about the grand boulevard.

From his high point of view, Pissarro makes it look like we are leaning out of a window looking onto the street below. The footpaths on either side of the street and the street level shops emphasize the high perspective. There is even an open coach that ferries people down the boulevard.

SISLEY
Landscapes, Landscapes and More Landscapes

Most of the Impressionists suffered financially early in their careers but Alfred Sisley (1839-1899) was different. During the 1860s, Sisley was in a better financial position than most of his fellow artists because he received an al-

lowance from his well-off father. But in 1870, his father's business failed because of the Franco-Prussian War. Sisley's financial circumstances changed drastically. His sole means of support became his art. But Sisley's paintings never sold very well even though he was accepted at the Salon in 1868. Exhibitions did not bring him financial or critical success. He lived in poverty until his death in 1899.

Sisley's art focused totally on landscapes painted en plein air. His work most resembles that of Pissarro. Both were great painters of rural scenes. He never changed direction like Monet and Renoir. Monet included figures in his early works and then moved on to an intense focus on the effects of light. Renoir painted portraits, figures, landscapes and urban scenes. But Sisley never deviated from landscapes. They fulfilled his artistic needs. In that regard, his work is overshadowed by Impressionists like Monet and Renoir. He was less gifted than either.

Sisley is often referred to as the "forgotten Impressionist." His scenes are neither complex nor dramatic. There is

7-4. After the Flood in Port-Marley by Sisley, 1876, oil on canvas, Musee d'Orsay, Paris.

no social or political content, no inclusion of contemporary people in his paintings. He spent his life content on depicting the undisturbed countryside and rural waterways. Some critics discredited him because they thought his painting lacked artistic personality in their sameness. Nevertheless, because of his infatuation with peaceful landscapes, his paintings provide an atmosphere of beauty and represent a high degree of pure Impressionistic accomplishment.

One of Sisley's most important paintings was *After the Flood in Port-Marley* (fig. 7-4). Painted in 1876, it is part of a series of works he did between 1872 and 1876 depicting the flooding of the Seine River in the town of Port-Marley. They are considered to be his masterworks. But even when painting a disaster scene Sisley's emphasis on peaceful beauty still comes through. There is a sense of tranquility in the piece.

The painting focuses our attention on the waters around a wine shop. The horizon line is low giving prominence to the sky and clouds. It is typical of Sisley to have the sky dominate the space in a painting. He was passionately interested in the sky.

There are two parts to the painting. On the left, we see how the flood affects the human environment, the architecture of the wine shop and the figures in the boats. On the right side is the natural environment.

Sisley is careful not to add any catastrophic elements to the painting that one might expect to see in the aftermath of a flood. There are no damaged buildings, no destroyed

bridges, not even any fallen trees. The sky is not threatening. The figures in the boats seem more like Venetian gondoliers than people trying to flee from a flood or trying to save their personal belongings.

Maybe there is a link between paintings like this one and Sisley's life. It is possible that he saw the flood as a reflection of his troubled situation. The unforeseen bankruptcy of his father resulted in financial difficulties for him. An unforeseen natural event like the flood of the Seine River caused trouble for the people of the quiet town of Port-Marley.

Sisley's work sold badly and for very little money. He was the only artist among the Impressionists whose paintings did not appreciate during his lifetime. His art often sold for 30 francs. He died destitute and too soon. In 1900, the year after his death *After the Flood in Port-Marley* sold for the enormous amount of 43,000 francs. Was that the ultimate injustice to an artist that had to live a wretched life because of his poverty? Or, was it a posthumous homage to him?

RENOIR
Dedicated To Scenes of Pleasure

Pierre-Auguste Renoir (1841-1919) was a master of color and texture. You can see it when he paints fabrics, skin and vegetation. Because of those common characteristics in his

7-5. *Moulin de la Galette* by Renoir, 1876, oil on canvas, Musee d'Orsay, Paris.

paintings some casual art observers see Renoir as the quintessential Impressionist staying with one style of painting throughout his career. But that is a misconception. His style of painting and selection of subject matter changed several times. In fact, by the mid 1880s he had broken with the movement and adopted a more disciplined and formal painting style.

He exhibited in the Impressionist exhibitions of 1874, 1876 and 1877. But in 1879 he gave up showing with them and exhibited at the Salon. His painting *Madame Georges Charpentier and Her Children* was a success there and that helped to launch his career. Nevertheless, he will always be regarded as a painter of snapshots of life notable for their vibrant light and saturated color.

Renoir began his career in 1854 at the age of 13 painting designs on fine china in a porcelain factory. He studied painting at night. He started exhibiting at the Paris Salon in 1864 after being rejected in 1863 but he did not receive much recognition for more than a decade.

Renoir formed a lasting friendship with Monet and Sisley and painted with them near the town of Barbizon. Renoir and Monet worked closely together during the late 1860s and their styles were virtually identical. It was Monet who helped him discover that while painting en plein air shadows are not brown or black but the re-

flected color of the objects around them. He was heavily influenced by Venetian color. There is often a glow that seems to come from within the painting.

Renoir was the Impressionist's most important colorist. He summed up his working method in this way: "I want my red to ring out like a bell. If I'm unsuccessful at first, I add more red and other colors, too, until I achieve the right sound ... I follow neither rules nor a specific method."

As time progressed, the paths of the two most important Impressionists Monet and Renoir diverged. Monet focused on the changing patterns of nature while Renoir became more entranced by people. Perhaps, more than any other Impressionist, Renoir identified with the beauty and charm of Paris. He was able to expertly depict delightful, intimate scenes of middle class people enjoying leisure time in the country or at cafes in Paris. Also, more than any other Impressionist he was able to blend the landscape style with figurative painting.

Renoir is probably one of the most beloved artists of all time because of his emphasis on pleasure and the style in which he painted it. There is a vitality and shimmering richness in his works. He chose subject matters that have an instant appeal like lovely women, flowers, beautiful scenes and pretty children. Degas abhorred pretty while Renoir embraced it. He once said, "Why shouldn't art be pretty. There are enough unpleasant things in the world without the need to manufacture more." His artwork conformed to that statement throughout his career.

He painted obsessively until just before his death. His health declined severely in his later years. In 1903 he suffered his first attack of rheumatoid arthritis which progressed to the point that some of his fingers became paralyzed. He was still able to grasp a paintbrush but an assistant had to place it in his hand. He was also confined to a wheelchair because of the effects of a stroke. When asked by Monet why he continued to paint under such adverse circumstances he responded, "The pain passes but the beauty remains." It is reported that when he died there were over 700 canvases in his studio.

Before he died in 1919, he experienced a supreme triumph. France had purchased his portrait *Madame Georges Charpentier and Her Children* (1877) that helped to launch his career. Despite very poor health, he traveled to Paris just four months before his death to see it hanging in the Louvre.

When Renoir painted *Le Moulin de la Galette* (fig. 7-5) he pursued his favorite themes of entertainment and pleasure.

It is one of his happiest compositions and one of his most important works in the 1870s. He had a proclivity for painting scenes of upper middle class recreation. This was no studio piece. It was painted on location. The scene is a Sunday afternoon dance hall in the Montmartre section of Paris.

Typical of Renoir in this period, there is a mood of relaxed informality with the figures. They are dappled in bright sunlight that shines through the cover of the trees. He was able to combine Monet's style of rendering light with his own penchant for figures. Renoir glamorized the scene by replacing some of the working class patrons with his artist friends and their models.

He provides a snapshot of real life and he enhances that image by cutting off the figures. This gives the feeling of an accidental image such as one might capture in a photograph. It also suggests that the scene continues beyond the frame. He brakes up the composition with mixtures of light that add to the vibrancy of the scene.

Notice how vibrant the colors are. The painting glows with light. He captures the movement of the crowd and the carefree attitude. It looks like everyone knows one another. It is all about pleasure.

7-6. *Luncheon of the Boating Party* by Renoir, 1881, oil on canvas, Phillips Collection, Washington, D.C.

7-7. *Dance in the Country* by Renoir, 1883, oil on canvas, Musee d'Orsay, Paris.

The innocence of the flirtations in the scene is enhanced by the presence of the children in the lower left hand corner. He is painting a sort of paradise. It is an idyllic image of a carefree age of innocence. That type of subject matter represents Renoir's essential notion of art and it has generated enthusiastic support among art lovers.

The French Salon saw it differently. They preferred artists to focus on classical rather than contemporary themes. The Salon did not appreciate dance halls depicted like this. Renoir and his Impressionistic friends wanted to paint the new and modern France, the life of leisure and pleasure. The French Academy wasn't ready for that.

It took six months for Renoir to finish the painting. There is no evidence that he created any preparatory drawings or that he made any preliminary sketches on the canvas. He developed the composition as he went along which was a common practice for Impressionists.

By the late 1870s, Renoir had moved on to a more respectable social environment, Restaurant Fournaise. He was a regular there between 1878 and 1881. He said, "I could find all the beautiful girls I wanted." But Renoir was not there to find beautiful women. He was there to gather information for a painting that he planned. In fact, an actress who had tried to seduce him when he painted a portrait of her said, "Renoir only loves women with the tip of his paintbrush."

The painting *Luncheon of the Boating Party* (fig. 7-6), also embodied his basic attitude toward art. It was his most important piece and was a complete success. Like his earlier work, it celebrates the triumph of youth with men and women enjoying themselves in a casual setting diffused with sunlight. It is a 14-person study of a group of Sunday pleasure boaters on the restaurant balcony by the Seine. This painting is another example of why Renoir is so beloved.

The women are beautiful. But, of course, that is a staple for Renoir. They attract one's attention because they look so relaxed and display a mischievous charm. Renoir was the only artist that could bring that out in women. There are a variety of activities and postures, all relaxed and some flirtatious. There is a couple chatting near the center of the painting. Aline, Renoir's future wife, is occupied by coquettishly holding the Pekinese dog. Behind her is a man lost in a world of his own. There is the marvelous still-life of the debris from the meal. Outside the awning we see the hazy brightness of the sunlight. Notice the fancy hats on the women. Renoir loved to paint them. Often he would have them specially made for his models.

The Luncheon of the Boating Party was a turning point in his career and work. It ends the series on Parisian social life and it is his last major work in the Impressionistic style, at least for a number of years. Renoir felt he had become saturated with Impressionism. Perhaps he thought he could

never top the success he had with *Luncheon*, at least in utilizing the same style. If he continued in the same direction he would have been repeating himself. He needed to explore new directions.

There was another complicating factor. Aline was talking about marriage. Apparently, that was something he wanted to delay as long as possible. After all, he was "only" 40 years old. Renoir told Aline he needed time to think it over (not exactly a romantic response).

He traveled first to Algeria where he was thrilled with the colors. This was a country associated with Delacoix who was also a colorist. Next he went to Italy to see the

7-8. *Dance in the City*, by Renoir, 1883, oil on canvas, Musee d'Orsay, Paris.

7-9. *Dance at Bougival* by Renoir, 1883, oil on canvas, Museum of Fine Arts, Boston.

Renaissance masters like Titian and Raphael. He was so impressed by their use of line that he decided he wanted to place a greater emphasis on drawing in his paintings.

When he returned from his travels he moved away from Impressionism. There is more preciseness in his use of line, his colors become cooler and his brushstrokes are more refined. This new method became known as his "dry period" or "Ingresque period" after Jean Ingres who was a master in the use of line. As far as Aline was concerned, she still had to wait. Their first son was born in 1885. Five years later Renoir finally gave up his penchant for bachelorhood and he married Aline in 1890. Renoir was nearly 50. She was 20 years younger. He didn't have his third son until he was 60.

Renoir's dance series is a collection of three paintings: *Dance in the Country* (fig. 7-7), *Dance in the City* (fig. 7-8) and *Dance at Bougival* (fig. 7-9) all executed in 1883. These paintings are an example of the new style he adopted after he returned from his travels. They represent the evolution of a painter who was trying to break away from Impressionism. With the greater emphasis on drawing his outlines became clearer. Renoir preferred to call the style "sharp." This early 1880s change in Renoir's style is regarded as the most experimental phase of his career.

Dance in the Country is probably the most popular of the three canvases perhaps because the life-sized figures seem so casual and are obviously enjoying themselves. The female is Renoir's future wife Aline Charigot. It was the custom at that time for a woman to carry a fan in an environment like this and, on cue, that is exactly what she does. Her suave dance partner is Paul Lothe a friend of Renoir who served as a witness at the artist's wedding. He also appeared as a model in *Luncheon of the Boating Party*.

This is the only canvas that Renoir painted with the woman enjoying herself, at least so noticeably. She has a wide smile. One of the artistic peculiarities of that period was that portraits of models with a smile would not be considered a serious work of art. But in this case, that did not matter to Renoir. He knew Aline enjoyed dancing and he wanted it to show. Renoir could probably see her dancing with him as her eyes looked directly at the painter instead of her partner. Renoir felt she was a wonderful dancer and portrays her so. He told his son John, "Your mother waltzed divinely. I'm afraid I stepped all over her feet."

Aline's pink country dress is complimented by the red straw hat trimmed with large purple fruit. Hats with fruit on them were the height of summer fashion. She wears thick leather gloves. There is an air of spontaneity in the piece

7-10. *The Large Bathers* by Renoir, 1884-1887, oil on canvas, Philadelphia Museum of Art, Philadelphia.

7-11. *The Girls at the Piano* by Renoir, 1892, oil on canvas, Musee d'Orsay, Paris.

painter Suzanne Valadon who was the mother of the artist Maurice Utrillo who became noted for his paintings of the Montmartre district of Paris. The woman wears a two piece white silk ensemble trimmed in lace and elegant white gloves. But with all the fashionable dress the couple does not seem to relish the activity at least not as much as in the first painting.

In *Dance at Bougival* Renoir leaves the elegant ball behind and returns to the outdoor café setting. This couple also doesn't seem to be enjoying themselves as much as in the first piece. The girl is shown with her mouth closed tightly almost in a grimace. Only part of the man's face is visible but you do not get the sense he is smiling.

In this painting the man's straw hat reappears from the first piece but it remains on his head and the woman's red bonnet makes an encore. She wears a pinkest ensemble with red piping and a white petticoat. In the background are people enjoying themselves in a wooded setting. The floor is littered with cigarette butts.

As a group these paintings accomplish what Renoir set out to do and that is to charm the viewer. They are likely to make you want to dance the night away very slowly with someone you like. It is hard to imagine three paintings that capture more of the romance and beauty of 19th century France. They evoke a panorama of fashionable modern life from Paris to Bougival. But later, Renoir decided to revert back to his style of freer brushstrokes and less emphasis on line.

Before he makes the move back, *The Large Bathers* (fig. 7-10) is another example of Renoir's effort to move beyond Impressionism and establish a link between modern art and the classical tradition of French painting. In so doing, he embarked on a path of experimentation and innovation. In a throwback to the past, he emphasized traditional drawing and moved to studio work. He described his new style as classical and decorative.

as if the dancers had suddenly arisen from their chairs after dinner and had taken to the dance floor. Their spontaneity is suggested by the man's hat that has dropped off in the foreground. Although everything looks casual and natural, the whole scene was carefully staged by Renoir including what his subjects wore, even down to the gloves.

The attire and mood in *Dance in the City* is much different. In this piece it looks like the couple is at a formal dance in an urban ballroom. They appear more restrained and there is an emphasis on elegance and glamour compared to the earthier and more vigorous atmosphere of *Dance in the Country*. The woman is Renoir's model and

7-12. *The Artist's Family* by Renoir, 1896, oil on canvas, Barnes Foundation, Philadelphia.

7-13. *Composition, Five Bathers* by Renoir 1918, oil on canvas, Barnes Foundation, Philadelphia.

His style change was not well received by all of his Impressionist colleagues. Some thought the work betrayed the cause of modern painting by retreating into classicism. In fact, Dr. Albert Barnes who established the Barnes Foundation where there are 181 Renoirs labeled this "dry period" as "his fall from grace."

The painting depicts a moment when one bather playfully threatens to splash another. It has a timeless quality. There are carefully drawn figures against a glowing landscape. The figures do not merge with the landscape but are disassociated with it. In his attempt to reconcile a modern piece with 17th or 18th century works, Renoir labored three years on the painting making a large number of preparatory sketches. This was a dramatic departure from the Impressionistic style of quickly painting one's immediate impressions.

The women are shown from three different views—front, back and side. This is a throwback to the classical approach when depicting the Three Graces. But these look like contemporary women frolicking on the banks of the Seine. One thing prevents the painting from being a whole-sale rejection of Impressionism. It is the loosely brushed colorful landscape in the background.

Renoir's career changes did not end here. Eventually, he abandoned the emphasis on drawing because it did not fit his disposition. Renoir liked to work quickly and spontaneously. The linear approach consumed too much of his time. He said, "I have gone back to my old soft style of painting with a light brush and I shall not give it up again."

In the 1890s, he entered his pearly period named for the flesh tones. Delicacy, form, color and light describe this style. His most famous work from this period was *The Girls at the Piano* (fig. 7-11). He reverted to a freer style, warmer colors and less emphasis on line. In this piece he is painting an idealized world with graceful young girls and a cozy, well appointed bourgeois interior. The two girls are involved in making music which was considered a highly respectable leisure activity.

The Artist's Family (fig. 7-12) is a portrait of the Renoir family as it existed in 1896. It is the largest portrait of his career measuring 68 x 54 inches. The location is the

Montmartre section of Paris where the family moved to in 1890 and lived for a number of years. The upscale attire of everyone is a reminder of Renoir's financial success at this stage of his career.

It has already been mentioned that portraits became more casual with the Impressionists and this is an example. Although everyone is dressed for the portrait, the only one posing is Renoir's wife Aline. Eleven-year-old son Pierre is on the left with his arm wrapped affectionately around his mother's. Gabrielle, the family nanny and cousin of Aline crouches down holding two-year-old Jean who clutches her sleeve. All of this adds to the naturalness and warmth of the portrait. Gabrielle was Renoir's favorite model for much of his career. A third son Claude (nicknamed Coco) is not in the portrait because he was born later in 1901.

The casualness of the portrait is enhanced by the pose of the young girl on the right, another Gabrielle who was a friend of the family. She flirtatiously toys with her hair because she knows she has caught the eye of Pierre. It seems nothing has changed among young people in that regard. Young Gabrielle hides a ball behind her back. Perhaps she is attempting to look more mature.

Renoir was a master of color and texture. It comes out in the color of the baby's dress which is expressive silvery white. It expresses or tells you at a glance that the fabric is silk or satin. There is the elaborate bonnet on the baby with impressive folds. Aline wears a fancy green hat. Even young Gabrielle has a hat. As already mentioned, Renoir loved to paint hats on women.

The portrait was painted in a garden near their home in the Montmartre section of Paris. Everyone is fashionably attired indicating Renoir's growing financial success and fame. The family had clearly become part of the bourgeoisie. He could afford a household servant and Aline could wear expensive clothes.

The piece was purchased by Albert Barnes, the great collector of Renoir's, in 1927 but it took him 12 years to close the deal. He made his first attempt to buy the work in 1915 when he wrote to Renoir's agent in Paris, Durand-Ruel, that he considered Renoir to be the greatest modern painter and he was assembling the largest collection of his works in the world. But Renoir refused to sell it because it was personal, a family portrait. Barnes finally bought it from Renoir's third son Claude after the artist had died. Perhaps Claude was willing to sell it because he was not in the painting. He was born in 1901 and the piece was executed in 1896.

In the post 1900 period, Renoir made one more change concentrating on a glorious outpouring of beautiful nudes with lush landscapes in the background. *Composition, Five Bathers* (fig.7-13) is an example of that style. This was his period of iridescent color that no other artist could match. Although painted late in his life it is easy to argue that his bather series may very well represent the pinnacle of his career.

These large, boneless, curvilinear female figures with velvet flesh painted in such lustrous color became Renoir's trademark in early part of the 20th century. They have a timeless appeal. With this theme Renoir leaves behind scenes of contemporary French life that were such an integral part of his career.

The idealized figures fill the canvas. The arms and torsos of the five figures seem intertwined. The foliage forms a frame for each of their bodies. Notice how it surrounds the standing figure on the left and the one climbing on the right. The skin tones match the landscape.

Emphasizing this subject matter is something that could be expected since he was always a great worshipper of the female form. When asked how did he know when one of his nudes was finished Renoir replied, "When I painted a women's bottom so I could touch it, then I know it is finished."

Unlike *The Large Bathers* there is a softer tone here and a more delicate handling of these nudes. Rather than being distinct from their surroundings, he softly fuses them into the landscape. The woman act free and uninhibited and have a timeless quality. There is a mischievous charm in these paintings. He was the only artist that could bring that out in women. There is little doubt that Renoir was using his models to charm the opposite sex.

Renoir had an ulterior motive for his concentration on painting nudes in landscape. He began to think about his legacy. He felt his paintings of contemporary French life were tied to a particular time and might not hold the interest of future viewers. Of course, we know that concern was entirely unfounded. Nevertheless, he focused on nudes because they are more difficult to associate with a particular time or place. Also, as he aged, he became more turned off by the spread of industrialization and became even more attracted to nature. What better response than to fuse his nudes with nature. He told Berthe Morisot, "They are one of the essential forms of art." When Matisse visited him late in his life he asked Renoir why he made a career out of painting such lovely young women. Renoir's response was that he considered them the supreme feat of God.

What is so impressive about this painting is that it was executed in 1918 when Renoir was 77 years old and a sick man. It was the year before he died. He was confined to a wheelchair from a stroke years earlier. He had arthritis so bad that the paint brushes had to be placed in his hands for him. The year of his death Matisse visited him and asked why he continued to paint when it caused so much pain. He replied that the pain passes but the beauty remains.

Composition, Five Bathers was painted in 1918 but was not exhibited until 1920 after Renoir had died. WWI prevented it from being shown before that. It was one of the hundreds of paintings that were still in the artist's studio at the time of his death. They were left to his three sons since Aline had died several years before Renoir.

If you want to have a moving experience you should go to Renoir's home and studio in Cagnes-sur-Mer in the south of France. There in his studio is his antique wheel chair placed in front of an easel. It is said that he was still painting until the day he died.

MONET
Devoted to Light and Pure Color

Manet called Monet "the Raphael of water." He could have gone further. Claude Monet (1840-1926) was a master of light and color. Monet and Renoir painted together and their styles were similar, at least early on. But as their careers progressed, their styles departed. For Renoir, figures become increasingly important. In Monet's works figures disappear completely.

Monet was the most adventurous of the Impressionists with his emphasis on reproducing the effects of light. Whereas Renoir, for example, was interested in painting a particular subject, Monet became more remote from the subject and concentrated exclusively on light. He spent nearly 60 years exploring the effects of light on the landscape and water and trying to capture those effects on canvas.

In the 1860s, Monet pursued a new style that he would stick with for the rest of his life. Rather than trying to reproduce the scene before him in detail, he recorded on the spot impressions from a momentary vision. It was the phenomena of the natural atmosphere and its color that captured his imagination. By eliminating black and gray from his palette, he entirely rejected the academic approach to landscape painting.

Monet was the Impressionistic painter who brought the study of the passing effects of natural light on its surroundings to its most precise expression. His experiments in this area became more daring as time progressed. Whether he was painting water lilies, haystacks or cathedral facades it was always about light and color.

Cezanne once said, "Monet is nothing but an eye, but what an eye." Clearly, Monet had the eye of an Impressionist but it was more advanced than the others. He had an incomparable talent to look at an image and to dissect it in order to single out shades and contrasts and set them down on canvas. More than any other painter, he was a slave to his eye when it came to permanently placing on canvas a moment of natural beauty.

THE COLOR WHEEL, COMPLIMENTARY COLORS AND THE "MONET EFFECT"

The role of Monet's painting Impression Sunrise (fig. 7-1) in naming Impressionism has already been discussed at the start of this chapter. It seems fitting that a painting by the prototypical Impressionist should also give the group its name. There is nothing in the piece that one would normally associate with a landmark painting: no clean lines, no smooth brushstrokes and no elaborate composition. In fact, there is little that can be clearly distinguished in the harbor view except the sun. But therein lays its importance.

What strikes you most about this painting? It is the orangey-red spot of the sun and its fragmented reflection on the water. But look what happens when you photograph the painting in black and white (fig. 7-14). The sun and its reflection disappear. Why is that? Because the brightness of the sun and its reflection are more or less the same as the background against which they are silhouetted. The sun's prominence is due solely to the difference in color between the orange of the sun and the bluish background. It is not due to the difference in brightness.

Brightness plays no part; it is all in the color contrast. This is called the "Monet effect." Essentially, it is a demonstration of the effect of contrasts of color or what we know as complimentary colors. An orange surface beside a blue one appears more orangey than beside a gray one.

Because color is so important to the Impressionists and to Monet in particular, it is worthwhile to briefly discuss color theory, the color wheel and complimentary colors. At one time or another, most people have seen a color wheel (fig. 7-15). The primary colors are red, blue and yellow. They are primary because they cannot be obtained by mixing other colors. The secondary or complimentary color to each primary color is the color opposite it on the color wheel. They are green for red, orange for blue and purple for yellow.

You can obtain each complimentary color by mixing the other two primary colors. In other words, the compliment to red is green and you get it by mixing blue and yellow. The compliment to blue is orange and you get it by mixing red and yellow. The compliment to yellow is purple and you get it by mixing red and blue.

Why does all of this matter? Because artists know they can get a more vivid effect when they place a primary color next to its compliment. Orange will appear more vivid when it is placed next to blue than if it is placed next to gray or brown. That is the effect you get in *Impression Sunrise*.

The sun's prominence is due to the use of complimentary colors or the orange sun against a blue background. If you remove the effect of complimentary colors by showing the piece in black and white, the sun's prominence completely disappears.

7-14. *Impression Sunrise* in a black and white photograph.

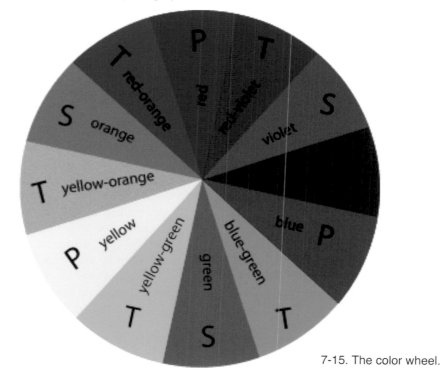

7-15. The color wheel.

7-16. *Terrace at Sainte-Adresse* by Monet, 1867, oil on canvas, Metropolitan Museum of Art, New York.

Monet's desire was to see without any bias. His goal was to base his paintings on his instinctive response to visual sensations. In short, he wanted his works to be free from assumptions. He believed that the first real look at the subject was likely to be the truest and most unprejudiced one. He said that he "wished he had been born blind and then suddenly gained has sight so that he could have begun to paint in this way without knowing what the objects were that he saw before him."

Monet did not paint a leaf but he painted a patch of green that he saw without worrying whether it was a leaf. He explained his approach this way:

> *"When you go out to paint try to forget what objects you have before you, a tree, a house, a field or whatever. Merely think, here is a little square of blue, here is an oblong of pink, here is a streak of yellow and paint it just as it looks to you, the exact color and shape, until it gives your naïve impression of the scene before you."*

Putting fleeting impressions on canvas were greatly at odds with the conventional approach to painting that set a premium on time consuming refinements to any work of art. Given that, it is not surprising that many critics dismissed his works as incomplete or preliminary studies to finished paintings.

In 1883, Giverny became his home base. It sits on the bank of the River Seine about 50 miles west and slightly north of Paris. Monet rented a house there and in 1890 was able to buy the property outright. He began to construct the water lily ponds (see fig. 7-18) and the magnificent gardens with wisterias and azaleas.

The river that flowed near his property was diverted to make a large pond in which water lilies could flourish. A Japanese bridge was added to enhance the scene. Over a period of more than 30 years, Monet constructed an inexhaustible source of inspiration for his painting. Step-by-step he created a garden paradise that became the perfect muse for his studies of light, color and water. He said, "I am good for nothing but painting and gardening."

At first he concentrated on the ever changing colors in the flower garden. Later, he turned almost exclusively to painting the weeping willows and the lilies in the pond.

7-17. *Haystacks at Sunset* by Monet, 1880-1881, oil on canvas, Museum of Fine Arts, Boston.

Whatever the subject, Monet was perfectly situated to explore the effects of changing weather on the light and color of his personally created landscape.

The Terrace at Sainte-Adresse (fig. 7-16) would have been a hard sell when it was painted in 1867. But exactly 100 years later in 1967 it sold for a new record price for a modern painting. That is because it encapsulates all the things that the public wants in an Impressionistic painting – blue summer skies, a sparkling sea, a garden full of flowers with rich red blooms, flags in the breeze and elegant women with parasols. How could you not like a painting like this?

Terrace shows how closely Monet's painting style in his early years paralleled that of Renoir. This looks like it could have been painted by Renoir, at least in terms of subject matter. Monet was delving into Impressionism but was a long way from the style for which he would become famous.

The piece was shown at the fourth Impressionistic exhibition in 1879. It was painted while Monet spent his summer at the resort town of Sainte-Adresse on the English Channel. The models were members of his family. His father sits in the foreground. Monet's cousin is at the fence with a parasol. His uncle is next to her and his aunt is seated in the foreground.

The composition of the painting was carefully worked out. The flagpoles, fence and horizon line all combine to provide a geometric design of verticals and horizontals. The elevated vantage point flattens out the space and emphasizes the two dimensionality of the painting. In contrast to the Renaissance artists that stressed depth, nothing recedes into space here.

The painting was probably done quickly with small dabs of color and short brushstrokes rendered to paint the flowers, leaves and waves. This fit into Monet's approach not to be concerned with the physical characteristics of some of the objects represented. That approach was not unique. Some artists used it in an effort to sketch a landscape's general appearance as part of the preparation for a finished work. But Monet used it as part of a completed painting. Hence, he had to endure the criticism that his paintings looked like they were not finished.

Although there is a great deal of emphasis here on the landscape, the figures play an even greater role. They tend to become the main subject to the painting. The sea becomes a backdrop to the relaxed, fashionable figures. But the sea does reflect something about the future. It shows Monet's growing interest in water.

There are a number of departures in this piece from his later works, not only in the subject matter and the use of figures. The sky is bright but is made up of few colors. The sea also gives the impression of a limited number of colors. Later, when painting nature, multiple colors blended together would vibrate throughout his paintings.

As is the case with a number of his works early in his career, the subject matter here is modernity. Later, nature would command all of his attention. Modernity can be seen in the fashion of the figures even to the point of the Panama straw hat worn by the man in the foreground that was very popular then. Compare that with the felt top hat worn by the other man. It seems out of place given the weather and time of year.

There is modernity in the steamboats in the distance. Nature looks organized and controlled with the cultivated flowers in the garden. The sea is dotted with boats. The sky, water and entire environment looks almost too good to be true. It is a very decorative setting with everything perfectly manicured. Later, Monet's depiction of nature would be quite different, climaxing with his almost wild and chaotic water lily series that would lead later artists to abstract canvases.

The next three paintings will show how Monet's style changed dramatically over his career. If one were to look at his late paintings it would be hard to imagine that *Terrace* could have been done by the same artist.

By 1890, Monet's approach to painting had changed forever. In his passion to capture the effects of sunlight, he created what became known as his haystack series. These were 25 paintings produced over the course of seven months between the summer of 1890 and the spring of 1891. *Haystacks at Sunset* (fig. 7-17) is one of those paintings. They are among his most notable works.

Most artists would have considered haystacks as an unimaginative subject to paint. But Monet, through careful thought and analysis, turned these ordinary forms into ones that showed shimmering vibrancy when examined carefully under changing light conditions. As the angle of the sun changed, the colors and shadows also changed. With the variations in the quality of the light, the shapes and mood of the subject would change. Monet painted exactly what he saw. By staying with the same subject, however mundane, he established the basis from which equal comparisons could be made in both direct and reflected light.

This was just the starting point for Monet. Over more than 30 years he concentrated on just a few subjects such as haystacks, poplars, the façade of the Rouen Cathedral and water lilies. In each case, his goal was the same, to capture the fleeting effects of changes in light on the same subject.

7-18. Photo of Monet's water lily pond in Giverny.

He had to rise very early in the morning to start the process. Fortunately, the haystacks were close to his home. Many of the works he did from 1883 until his death were scenes within two miles of his home. He worked quickly to capture the "moment" before it passed. He would work on several canvases at the same time, perhaps devoting no more than a few minutes to any one of them. His stepdaughter Blanche assisted him by carrying out more canvases in a wheelbarrow and sliding them onto his easel. When he started the process he believed that two canvases would be enough, one for sunny weather and one for overcast weather. But that changed.

Prior to the Impressionists, color was thought to be essentially the same under all conditions. Oranges were essentially orange and lemons were essentially yellow. But Monet did more to change that perception than any other Impressionist. He showed that the color of each haystack is different because the light shining on the haystack is different.

What Monet accomplished is that he became the first artist in history to show the different effects of light on the same subject across various times of day, seasons and types of weather. These works demonstrate what a perfectionist he was in the study of light.

For the first time, there was no hostile reaction to his work. The pieces received unanimous praise and they sold quickly. This allowed Monet to achieve financial success at the age of 40, a rarity among his fellow Impressionists. It allowed him to buy his home and grounds at Giverny and to start constructing a water lily pond. This set the stage for his most inspirational artistic venture, the interaction between light and water demonstrated in his water lily paintings.

Giverny sits on the bank of the River Seine about 50 miles west and slightly north of Paris. After he bought the property outright in 1890 he began to construct the water lily ponds (fig. 7-18) and the magnificent gardens with the wisterias and azaleas.

Water Lilies 1920-1926 (fig. 7-19) is one of Monet's most celebrated paintings in the series as well as one of the most iconic images of Impressionism. It is a theme that dominated his late work. Monet said it was by chance that he started painting the water lilies. "I planted them purely for pleasure; I grew them with no thought of painting them. . .all at once I had a revelation – how wonderful the pond was – and I reached for my palette. I've hardly had any other subject since." Monet revisited the subject over and over. From 1899 until his death in 1926, he produced more than 250 paintings devoted to the water lilies.

In this piece, Monet focuses entirely on the water surface. The picture plane is filled with light and color on the surface of the lily pond. There is no horizon, no

7-19. *Water Lilies, 1920-1926* by Monet, 1920-1926, oil on canvas, Musee de l'Orangerie, Paris.

7-20. *The Japanese Footbridge* by Monet, 1920-1922, oil on canvas, Museum of Modern Art, New York.

figures, sky or land to break one's gaze into the soothing scene. You can become immersed in it as you gaze from the edge of the pond. If you stare at the piece, it becomes almost hypnotic. Given that it was painted nearly 100 years ago, it seems amazingly modern because of its almost abstract qualities.

There are bits of color everywhere. The lily pads have splotches of red, yellow or white in the center representing flowers. They float on water that varies in color with different tones of blue and pink intermingled with green foliage.

This type of depiction of water lilies was only the start for Monet. Eventually, form almost totally dissolves into color. *The Japanese Footbridge 1920-22* (fig. 7-20) is an example of this. The original subject of the footbridge almost disappears. Only the vague shape of it is visible. It is submerged in an explosion of orange, gold and burgundy hues. These are hot colors that are unique to Monet's palette. They are a far cry from his creamery blues, pinks and greens of many of his water lily paintings.

Perhaps the change was due to color distortions because of his cataract problems that began to develop and, for a time, changed his world of color. He was fearful that surgery might leave him blind. His friend Mary Cassatt did poorly with surgery. But he finally acquiesced and had successful surgery in 1923. Or, perhaps a painting like this represented a formal experiment or maybe an emotional outburst. We really do not know. But it would be unfortunate to suggest that the painting was simply the result of Monet's diminished eyesight. Whatever the cause, works like this are gripping in their color intensity. They represent a new vista in his art.

This detachment from the more realistic world enabled one of the founders of Impressionism to become an artist that transcends Impressionism. He is also pointing into the future. His art is establishing an important precedent for the development of abstract painting. Almost devoid of subject, the space is filled with color. Such spaces of color were unprecedented in his lifetime. Monet said, "These views of water and re-

7-21. Photo of Monet's Nympheas at Musee de l'Orangerie.

flections of light have become an obsession with me." And so it was!

If Manet begins modernism then Monet carries it to the next generation. Then the heirs to an Impressionist like Monet become the Abstract Expressionists of the 1950s, even painters like Jackson "the dripper" Pollack. But Monet was never an abstract painter. Color was never an end in itself but the means by which to represent the interplay between light and color.

The best place to see Monet's water lilies is at Musee de l'Orangerie which is located at the end of the Tuileries Gardens next to the Place de la Concorde in Paris. He spent the last 12 years of his life, from 1914 to 1926, preparing paintings specifically for the museum. There you will see eight awe-inspiring canvases up to 20 feet long displayed in two oval rooms. His designs for l'Orangerie specified that the canvases be displayed on curved walls to enhance the impression that you are walking along the edge of the pond (fig. 7-21).

It all started with a note he wrote to his friend Georges Clemenceau in 1918: "I am on the eve of finishing two decorative panels which I wish to sign on the day of victory, and am asking you to offer them to the state...It's not much, but it's the only way I have of taking part in the victory."

In 1922 Monet signed a contract donating eight giant canvases to the French government as a monument to the end of World War I. His conditions were that a suitable place had to be found in which to display the paintings and the exchange would not occur until after his death. The artist felt he could not be separated from his work. Monet died in 1926 and his water lily paintings, known as Nympheas, were displayed at the redesigned Musee de l'Orangrie in 1927.

When Monet died, he was the last of the great giants of 19th century painting. His instructions to his family were that there should be no flowers. He said, "It would be a sacrilege to plunder the flowers of my garden for an occasion such as this." Clearly, here was a man that loved nature and his gardens. Monet summarized his life work as follows: "All I did was to look at what the universe showed me, to let my brush bear witness to it." What better way to sum up his career.

DEGAS
The Preeminent Draftsman

Edgar Degas (1834-1917) is almost always included in discussions of the group of Impressionists. But there are a lot of reasons why he does not fit with the general definitions of Impressionism. Degas never liked the term Impressionists particularly when it was applied to his paintings. He preferred to be called a Realist. By 1879, he persuaded the group to give up the label and refer to themselves in the exhibitions as "the group of independent artists."

Initially, Degas wanted to be a history painter and he was well prepared for it given his academic training and his studies of the Renaissance masters. In his 30s he shifted to a more contemporary subject matter. He became a classical painter of modern life which is a different approach than the one used by Impressionists.

Degas did not paint peasants in the fields. He was a life-long studio painter. He belittled the Impressionist's practice of painting en plein air. He was attracted to what he called "artificial life," the world of dancers, opera and horse racing. He told his Impressionistic friends, "You need nature, I need artificial life." He said, "Boredom quickly overcomes me whenever I even look at nature." Although he sometimes used bold colors, he never adopted the Impressionists style of applying flecks of color. Instead, he urged them to emphasize drawing rather than color.

The Impressionists focused on spontaneity in their art. Degas said, "No art was less spontaneous than mine." That was a result of intense study of the masters and the subject matter he was intending to paint. Rather than creating a piece spontaneously, he always did numerous preparatory drawings. His interpretation of Impressionism was creating an image based on memory. He felt it was acceptable to copy what you see but it was better to draw what you see in your memory. In other words, reproduce what has made an impression on you.

Given all of these differences, why is he grouped with the Impressionists? One reason is as a matter of convenience because it is hard to assign him to any other movement. But more importantly, he can be identified with the Impressionists in a number of ways. His bond with the Impressionists was not a likeness in style. He was a great draftsman and had a preoccupation with drawing, something the Impressionists did not focus on. But where they

7-22. *The Rehearsal on Stage* by Degas, 1874, pastel on paper, Metropolitan Museum of Art, New York.

7-23. *Dance Class* by Degas, 1874, oil on canvas, Metropolitan Museum of Art, New York.

were most closely connected was in their common revolt against the established art conventions of the day. Degas was the fiercest opponent of the Salon.

He was instrumental in organizing the first Impressionistic exhibition and participated in seven of the eight. The last exhibition was held in 1886. By then, most of the original participants had departed. Only Pissarro, Morisot and Degas remained steadfast to the very end. It is for these reasons that Degas is labeled an Impressionist.

Degas was basically antisocial. He believed an artist should sacrifice social life and devote himself to his work. So he immersed himself in it. That is probably one reason

why he never married. He became more and more isolated over time.

The last 20 years of his life were miserable. His eyesight began to fail and he spent years quarreling with everyone. His disagreeable nature was deplored by Renoir who said, "What a creature he was, that Degas. All his friends had to leave him. I am one of the last to go but even I couldn't stay to the end." Even Mary Cassatt, his closest friend, said of him late in his life, "You don't know what a dreadful man he is, he can say anything."

At the time of his death he was nearly totally blind and did not create any new paintings for the last ten years of his life. When he died in 1917, despite all his notoriety, few people attended his funeral. One was the aged Monet who made the effort in memory of better days.

Degas was fascinated with movement. That is why more than half his works were devoted to the ballet. It was also why he loved to paint racehorses. There was movement plus, like ballerinas, they met his conditions of style, elegance and precision all in one body. But most of all, he was interested in the female figure. He never painted male dancers.

Over his career, Degas was increasingly attracted to photography and this influenced his paintings in that he often chose an off-kilter perspective. He would depict his subjects from unusual viewpoints, from above or below or from the distance. This would reflect a distant observer or a voyeur. Painting in this candid-camera fashion provided a sense of spontaneity to his works. In this regard, he was painting in a spontaneous manner but it was different from the Impressionists.

He would balance crowded and empty spaces in the same piece or move his figures to one side of center. Degas would cut off figures at the edges of the painting to give the viewer the feel of an accidental image such as you might get in a snapshot.

He painted the spectacle of the ballet with its elegant costumes and scenery over and over again. It was the ideal subject for him because of his interest in studying the human body. Also, given his preoccupation with drawing, he could draw and redraw the figures. But because he considered himself a realist, he would not always show the ballerinas as beautiful icons. Sometimes he depicted the truthfulness of the trade (see the discussion immediately below). Degas would paint off guard moments of the ballerinas like stretching, gossiping or adjusting their costumes. They might be shown exhausted after a tiring practice session.

A good example of his attraction to the ballet and that he was an observer of all aspects is *The Rehearsal on Stage* (fig. 7-22). This is a practice session, not a glamorous performance. The rehearsal is viewed from an opera box slightly above the stage. By shrinking the size of the figures in the rear of the

painting (foreshortening) he is adding depth. The figures at the left are cut-off as he applies his cropping technique. The right side of the painting is nearly empty but the left side is crowded with "opera rats." They were called that because of the way they scurried around the stage in tiny fast moving steps and also because they always seemed to be looking for food.

The ballet was not always as innocent as it seemed and Degas was aware of that. However subtly, he is exposing the dark side of the ballet in this painting. Notice on the right side of the painting at the back sit two well-dressed middle-aged men. They were probably "protectors" or lovers of one of the young dancers. Because ballerinas generally came from lower-class families and exhibited their

7-24. *L'Absinthe* by Degas, 1876, oil on canvas, Musee d'Orsay, Paris.

scantily clad bodies in public, something a "respectable" bourgeois woman would not do, they were widely assumed to be sexually available. They often attracted the attention of wealthy men willing to support them in exchange for sexual favors. Sometimes Degas would include mothers of the dancers who were there to protect their daughter's virtue.

Dance Class (fig. 7-23) is another example of Degas showing the world of the ballet with a new kind of truthfulness. It is also an example of how astonishing it is that so few of his ballerinas are actually dancing in his pieces. In this painting some of the figures are rendered in an awkward way. In the front of the group there is a dancer hiking her tutu. Behind her is a girl biting her nails. The rest of the girls seem to be hanging out waiting for their turn to audition. The lone exception is the single dancer near the center of the composition. She extends herself on one foot while stretching out the other leg behind her.

In all there are twenty-four ballerinas and their mothers. The dancers wait their turn to be evaluated by the ballet master Jules Perrot. He is one of the best known ballet instructors in Europe. The mothers chaperon their daughters during the rehearsals. Mostly they are there to protect the girls but, in some cases, they may be willing to introduce them to wealthy patrons who visited the dance halls and watched the rehearsals.

In a painting like this, it is as if the viewer has a backstage ticket. Everything looks unchoreographed, not like the ballet itself. But that does not mean Degas painted it in a casual way. Sometimes the more spontaneous a work looks the more difficult it is to paint. Degas made countless preparatory drawings in the studio and numerous dancers posed for him.

As was often the case with Degas, the off-center composition, with the larger figures crowded into a small space in the front of the painting, provides a sense of an accidental image which adds to the reality of the piece...His life-

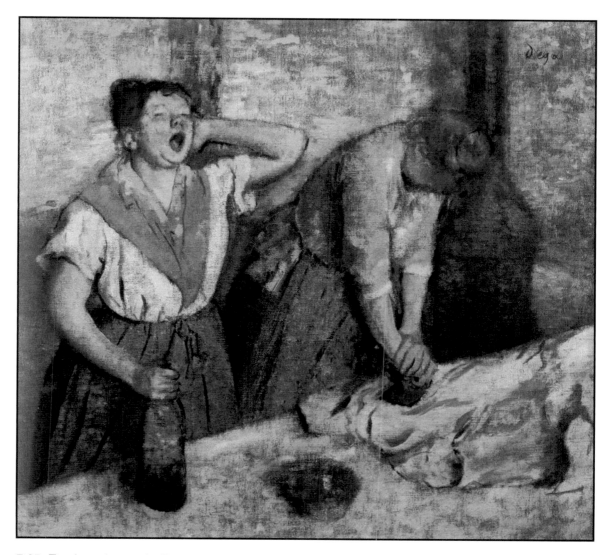

7-25. *Two Laundresses* by Degas, 1882, oil on canvas, Musee d'Orsay, Paris.

7-26. *The Little Dancer of Fourteen Years* by Degas, 1881, wax and then bronze in 1922, various museums with the largest collection in the National Gallery of Art, Washington, D.C.

long friend Mary Cassatt said that in this painting Degas surpassed Vermeer.

In his portrait *L'Absinthe* also known as *The Absinthe Drinker* (fig. 7-24) Degas painted the under side of society. Like Renoir, he was a great painter of women but he used his models differently. Renoir, particularly in his bather scenes, used his models to charm the opposite sex. With Degas, the models simply become part of the painted scene with no effort to make them more physically appealing. Certainly, there is nothing charming about the woman in this scene.

The painting provides another example of the off-center placement of the figures. There is a large area of space in the foreground. The unusual composition creates a "slice of life" feeling like a candid photo. The woman stares vacantly downward at a glass filled with the 130 proof greenish anise-flavored aperitif with her arms slack at her sides. The man turns from the woman looking out to the right edge of the painting. You get the sense that both have come to find solace for their mutual loneliness and despair. Later, the drink was banned in a number of countries because of the view that it was dangerously addictive and could have hallucinogenic effects and even cause madness when consumed in excess.

Degas is not seeking to send a moral message in the painting. In fact, the drink became the rage in France starting around 1850. It was used in the intellectual and artistic communities because it was thought to stimulate creativity. Among the famous people that were said to have drunk absinthe were Picasso, Van Gogh and Hemingway.

The appearance and facial expressions of the figures make them a metaphor for the darker side of modern life in the big city. At its first showing in the 1876 Impressionist exhibition, the critics called the painting "ugly and depressing." It was put in storage for 16 years. Now it is considered a classic. Two years later, Manet would paint the same couple in *Au Café* but it was a more pleasant scene. In the 20th century, Picasso would paint his version of the same subject.

Women at work provided inspiration to Degas to become a classical painter of modern life. Often his portrayals involved those at the lower end of the social spectrum. To an extent, Degas' laundress paintings parallel his more famous ballet series. In both, he captured the precise movements of women at work. In *Laundresses Ironing* (fig. 7-25) he shows two women frozen in a moment of movement. He portrays in an instant the difficult lives of these women. They worked long, hot hours for low wages. Because of the social class they represented and because they often delivered the laundry directly to male customers, they were sometimes considered as women of easy virtue. But, fortunately, Degas avoids that association. He shows them as women hard at work, strained almost to the point of physical exhaustion. This is a long way from Renoir's idealized female figures.

This is not a "pretty" painting. But then Degas was not into pretty. When asked why he never married he said, "I would be afraid when finishing a painting to hear my wife say what you have done is pretty." Note the bottle in the painting. At the time it was incorrectly identified as containing wine, a disparaging reference to the class of workers. But that was not the case. It was used as a mold for the rounded starched shirt cuffs.

The model for *The Little Dancer of Fourteen Years* (fig 7-26) was a young dance student named Marie van Goethem. It was the only sculpture Degas would exhibit in public. He had no formal training in sculpture. Marie was one of the many "opera rats." As was the case with most ballet students she came from a working class background. Her father was a tailor and her mother a laundress.

The piece was shown at the 6th Impressionist exhibition in 1881. It was made in wax. But after Degas' death his heirs had 27 cast in bronze. The original piece was fitted with a wig of real hair and fabric dance slippers. The upper part of her outfit was silk and she was dressed in a tutu and had a ribbon for her hair. The entire piece was covered in wax except for the ribbon which was given to him by the model. Degas had the piece placed in a glass showcase.

The work received mixed reviews. Some critics found it shocking and thought it was ugly. Her face was compared to a monkey. Because of the glass case, some thought she looked like a medical specimen or that Degas bordered on being an anthropologist. But other critics applauded it as innovative and a ground breaking piece. Now she is one of the most beloved works of art.

What Degas wanted to do was to change the way one looks at beauty. He chose not to sculpt a tall, slender ballerina in the midst of a complicated maneuver. Instead, he chose to sculpt a young dancer who was still learning and struggling with her trade. Although some critics disregarded the piece because she was not pretty, Degas was trying to show that there is beauty in truth.

He was aware of the derogatory association of "opera rats" with dirt and sewage and the predicament the *Little Dancer* was in being the potential target of "male protectors." So he showed her with head held high and arms stretched behind her back to provide a measure of dignity. Unfortunately, Marie never became a ballet star. She left the dance class at the age of 17.

IMAGES

7-1. *Impression Sunrise* by Monet, 1872, oil on canvas, Musee Marmotten Monet, Paris.

7-2. *Garden of Pontoise* by Pissarro, 1877, oil on canvas, private collection.

7-3. *Boulevard Montmartre, Afternoon Sunlight* by Pissarro, 1897, oil on canvas, Hermitage, St. Petersburg, Russia.

7-4. After the Flood in Port-Marley by Sisley, 1876, oil on canvas, Musee d'Orsay, Paris.

7-5. *Moulin de la Galette* by Renoir, 1876, oil on canvas, Musee d'Orsay, Paris.

7-6. *Luncheon of the Boating Party* by Renoir, 1881, oil on canvas, Phillips Collection, Washington, D.C.

7-7. *Dance in the Country* by Renoir, 1883, oil on canvas, Musee d'Orsay, Paris.

7-8. *Dance in the City*, by Renoir, 1883, oil on canvas, Musee d'Orsay, Paris.

7-9. *Dance at Bougival* by Renoir, 1883, oil on canvas, Museum of Fine Arts, Boston.

7-10. *The Large Bathers* by Renoir, 1884-1887, oil on canvas, Philadelphia Museum of Art, Philadelphia.

7-11. *The Girls at the Piano* by Renoir, 1892, oil on canvas, Musee d'Orsay, Paris.

7-12. *The Artist's Family* by Renoir, 1896, oil on canvas, Barnes Foundation, Philadelphia.

7-13. *Composition, Five Bathers* by Renoir 1918, oil on canvas, Barnes Foundation, Philadelphia.

7-14. *Impression Sunrise* in a black and white photograph.

7-15. The color wheel.

7-16. *Terrace at Sainte-Adresse* by Monet, 1867, oil on canvas, Metropolitan Museum of Art, New York.

7-17. *Haystacks at Sunset* by Monet, 1880-1881, oil on canvas, Museum of Fine Arts, Boston.

7-18. Photo of Monet's water lily pond in Giverny.

7-19. *Water Lilies,1920-1926* by Monet, 1920-1926, oil on canvas, Musee de l'Orangerie, Paris.

7-20. *The Japanese Footbridge* by Monet, 1920-1922, oil on canvas, Museum of Modern Art, New York.

7-21. Photo of Monet's Nympheas at Musee de l'Orangerie.

7-22. *The Rehearsal on Stage* by Degas, 1874, pastel on paper, Metropolitan Museum of Art, New York.

7-23. *Dance Class* by Degas, 1874, oil on canvas, Metropolitan Museum of Art, New York.

7-24. *L'Absinthe* by Degas, 1876, oil on canvas, Musee d'Orsay, Paris.

7-25. *Two Laundresses* by Degas, 1882, oil on canvas, Musee d'Orsay, Paris.

7-26. *The Little Dancer of Fourteen Years* by Degas, 1881, wax and then bronze in 1922, various museums with the largest collection in the National Gallery of Art, Washington, D.C.

BERTHE MORISOT AND MARY CASSATT:

The Woman's Touch To Impressionism

8

Berthe Morisot (1841-95) was born in the same year as Renoir. She was the first woman in the Impressionist movement and she participated in seven of the eight exhibitions remaining loyal to the group after others had abandoned the movement. The only one she missed was when her daughter Julie was born. She almost single-handedly organized the final show in 1886.

When a critic assailed the first Impressionist exhibition in 1874 by stating, "Five or six lunatics, one of whom is a woman, deranged by ambition," the woman he was referring to was Berthe Morisot. But not all the responses to her work were negative. Another critic wrote, "There is but one real Impressionist in the group and that is Berthe Morisot. Her painting does truly give the idea of an impression."

The fortune Berthe Morisot inherited in 1873 resulted in the criticism that she was a woman that painted rather than a woman painter. It was untrue. She was a committed artist. Along with Monet, Sisley and Pissarro she could be considered as being among the purest Impressionists. Hers can also be considered among the most refined and delicate of the Impressionistic paintings. She was the first woman in

8-1. Berthe Morisot Reclining by Manet, 1873, oil on canvas, Musee Marmotten Monet, Paris.

the history of French art to have a career comparable to the best of her male colleagues. Yet, early in her career, many of her paintings were criticized as being messy, sloppy and incomplete. But, after all, that was the same type of criticism directed at all of the Impressionists.

The world that Berthe Morisot represented in her art was one of refinement, beautiful gardens, wonderful interiors and expensive clothing. It was a world almost exclusive to the women represented by her social position in the fashionable bourgeoisie. Her paintings of women were different from those of male artists. There were no nudes, certainly no street walkers or entertainers and there were few city scenes. Boredom was one of her subjects because she understood it. Upper class women had little to do in that era. She was, in effect, through her art allowing men private access to feminine activities and their effects like clothing, flowers and jewelry.

She started her training as a copyist at the Louvre copying masters like Veronese and Rubens. At 20 she met Corot and it was under his influence that she took up plein air painting. She exhibited for the first time at the French Salon in 1864 at the age of 23. Her work was accepted at six subsequent Salons until 1873 when, after an invitation by Degas, she joined the Impressionists at their first exhibit in 1874.

Berthe Morisot played two roles in the art world of that day. First and foremost, she was an accomplished painter. But there is another part of her life that attracts you to her. That is as a muse for the art of Edouard Manet and her relationship with him.

Morisot first appeared in one of Manet's works *The Balcony* (see fig. 6-15). Although she is shown as a very attractive woman in that piece, her beauty and sensuality really come across in the 11 portraits that Manet did of her. The portraits also reflect something about the mystery of their relationship. You get the sense that it was one of the great unfulfilled love stories among artists.

She met Manet in 1868 at 27 while copying a Rubens painting at the Louvre. It marked a turning point in her career. It was difficult for women to move within the male dominated art circles at that time. Although she had seen him at exhibits and knew his work, it was unacceptable for Berthe to introduce herself. In accordance with etiquette she had to wait for a mutual friend to introduce them. After all, Manet was married and she was single.

It was four years after *The Balcony* that Manet painted the beautiful portrait *Berthe Morisot Reclining* (fig. 8-1). Here the element of seduction is unmistakable. There is her seductive gaze. Her dark eyes seem to follow the viewer around the room. Her reclining pose is provocative. Manet often painted her skin as luminously white against either a dark background or her black clothing. Here he does both.

The sheer number and beauty of the portraits has aroused curiosity about the relationship between the two. In them there is a charged connection between the artist and his beautiful subject. They are among his most moving works probably because of his fascination and emotional involvement with her.

There was a play in a theater in Boulder, Colorado called *Berthe Morisot Reclining*. In it, Degas calls the bond between Morisot and Manet, "The greatest relationship ever recorded on canvas." Looking at this piece that may be correct and, just imagine, there are ten others.

The relationship between the two was more than just about portraits. Although Manet could be considered the mentor and she the pupil, there was reciprocity in their relationship. It was Berthe who drew Manet into the wide circle of Impressionists. She even encouraged him to abandon black although that was never completely possible for Manet. She convinced him to attempt plein air painting. They also interacted in subject matters in several paintings.

Nevertheless, Manet could adopt a patronizing tone that the two sisters (Berthe had a sister Edma who was a painter before she married) could make use of their feminine charm. It was a sign of the times. The year they met and before he began the portraits of her he said, "The young Morisot girls are charming, it's a pity they are not men. But being women they could still do something in the cause of painting by each marrying an academician and introducing discord into the camp of those old dodderers, though that would be asking for considerable self-sacrifice."

Perhaps Manet's greatest influence on Morisot was the introduction of her to his brother Eugene. According to Julie, her daughter, it was on the occasion of painting one of her portraits in 1872 that Manet suggested Berthe marry his brother. The marriage took place in 1874. After her marriage to Eugene, Manet did not paint any more portraits of her.

Here is where all the speculation begins. If it was simply a platonic relationship, one has to wonder why he did not continue to paint his sister-in-law after she married his brother. Did she marry Eugene because she could not marry Edouard? Is there any doubt they would have married if Manet had not already been married. At the very least, Manet's portraits reveal not only the talent of the painter and the beauty of the model but also a bond between them.

That bond is also revealed in another portrait by Manet, *Repose* (fig. 8-2). Here the color patterns are reversed. Berthe wears a white dress. There is a more dreamy, pensive aspect to her character but her beauty is what Manet clearly brings out.

The fingers of her left hand are spread between her white handkerchief and the star-shaped indentations of the sofa buttons. In her hand she is holding a fan that helps accentuate her femininity as if there was a need to do so. Her black hair hangs below her shoulders.

Does anyone have such a narrow waist? It is accented by the black sash. Her calm demeanor contrasts with the swirling brushstrokes of the painting above her head. Ob-

8-2. *Repose* by Manet, 1870, oil on canvas, Rhode Island School of Design, Providence.

viously, this piece was carefully staged by Manet to take advantage of all of Berthe's charms. Later, she told her daughter Julie that her left leg that was drawn back under her skirt used to stiffen painfully but Manet would not allow her to move lest the skirt would be disarranged.

Perhaps more than any other of the portraits, the haunting, indefinable bond between the two artists comes out in *Berthe Morisot with a Bunch of Violets* (fig. 8-3). Rather than using uniform light, Manet chose to light his model from one side. That makes Morisot's face appear to be half in light and half in shadow. Notice another detail, the ribbons hanging down from her hat accentuate her scattered strands of hair.

It is a spellbinding portrait. What strikes you again is the intense black that could only be Manet's. There is a black hat, black scarf and black dress. All of this enhances her "Spanish" beauty which is the image she presented in *The Balcony*. A bunch of violets can barely be seen. It is nestled in the clasp of her jacket.

She is posed against a plain gray curtain. The neutral background dramatizes the effects of the black and accentuates the aura of mystery in her look. But it is Manet's depiction of her eyes where he works the most magic. He paints them deep pure black; forget that they were actually green.

Perhaps Manet had an ulterior motive in using so much black. Maybe he was reminding his model of the stunning possibilities that the color held. After all, this was done when Morisot's own paintings were taking on a lighter tone as she was following the path to Impressionism. Black was not a color that the Impressionists had on their palette.

Berthe is never more alive in this portrait. She is directly engaging us. Or perhaps her look is directed at the artist, maybe she is even flirting with Manet. Later, her daughter Julie would say that the painting was done in just two sittings and that mama told me when it was finished Manet told her she ought to marry papa who was his brother.

8-3. *Berthe Morisot with a Bunch of Violets* by Manet, 1872, oil on canvas, Musee d'Orsay, Paris.

What does the delightful, tiny intimate still life *A Bouquet of Violets* (fig. 8-4) painted around the same time say about their relationship? If you could examine the original piece very closely you would find that Manet addressed a folded note to "Mlle Berthe" and signed it "E. Manet." He placed a red-lacquer fan and a small group of violets beside it. The violets relate to the corsage she wore in the ravishing portrait described above. The red fan is the same one that Berthe held in *The Balcony*.

Berthe Morisot and her sister were both artists. But in that era, although artistic ability was respected and even encouraged among young women, there was a thick line

8-4. *A Bouquet of Violets* by Manet, 1872, oil on canvas, private collection.

drawn between being an amateur artist and a professional. Yet, their mother Marie Cornelie Morisot and their father both enthusiastically supported their efforts to become professional artists. Their father had a studio built for them in the garden and their mother told her daughters to carry on with their careers even if it meant they had to paint twice as well as their male counterparts to get recognized.

The twelve-year painting partnership of the two sisters ended in 1869 when Edma married. She decided to forego her art career. But this did not deter Berthe. She was a perfectionist in her art and totally committed to her career as a painter. *Mother and Sister Reading* (fig. 8-5) is a family portrait but different from most you will find. The setting is the family drawing room where the mother is reading and Edma sits close by. Edma is in the late stages of her first pregnancy.

What is unusual about the piece is that the mother looks oblivious to her daughter's presence. Edma is shown with an almost dazed expression or perhaps in a dream like state as if she is in a world of her own. Why would Berthe depict them in this manner? It is certainly lacking in the type of warmth one would expect in a portrait of this type.

Perhaps Berthe is capturing things in the reality of the moment that we are not aware of. Maybe Edma is simply lost in thought over the arrival of her first child and what the future holds. Maybe her mother is reading out aloud and Edma is concentrating on her mother's words.

Morisot paints Edma's white dress is such a full way that it almost hides the fact that she is pregnant. This may be because Berthe was planning to have this piece accepted at the Salon. She probably realized that depicting a pregnant woman might not please the jurists and thus reduce her chances of acceptance. Edma's white dress contrasts sharply with the black one worn by her mother who might be in mourning over the death of her own mother earlier in the year.

This work is also an example of the interaction in painting between Morisot and Manet. Occasionally, they painted similar subject matters or Manet would critique her work. But, in this case, he went too far. She craved his admiration more than anything. But sometimes he could be arrogant and overbearing much like Degas with Mary Cassatt which will be discussed later.

On the occasion of this painting, Manet carried his dominance too far. When Berthe completed the work she asked Manet for his opinion. Instead of telling her what he would suggest, he took the brushes and began to retouch it and got carried away.

Manet arrived on the same day that Berthe had arranged for the Salon to pick up the painting. She described what occurred in a letter to her sister Edma parts of which are presented below:

"...he came about one o'clock; he found it very good, except for the lower part of the dress. He took the brushes and put in a few accents that looked very well. ... That is where my misfortunes began. Once started, nothing could stop him; from the skirt he went to the bust, from the bust to the head, from the head to the background. He cracked a thousand jokes, laughed like a madman, handed me the palette, took it back; finally at five o'clock in the afternoon we made the prettiest caricature that was ever seen. The carter was waiting to take it away; he made me put it on the hand-cart. ... And now I am left confounded. My only hope is that I shall be rejected. My mother thinks the episode funny, but I find it agonizing."

She resented the imposition of his style on her own work. It turned out that the Salon jury did not reject the piece but it did not sell. Later she showed it at the first Impressionistic exhibition in 1874.

The Cradle (fig. 8-6) was her most celebrated piece and received favorable comments at the first Impressionist exhibition in 1874. Some of the critics commented on its grace and elegance. It is certainly an enchanting work. Nevertheless, it did not sell and Morisot withdrew it from display and it stayed with the family until the Louvre bought it in 1930.

One of the reasons Morisot cast her lot with the Impressionists was because of their interest in genre paintings. This certainly qualifies as a genre scene. It is her first image of motherhood which would become one of her favorite subjects. She also liked to use family

8-5. *Mother and Sister Reading* by Morisot, oil on canvas, 1870, National Gallery of Art, Washington.

and friends as models. This is her delicate celebration of her sister Edma and her sleeping newborn daughter Blanche.

Although there are many interesting aspects to the painting, the primary focus is the intensity of the mother's gaze fixed upon the baby as she reflectively rests her chin on her hand. It makes the viewer try to guess what she is thinking. Morisot symbolizes the bond between the mother and her child by the diagonal formed by the bend in the mother's left arm and her baby's arm. It links the mother and child. There is also Edma's gesture of drawing the curtain of the cradle between the viewer and the baby. It reinforces the feeling of intimacy expressed in the painting.

Morisot also took note of current trends in nursery furniture. There is the diaphanous white net trimmed with a pink ribbon. The mother wears a dark dress that is heightened by the white background. The infant is blurry-featured in typical Impressionist manner. Because of Berthe's sensitivity to this type of subject matter along with her attention to fashion, she attracted a large female following.

Summer's Day (fig. 8-7) is another one of her most important works. It was shown in the fifth Impressionist exhibition in 1880. In terms of subject matter, it is typically Impressionistic in its depiction of modern urban leisure.

It shows two fashionable young women in a boat floating on a lake. We, as the viewer, sit opposite

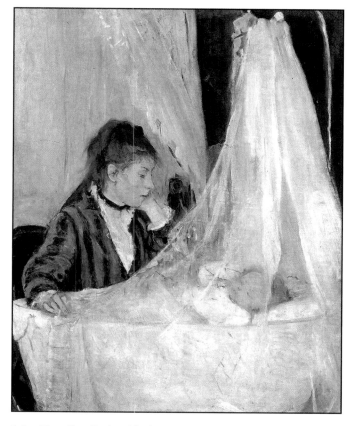

8-6. *The Cradle* by Morisot, 1872, oil on canvas, Musee d'Orsay, Paris.

8-7. *Summer's Day* by Morisot, 1879, oil on canvas, National Gallery, London.

MANET AND MORISOT: MENTOR, COLLEAGUES, FRIENDS AND ROMANCE?

There have been more famous couples in the art world such as Georgia O'Keeffe and Alfred Stieglitz or Frida Kahlo and Diego Rivera. But they were married. The nature of the relationship between Manet and Morisot is more elusive because they were not married.

Manet and Morisot were certainly artistic colleagues and he could be considered her mentor although she was never officially his student (she did study in her teens under the Barbizon master Corot). They were also friends. But how much more than friends could they be given that Manet was married and off limits to a single woman who was protected by the strict rules and oversight of her close family circle?

Despite the constraints, when looking at The Balcony and the series of eleven portraits done from 1870 to 1874, three of which are depicted in this book, one has to wonder how much more than friends they were. After all, there is a sense of something very personal in the portraits that transcends friendship, perhaps even implying romance.

Then there is the most intimate still life in the history of art painted by Manet, *A Bouquet of Violets* (see fig. 8-4). It was painted in 1872 the same year that Manet completed his portrait *Berthe Morisot with a Bunch of Violets* (see fig. 8-3). Is the note in the painting simply a token of thanks to a good friend for being such an excellent model? Or, does the combination of such Victorian symbols—violets, a fan and a letter—represent a cloaked love message? Most of all, one has to wonder how Morisot reacted to the painting. If we knew that we would have the answer to the question about their relationship.

8-8. *Eugene Manet and His Daughter at Bougival* by Morisot, 1881, oil on canvas, Musee Marmotten Monet, Paris.

8-9. *In the Garden* by Morisot, 1883, oil on canvas, Art Institute of Chicago.

which was typical of Morisot and there are her characteristic whirling brushstrokes.

The most impressive part of the work is the details. The garden is confined by a blue gate in the back and it is alive with red flowers. Eugene gazes down at Julie who rests her toy village on his knees. He is fashionably dressed with a bowler hat, blue cravat, fawn-colored jacket and blue trousers. Julie has delicate features, long blond hair and bangs. She wears a yellow sunbonnet tied with a ribbon under her neck and a long, pink frock. Fashion is everywhere.

Eugene observes her as she plays with the tiny pieces. Both seem to be absorbed in the game. This is everything you would expect from a father and daughter.

In the Garden (fig. 8-9) is an example of the intimate images of women in the privacy of their homes or gardens that Morisot painted. It reflects the comfort of family life. It is all about the impression she gives you of the style of the upper class at that time.

In the background is Julie again. She was probably the most documented child in the history of art. This is an interesting portrayal because the woman's tool is really the fan she holds, not the rake in the background. That is probably for the gardener because it is something she would never use.

Edouard Manet died in 1883 from complications after he had a leg amputated due to syphilis. Berthe Morisot was at his side when he died and wrote to her sister: "These last days were very painful; poor Edouard suffered atrociously. His agony was horrible. In a word, it was death in one of the most appalling forms that I witnessed at very close range."

"If you add to these emotions my old bonds of friendship with Edouard, you will understand that I am crushed. I shall never forget the days of my friendship and intimacy with him, when I sat for him and when the charm of his mind kept me alert during those long hours."

Berthe Morisot died in 1895 of typhoid fever at the age of 54. During her career she wanted to be treated as an equal. She said, "I don't think there has ever been a man who treated a woman as an equal and that is all I would ask, for I know I'm worth as much as they." But she lived in a time when equal treatment was rare. Even though she produced more than 800 paintings, her death certificate stated she had "no profession."

For a long time she was known as much for being a friend and model for Manet than an artist in her own right. It took almost a century for her work to receive the credit it deserved.

them and seem to be invited to share their enjoyment. The painting is intentionally executed in a sketchy manner. The bold, rapid brushstrokes are characteristic of her work. The figures almost dissolve into a flurry of feathery brushstrokes that pushes the Impressionist technique to the limit. They define form but almost dissolve into abstraction.

The painting is an example of how the overall effect and atmosphere of a scene is more important than the details. The precise subject matter becomes secondary to the mood of the painting. It is a mood that Morisot is trying to capture and she does it wonderfully. In the process, the academic traditions of how to paint fall by the wayside.

Men appear infrequently in Morisot's paintings and that applies to her husband Eugene. But *Eugene Manet and His Daughter at Bougival* (fig. 8-8) is an exception. We get a view of her husband with their daughter who would have been near three at the time. The piece is bathed in light

Mary Cassatt (1844-1926) lived a life of paradoxes. She was born in the U.S. but lived and painted in France. She was a classically trained artist but became involved in what was considered at the time as a group of radicals. She never married but became known for her paintings of mothers and children.

Both Berthe Morisot and Mary Cassatt came from similar upper-class backgrounds and did not have to sell their art to support themselves. But their personalities were quite different. Morisot was feminine, charming and sensuous. Cassatt was homely, caustic and austere. Morisot was filled with doubts when it came to her art. Cassatt was more confident about exhibiting and selling her work.

Morisot was helped by her husband. Cassatt had to help herself. Although Morisot was sympathetic and discreet, Cassatt brusque and frank with a sharp tongue, they became friends and exhibited together. Both had mentors who importantly influenced their careers. For Cassatt it was Degas.

Mary was one of the two women in the Impressionistic movement but the only American. She came from wealth. She was born in Lancaster, Pennsylvania and moved to the West Chester

8-10. *La Loge* by Renoir, 1874, oil on canvas, Courtland Institute Galleries, London.

area outside of Philadelphia where she lived with her family for a number of years. Her brother was chairman of the Pennsylvania railroad. At 16 she enrolled in the Pennsylvania Academy of the Fine Arts where she was a fellow student of Thomas Eakins. She traveled to Paris on numerous occasions with her family and had additional training in art there. Mary felt she could not be a great painter in the U.S. so she went to live in Europe – Spain first and then to Paris in 1866 at the age of 22. Like Berthe Morisot she was a copier of old masters at the Louvre.

When she saw some pastels by Degas in a Paris gallery window in 1875 she said, "I used to go and flatten my nose against the window and absorb all I could of his art." Later she recalled, "It changed my life." Because of Degas' influence she became extremely proficient in the use of pastels.

The two became life-long friends. She was the only woman Degas had a close relationship with. He became devoted to her, at least as much as Degas could be devoted to anyone. Although they were close, there is no suggestion their relationship approached that of Berthe Morisot and Manet even though both remained single through their lives.

Mary was the perfect female counterpart to Degas in temperament. Both could be opinionated and abrasive. For example, although she admired Renoir's courage to paint late in his life despite very ill health, she described his bather's paintings as "enormously fat, red women with very small heads." She said Monet's water lily paintings looked like "decorative wallpaper." Regarding the avant garde movements early in the 20th century she said, "No sound artist ever looked except with scorn on these Cubists and Matisse."

8-11. *At the Ball* by Morisot, 1875, oil on canvas, Musee Marmottan Monet, Paris.

became a studio painter and was not interested in plein air painting.

She recalled her enthusiasm when asked by Degas to join the Impressionists and why she was so attracted to the movement:

"It was at that moment that Degas persuaded me to send no more to the Salon and to exhibit with his friends in the group of Impressionists. I accepted with joy. At last I could work with complete independence without concerning myself with the eventual judgment of a jury. I already knew who were my true masters. I admired Manet, Courbet and Degas. I hated conventional art. I began to live."

From the beginning, her art was about modernity. She liked subject matter drawn from contemporary life, rather than painting mythological or historical scenes. Mary Cassatt's art falls roughly into three categories. From the 1870s to mid 1880s she focused on female family members at tea, the opera, etc. In 1889 and the early 1890s, oils and pastels of mothers and children became her favorite subject matter. She also began to focus on making color prints inspired by Japanese woodblock prints.

Women attending social events like the opera, ballet or a ball were a popular artistic theme at the time. But there was a distinct difference regarding how the subject was handled depending on whether it was from a woman's point of view like Morisot or Cassatt or from a man's perspective like Renoir. But one thing that the artists discussed here had in common was that they all focused on the spectators not the onstage performers which was the way Degas handled the subject.

As you might expect, Renoir presents the scene of Parisian modern life in *La Loge* (fig. 8-10) from the male point of view. His brushstrokes are loose, a typical Impressionist technique but that does not prevent him from providing a lot of detail.

The woman sits at the front of the box so she can be seen. Her social status is unclear but given her rather showy black and white stripped dress, her adornments and

By the turn of the century, she resisted anything that was new. She could not understand Cezanne's growing reputation and influence. She condemned Monet's late work and objected to the squalid, low life subjects of Toulouse Lautrec.

Given those opinions, her reaction when she went with a friend to the Paris apartment of Gertrude Stein to see her great collection of modern art should not be surprising. She said, "I have never in my life seen so many dreadful paintings in one place. I have never seen so many dreadful people gathered together."

In 1877, her works were rejected by the Paris Salon. For the first time in seven years she had no showings there. Degas invited her to show with the Impressionists in 1879. She participated in each of the last four exhibitions from 1879 to 1886. Because of his influence she

8-12. *Woman With a Pearl Necklace in the Loge* by Cassatt, 1879, oil on canvas, Philadelphia Museum of Art, Philadelphia.

the heavy use of cosmetics she is likely a courtesan, not the man's wife. Her face is painted white and lips red. She wears glistening pearls around her neck, a gold bracelet and earrings. There is a flower in her hair and she has a corsage tucked into the center of her low cut dress. She holds a handkerchief and fan in one hand. All of this is an example of Renoir's sharp eye for minute details. The touches that he adds enhances the realism of the painting.

Renoir he did not have any scruples about using black in the piece. It is a color that Impressionists frowned upon. But he probably used the bold black stripes on the woman's dress to provide contrast between the two characters.

The female is a model from Montmartre named Nini Lopez but also known as "fish face" for some reason. The male is Renoir's brother Edmond. The woman lowers her opera glasses revealing herself to all the potential admirers in the theatre. Her expression makes it look as if she is lost in a daydream. But her passive demeanor has a purpose. She is signaling her availability and displaying her charms for all to see.

Her bearded male companion sits behind her so he can use his glasses to survey the audience, perhaps looking for a new partner. In a nutshell, the painting is about seeing and being seen. Renoir is providing a slice of the spectacle of modern life in the city. He presents the theatre as a social stage where relationships are on public display.

An interesting sidelight is that although this painting is highly regarded today, when it was exhibited in Paris in 1874 it did not sell. Later it was bought very inexpensively. Renoir sold it for the exact amount he needed to pay his rent. He was 33 and it provides a glimpse into his financial circumstances at the time.

Berthe Morisot was probably aware of Renoir's *La Loge* when she painted *At the Ball* (fig. 8-11) the following year. As we might expect, she is making a contradictory statement to the one made by Renoir. We see another beautiful woman in an evening gown, wearing flowers but with little makeup. She is in a dress that is subtle and the flowers are not there to draw attention to her. In fact, they seem to symbolize her innocence.

This is a respectable, upper class female at a ball with no male escort shown. She is beautiful but presented as a thinking woman. Hers is a more elegant world. Morisot is out to impress us with her intimate world of delicate femininity.

Mary Cassatt's presentation of women out and about was very different from male painters. These were not the

8-13. *Little Girl in a Blue Armchair* by Cassatt, 1878, oil on canvas, National Gallery of Art, Washington, D.C.

vulnerable lower class women often painted by Degas or the entertainers and prostitutes of Toulouse Lautrec. Nor do they emphasize the mischievous charm of Renoir's bathers. *Woman With Pearl Necklace in the Loge* (fig. 8-12) is a good example.

This piece was singled out for praise at the fourth Impressionistic exhibition in 1879. Like Berthe Morisot, Mary Cassatt often used her sister as a model. Unlike Degas, who often shows what is happening on stage, we see a beautiful woman watching and being watched. Notice the barely visible men in the first and second boxes on the right focusing on her with binoculars. But she is not inviting anyone to join her.

This is another painting about the culture of display in modern Paris. The stage here is not for performers. The stage is the audience. They are on display. Cassatt presents her sister Lydia. She is seen as the audience would see her. Lydia appears as a woman with a great deal of freedom. But that is not entirely the case. This type of event was one of the few that she could attend unescorted. For a change, she has the same access that a man does.

There is a feminist element to this painting. She is shown as intelligent, alone and probably self-sufficient. There is no male escort. She leans slightly forward as if she is presenting herself to the audience that Cassatt cleverly reveals through the mirror in back of her. The luminous color and fluid brushstrokes are synonymous with Impressionism. Then there are the effects of the artificial lighting on her skin tones. The light picks up the side of her face, the front is in shadow.

Cassatt's words about one year earlier are echoed in this painting. "Oh, I am independent! I can live alone and I love to work." Unfortunately, this lifestyle and her view of it did not adhere to the traditional ideas of the role of women near the end of the 19th century.

Little Girl in a Blue Armchair (fig. 8-13) is a painting that Degas advised her on and even worked on the background. It shows his influence in that the little girl, who is the focus of the composition, is placed off-center. Also, the painting is cropped at the edge of the canvas to enhance the feel of an accidental image like you might get with photography. These are all characteristics representative of Degas.

The piece demonstrates Cassatt's keen powers of observation. The young subject is sprawled in an overlarge chair with her legs dangling. She has a carefree attitude. The girl's pose has the naturalism of childhood. This is something that would characterize many of Cassatt's paintings of children. Cassatt wrote, "I love to paint children. They are so natural and truthful."

Notice the details that emphasize the realism of the piece even if it is Impressionism. Around her waist is

8-14. *At the Opera* by Cassatt, 1879, oil on canvas, Museum of Fine Arts, Boston.

a tartan shawl that is echoed by the falling down socks and the ribbon in her hair. The armchairs encircle an oddly shaped patch of gray floor in the middle of the painting.

She is in her own private world of boredom. She has the same self-satisfied expression as the dozing dog stretched out on the nearby chair. The realistic mood makes this piece one of the great representations of a child in art. But it is also about modern life, new furniture and fashion in that everything matches.

When the painting was refused by the Paris Salon in 1878, Cassatt said she was furious, all the more so since Degas had worked on it. It was this reaction that helped propel her into the Impressionist exhibit the next year.

In *At The Opera* (fig. 8-14) Cassatt returns to the theme of watching and being watched. She captures a fleeting moment at a cultural event. Cassatt did not always depict fashionably dressed, beautiful women at these events. In fact, here you get the sense that this woman could be a widow because she is dressed entirely in black. You also could speculate that it was done in response to *La Loge* by Renoir because this piece is the antithesis of Renoir's. The contrasts are almost two numerous to list. The two women are worlds apart in their appearance. Unlike the woman

in *La Loge*, Cassatt's female is genuinely unconscious of what is happening.

The woman is seen in her own theatre box assertively using her opera glasses to see what is happening on the stage or perhaps in the audience. She is unaware that she is the object of intense scrutiny by a man in another box. He is so frantic to get a good look at her that he leans out over the ledge of the box with his binoculars glued to his eyes.

Here is a fiercely independent woman, not chaperoned, attending the opera and taking on the male role of observing. There is no feminine softness here. There is even a masculinity in the way she holds the binoculars and how she places her elbows on the rail to steady her glasses just as the man does. The red velvet covered rail which runs along the loges links the two viewers. She looks alone in the box conveying independence. Her posture seems to trivialize the man looking at her. She is definitely not inviting anyone to join her.

Five O'Clock Tea (fig. 8-15) is an example of the world Mary Cassatt had access to – the domestic and social life of well-off women. The painting is about the ritual of tea. It is reminiscent of a Victorian Era English afternoon tea but painted in France by an American in 1880.

8-15. *Five O'Clock Tea* by Cassatt, 1880, oil on canvas, Museum of Fine Arts, Boston.

8-16. *Self Portrait* by Cassatt, 1878, gouache on paper, Metropolitan Museum of Art, New York.

There is a visitor and the hostess. One is finished and the other is still drinking. The two gaze out to the right as if they are looking at someone beyond the canvas. Notice the difference in clothes. One is dressed to go out with long yellow gloves and she still wears her hat. She is the obvious visitor. The other, as the hostess, is without a hat. The visitor, with extended little finger, sips daintily from the blue-rimmed cup. The atmosphere is proper and fashionable, silent and stiff. Although the two women are sitting next to each other, there is no warmth. It appears to be a tedious social ritual.

The painting is also about a meticulously decorated interior. There is the richly furnished drawing room with striped wallpaper and a chintz sofa. A bell rope for summoning servants fades into the stripes. There is the gleaming silver tea service with light reflecting off it. The gilt mirror and marble fireplace also add to the setting.

It is safe to say that not everything went smoothly in the relationship between Degas and Cassatt. It was a close but turbulent friendship. For example, regarding his critique of her work she said:

8-17. *Portrait of Mary Cassatt* by Degas, 1884, oil on canvas, National Portrait Gallery, Washington, D.C.

"I have been half a dozen times on the point of asking Degas to come and see my work, but if he happens to be in the mood, he would demolish me so completely that I could never pick myself up in time to finish for the exhibition."

In 1884 he pushed things too far. When Degas did a portrait of Mary that year, in her opinion he degraded her. Six years earlier Mary Cassatt did a self portrait (fig. 8-16). As might be expected, she painted an idealized piece. She portrays herself in dangling earrings, a ruffled white gown and white gloves all in line with her upper class social status. Her hat is trimmed with red flowers and tied with a black ribbon around her neck. She leans on a soft, red stripped chair and looks away.

In *Portrait of Mary Cassatt* (fig. 8-17) Degas portrays her looking much older. She wears a black dress instead of the ruffled white gown. She is sitting on a hard chair, leaning forward with elbows on her knees in an unflattering, hunched-forward position holding three cards and looking down at them suggesting, in her opinion, a gypsy fortune-teller.

Mary was ashamed and revolted by the portrait. Later, in letters to her agent Durand-Ruel she insisted, "I do not want to leave it with my family as being of me. It represents me as such a repugnant person that I could not want it known that I posed for it." To avoid the painting being recognized as her portrait, she wanted it sold to a foreigner

8-18. *Helene de Septenil* by Cassatt, 1890, oil on canvas, private collection.

In fact, mother and child themes were extensively explored by both Cassatt and Morisot in their artistic careers. It is one of the many things they had in common in their artwork.

Notice the marvelous way Mary paints the pressing of the woman's cheek against the cheek of the child. The infant shares a tender moment with its adoring mother. It is a scene of daily intimacy. With the embrace, Mary is showing the bond between a mother and her child. Given that Mary never married and had no children it is impressive that she could paint such a scene. You get the sense that this is Cassatt's modern response to the tradition of the Madonna and Child paintings of the Renaissance.

In paintings like this she was able to document the intimacy of private moments of women in ways that male artists never could. In short, she had a competitive advantage here. Notice that fathers seem to play no part in the families. They are always absent in her paintings.

Young Women Picking the Fruit of Knowledge (fig. 8-19) is more hard edged and linear than most of Cassatt's works. Degas was a great draftsman so, understandably, he praised her drawing in this piece.

Both Morisot and Cassatt were occasionally criticized for their repetition or so called monotony of their subject matter in terms of tea, clothes, gardens, mothers and children. Of course, this came from male critics who did not understand or appreciate the world they were representing. Their subject matter was because of their limited access to the aspects of society that men had – city life, taverns, nudes, etc. In short, women's lives were different from men and both Morisot and Cassatt depicted them as such.

This painting is a departure for Cassatt in terms of subject. It is highly symbolic and feminist charged. According to her, the pear tree shown in the painting represents the tree of knowledge. One of the women sits meditatively holding a pear in her lap. According to the artist, in plucking the fruit from the tree of knowledge, these

without her name on it. It is in the National Portrait Gallery in Washington.

Consider the difference between Degas' approach and when Manet did his passionate portraits of Berthe Morisot. They expressed his deep feeling and his attraction to her. In contrast, Degas' cool portrait of Mary Cassatt revealed the constraints in his relationship with her.

Helene de Septenil (fig. 8-18) is an example of the mother and child theme that Cassatt adopted in the 1890s.

women express their desire for equality and intellectual recognition.

In 1892, Mary Cassatt was commissioned to do a huge mural 12 x 58 feet for the Woman's Building at the Chicago World's Columbian Exposition in 1893. The goal of the building was to showcase the advancement of women throughout history. Her mural was titled *Modern Woman*. She took the fruit picking theme for the center panel. Unfortunately, the mural did not survive. It was lost when the building was destroyed.

In *The Letter* (fig.8-20) Mary Cassatt takes the daily mundane activity of licking an envelope but enlivens it with a Japanese inspired composition and design. It is one of her most popular and frequently reproduced works.

At first glance, one might wonder why Cassatt would paint a subject that seems like such a trivial domestic activity. But in her time letter writing consumed a large part of a woman's day. A woman not only wrote to friends and acquaintances but she was responsible for answering invitations and dealing with the daily domestic chores of the household. Also, Cassatt, who was an American expatriate living in Paris, probably spent a lot of time keeping in touch with family and friends back home. Thus, letter writing probably held special significance for her. The drop leaf desk belonged to her family so at one time she might have used it to write letters.

8-19. *Young Women Picking the Fruit of Knowledge* by Cassatt, 1892, oil on canvas, Carnegie Museum of Art, Pittsburgh.

Mary became attracted to Japanese prints after seeing them in a show in Paris in 1890. She became entranced with their themes of everyday activities and their sparse beauty. She was influenced by them more than any other Impressionist.

Japanese woodblock prints date to the 8th century and became very popular in France in the second half of the 19th century. This piece has many of the com-

mon characteristics of a Japanese print. They often depict everyday life activities of commoners. There is a flat two-dimensional space with the figure in a direct frontal position that is placed against decorative patterns in the background.

There is the downward gaze of the woman that recalls Japanese modesty. The female subject even looks faintly Japanese in her features and skin color. It is interesting that Cassatt chose this subject matter for her experimentation

8-20. *The Letter* by Cassatt, 1891, drypoint and aquatint on paper, National Gallery of Canada, Ottawa.

Cassatt's response to the death of Degas was cooler. She mourned him as a friend and a brilliant artist whose passing signaled the end of an era. She wrote, "Degas died at midnight. His death was a deliverance. I am sad since he was my oldest friend here and the last great artist of the 20th century. I see no one to replace him."

Mary Cassatt died in 1926 at 82. She lived in France for 55 years and made only three trips back to the U.S. partly because traveling by sea made her ill. As she aged she endured serious eye problems. By 1919 she had five cataract operations. Thus she shared a tragic bond with the man with whom she was friends for a large part of her life. Both Cassatt and Degas died nearly totally blind. Neither was able to produce any new paintings over the last decade of their lives. It must have been very difficult for them.

In addition to her art, Mary Cassatt played another important role in the Impressionist movement. She was instrumental in promoting the works of the Impressionists in the U.S. largely through her brother Alexander who was president of the Pennsylvania railroad. She persuaded him to buy works by Monet, Manet, Morisot, Renoir and Pissarro making him the first important collector in the U.S. She also encouraged her friends to buy.

IMAGES

8-1. *Berthe Morisot Reclining* by Manet, 1873, oil on canvas, Musee Marmotten Monet, Paris.

with Japanese-style prints. Perhaps a novel subject was appropriate for such a novel technique.

When Edgar Degas died in 1917 at the age of 83, Mary Cassatt's reaction was different from that of Berthe Morisot on the death of her close friend Manet. As discussed earlier in this chapter, Berthe's letter to her sister was personal and emotional. It emphasized his charm and her crushing loss.

8-2. *Repose* by Manet, 1870, oil on canvas, Rhode Island School of Design, Providence.

8-3. *Berthe Morisot with a Bunch of Violets* by Manet, 1872, oil on canvas, Musee d'Orsay, Paris.

8-4. *A Bouquet of Violets* by Manet, 1872, oil on canvas, private collection.

BERTHE MORISOT AND MARY CASSATT: HOW GOOD WERE THEY?

Berthe Morisot and Mary Cassatt were the only prominent women painters of the day. They worked in a field dominated by men. But how accomplished were they? Where might they rank among the artists of that era?

There have been critics that have suggested the lack of women artists in the 19th and early 20th centuries was, quite simply, because of their lack of ability. The inference being that Berthe Morisot and Mary Cassatt fall into that category. There has even been the suggestion that their wealth and the desire of the Impressionist movement to publicize its modernism by taking women into its ranks were responsible for their acceptance and success. Both have been criticized because the subject matter of their paintings was associated with women and their lives and, therefore, not very original.

This writer does not think those types of criticisms apply. These women faced enormous obstacles trying to make their way in a male dominated profession in the 19th century. One perspective was that the most important contribution to the art profession that a woman could make was to be the mother of an artistic genius. These were exceptional women to overcome such obstacles. They had to be anomalies and very talented to achieve such a level of success.

Here is a quote that is representative of the thinking about the place of women painters in that era. "No respectable, refined lady could be a professional artist. Ladies were permitted to paint roses or pansies on china plates, even to make pencil sketches or watercolors in their enclosed gardens. But to study art seriously, learning anatomy from nude models and having a studio of their own, it was never done and therefore unthinkable."

Having said all of that and even though biases against women have long since fallen by the wayside, art history has still not elevated either of the two women to the level of the most prestigious painters of that period. Their accomplishments do not match those of the so called "masters."

That means you are left with a "pecking order" as is usually the case. But I do not think it is based on any bias against women artists. Essentially, Berthe Morisot and Mary Cassatt rank in the second tier and that is not bad. They are below the masters like Renoir, Monet and Degas. They vie for prominence with names like Sisley and Pissarro. But as far as American born woman artists are concerned, Mary Cassatt may well be the most distinguished.

8-5. *Mother and Sister Reading* by Morisot, oil on canvas, 1870, National Gallery of Art, Washington.

8-6. *The Cradle* by Morisot, 1872, oil on canvas, Musee d'Orsay, Paris.

8-7. *Summer's Day* by Morisot, 1879, oil on canvas, National Gallery, London.

8-8. *Eugene Manet and His Daughter at Bougival* by Morisot, 1881, oil on canvas, Musee Marmotten Monet, Paris.

8-9. *In the Garden* by Morisot, 1883, oil on canvas, Art Institute of Chicago.

8-10. *La Loge* by Renoir, 1874, oil on canvas, Courtland Institute Galleries, London.

8-11. *At the Ball* by Morisot, 1875, oil on canvas, Musee Marmottan Monet, Paris.

8-12. *Woman With a Pearl Necklace in the Loge* by Cassatt, 1879, oil on canvas, Philadelphia Museum of Art, Philadelphia.

8-13. *Little Girl in a Blue Armchair* by Cassatt, 1878, oil on canvas, National Gallery of Art, Washington, D.C.

8-14. *At the Opera* by Cassatt, 1879, oil on canvas, Museum of Fine Arts, Boston.

8-15. *Five O'Clock Tea* by Cassatt, 1880, oil on canvas, Museum of Fine Arts, Boston.

8-16. *Self Portrait* by Cassatt, 1878, gouache on paper, Metropolitan Museum of Art, New York.

8-17. *Portrait of Mary Cassatt* by Degas, 1884, oil on canvas, National Portrait Gallery, Washington, D.C.

8-18. *Helene de Septenil* by Cassatt, 1890, oil on canvas, private collection.

8-19. *Young Women Picking the Fruit of Knowledge* by Cassatt, 1892, oil on canvas, Carnegie Museum of Art, Pittsburgh.

8-20. *The Letter* by Cassatt, 1891, drypoint and aquatint on paper, National Gallery of Canada, Ottawa.

POST-IMPRESSIONISM

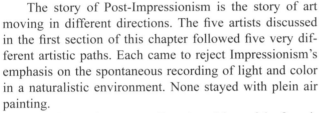

The story of Post-Impressionism is the story of art moving in different directions. The five artists discussed in the first section of this chapter followed five very different artistic paths. Each came to reject Impressionism's emphasis on the spontaneous recording of light and color in a naturalistic environment. None stayed with plein air painting.

All of the painters were French and four of the five either started as Impressionists or were heavily influenced by them. But, in each case, they rejected Impressionism and went down a path to form their own highly personalized style. In their minds, they were seeking a more ambitious way to express their art.

Each of the Post-Impressionists chose their own form of artistic expression. They did not agree on a way forward. For example, Gauguin and Van Gogh focused on an emotional approach in portraying the subject. Cezanne and Seurat were more interested in the structure of a painting.

This does not mean that all of them totally disregarded Impressionism. At least implicitly, some admitted their debt to the group in their use of pure, brilliant colors or in their departure from traditional subject matter. But they wanted to extend Impressionism and move beyond what they considered its limitations. They continued to use vivid colors, thick application of paint, distinctive brush strokes and real life subjects. But they also rejected Impressionism by emphasizing geometric shapes, distorting for emotional effects and applying unnatural and arbitrary colors.

Unlike the Impressionists, these artists painted mainly alone and were not heavily influenced by what others were doing. Cezanne painted in isolation in Aix-en-Provence. Gauguin matched Cezanne's solitude by going to Tahiti in 1891. Van Gogh painted in the countryside in Arles and, at the end, in Auvers. Toulouse Lautrec preferred to immerse himself in the night life of Paris.

Although labeled as Post-Impressionists, they did not have much in common. There was no specific style or formal movement at the time which bound the artists together. Each, in his own way, was rebelling against what he considered to be the limitations of Impressionism. Their focus ranged from the emotional to the structural, to the symbolic and even spiritual elements that they felt were missing from Impressionism. They pushed the boundaries of the Impressionistic style in different creative directions and, in the process, laid the foundations for art in the 20th century.

If Impressionism was the first movement in the body of modern art, then the Post-Impressionists set the stage for a series of later movements.

Post-Impressionism covered a relatively short period of time. One starting date can be assigned to 1886, the year of the last Impressionistic exhibitions. It extended to approximately 1914. By then Cubism and Fauvism had taken hold and both represented a fresh start for the world of art. Also, war broke out in Europe in 1914 and that represented a temporary but major break in French cultural history.

Whatever the start and end dates for Post-Impressionism, the painters formed a basis for a number of contemporary trends that led to 20th century modernism. Gauguin had an important influence on Fauvism. Cezanne can be linked to the start of Cubism. Seurat's Pointalism influenced artists to take a more calculated approach to painting leading to the development of abstraction. The art of Van Gogh had an influence on Expressionism. The direct descendants of Toulouse Lautrec's graphic art are the advertising posters that publicize events and make faces and products familiar and famous.

CEZANNE
The Father of 20th Century Modernism

Paul Cezanne (1839-1906) was even more of a loner than Degas and he became increasingly so over the years. That was partly because he became tormented by doubt. He was deeply hurt by the lack of even the faintest signs of recognition of his artistic efforts. His temperament became unbearable. He turned into a hermit, driving away all of his friends.

Despite his personal problems, no artist had a greater impact on the next generation of modern painters than Cezanne. Yet, he had little professional success until the last years of his life. He showed with the Impressionists in the first and third exhibitions in 1874 and 1877. Although his objective then was to paint the sensations of nature, he never sought to capture the transitory effects of light and color like the Impressionists.

Cezanne went through a number of important changes in art style over his career. It is safe to say that it took him quite a while to mature artistically. His paintings in the 1860s were peculiar, showing little resemblance to what would come later. There were signs of a great deal of energy in them. But they were dark and the paint was thick, sometimes applied with a palette knife. The subject matter was gloomy with a sense of melancholy. There were violently deformed shapes. He depicted dreams, fantasies and religious subjects often in a distorted manner. These works exhibited few of the features of his later paintings. These were works by an artist who could be either a madman or a genius. Fortunately, Cezanne would evolve into the latter.

Next in line for Cezanne was a shift into Impressionism. He was an Impressionist for five years from 1872 to 1877. He painted landscapes often working with Pissarro. In fact, he described himself as Pissarro's pupil. He said, "We all stem from Pissarro." It was Pissarro who succeeded in convincing him to choose lighter colors and it was because of his influence that he participated in two Impressionistic exhibits.

At this stage of his career, Cezanne became convinced that one must paint directly from nature. His somber palette gave way to fresher more vibrant colors. It was Pissarro that gave him the advice that changed his career. He told him, "Don't look for something new in the subject matter, only in the way you express it." Cezanne took that advice and ran with it. After that, he became Cezanne.

Eventually, the emotional experience of painting in the Impressionistic style was not enough to satisfy him. He believed that the Impressionists lacked one of the important strengths of great art: structured compositions. He also believed the Impressionist's style was limited because they had to work quickly to capture the fleeting effects of changing color and light. Cezanne wanted to paint art where the compositions were organized and solid.

He was not concerned with "sensations" or communing with nature that was the staple of the Impressionistic approach. Rather, he wanted to analyze nature. He became obsessively preoccupied with form. He said that he began to see nature in terms of geometric forms – cubes, spheres, cones and cylinders. For example, a tree trunk could be conceived as a cylinder and an apple as a sphere. He often painted one of his favorite subjects, Mont Sainte-Victoire, as a cube.

After participating in the early Impressionist exhibitions he gradually withdrew from his colleagues. He did not exhibit for almost 20 years. He worked increasingly in isolation at his home in southern France. One reason for his withdrawal was that his work began to go in a direction not aligned with that of any of the Impressionists.

Often the question comes up: What makes a painter important? If you create a new tradition in art, a new way of seeing art you become very important. For example, Matisse created a tradition of decorative color while Braque and Picasso created Cubism, new ways of seeing art. All of them became very important in art history. But Cezanne created no new school of art. Yet, Picasso called him "the father of Cubism" because Cubism is about geometry and shapes.

Cezanne studied his subjects intensely and struggled to deal with issues associated with visual perception. Likewise, Braque and Picasso went on to experiment with more complex views of the same subject. His decision to defy the laws of perspective (and sometimes gravity when it came to his still-life's) influenced the invention of Cubism.

Matisse said "Cezanne is the father of us all." If you do not create a new tradition of art you can also become important because of the influence you have on other artists. Cezanne has inspired generations of modern artists and has been the impulse to many new movements since his death more than 100 years ago.

Many leading modern painters develop a single idea that has great impact. But there is no one element in Cezanne's work that can be singled out as having a powerful effect. Rather, you are struck by the comprehensive nature of his art. Cezanne's greatness is not associated with one or two masterpieces. It is the quality of the overall body of his work that is important.

Until Cezanne came along, painters tried to represent the visible work pretty much as it was. A man looked like a man and a cup looked like a cup. But Cezanne changed the visible world. Suddenly, dishes are lopsided, fruit is oddly shaped, figures look different and tables slope downward. Unlike artists like Renoir, physical beauty is not part of his work. Renoir is easy to look at but Cezanne is not always easy to look at. But beauty is not always the criteria for importance and that is certainly the case with Cezanne.

Cezanne changes your perspective. His distortions opened the way for Cubism and abstract art. His artistic endeavors laid the foundation to the radically different art of the 20th century. He is the father of modernism and that is what makes him so important.

His greatest work came in the last 25 years of his life. He developed an almost architectural style of painting. For example, in a painting of Mont Sainte-Victoire he developed a system of horizontal planes which add to the scope of the work and draws the viewer into the landscape. He used the same approach in his still-life paintings. Rather than following the traditional way of providing perspective from a single fixed point, he portrayed objects from shifting viewpoints.

Although Cezanne's artistic approach befuddled the public and the critics for most of his career, he began to be mentioned with increasing admiration within the circle of young painters. Finally, he had his first one-man exhibition at the age of 55. The hostility of the press remained a given but to an increasingly number of artists he was seen as their master. He was what can be called a painter's painter. The artists of his day understood how important he was before the critics and the public.

Was Cezanne aware of this belated recognition? In a letter to the dealer Vollard in 1903 three years before his death he wrote, "I can see the promised land...Why has it come so late and so painfully?" The brilliance of the artist

9-1. *Mont Sainte-Victoire* by Cezanne, 1885-1887, oil on canvas, Courtauld Institute of Art, London.

was finally established when a retrospective of his works was held in Paris in 1907. Unfortunately, it was a year after he died.

Cezanne's aim was to make art that was "solid and durable like the art of museums." His painting *Mont Sainte-Victoire* (fig. 9-1), a subject he painted over and over again, is representative of his effort to create a "solid and durable" landscape. He used geometry to describe nature and different colors to achieve depth.

There is something timeless about this landscape. Unlike the Impressionists, there is no emphasis on capturing a fleeting moment in the ever-changing world of nature. There is the illusion of three-dimensions. Depth is suggested by the tree and branches that draw one's eye into the valley and the distant mountain. It is also suggested by the gradual transition from greens, oranges and yellows in the valley in the foreground to the paler colors of the mountain with patches of blue. Cezanne divides the canvas into a series of overlapping planes that lead stepwise to the mountain adding to the sense of depth.

Breadth, height and depth are all balanced in the painting providing a feeling of calmness. There is the vastness of space in the valley. Depth is measured by the distance from the home in the left foreground to the mountain top. Height is added by the tree that reaches from the lower to upper edges of the canvas.

The majesty of the mountain is actually reduced by the tree in the foreground and the width of the valley. There is a great emphasis on artistic construction here. What emerges is a landscape painting that depicts a solid world of endless expanse.

The Bather (fig. 9-2) is an example of Cezanne challenging your perspective. It is one of his most mysterious works of a figure. It fuses his interests in artistic tradition (bathers have an extensive history in classical art) with an attempt to be thoroughly modern.

Cezanne has created a statue in a landscape. It is really not a bather but a man looking down absorbed in deep thought. He seems unaware of the world around him. Cezanne has moved the figure as far as he can into the foreground. He has pushed him up to the front of the picture plane as if he is giving the viewer the best opportunity to scrutinize him.

The figure is united to his surroundings. The color of his flesh is like the ground and the shadow tones of blue on his body are like the water and the sky. Verticals

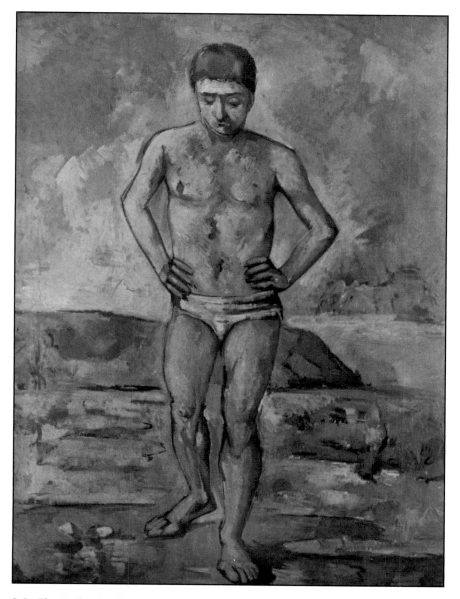

9-2. *The Bather* by Cezanne, 1885, oil on canvas, Museum of Modern Art, New York.

There is a strange dark shadow on the right side of his face that seems to eliminate his mouth. He looks like half boy and half man. Part of the sky seems to radiate out from his body creating a sort of halo. The surface beneath him looks like water but he stands not in the water but on it. His knees are bent with one foot ahead of the other like he is taking a step. But, somehow, we know he will never move.

Such distortions have been characterized as being modern. Although Cezanne had respect for tradition, he did not represent his figures the way classical or Renaissance artists did. What Cezanne does in this painting is a revelation to young artists and helped to liberate them in their artwork.

Between 1890 and 1897, Cezanne created five versions of The Card Players. The one in figure 9-3 is the most heroic of the group. It is the only one that contains five figures. With Cezanne, a lot is conjecture and that is the case concerning the order that he painted the five works. No one is quite sure of the exact order. He did not date his paintings and, for the most part, he worked in isolation.

One thing that is sure is that this was an important subject matter for Cezanne. It is as if he wanted to make it his own just as he did with Mont Sainte-Victoire and his series of nudes in landscape. Cezanne's approach to the theme was different. Card players had long been a subject that attracted artists going back to the 17th century Dutch masters.

There are none of the rowdy, drunken gamblers sometimes with their wenches revealing in a tavern. These men are still and look solid like trees or even Mont Sainte-Victoire that Cezanne so often depicted. They seem frozen in a quiet moment. There is an ageless, timeless quality to them. The subject is everyday life and the individuals who live it. This is what a genre painting is all about: intimate scenes of ordinary people in everyday life. These are ordinary people studiously concentrating on the game. The men may have modeled individually for the piece in Cezanne's studio. Probably they all worked as laborers on the family estate, Jas de Bouffan outside Aix-en-Provence.

and horizontals come together. His large vertical form is presented against a background of a series of horizontal panels. The figure and the landscape echo each other. Two parts of the landscape match the divisions of the figure. His upper body is in the sky and the lower body is on the earth.

Look how the figure diverges from normal. His body is uneven. The left side is higher than the right and the right arm is longer than the left. Both arms are stick like with almost no muscles. They look fragile enough to snap. Yet, the rest of his body, particularly the thighs and calves, looks massive with great volume. These two opposed themes also appear in the sky and earth. One is like a vapor and the other looks solid.

9-3. The Card Players by Cezanne, 1890-1892, oil on canvas, Barnes Foundation, Philadelphia.

9-4. *The Basket of Apples* by Cezanne, 1895, oil on canvas, Art Institute of Chicago, Chicago.

There is an extraordinary sense of stillness that is enhanced by the balance that Cezanne provides to the composition. The bare-headed player is flanked by the two men each with broad-brimmed hats. The man in the middle sits exactly at the center of the composition. His upper body with the downward sloping arms creates a triangle which mirrors his V-shape of his legs beneath the table. That V-shape anchors the whole group of card players to the scene.

In effect, everything seems to radiate out from the triangle formed by his legs. In the back, a young girl, who is probably the daughter of one of the players, sits with her white face and a gaze that draw the viewer into the scene.

Cezanne is a master of subtle embellishments in this piece. Some things seem out-of-kilter. The man standing in the back looks out of scale compared to the other fig-

ures. At first glance, the table is presented as one would expect. But under closer inspection its surface appears to tilt slightly down toward the viewer. This allows us to get a clear view of the items on the gaming board. The items add a decorative element to the piece. There is a white pipe that comes from the pipe-rack on the wall. One card faces up, perhaps a red king or queen.

The men's bulky clothes are painted with deep folds. The color of the garment worn by the player on the right matches the standing smoker's blue smock. Both blues set-off the golden color of the drape. It appears to have great weight with even deeper folds than the ones on the men's garments.

In 2011 one of the five versions of *The Card Players* was purchased reportedly for the astronomical amount of $250 million. That sets the highest price ever paid for a work of art. It seems insane that the purchase price could top the previous

9-5. *The Large Bathers* by Cezanne, 1906, oil on canvas, Philadelphia Museum of Art, Philadelphia.

record of $140 million for a Jackson Pollock painting by such a wide margin. With that purchase, in a single stroke, the tiny oil rich nation of Qatar that is in the midst of building a museum empire joined the exclusive club of other *Card Players* owners the Metropolitan Museum of Art, Musee d'Orsay, the Courtauld Gallery and the Barnes Foundation.

There is nothing coherent or orderly in the perspective that Cezanne offers in *The Basket of Apples* (fig. 9-4). One cannot imagine a situation in daily life that objects such as those depicted would come together in this way. Yet, the composition as a whole comes off as balanced even though it is unbalanced in its parts.

There is the appearance of randomness to the placements but this is no accidental grouping. The painting is a construction where everything is carefully intended. There are a large number of appealing, densely colored fruit. Yet, that reality is contradicted in the details. There is a total disregard for normal perspective. It is that approach by Cezanne in paintings such as this where he forms a bridge between Impressionism and Cubism.

The right side of the table is higher than the left. The pastries on the plate on the right are tilted upward. There is an oddly shaped bottle tilting to the left. But it seems to fit with the rest of the still life.

The whole composition seems on the verge of collapse but that adds a sense of tension to the work and prevents the "still" life from being static. The pastries look like they could levitate. The bottle is precariously balanced. The contents of the fruit basket appear as if they are about to spill out. Only the folds in the table cloth seem to prevent the apples from rolling off the table onto the floor.

All of these improbable relationships are carefully designed by Cezanne, not as a representation of nature but as a construction of nature. He would characterize them as "something other than reality." But one could say the same thing about the art that followed Cezanne in the 20th century. It is often something other than reality. He is pointing the way to that type of art with paintings like this.

The Large Bathers (fig. 9-5) is a monumental scene of nude figures in a landscape setting. It is his largest composition measuring roughly 7 x 8 feet. Like Mont Sainte-Victoire, it is a subject that preoccupied him throughout his career. He worked on the painting for seven years and it was still unfinished at the time of his death. It is considered one of the masterpieces of modern art.

The figures are presented in a stage like setting. These are not images of modern French women at a picnic. Rather, they suggest goddesses in a remote setting involved in some sort of ritual. The figures in the background watch their actions. There is a lot of activity yet there is a profound sense of calm added to by the tranquil lake and church tower in the distance. The arched trees act as a cover to the stage.

Since the Renaissance, the human body was considered sacrosanct, a thing of beauty. But Cezanne deconstructs the human body before Picasso. In that sense, he

makes it modern. The bodies look unfinished and are not sensual. The setting is classical, inspired by Titian's *Diana and Actaeon* but Cezanne modernizes it.

There is a sense of symmetry to the painting. The nudes are arranged in two triangular shaped groups on each side of the painting. They are framed by a group of triangular shaped trees. The bathers do not appear life like. They are created out of Cezanne's imagination because he worked far too slowly to use real models. There is a sharp contrast to the stiffly drawn almost abstract figures and the blue sky.

In creating works like this, Cezanne was trying to give a timeless quality to his art. He did not want to follow fashionable trends or be pressured by current day artistic methods. With Cezanne, art is not merely a matter of copying what one sees. In following this path, he set the stage for future artists to diverge from current trends and to paint pieces that would appeal to all generations. For example, comparisons have been made between this work and another famous group of nude women that were painted about a decade later, Picasso's *Les Demoiselles d'Avignon* (see fig. 11-6).

SEURAT

A New Structure In Painting

Georges Seurat (1859-91) put it best when discussing his art. "Some say they see poetry in my paintings. I see only science." His painting style was even more structured than Cezanne's. His approach has been called "scientific Impressionism." Although he participated in the last Impressionistic exhibition in 1886, he was at the forefront of the challenge to Impressionism in the 1880s. But one thing he had in common with the Impressionists was that he painted the new and modern France, people enjoying their leisure time.

Seurat did not like the Impressionist's style of using vivid brushstrokes. He wanted to turn painting into a science. Although Seurat could draw beautifully, the challenge for him was to render line purely through color and, at the same time, make the colors more brilliant and powerful than when applying standard brushstrokes.

To meet these challenges, Seurat undertook a rigorous study of optics and color. The Impressionists did not develop a color theory of their own but used their judgment on how to apply colors. In contrast, he based his decisions on the principle of complimentary colors with the goal of achieving as much luminosity as possible. (See the discussion in the information box in Chapter 7 on the color wheel and complimentary colors).

His technique was to paint pictures with thousands of dots of primary colors and their complimentary colors. He would arrange the paint on his palette in the order in which they appear in the color wheel: blue, blue-violet, violet,

9-6. *A Sunday Afternoon on the Island of La Grande Jatte* by Seurat, 1884-1886, oil on canvas, Art Institute of Chicago, Chicago.

violet-red, red, etc. Although usually described as dots, in reality they were small brushstrokes.

The colors located opposite one another on the color wheel create the strongest contrasts. For example, red and its compliment green, blue and orange, yellow and violet provided the greatest intensity when placed next to one another. In Seurat's method of painting, mixing colors was not the task of the painter; it was the task of the eye.

Seurat carefully calculated which colors should be combined and in what proportion to produce the effect of a particular color. He then set the colors down in dots next to one another. The technique became known as Pointillism or Neo-Impressionism although Seurat preferred the term Divisionism because of the method of separating colors. For example, instead of tying to mix the perfect color of purple, he would put red and blue next to one another and let the eye do the mixing. It is called "optical mixture."

In theory, the juxtaposed dots would merge in the viewer's eye to produce the impression of other colors which would be seen as more intense or luminous. However, in Seurat's work the optical mixture does not work as completely as thought because the dots of color are large enough to remain separate in the eye, giving a grainy appearance to the painting.

Seurat spent nearly two years painting *A Sunday Afternoon on the Island of La Grande Jatte* (fig. 9-6). The scene is not one that comes from his imagination but was preceded by dozens of preparatory drawings and many days spent in the park observing the people. But the final piece was painted in the studio.

In effect, he took Impressionism and turned it on its head. There is nothing spontaneous about this painting. It looks organized and structured. The only similarity with Impressionism is that he focused on the same theme of leisure but everything ends there.

The painting is beautifully balanced with a formal elegance. There is no disorder here. Everyone seems alone even those in pairs or groups. Even though the theme is leisure, you end up with a stiff formality of figures that is at odds with the casualness of Impressionism. They look artificial, like chess pieces that you can move around. You have a contemporary subject matter presented in a highly formal style recalling art of ancient Egypt. Nevertheless, to make the painting appear even more vivid, he surrounded it with a frame of painted dots.

The Grande Jatte is a small island in the Seine River. Accounts about the island at the time Seurat painted it were that it was a noisy, littered and chaotic place. By painting

9-7. *The Models* by Seurat, 1886-1888, oil on canvas, Barnes Foundation, Philadelphia.

it in this manner, maybe he intended to show how tranquil it should be. Perhaps he was suggesting there should be a more civilized way of life in a modern city like Paris.

Often, we all feel harried by life's pressures and the speed at which things occur. From time-to-time we may even think: "stop the world." You get the sense in this painting that Seurat has "stopped the world." He revealed to us a beautiful sunlit and silent world. It looks like it would be a nice place to spend some time, perhaps a Sunday afternoon.

Unfortunately, there are not many Seurat Pointillist paintings to see partly because of the time it took to compose such a work of art but more importantly because Seurat died at the early age of 32 after contracting diphtheria. But fortunately, two years after *La Grande Jatte*, he continued his effort to bring science to Impressionism by applying optical theory with *The Models* (fig. 9-7). He chose to do it on a similar sized monumental canvas. He varied the application of dabbed paint from the pinks and

blues that cover the walls to a more dense treatment of the women's flesh. The canvas *La Grande Jatte* is pinned to the wall behind the women. It presents a contrast of color from *The Models* which Seurat believed expressed a different mood.

One objection to *La Grande Jatte* was that Seurat's Pointillist technique was suited, at best, to outdoor images of light, water or foliage, not necessarily the human figure painted in large-scale interiors. Thus, the assumption was that such a traditional subject matter would represent a serious challenge to his revolutionary technique. With *The Models* Seurat set out to disprove such challenges by applying Pointillism to one of the most distinguished subjects in art history, the nude.

His compositional approach was indeed challenging: nudes in a studio pose before the painting *La Grande Jatte* that rests behind them. It becomes a painting-within-a-painting. The artist then goes on to exploit a number of possible connections between the two themes in his compositions. The nude women could be models from *La Grande Jatte* where they appear fully dressed and have returned to the studio to disrobe. Strewn throughout the studio are articles from *La Grande Jatte*: hats, shoes, parasols even a small basket of flowers.

The scene also raises the question of whether this is three models at work or a single model in three different stages of activity: disrobing, dressing and posing. In the process he provides three views of the nude, from the front, back and side. By placing his models in front of *La Grande Jatte* he allows the viewer to compare an interior and exterior scene as well as nude women and fully clothed women.

The painting is out of the Florentine art tradition with its cool colors. The figure in the center of the painting recalls the central figure in Botticelli's *Birth of Venus*. Botticelli was a late Florentine artist.

Figure 9-8 shows a detail of one of the figures in *The Models* to more clearly provide a perspective on what Pointillism looks like up close. Here the dots and dabs of paint are more clearly visible. It shows how Seurat was trying to render line through the use of color. There are no lines drawn on the canvas but you get the appearance of lines through the dabs of color next to one another that represent the Pointillist technique.

Both *La Grade Jatte* and *The Models* are examples of how art history progresses. Seurat was part of a new generation of artists that challenged the art of his day. He tried to create something new. It is that challenge that drives the avant-garde artists who, in turn, drive the history of art.

GAUGUIN
The Symbolist

When Matisse and Picasso were inventing modern art in the 20th century, three names were on their lips: Cezanne whose career has already been discussed; Van Gogh whose art will be discussed shortly and Paul Gauguin (1848-1903). Gauguin had an artistic style that was the antithesis of Pointillism. Rather than applying dots, he worked in large flat areas of vivid color. He wanted to go back in time and try to rediscover man's purity and simplicity before the emergence of science. In contrast, Seurat was trying to apply science to art.

Although Gauguin participated in the last four Impressionistic exhibitions he eventually rejected Impressionism altogether. The Impressionists painted the new and modern France but Gauguin reacted against modernity to the point that he left France and lived in more primitive cultures. He wanted to observe innocent behavior in a primitive society still relatively uncorrupted by civilization.

Gauguin was the master of exotic and decorative painting and he had the background for the exotic. Although born in Paris, his family sailed for Peru when he was 18 months old. He joined the merchant marine at 17 and then the French navy circumnavigating the globe twice. Gauguin married a Danish woman named Metta and supported his family by being a stockbroker until 35. He was a "Sunday painter" and then decided to become a full time artist. But his marriage fell apart and his wife returned to Copenhagen with their five children.

He left Paris for Brittany to study peasant life. Gauguin believed that the people of this deeply religious region of France were closer to nature than those in Paris. He was also attracted to the expressiveness of the peasant costumes.

He went to the French Caribbean island of Martinique in 1887. As part of his constant search for an untouched land of simplicity and beauty he traveled to more remote destinations where he could live easily and paint the purity of the country. He went to Tahiti in 1891 but returned to France in 1893. He sailed again for Tahiti in 1895 and

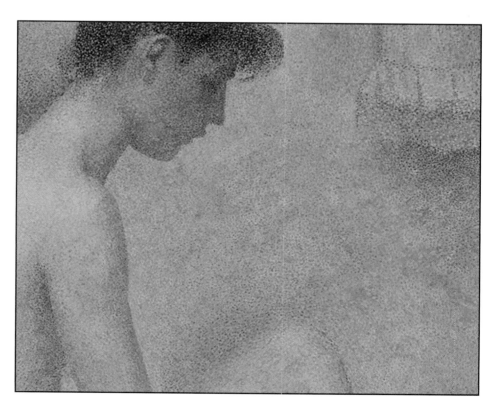

9-8. *Detail of The Models* by Seurat.

9-9. *Vision After The Sermon* by Gauguin, 1888, oil on canvas, National Gallery of Scotland, Edinburgh.

finally to the Marquesas Islands 900 miles from Tahiti. He was in constant search for a kind of Eden.

Unfortunately, wherever he traveled, he did not find the pure race of people who lived close to the earth, those not tainted by European materialism. What he did find were cultures subjected to European influences like alcohol, prostitution and venereal diseases. Nevertheless, it did not deter Gauguin. Instead of focusing on the subject in the world that actually confronted him, he painted his ideal of natives living in a paradisiacal environment. His paintings show the world as he imagined it should be rather than as it actually was.

His artistic style in the islands represented a dramatic departure from his Impressionistic years. The Impressionists were concerned with modernity and what they saw in that modern environment. Gauguin's art, rather than representing what he saw, is about primitivism, imagination and fantasies. Instead of relying on short, sharp brushstrokes he used long brushstrokes, large patches of flat, non-naturalistic saturated color. His forms are clearly defined. He

completely eliminated subtle graduations of color thereby dispensing with one of the characteristic principles of Impressionism. He depicted exotic themes and images with an emotionally charged emphasis on symbolism.

In his travels, Gauguin was always in search of artistic freedom and probably sexual freedom as well. He found both but along the way he contracted syphilis which ravaged his eyesight and mind. At one point, he tried to commit suicide by taking arsenic. He died in poverty in the Marquesas Islands at the age of 55.

For such a solitary figure, Gauguin left a rich legacy of followers. His innovations inspired generations of artists. The Fauves and Matisse benefited from his use of color in their own daring compositions. Gauguin was a mentor to Van Gogh. He helped in the transformation of Van Gogh from a painter who used dark, drab colors to one who emphasized a rich, vibrant palette. Like Gauguin, rather than painting reality, Van Gogh began to paint an exaggeration of reality. Gauguin helped to inspire a

GAUGUIN AND VAN GOGH IN ARLES

Gauguin and Van Gogh are the odd couple of the art world. They had a rocky relationship in the limited time they spent together. For nine weeks from October to December 1888 they lived together in the Yellow House in Arles in the south of France. Earlier that year an uncle died and Vincent's brother Theo was named as the main heir. Theo shared the windfall with Vincent and the money was used to spruce up space in the Yellow House to accommodate Gauguin. But things did not work out as Vincent Van Gogh hoped.

Vincent was intent on establishing his "Studio of the South" in Arles. He hoped their creativity would be spurred by their association. But few men have struggled so much with their demons and suffered so much for their art. Van Gogh's experiment was doomed to failure but not as completely as it might seem.

When Gauguin arrived, Vincent insisted they work en plein air like the Impressionists. But Gauguin was already on his way to rejecting Impressionism. The month before he arrived in Arles he had painted *Vision After The Sermon*. He was moving decisively away from painting natural appearances and was relying more on depicting images from his mind. In short, he was transitioning from being a second-generation Impressionist to a Symbolist.

As Gauguin became more disillusioned with Impressionism his quarrels with Van Gogh intensified. On the evening of December 23, 1888 Van Gogh confronted Gauguin with a razor and then, according to legend, fled to a local brothel and cut off the lower part of his left ear lobe. He wrapped it in a newspaper and handed it to a prostitute named Rachel. Gauguin left Arles shortly later and they never saw each other again although they continued to correspond. Hollywood's best interpretation of the incident was presented in the 1956 movie *Lust For Life* starring Kirk Douglas as Van Gogh and Anthony Quinn as Gauguin.

Although the incident started Van Gogh on a painful descent into madness that ended 1½ years later when he committed suicide, he probably gained the most from the volatile relationship between the two artists. A lost soul can sometimes, if only temporarily, find a new path. Gauguin's powerful image of spiritually in Brittany in *Vision After The Sermon* inspired Van Gogh to be even bolder in his use of color. It was Gauguin who urged Van Gogh to rely more on his imagination rather than working en plein air in front of his subject. After the mutilation of his ear incident, Van Gogh's terrified neighbors insisted that he spend some time in a mental hospital. It was in the asylum in San Remy that Van Gogh produced some of his best works including *Starry Night*.

Perhaps more than anything else, two paintings that Van Gogh did in 1888 provide some insights into how he viewed his relationship with Gauguin and how their personalities differed. *Gauguin's Armchair* (fig. 9-10) is more stylish and is placed on a carpet of flowers. A candle illuminates two books that lie on it. The books make a statement about Gauguin's intellect. The green wall is lit by a blazing lamp. The lights are said to serve as sparks of inspiration.

Vincent's Chair (fig. 9-11) is plain and sits in the kitchen on old brown tiles. A box of onions is on the floor in the background bearing his signature. The chair has thick uneven legs. A pipe and some tobacco wrapped in a scrap of paper lie on the chair. The somber room is filled with natural light compared to the artificial light that illuminates Gauguin's more luxurious room. Van Gogh's chair is yellow which is regarded as his signature color.

Van Gogh sees himself as closely tied to the hard working poor peasants that he painted so often. His chair shows him as simple and unsophisticated. In contrast, he viewed Gauguin as more worldly and sophisticated. The darker, more somber tones of Gauguin's chair may suggest his imminent departure from the Yellow House.

There is even symbolism in the way the paintings are displayed when shown together. Generally, the works are displayed the way they are shown in this book. That is, *Gauguin's Armchair* is on the left and *Vincent's Chair* is on the right. Then they are facing away from each other symbolizing the conflicting nature of the two artists and the turbulence in their association. However, if the paintings are displayed in the reverse order they would be facing one another symbolizing mutual respect.

young Picasso in his appreciation of African art. Because of his imagination and use of symbols, he was a precursor to the Surrealistic movement. All in all, his is an impressive resume.

Vision After The Sermon (fig. 9-9) also known as *Jacob Wrestling the Angel* is important for its pivotal role that it played in Gauguin's career. His use of clear-cut shapes of black and white against a dramatic red background is a sharp departure from his prior work. He had considered himself an Impressionist. But the red ground, a shrunken cow and large praying women in black and white make the painting the antithesis of Impressionism. In addition, Impressionism did not deal with religious themes. Here he begins to develop his signature style of

9-10. *Gauguin's Armchair* by Van Gogh, 1888, oil on canvas, Van Gogh Museum, Amsterdam.

9-11. *Vincent's Chair* by Van Gogh, 1888, oil on canvas, National Gallery, London.

large blocks of bright, saturated color. This is one of his first symbolist paintings.

At first glance, there is simplicity in the work. But that gives way to layers of complexity in meaning and interpretation. In fact, Gauguin's imagination and use of dream type images have linked him to the Surrealist art movement in the 20th century.

The painting depicts a very physical encounter between Jacob and an angel. This story has been portrayed often in art history. It comes from the Old Testament's Book of Genesis. In theology, the notion is that Jacob's struggle with the angel represents the inner struggle that takes place in every Christian which is the struggle that many have with their faith.

Gauguin depicts the struggle against a feverish red background. In the foreground are a group of pious women in their national costume of Brittany, France. They are reflecting on a sermon they have just heard. The cropped head of the priest at the far right is thought to be a self portrait of Gauguin.

Jacob is desperate to convince the angel that he has repented of his sins and will not let the angel go until he has succeeded. Gauguin uses compartmentalization in the form of a tree to separate the women from the wrestling match which supposedly mirrors their own hidden tor-

ments over the struggle they are having with their conscience.

The bright and vibrant colors represent purity and divinity. Color functions symbolically as a separating device. The common people are in drab color which separates them from the ground and the angel that vibrate with bright color. Given that both Jacob and the self portrait head on the far right wear similar caps, the scene could represent Gauguin's own struggle with faith.

Day of the God (fig. 9-12) is one of Gauguin's paintings that laid the foundation for abstraction. There are three horizontal zones from top to bottom with the bottom zone of water filled with curious amoeba-like shapes that are abstract. The colors are non-naturalistic and they do not seem to correspond logically to other colors in the painting. The composition deals with Polynesian mythology. At the center is the image of an idol which reflects Gauguin's fascination with religion. In the idol's honor, gifts are being brought by two maidens on the left. There is a flute player and two girls on the right perform a ritual dance.

All of this is background to the subject of the painting, which is the three women in the foreground at the pool. There Gauguin shows that the purpose of his art is to evoke symbolism rather than represent the real world. The three women represent the stages of mankind – birth, life and death. The

WHAT IS SYMBOLISM IN ART?

Symbolist painters believed that art should reflect an idea or an emotion rather than be an objective representation of the natural world. Unlike the Impressionists, the Symbolists who emerged in the 1880s were a diverse group of artists often working independently with varying artistic goals. They were united by a shared weariness of the decadence they saw in modern society. They sought to escape reality, expressing their personal visions and emotions through color, line and composition.

Symbolism allowed free access to the artist's inner world and provided for freedom from the boundaries of artistic style at the time. The painters generally had a preference for broad strokes and flat, unrestrained color. These types of artistic techniques seemed to fit with their emotional approach to art.

The surge in Symbolist imagery at the end of the 19th century represented a reaction against the effects of urbanization and materialism that accompanied the Industrial Revolution. It was also a reaction to the more realistic approach of Impressionism. It focused on spirituality, imagination and dreams.

Gauguin's brand of Symbolism was unique and highly personalized in that he actually sought to escape from civilization to more primitive cultures. Unlike the others, his paintings did not reflect an imaginary dream world. His search for a lost paradise led him to the South Seas where he produced highly personal and esoteric imagery that often avoids a clear interpretation.

Symbolism had a significant influence on Expressionism and Surrealism. Both of these 20th century movements can look back and see that their roots lie with the late 19th century Symbolists. Picasso embraced Symbolism in his early years, particularly his Blue Period works that depict downtrodden characters in a simplified style.

9-12. *The Day of the God* by Gauguin, 1894, oil on canvas, Art Institute of Chicago, Chicago.

9-13. *Where Do We Come From? Where Are We? Where Are We Going?* by Gauguin, 1897, oil on canvas, Museum of Fine Arts, Boston.

central figure, representing life, has both of her feet in the pool. The figure on the left represents birth. She has only her toes in the water while the figure on the right, symbolizing death, turns completely away from the water. There is nothing simple in the representations here. The symbols are complex and Gauguin's full intent in the painting is not clear.

Gauguin considered his monumental painting (4½ x 12 feet) *Where Do We Come From? Where Are We? Where Are We Going?* (fig. 9-13) the culmination of his artistic career. It is his most ambitious painting in terms of size, number of people and in the overlay of meanings. The work deals with human destiny.

He said that the painting should be read right to left. There are three groups of figures relating to the questions posed in the title. Barely visible, those questions are written in the upper left hand corner of the painting.

Everything takes place in a paradise of tropical beauty. It is a Garden of Eden tropical setting. The three women with the sleeping baby on the right represent the beginning of life. The standing figure in the center is picking fruit, perhaps from the tree of knowledge, that symbolizes the daily existence of young adulthood. On the left there is an old woman approaching death. Scattered throughout the piece are animals with which we share the world.

In the background, there is a large foreboding idol that represents "the Beyond," a god like figure according to the artist. The painting invites us to contemplate life; why we are here and where we are going. Gauguin himself was filled with self-doubt because of the lack of recognition and compensation for his art work. It was also a time of personal turmoil. His health and mental state had deteriorated due to the effects of his alcoholism and syphilis and he was recovering from a failed suicide attempt.

TOULOUSE-LAUTREC
Painter of Parisian Night Life

Henri de Toulouse-Lautrec (1864-1901) was one of a number of tragic figures in the art world of that era. He came from an aristocratic background but his parents were first cousins. He suffered from a congenital health condition attributed to inbreeding. That situation was compounded when he fractured his right leg at 13 and his left leg at 14. The breaks did not heel properly and his legs ceased to grow. This left him as a dwarf and crippled.

Given his family background, he could have supported himself painting Paris high society. But he preferred the bistros and brothels of Montmartre. He dedicated himself to depicting the late 19th century bohemian lifestyle of Parisian cafes, theaters, dance halls and brothels. He thought this is where one found "real life."

Whether painting cabarets or brothels, Toulouse-Lautrec made no attempt to glamorize his subjects. With his decorative and intense colors, the orange hair of the entertainers and prostitutes, he caught the atmosphere of the night life in Montmartre. He was a master at painting crowd scenes in which figures become highly individualized.

Toulouse-Lautrec said he preferred "real life" to genteel refinement. He explained it by saying, "A professional model looks like a dummy, these women are real." Frequently his models were red heads. Someone asked him why

9-14. *At The Moulin Rouge* by Toulouse-Lautrec, 1892-1895, oil on canvas, Art Institute of Chicago, Chicago.

he preferred red headed models. He said that he preferred to paint them because "they are so alive." That may have been the case but it is also true that many of his models were prostitutes and entertainers and they were frequently red heads.

Perhaps the artist that had the most direct influence on Toulouse-Lautrec was Degas. This can be seen in his indirect viewpoints and cutting off figures at the edges of the canvas, trademarks of Degas. Also, he excelled in capturing people in their working environment as Degas did with his ballet dancers.

With Toulouse-Lautrec, like his friend Van Gogh, there was the urge to work fast. It was as if he was in a frantic race against time and maybe he was. His work often takes on the appearance of swift sketches. To record the activities of his working-class women he had to paint fast in order to capture the moment. In this regard, his technique was the complete opposite of Cezanne's.

His greatest contemporary impact was his series of 30 posters he did from 1891 to 1901 which transformed the beauty and artistic appreciation of poster art. He realized that if the posters were to be successful, their message had to make a forceful impact on the passerby. He designed them with that in mind.

Toulouse-Lautrec became the father of the modern large-scale poster. His best ones were those that advertised entertainers at Montmartre cabarets. When the Moulin Rouge opened up, he was commissioned to produce a series of posters. They were so successful that the cabaret reserved a seat for him and would display his paintings.

Because of his deformity, Lautrec knew pain and suffering during his brief life time. He was often mocked because of his short stature and physical appearance. Unfortunately, art could not completely offset that. He needed a stronger remedy and found it in alcohol. It is said he invented the cocktail called "the earthquake." It was a potent mixture of half the 130 proof liqueur called absinthe and half cognac. Alcoholism and syphilis caught up with him early. He died at the age of 37 at his family estate.

At the Moulin Rouge (fig. 9-14) is an example of Lautrec painting people in the gaudy Parisian night life. He was able to accurately paint such images because he was a frequent visitor to the Moulin Rouge.

This is a partial self portrait because Toulouse-Lautrec is shown at the back of the painting moving to the left. He is accompanied by his cousin and frequent companion wearing a top hat. In fact, the visual line along the top hats leads directly to the entertainer with the turquoise face and orange hair. There are two women at the adjacent table, one with a white face and the other with bright red hair. The artist uses such strong colors to give vitality to the painting. The woman standing in the back dressed in black is the famous dancer La Goulue (The Glutton) who is said to have created the French can-can.

Notice the railing that separates the spectators from the scene and how the figure at the right is cut-off. Both are characteristics developed by Degas but picked up by Lautrec. In fact, at some point either the dealer or the artist cut down the canvas to remove the garish face on the right from the composition. Perhaps this was because her shocking appearance made the piece hard to sell. Later, the cut section was reattached to the painting.

In *Jane Avril* (fig. 9-15) Toulouse-Lautrec created a poster of the famous dancer doing her specialty, the can-can. It is an excellent example of how innovative he was in developing posters. This was supposed to be a promotional advertisement and, indeed, it filled that role by helping to make her famous. She became one of the most recognized names of the Parisian night life scene.

Lautrec shows Jane performing with one leg up in the air and her skirt flowing. He is able to depict the dancer's rustling petticoats by simply adding a few skillful stokes to the lithograph.

Below Jane is the diagonally placed hand of the musician playing his instrument. It is done in gray tones so as not to detract attention from the dancer. Toulouse-Lautrec demonstrates his remarkable originality by extending each end of the bass viola so that they curve around the scene and create a frame. This connects her visually with the musical accompaniment.

The artist contrasts the dancer's slender leg with the thick neck of the bass viola in the foreground. He shows more of his creativeness by adding an unusual perspective. The performer is seen from the vantage point of an orchestra member. It allows Lautrec to show how tired and bored she looks close-up. It is as if she is dancing entirely for the

9-15. *Jane Avril* by Toulouse-Lautrec, 1893, lithograph, San Diego Museum of Art, San Diego, California.

audience's pleasure and not her own. In addition, this perspective adds to the illusion of depth in the poster.

VAN GOGH
All About Color, Intensity and Originality In Art

Vincent Van Gogh (1853-1890) is the art world's favorite martyr. His life is almost as legendary as his art. He became the prototype of the misunderstood, tormented artist who sold just one painting in his lifetime. His is the legacy of the mad genius.

9-16. *The Potato Eaters* by Van Gogh, 1885, oil on canvas, Van Gogh Museum, Amsterdam.

Van Gogh did not start painting until 28. His career spanned just nine years until his suicide at 37. But in that short period he made unprecedented progress in color, intensity and originality of his art. That is what makes Van Gogh so important.

His paintings became ever more decorative and they moved further and further away from reality. He shows us a world transformed by his own personal use of color and form. He used bold colors and vibrant, swirling brush stokes to convey his feelings and state of mind. His art becomes more and more exciting and emotional and, in the process, more endearing and universally irresistible.

Van Gogh eventually embraced the vivid colors of Impressionism and went even further. But he did not follow their lead of carefully capturing the effects of color and light in nature. For Van Gogh, this was too scientific an approach. He used his basic instincts in capturing the emotional power of color choosing them almost arbitrarily. For him, it was all about what he felt, not what he saw. This pushed his art toward Expressionism or toward an exploration of the emotional side of art.

It wasn't always like this for Van Gogh. At the start, there was a "dark" style to his art. His early images of

Dutch peasant life were characterized by impasto (i.e. heavy brush strokes) and dark, earthy tones. They were the colors of mud and they echoed the lives of his subjects.

In 1878, the humanitarian side of Van Gogh took over. He went to work as a lay preacher among the impoverished coal miners in a grim district of Belgium. But, as in all things, he showed too much enthusiasm. Because his eccentricities alienated the miners, he was dismissed in 1879.

In 1886, he moved to Paris where he met Pissarro, Degas, Gauguin, Seurat and Toulouse-Lautrec. He fell under the influence of Impressionism and his painting underwent a striking change. It was Pissarro who persuaded Van Gogh to give up the gloomy tones of his Dutch period. He switched to brighter, more vivid colors. But he went even further than the Impressionists as a colorist in that he became obsessed with the symbolic and emotional values of colors. Van Gogh said, "I use color more arbitrarily so as to express myself more forcefully."

Van Gogh stayed in Paris until 1888. Although his painting style benefited enormously during his stay, the frenzied life style of the city was too much for him. He wanted to paint in a calmer environment where there was light, color and warmth. He left for Arles in southern France.

This was an extremely productive period for him despite personal tragedy. In 15 months he painted over 200 pictures. In the sunshine of Arles he created his own style, one of strong color, heavy impasto and dark outlines.

Then tragedy struck. Van Gogh had invited Gauguin to join him in Arles so they could paint together, learn from each other and, hopefully, establish an artistic community where other artists could join them. But Gauguin spent only nine weeks there before deciding he could not take Van Gogh's emotional instability anymore. When he announced his decision to leave, Van Gogh threatened him with a knife and later mutilated his own left ear.

At this point, Van Gogh realized he was a threat to himself and possibly others so he admitted himself to a mental hospital in Saint-Remy. In the year he spent there, Van Gogh worked feverishly and his art style changed. The paintings became more disturbing. His colors lost the intensity of the Arles period. The paint was applied with even thicker impasto. Perspective became more distorted.

The last phase of his career came after he left the asylum and settled in Auvers just outside of Paris on the advice of Pissarro and his brother Theo. He went there to submit to the care of Dr. Gachet who was a friend of Pissarro and Cezanne.

His frenzied painting activity continued. In the last 70 days of his life he finished over 70 pieces. On July 27, 1890 he shot himself in a field and died two days later. His brother Theo and Dr. Gachet were at his side when he died.

The Potato Eaters (fig. 9-16) is a perfect example of Van Gogh's dark works when his style was reminiscent of the Dutch master Rembrandt. The similarity was not accidental. Van Gogh was well aware of his Dutch heritage. But in this case he was trying to be a true "peasant painter" such as the French artist Millet whose idealizations of the rural poor he admired. Van Gogh wrote to his brother Theo, "I have tried to emphasize that these people eating their potatoes in the lamp-light have dug the earth with those very hands they put in the dish, and so it speaks of manual labor, and how they have honestly earned their food."

The Potato Eaters is his tribute to the working classes, the group he thought to be closest to Christ. He believed that these God fearing, hard working people that are the "salt of the earth" are more deserving of salvation. It is the only time he painted a piece featuring a large number of people. He felt more at ease with one-on-one portraits or peasant figures involved in individual endeavors.

The emphasis here is on the brutalization of hard labor. The interior of the room almost resembles a cave. Looking at the faces of the individuals, he renders them almost like a

9-17. *Sunflowers* by Van Gogh, 1888, oil on canvas, Neue Pinakothek, Munich.

caricature. Yet, he also captures a sense of fellowship and a warm community where people are willing to share.

In 1888, for a time, Van Gogh's mood improved. Ironically, the person who was responsible for this was Gauguin. During this period of rare optimism, Van Gogh painted a series of sunflower pieces. Gauguin had decided to move into Van Gogh's Yellow House in Arles. He intended to use *Sunflowers* (fig. 9-17) to decorate the bedroom where Gauguin was supposed to stay.

Some critics have gone so far as to say that Van Gogh's sunflowers are among the best still lifes in the history of art. The flowers are rendered with thick brushstrokes. The multiple shades of yellow seem to enhance one another.

The composition is bold and alive. Unfortunately, life does not always imitate art. The two artists quarreled violently. Afterward, when Gauguin left, Van Gogh's fits of depression returned and he soon headed for a one-year stay in an asylum.

Starry Night (fig. 9-18) is one of Van Gogh's most famous works and one of the most well known images in modern art. It is a painting that is instantly recognizable because of its unique style. Along with *Wheatfield With Crows* that is discussed below, it is a painting that has been subject to an enormous amount of interpretation.

Does the painting simply sing the praises of God's creation? Or, given the turbulence in it, is it Van Gogh's way of communicating that he is considering suicide? There are eleven stars in the sky. Perhaps this may refer to a statement by Joseph in Genesis 37:9, "I had another dream and this time the sun and moon and eleven stars were bowing down to me."

One thing is sure, the painting points toward the Abstract Expressionist movement of the 1940s and 1950s. There are Van Gogh's broad, gestural brushstrokes. The whole painting seems to be engulfed by an outburst of circular movements. Rather than using a brush, he probably applied some of the paint directly from the tube giving the thick whirly appearance. You can almost see his gestures on the canvas.

9-18. *Starry Night* by Van Gogh, 1889, oil on canvas, Museum of Modern Art, New York.

Expressionism is when the artist's emotions override any attention to reality. Unlike the Impressionists who paint what they see with their eyes, Expressionists paint what they see with their mind. He clearly took the advice from Gauguin who told him to paint from his imagination. *Starry Night* qualifies as an Expressionist painting. It looks like he did it in a fit of passion. He painted it from memories he had of the night sky after observing it from his window in the asylum at Saint-Remy.

There is the small, peaceful cluster of homes of the village of Saint-Remy with the typical church spire. But what is the subject matter? One explanation is that the subject was taken from a theory at that time that, after death, people journeyed to a star where they could continue their lives. This would have been an appealing thought to Van Gogh given all the turmoil in his life. Perhaps he contemplated immortality and even suicide in a letter when he wrote, "Just as we take a train to get to Rouen, we take death to reach a star." Less than a year later he was dead.

Some credence to that idea can be found in the very visible form of a large cypress tree in the painting. It is a traditional symbol of death and eternal life. It is a tree often found in graveyards. Here it dramatically rises as if it is linking the land with the heavens.

Of course, all of this is speculation. Van Gogh may have simply been paying tribute to nature and the way God can create such stunning skies. He was always fascinated with the night. In 1888 he created at least two other pictures with a starry night theme: *Starry Night Over the Rhone* and *Café Terrace on the Place du Forum*.

Portrait of Dr. Gachet (fig. 9-19) is one of the most revered paintings by Van Gogh. At one time, it held the record for the most expensive painting ever sold at auction. In 1990, it sold for $82.5 million to a Japanese collector who joked about his wish to have the famous painting cremated with him. The previous record auction price was for another Van Gogh painting *Irises*. Even given the huge surge in art prices in recent decades, in inflation adjusted terms, it is still the priciest painting ever sold at auction.

Dr. Gachet knew many of Van Gogh's contemporaries and treated some. In fact, it was Pissarro who recommended him to Vincent's brother Theo. Gachet was a rather eccentric homeopathic doctor. Regarding how Vincent responded to him, he wrote to his brother Theo in an almost humorous manner, "I think that we must not count on Dr. Gachet at all. First of all, he is sicker than I am, I think, or shall we say just as much, so that's that. Now when one blind man leads another blind man, don't they both fall into the ditch?"

Many people do not connect Van Gogh to portraiture. But despite classic paintings like *Sunflowers* and *Starry Night* his first love was portraits. He wrote, "What impassions me most is the portrait." Van Gogh sought to create an unconventional and modern portrait. He succeeded and therein lays its appeal.

Dr. Gachet is painted sitting at a red table and leaning his head on his right arm. He wears a white sailor's cap. Two yellow books are displayed on the table. His status as a homeopathic doctor is highlighted by a foxglove plant in front of him. It is a plant from which digitalis is extracted for the treatment of various ailments.

These details are important but the focus of the painting is on Gachet's

9-19. *Portrait of Dr. Gachet* by Van Gogh, 1890, oil on canvas, private collection.

9-20. *Wheatfield With Crows* by Van Gogh, 1890, oil on canvas, Van Gogh Museum, Amsterdam.

face. His blue eyes reflect a compassionate but melancholy man. Van Gogh emphasizes sensitivity and expression rather than attempting a perfect likeness. He wrote to Gauguin about wanting his portraits, "to portray the sorrowful expression of our age." And so he did with *Portrait of Dr. Gachet.*

Finally, in explaining the portrait Van Gogh wrote to his brother:

> *"I've done the portrait of M. Gachet with a melancholy expression, which might well seem like a grimace to those that see it... Sad but gentile, yet clear and intelligent, that is how many portraits ought to be done... There are modern heads that may be looked at for a long time, and that may perhaps be looked back on with longing a hundred years later."* And so it is.

Wheat Field With Crows (fig. 9-20) carries with it a great deal of speculation over whether it was Van Gogh's final work and, as such, his "suicide letter" on canvas. But the identity of his last painting is not known for sure. What is known is that this work was painted in the last weeks of his life.

One reason why some connect it to his suicide is because of its foreboding nature. It shows ominous overtones of distress for the troubled genius. It serves as a compelling and poignant expression of the artist's state of mind. He had reasons to be depressed. He probably realized that his mental illness might never be cured. He felt that he was becoming an increasing financial burden on his brother who now had a son to support.

Van Gogh described the painting as representing a vast field of wheat beneath troubled skies. Then there are the three paths going in different directions. The most prominent path is in the center of the painting with contrasting colors of red and green. Does this path go anywhere? Does it go through the wheat field and lead to new horizons? Or, does it terminate and represent a dead end?

There is no doubt that the dramatic, cloudy sky filled with crows over a wind-swept wheat field suggests the turbulence and loneliness in the life of the painter. But, on the positive side, there is nothing in Van Gogh's late writings to suggest suicide was imminent. In fact, in regard to his recently painted wheat field canvases he wrote to his brother, "I hope to bring them to you in Paris as soon as possible." He also wrote of "the health and restorative forces" of being in the country.

Van Gogh lived in a topsy-turvy mental world and because of that, it is understandable that some art historians would look for subliminal messages in his works. But there is no evidence from earlier works that is something Van Gogh hid in his paintings. To try to connect images in this piece with a message about his intentions is an exercise in futility.

Wheat Fields With Crows is an extraordinary painting whose vivid colors and turbulent brushstrokes result in a work of enormous vitality. Admire it for those qualities rather than focusing on trying to uncover abstract secrets that will detract from the appreciation of the artistic value of the work.

There is a question about Van Gogh's work that has no answer. Was he a great painter in spite of his illness? Or, perhaps, because of his tortured mind that is the way he saw the world. He lived his short life in fear of his fits and hallucinations. But without them we might not have had such creative images.

By the accident of history, four of the leading painters of the younger generation who were all Post-Impressionists (i.e. Van Gogh, Seurat, Gauguin and Toulouse-Lautrec) died before their elders Cezanne, Renoir, Degas and Monet who were leading the way for them. For some reason, the art world seems to encounter more than its share of misfortune. In committing suicide, Van Gogh joined the list of tortured artists of the 19th century that were beset with tragedy. In fact, three of the successors to Impressionism covered in this part of the chapter died in their 30s.

POST-IMPRESSIONISM BEYOND FRANCE

The two artists covered in this section painted around the same time period as the Post-Impressionists discussed above and their art shares some of the same characteristics. But they are rarely linked directly to the group. That is because they are not French and never had contact with the Impressionists. They painted in Norway and Austria, far from Paris and the French countryside where

9-21. *The Scream* by Munch, 1893, tempera and pastel on cardboard, private collection.

the Impressionists and Post-Impressionists flourished. Nevertheless, the two artists discussed immediately below shared the Expressionist and Symbolist characteristics of artists like Gauguin and Van Gogh. In addition, their art has been highly sought after by the most prominent collectors in recent years. The prices of their paintings have established new records in the art world.

Norwegian artist **Edvard Munch** (1863-1944) is regarded as a pioneer in the Expressionist art movement. His most famous painting *The Scream* (fig. 9-21) has sometimes been described as the first Expressionist painting. One way to describe Expressionism is when the emotion showed in the painting overrides any attention to reality. That certainly is the case with *The Scream*.

During the early part of his career, Munch experimented with Impressionism. But he felt it did not allow him sufficient expression. He needed something deeper that enabled him to explore subjects that had greater emotional and psychological content.

The Scream, which was originally titled *Despair*, has become part of the popular culture with the image appearing on T-shirts, coffee mugs, neck ties etc. It is one of the few paintings that immediately communicates a specific meaning to almost anyone that sees it. It is an unforgettable image that reflects the turmoil and angst that all humans feel one time or another. It uniquely combines the suggestiveness of Symbolism with the intense emotion of Expressionism.

In May 2012, *The Scream* was sold for $120 million, the highest price ever paid for a work of art at auction. Between 1893 and 1910, Munch painted four versions of "The Scream." The one sold at Sotheby's in 2012 was painted in 1895. It was the only one of the four that was owned privately. Two of the paintings had been previously stolen but both were recovered.

The painting of an amoeba-like figure with an agonized expression holding his head and screaming under an electric, blood-red streaked sky is one of the art world's most recognizable images. It has become a modern symbol of universal anxiety and dread. The colorful abstract sky reflects the influence of the Symbolist painter Gauguin.

The setting is along Oslo's U-shaped bay where, at the time, a passerby might hear screams from a nearby slaughterhouse and an insane asylum in the area. In fact, it has been suggested by some art historians that the character is not howling but he is blocking the sounds of the screams around him with his hands.

The work has a mix of 12 colors including one blue and one brown nostril. What adds to the unusualness of this piece is that the frame is inscribed with a hand-painted poem by Munch that describes his inspiration for the image:

> I was walking along a path with two friends
> – the sun was setting – suddenly the sky turned
> blood red – I paused, feeling exhausted, and
> leaned on the fence – there was blood and tongues
> of fire above the blue-black fjord and the city –
> my friends walked on, and I stood there trembling
> with anxiety – and I sensed an infinite scream
> passing through nature.

Like Munch, Austrian painter **Gustav Klimt** (1862-1918) can be associated with both Symbolism and Expressionism. He can also be tied to the Art Nouveau style. But above all he can be considered a thoroughly modern painter.

Art Nouveau is French for "new art." It represented part of the transition from late 19th century art to 20th century modernism. It is a richly decorative form of art with a distinctive appearance that includes curved lines, patterned surfaces and visual flatness. It was fashionable from roughly 1890 to the early part of the 20th century. The Art Nouveau style had an important impact on graphic arts including the type of poster design practiced by Toulouse-Lautrec.

Klimt is noted for his complex portrayals of female sexuality in his portraits of beautiful socialites. He traveled to Venice and Ravenna, Italy in 1899 and 1903 where he was inspired by the flickering gold in Byzantine mosaics. Those visits plus his memories of his late father's work as a goldsmith were responsible for the highly successful "Golden Phase" of his career that began at the start of the 20th century.

The paintings were characterized by almost psychedelic swirls of color and gold leaf. One of the first examples of his use of gold leaf was his partially nude contemporary rendering of the Old Testament biblical heroine Judith in 1901. It was a far cry from the Renaissance paintings of the same woman.

Klimt's most famous portrait was *Adele Block-Bauer I* which was sold privately to Ronald Lauder in 2006 for $135 million, then the most ever paid for a painting. The work along with others was recovered after a long, contentious suit against the Austrian government.

The high point of Klimt's "Golden Phase" came in 1907-08 with the painting The Kiss (fig. 9-22). He depicts a couple locked in a passionate embrace. It is a very sensuous image yet there is a tenderness that is missing from his portrayals of women in other paintings. She passively awaits the kiss with her eyes closed while there is an intensity of desire in the man's embrace.

The decorative aspects of the painting with the flat pattern of extravagant, shimmering gold leaf are clearly tied to Art Nouveau. The man wears a crown of vines while the woman's hair is sprinkled with flowers. The scene takes place at the edge of a flowery meadow. There is a large swirl of gold studded with colored designs. All of this adds to the intricate, ornamental quality of the work. The painting is a perfect square although it has often been shown as a rectangle when it is presented focusing only on the two embracing figures. It is another one of those iconic, immediately recognizable works of art.

Klimt painted *Adele Block-Bauer I* (fig. 9-23) the same year as *The Kiss*. He was at the height of his artistic creativity. It was the first of two portraits he did of the wife of a wealthy Austrian industrialist. She became the only society lady that he painted twice probably because she had a lengthy affair with Klimt. Adele Block-Bauer also posed for two highly erotic paintings of the Old Testament heroine Judith. In addition to using gold leaf in his paintings, Klimt was noted for the eroticism of his works.

In June 2006, *Adele Block-Bauer I* was sold for a reported $135 million to Ronald Lauder for his Neue Galerie in New York. It held the record for the world's most expensive painting for five months until Willem de Kooning's *Woman II* was sold for $137.5 million. Later, Jackson Pollock's *No. 5, 1948* and Cezanne's *The Card Players* set new records.

The painting had a storied past spanning more than 60 years before getting to the U.S. Adele Block-Bauer died in 1925. When the Nazis invaded Austria her widowed husband had to flee to Switzerland and the Nazis seized his art collection. In his 1945 will Ferdinand Block-Bauer designated his nephew and nieces including Maria Altmann as inheritors of his estate. Nevertheless, the painting remained in the national museum of Austria for the next 60 years. But after a protracted court battle Maria Altmann and the other heirs were established in 2006 as the rightful owners of

9-22. *The Kiss* by Klimt, 1907-1908, oil and gold leaf on canvas, Osterreichische Galerie Belvedere, Vienna, Austria.

9-23. *Adele Block-Bauer I* by Klimt, 1907, oil and gold leaf on canvas, Neue Galerie, New York.

the painting as well as four others by Klimt. Lauder purchased the portrait shortly later from the heirs.

The pale skin of Adele Block-Bauer's face, neck and arms are framed by a decorative gown and a background with a thin layer of gold and silver. Her large brown doe-like eyes, upswept dark hair and vivid red lips all add to the restrained sensuality of the model. The woman also has an air of sophistication. The awkward pose of her hands hides a deformed finger. The pose also provides her with a sense of nonchalance and naturalism.

Judith 1 (fig. 9-24) is a great example of how artists can treat the same subject in radically different ways. The biblical story of Judith and Holofernes was a popular subject with Renaissance artists. Donatello did it in bronze in 1456. He showed Judith holding the head of Holofernes. Botticelli did it in two parts in 1470. In part one the decapitated corpse is discovered by soldiers. It is a gory scene. In part two, Judith is shown returning to her people while her servant carries the head of Holofernes.

For comparison's sake, Giorgione's *Judith* painted around 1504 is shown in figure 9-25. Here, Judith is presented as a female David with the head beneath her foot. The scene is less graphic than some of the other renditions because a sweeping view of the landscape is included. This addition is typical of Venetian art. Also, Judith's bare leg is revealed presenting her in a somewhat seductive manner. Nevertheless, the focus of all three of these renditions is on the grizzly deed of decapitating the villain, Holofernes.

By way of background, here is how the biblical story goes. In roughly 590 BC, the beautiful Jewish widow saved the city of Bethulia from siege by the Assyrians by venturing into the enemy camp to rendezvous with the Assyrian general, Holofernes. He invites her into his tent for a feast intending to seduce her. While they are alone Judith takes advantage of his drunken stupor by decapitating him with his own sword. She returns to Bethulia with his head in a sack thus rallying the citizens to rout the enemy.

The account appears in the Apocryphal Books that are not part of the traditional Bible in that they fall between the Old and

9-24. *Judith I* by Klimt, 1901, oil and gold leaf on canvas, Osterreichische Galerie, Belvedere, Vienna.

9-25. *Judith* by Giorgione c. 1504, oil on canvas transferred from panel, Hermitage Museum, Saint Petersburg, Russia.

New Testaments. Judith is the second book. In chapter 13 versus 6 to 10 the gory incident is described:

> *"She went up to the bedpost near Holofernes head and took down his sword that hung there. She came close to his head and said, 'Give me strength today, O Lord God of Israel!' Then she struck his neck twice with all her might, and cut off his head.*

> *Next she rolled his body off the bed and pulled down the canopy from the posts. Soon afterward she went out and gave Holofernes head to her maid, who placed it in her food bag."*

The story is an example of virtue overcoming vice in a violent way. But Klimt hardly paints Judith as a virtuous women. His portrayal is far removed from anything done by the Renaissance masters such as Giorgione's *Judith*. But then we should expect that from Klimt. Rather than the biblical image of Judith as a virtuous heroine, Klimt portrays her as a Viennese femme fatale. This is in line with other erotic female images that he often depicted. After all he is quoted as saying, "All art is erotic."

His life style mirrored his art. He was known for having slept with many of the women whose portraits he was commissioned to paint including Adele Block-Bauer. It has also been said that he fathered as many as 14 children with a number of different women.

Klimt fused several styles in his art including Byzantine mosaics, Egyptian designs and avant-garde ornamentation. Judith reflects his eclectic approach. Scandalous pictures were often the embodiment of Art Nouveau that was a revolt against the traditional style.

Klimt renders Judith in an explicitly sexual way. So much so that some critics thought he had mistaken her for Salome, a widely accepted femme fatale. Her hair is shown up in a full bouffant. She wears an ornamental vest where there is one breast exposed. But with all of this she is not the image of the type of female beauty that appealed to Renaissance painters. With all the sensuality this is still the image of an empowered woman. She is not someone to be taken lightly.

It is as if she glows in her accomplishment and seems to be in a state of ecstasy. Her eyes are nearly closed and her mouth is open. Klimt paints her in a moment of rapture. She is clearly taking pleasure in what has occurred. Her almost orgasmic expression tells us that. She even appears to be stoking the hair of Holofernes with her right hand. The artist is obviously fascinated by the subject of death and sexuality. He was not alone. His Austrian contemporary Sigmund Freud shared the same interest. Eight years later he would paint another Judith in the same sexual mode.

The theme of decapitation is carried further by Judith's gold choker. It is rendered in the same gilded style as the background of the painting. It is as if it separates her own head from her body. Whatever you think of this image it is truly avant-garde art and that is what Klimt intended. This piece goes beyond being merely decorative.

That Klimt would paint such unusual works as *The Kiss, Adele Block-Bauer I* and *Judith 1* might be expected because he was the first president of the Vienna Secession. This was a movement founded in 1897 that objected to the prevailing artistic conservatism in the country. They wanted to create a new style of art that owned nothing to historical influence. It is safe to say that was exactly what Klimt accomplished with his paintings.

ADDENDUM TO CHAPTER NINE
About the Barnes Foundation

The Barnes Foundation houses one of the largest Impressionist and Post-Impressionist art collections in the country. It is also an art educational facility. As of mid 2012 it had moved from Merion, Pennsylvania to its new location in downtown Philadelphia.

Albert Barnes (1872-1951) did not come from money. He came from a middle-class background. He was raised in Kensington, Philadelphia, a blue-collar neighborhood. His father was a butcher. But he went to Central High, one of the preeminent public secondary schools in the U.S. and then to the University of Pennsylvania Medical School where he received a medical degree. But Barnes decided he was not interested in practicing medicine. He took a job in advertising and sales with a pharmaceutical company and also studied pharmacology.

Along with a German chemist Hermann Hille, they developed a silver based compound called Argyrol. In 1902, they established the firm Barnes and Hille. Argyrol was used to counteract upper respiratory infections and was an effective treatment of eye inflammations in newborn babies. The partnership was dissolved in 1907 and Barnes established his own company the following year. It became the source of his wealth.

Despite running a successful business, Barnes' real interest was in collecting art and educating others in art. He collected works by American painters like William Glackens (who had been a student with Barnes at Central High) and Maurice Prendergast. He would display paintings in his company for study and observation by his employees and he would conduct art appreciation seminars for them on company time. Barnes' philosophy was that if you could learn to appreciate art it would enrich your life. It was that philosophy that eventually led to the establishment of the Barnes Foundation.

Fortuitously, Barnes sold his company in 1929 so he could devote full time to the Foundation. The sale occurred just months before the stock market collapse and the onset of the Great Depression. That timely transaction allowed Barnes to continue to buy art in the 1930s and beyond when many prominent collectors were selling off their art to restore some of the money they lost during the great stock market panic.

Barnes' emerging art collection took a major turn in 1912 when his artist friend William Glackens agreed to travel to Paris to purchase some of the new avant-garde art coming on to the market. Glackens returned with 33 oil paintings, watercolors and prints spending about $20,000. Barnes returned 13 and kept 20 pieces including works by Renoir, Cezanne, Van Gogh and Picasso. That may seem like an incredible value and it was by any standard. Nevertheless, it was a substantial amount of money at the time. In today's dollars it would be more than $400,000.

After that, Barnes made all the buying trips to France himself. He established contacts with a number of dealers. For example, he purchased his first two Matisse paintings from Leo Stein, brother of the famed American born writer and art collector Gertrude Stein. Since Barnes was captivated by color he was particularly attracted to Renoir. He wrote to Leo Stein, "I am convinced that I cannot get too many Renoirs…" It was a prophetic statement. There are 181 Renoirs at the Barnes, more than anyplace else in the world.

The Barnes Foundation was formed in 1922 as an educational institution. In his teachings, Barnes concentrated on the way artists used color, light, line and space and on their relationship to each other. He termed them the "plastic means" because they are malleable or capable of being manipulated.

In 1925, Barnes built a 23 room gallery with his home attached in Merion, Pennsylvania. At first glance, the wall arrangements in the gallery are challenging. They have been described by some as "quirky." There is a lot of mystery in the hangings. But it peaks your interest and challenges you to figure out the presentations. Old master paintings are hung beside modern ones. Major works may be shown next to minor ones. The result is that there seems to be no historical continuity or thematic ordering in the presentation of the art. Sometimes, it all comes off as somewhat maddening. But each wall arrangement is a work of art itself.

In the main gallery *The Artist's Family* by Renoir is flanked by two paintings by 16th century Venetian artists. In arrangements like this, Barnes is drawing on the effects of past traditions on an artist. The Venetians were noted for their rich color and Renoir was greatly influenced by their use of color in his own paintings. Therein lays one reason for the arrangement of the three paintings in the ensemble that may look arbitrary. It also demonstrates a fundamental philosophy of Barnes that modernism, as represented by art movements like Impressionism, does not constitute a complete break from the past. Rather, it is a continuation of earlier traditions and builds on them.

There are even paintings in the collection that Barnes was not enthusiastic about, at least at first. For example, in Gallery V hangs Renoir's *Woman with Fan*. It has cooler colors and a greater attention to line than most Renoirs. The typical feathery brushstrokes are missing. It was painted during a period when Renoir was reevaluating his artistic style. It was a span of time that came to be known as his "dry period."

After visiting Rome he was impressed with the great drawing techniques of the Renaissance masters such as Raphael. He temporarily adopted a style where he put a greater emphasis on line and less on color. Barnes was not impressed. He called this change in style "his fall from grace." Nevertheless, he added paintings to his collection that he did not necessarily approve of so viewers could evaluate how the artist's style changed over time. No other collector would buy a painting he did not like. But Barnes' goals were different. Remember this is a teaching institution. In another case he described the large Renoir painting *Bather and Maid* as, "Banal and academic, lacking in a spark of life." Yet, it hangs in a prominent place in the collection.

While in Gallery V if you look to the far left of *Woman with Fan* on the same wall you will see another Renoir *Apple Vendor*. It doesn't even look like it was painted by the same artist. The colors are lush not cool. It has all the characteristics that come with Impressionism. But that is exactly the point that Barnes is trying to bring out in the arrangement. The two paintings demonstrate different phases of Renoir's career.

That same grouping is anchored at the center by a painting by the 17th century Dutch master Frans Hals' *Portrait of a Man Holding a Watch*. Typical of Dutch paintings of the era it is dark with the predominant color being black. The color is in sharp contrast with the lively hues of the Renoirs that surround it. But although the Hals portrait was painted more than 200 years earlier it has at least one striking characteristic that links it to the Renoirs on the same wall, particularly *Apple Vendor*. That is the vivid, expressive brushstrokes of the man's beard. They echo the brushstrokes of Renoir and his expressive color. So the similarities and contrasts of the arrangements of paintings go on and on. All the time Barnes is showing how newer and older art traditions, rather than being separate, are linked together.

Although the groupings may look confusing, when Matisse visited the Barnes in 1930 he said, "The Barnes galleries are the only sane place to view art." He was certainly onto something because there is a structure to the arrangements unlike any other place in the world.

The arrangements, where paintings are hung one above the other but symmetrically, are not because of space limitations and they are not arbitrary. As already noted directly above in the discussion of gallery V, they are designed to draw attention to similar and contrasting styles of artists and to the traditions of art – Greek, Byzantine, Gothic, Florentine, Venetian, etc. They allow you to see how artists were influenced by the traditions. Viewers have the opportunity to look for repetition in colors and shapes. These arrangements are one of the great advantages of studying art history at the Barnes. Power Point presentations can be great but they are no substitute for being in the galleries and looking at the real thing right in front of you.

The presentations of art in the Barnes' galleries are unlike any in a museum. In a museum, you are encouraged to look at a single painting. But the Barnes is an educational institution so you are encouraged to look at an entire wall of paintings to study the arrangements that are for the purpose of contrast and similarity.

Although there are now booklets in each gallery providing information on the title of each work along with the date painted and the name of the artist that was not always the case. There are still no text panels or explanatory wall labels. Barnes avoided providing titles because he believed that would draw attention to the subject of the painting. He wanted students to concentrate on the plastic elements and the arrangement of the art.

Around 1935, Barnes began to acquire early American furniture to place in front of the wall groupings. This was augmented by a huge array of unique antique wrought-iron objects like spoons, keys and door hinges whose placement was designed to accent or set off the art. In some cases, the metalwork becomes a matter of the viewer's interpretation of how it relates to the paintings. But often it is there to call attention to the lines of the painting nearby.

When hanging the paintings in the galleries, Barnes ignored the usual approach. He did it his way. He was not interested in the opinions of others. Although the arrangements of the paintings are most striking in the two story main room that is crowned by Matisse's huge mural *The Dance*, even in the smaller rooms the viewer is immediately aware that something is very different. In museums, the collections are typically arranged by artist, chronologically, artistic movement (e.g. Impressionism, Cubism, Surrealism, etc.) or subject matter. That does not occur at the Barnes.

Once again, Gallery V serves as a good example of the mixture of art works. There is a copy of a Bosch painting whose career spanned the 15th and 16th centuries. There is a 1643 portrait by the Dutch master Frans Hals who painted in the tradition of Rembrandt. There is also a work by Peter Paul Rubens, the 17th century Flemish Baroque master. Yet, mixed in with these pieces are works by more modern painters like Renoir, Seurat and Soutine.

All of this may look arbitrary but it isn't. The placement of each piece was well thought out by Barnes. Perhaps he is showing the links between old and newer traditions. Or, as is the case in Gallery V, the viewer can follow the evolution of portraiture from Hals to Renoir to Soutine. Often, Barnes' "plastic means" of light, line, color and space are the determining factors in where paintings are placed.

The arrangement of art, furniture and ironwork is called a wall ensemble. There are over 90 wall ensembles at the Barnes. He wanted each person to look at an entire wall of paintings and view each ensemble as a blackboard for teaching the traditions of art, comparing the styles of artists and focusing on the "plastic means." Above all, the ensembles are designed to show the continuity of art history. That is, how each tradition of art is indebted to an earlier one.

Although there are more than 800 paintings, the Barnes collection is not huge by the standards of a number of museums in major metropolitan areas. But that is because it is one man's private collection. Nevertheless, some of the numbers regarding holdings of specific artists are daunting. For example, there are more paintings by Renoir and Cezanne in this collection than any in the world. There are 181 Renoirs, 69 Cezannes, 59 Matisses, 44 Picassos, 18 Rousseaus, 16 Soutines, 15 Modiglianis, 11 Degas and 7 Van Goghs.

The main gallery is overwhelming. When you first enter it you may feel like you are confronted with visual overload. But then you realize you are surrounded by huge paintings by the superstars of early modernism so you had better take advantage of it. There are works by Renoir, Cezanne, Matisse, Picasso and Seurat. As you move through the galleries you will find one room filled with so many Renoirs that it looks like a retrospective on him. Seven of the paintings at the Barnes are discussed in some detail in this book.

There are countless examples of peculiar arrangements. For example, in Gallery VI there is a pewter teapot that sits atop a German chest that dates to 1769. The arrangement fronts a painting by Paul Gauguin. It turns out that the spout of the teapot mirrors the shape of a stick that appears in the painting. In another part of the room there is a large door latch above paintings by Renoir and Cezanne. In the Renoir painting a young girl ties the bow on her bonnet. Her hand is partially open. In the Cezanne piece, an older woman tightly grips a book in both hands. How does the door latch relate to all this? Since a door latch opens and closes, it becomes a metaphor for the open and closed hands of the women in the paintings below. The intriguing relationships go on and on at the Barnes. They are something to behold.

Gallery III is one of the twelve smaller rooms. There you will find *Sleeping Shepherd*. It is a long, narrow horizontal panel attributed to the Renaissance master Titian and painted at the start of the 16th century. It presents a beautifully colored panoramic landscape view with goats on the left and a sleeping shepherd near the center of the composition.

Above it is *Crucifixion* painted on panel in tempera and gold by an Austrian artist in the early part of the 15th century. It forms its own small ensemble. At the foot of the cross there is the skull of Adam which commonly appears in such scenes painted in that era. Barnes creates the ensemble by adding a tiny still life of apples by Renoir above the painting. The apples allude to the sin of Adam and the fall of man. Finally, above those two pieces there is metalwork with a birdlike shape to evoke an image of the Holy Spirit.

There is a sense of quirkiness and humor in the presentation of some of the metalwork. For example, in gallery VI there are two rather ample female nudes by Renoir at each end of the same wall. Above each nude there are two identical pieces of metalwork that mirror the shape of their derrieres. In gallery IX there is a 19th century cookie cutter on the wall whose image is repeated at the bottom of a late 18th century wooden Pennsylvania German chest across the room.

All of this vast accumulation of art was accomplished with a different purpose in mind than almost any other collector. Most collectors have an investment oriented approach to accumulating art or, their purchases may be related to prestige. Barnes did not chase the latest fad or hot artist. He was not interested in prestige. For him, it was about educating others. He was not building a monument to himself.

For many years, while located in Merion Pennsylvania, the Barnes Foundation seemed like an inaccessible fortress guarding its treasures. It was open to the public only a few days per week and the number of entrants was strictly limited. The paintings were not permitted to travel to other exhibits (that is still the case). No color reproductions of the art were allowed in magazines, etc.

That fort like situation has changed dramatically. The new Barnes opened in a state-of-the-art facility in the center of Philadelphia in mid-2012. The architecture is truly amazing. It is open six days a week. But one thing has not changed. Some of the mystery about the Barnes remains and that is a good thing. The arrangements of the paintings and ironwork in the 23 galleries are exactly the same as in the original Barnes. That means visitors will get the same awesome, overwhelming feeling as was the case in the past. The educational aspect of the Barnes remains in place.

This is a totally different art experience. The visual effects in the main gallery are truly mind-boggling. As you go through the galleries you might ask how many masterpieces can be crammed on a single wall. It takes time to acclimate oneself to the arrangements but it is time well spent that will be richly rewarding.

There was nothing quite like the Barnes when it was located in Merion. That is still the case now that it is in Philadelphia. The new Barnes does not replicate the old one; it pays homage to it. There is a soulfulness unmatched by most other art facilities. It is one of the purest art experiences available. You can ponder the art, immerse yourself in it and maybe even meditate over it. Some have. There is so much going on with the art and its presentation that it is impossible to do it justice here. It is a light filled jewel box of art that you have to experience in person.

IMAGES

9-1. *Mont Sainte-Victoire* by Cezanne, 1885-1887, oil on canvas, Courtauld Institute of Art, London.

9-2. *The Bather* by Cezanne, 1885, oil on canvas, Museum of Modern Art, New York.

9-3. *The Card Players* by Cezanne, 1890-1892, oil on canvas, Barnes Foundation, Philadelphia.

9-4. *The Basket of Apples* by Cezanne, 1895, oil on canvas, Art Institute of Chicago, Chicago.

9-5. *The Large Bathers* by Cezanne, 1906, oil on canvas, Philadelphia Museum of Art, Philadelphia.

9-6. *A Sunday Afternoon on the Island of La Grande Jatte* by Seurat, 1884-1886, oil on canvas, Art Institute of Chicago, Chicago.

9-7. *The Models* by Seurat, 1886-1888, oil on canvas, Barnes Foundation, Philadelphia.

9-8. *Detail of The Models* by Seurat.

9-9. *Vision After The Sermon* by Gauguin, 1888, oil on canvas, National Gallery of Scotland, Edinburgh.

9-10. *Gauguin's Armchair* by Van Gogh, 1888, oil on canvas, Van Gogh Museum, Amsterdam.

9-11. *Vincent's Chair* by Van Gogh, 1888, oil on canvas, National Gallery, London.

9-12. *The Day of the God* by Gauguin, 1894, oil on canvas, Art Institute of Chicago, Chicago.

9-13. *Where Do We Come From? Where Are We? Where Are We Going?* by Gauguin, 1897, oil on canvas, Museum of Fine Arts, Boston.

9-14. *At The Moulin Rouge* by Toulouse-Lautrec, 1892-1895, oil on canvas, Art Institute of Chicago, Chicago.

9-15. *Jane Avril* by Toulouse-Lautrec, 1893, lithograph, San Diego Museum of Art, San Diego, California.

9-16. *The Potato Eaters* by Van Gogh, 1885, oil on canvas, Van Gogh Museum, Amsterdam.

9-17. *Sunflowers* by Van Gogh, 1888, oil on canvas, Neue Pinakothek, Munich.

9-18. *Starry Night* by Van Gogh, 1889, oil on canvas, Museum of Modern Art, New York.

9-19. *Portrait of Dr. Gachet* by Van Gogh, 1890, oil on canvas, private collection.

9-20. *Wheatfield With Crows* by Van Gogh, 1890, oil on canvas, Van Gogh Museum, Amsterdam.

9-21. *The Scream* by Munch, 1893, tempera and pastel on cardboard, private collection.

9-22. *The Kiss* by Klimt, 1907-1908, oil and gold leaf on canvas, Osterreichische Galerie Belvedere, Vienna, Austria.

9-23. *Adele Block-Bauer I* by Klimt, 1907, oil and gold leaf on canvas, Neue Galerie, New York.

9-24. *Judith 1* by Klimt, 1901, oil and gold leaf on canvas, Osterreichische Galerie, Belvedere, Vienna.

9-25. *Judith* by Giorgione c. 1504, oil on canvas transferred from panel, Hermitage Museum, Saint Petersburg, Russia.

MODIGLIANI:

The Accursed Painter

10

This is one of three chapters in the book dedicated to specific artists (Picasso will be singled out in the next chapter and Mary Cassatt and Berthe Morisot were discussed in chapter 8). Certainly, there are many other artists to which a chapter could have been devoted. Why choose Modigliani? One reason is because he is hard to group with other artists or a particular school of art. He left no followers and was not at the forefront of forming a new art movement. He does not qualify as a Post-Impressionist nor does he fit in with the avant-garde groups of artists and their movements that come along in the 20th century that will be discussed in the final chapter.

Most of all, I am devoting a chapter to Amedeo Modigliani (1884-1920) because his art fascinates me. He had a unique style. In a sense, he stands alone. But I am also signaling him out because he was at the center of one of the greatest tragedies in art history. I hope his art and life will fascinate you too.

Why is Modigliani so popular today? One reason is because of the uniqueness of his art. But his popularity is also because everyone loves a good story particularly when it includes despair and tragedy. Modigliani, in life and death, had more than enough of that to satisfy anyone's curiosity. Here is his story and his art.

Modigliani was one of just three artists of his generation to achieve distinction in three different media: painting, sculpture and drawing. The other two were Matisse and Picasso. That puts him in extraordinary company.

As you can see from the photo (fig. 10-1) Modigliani was extremely handsome and could easily attract women although he was rather short at 5'5" or 5'6" tall. He was one of modern art's fabled beauties if "beauty" is a term that can be applied to a man. His frequent affairs with women, his drinking and his self-destructive life-style became part of his legend. In Paris he was known as Modi from which, by linguistic corruption, the French referred to him as "paintra maude" or accursed painter.

There were two Modigliani's. As you will read later, his lover Beatrice Hastings, described him as a "swine and a pearl." Sober he was graciously timid and charming. He was a man who could quote Dante and recite poems. Drunk he was a bitter, angry person.

He has been characterized as a dashing, irresistibly handsome, penniless, drug abusing, womanizing vagabond. All of that is probably accurate. In short, he has become the very embodiment of the Bohemian artist.

10-1. Photo of Modigliani.

Modigliani was a compulsive womanizer. He once said, "To paint a woman is to possess her." One characterization was that, when he painted nudes, women undressed so Modigliani could paint them and he undressed to paint them. His posthumous legend, although for different reasons, is almost as great as Vincent Van Gogh.

He was born in Livorno, Italy into a strict Jewish family in 1884. He was beset with health problems early. These included an attack of pleurisy at 11 and typhoid fever at 14. As he lay in bed, feverishly raving about the Italian Renaissance and his longing to paint, his mother promised to send him to art school.

He began his formal training locally at 14 in 1898. He contracted tuberculosis at 16. Nevertheless, he studied in Florence and Venice in 1902 and 1903. It was in Venice at the age of 18 that he began to experiment with hashish but, at least then, perhaps only as a rebellious teenager. Modigliani moved to Paris in 1906 and, within a year, was an alcoholic and drug addict.

It is possible that his self-destructive tendencies may have stemmed from his TB and the knowledge that the disease marked him for an early death. He told his friend, Jacques Lipchitz, he sought "a brief but intense life." So it was to be!

Modigliani's behavior stood out even in his Bohemian surroundings. He became the epitome of the tragic artist. One of the ironies of his life was that such a tortured artist could produce such a serene body of work.

During his life, the going rate for his paintings was less than $10 and there were few takers. A landlord who confiscated his work in lieu of rent used the canvases to patch old mattresses. He died penniless and destitute in 1920 at 35, managing only one solo exhibit in his life and often giving his works away in exchange for meals and drinks.

Modigliani started his formal artistic career when he met renowned master sculptor, Constantin Brancusi in 1909. Brancusi had a big impact on him and influenced his style and his choice to sculpt in stone. Figure 10-2 shows Modigliani's Tete, a limestone bust sold at auction in June 2010 at a record for the artist of $52.8 million. His sculptures are coveted because they are so rare. There are only 27 confirmed pieces. Ten are in private collections and 17 are in museums. One of them is at the Barnes Foundation in Philadelphia.

The piece is particularly interesting because it incorporates two important influences on his art – the fine features and a bulb of hair in the back that is typical of Egyptian art along with the haunting mystery of an African mask. Often, these influences were carried over into his paintings such as the effect of African masks, long necks, elongated noses and small mouths.

Why are there so few sculptures? One reason is because his career in sculpture lasted only a short time, about two years. Because of his bouts with pleurisy and his TB, he did not have the strength to continue. The dust from the stone and wood he used badly affected his lungs.

10-2. *Tete* by Modigliani. A limestone sculpture sold at auction in 2010.

There was another reason. Modigliani destroyed many pieces or left them behind. His curved heads and bodies were too strange to attract buyers. So he sometimes used them as giant candleholders in his disheveled studio where he slept. He abandoned one piece in a vacant lot. It was found shortly after his death and is now in the collection of the MOMA in New York.

There is a legendary story that when he showed some of his sculptures to his friends who ridiculed them and jokingly dared him to toss them into a canal. Modigliani loaded them into a wheelbarrow and dumped them into a canal in Livorno, his home town.

Seventy-five years later the curator of the museum in Livorno persuaded the city council to spend $200,000 to dredge the canal in search of the works. It looked like the dredging paid off when three elongated heads with slit eyes were pulled from the water. Art historians and curators gathered and were quick to authenticate the pieces. The head of the search mission cried when seeing the pieces saying, "They are so beautiful."

Unfortunately, in the world of art, things are not always as they seem. The celebration was short lived. It was soon discovered the pieces were forgeries. Four men admitted that, motivated by the media frenzy over the proposed dredging, they carved the heads with a screwdriver and a Black & Decker electric drill and sunk them in the canal.

Several weeks later, the forgers accurately reconstructed the sculptures in three hours on live TV. The one beneficiary of the fiasco was Black & Decker who launched an advertising campaign with drawings of the heads and the slogan: "It's easy to be talented with a Black & Decker." It is an interesting story that provides an example of art history's limitations and failings.

Although Modigliani devoted himself almost exclusively to sculpture from 1910 to 1912, as already been mentioned, because of health issues this phase of his career was short lived. He turned to painting but he often carried the characteristics of his sculptures over into his portraits.

10-3. *Woman in a Yellow Jacket* by Modigliani, 1909, oil on canvas, private collection.

One has to ask how an artist can become so famous yet paint only one subject matter, portraits. He did no still lifes and only four landscapes. It is because he reinvented portraiture. It became avant-garde art in his hands. He succeeded in far distancing himself from the stiff, academic style of the 19th century.

Not everyone appreciates Modigliani's portraits. One of the criticisms is that of sameness or repetition in his portraits. He carries the same characteristics from his sculp- tures into portraiture – long swan necks, oval shaped faces, tiny puckered mouths, mysterious puzzling eyes, elongated ski-sloped noses and often blank or melancholy expressions. In short, the lines look the same and there is often a uniform mood. But it would be a mistake to assume his style is one of sameness. Even when he does repeat those characteristics, he gets different personalities in his portraits.

The fact is, Modigliani's portraits are specific to the sitter's personality and mood. Sometimes he achieved that

10-4. *Portrait of Juan Gris* by Modigliani, 1915, oil on canvas, Metropolitan Museum of Art, New York.

Modigliani was improvised throughout his brief life so this commission would have been a windfall for him. But even when he had a chance to make money things did not seem to work out for him. In this case, the sitter posed for many hours. Finally, she became rebellious and gave Modigliani an ultimatum to finish the piece. He complied by painting over the red riding jacket she was wearing in yellow. Marguirite was so infuriated that she refused to take it.

Perhaps that is not the only reason she rejected the portrait. It does not show a sympathetic woman. She is shown as being too independent for comfort. She stands with hand on hip with bold conviction. There is more than a sense of self-confidence here, she borders on arrogant. Given that the Baroness harshly rejected the painting and refused to pay for it may confirm that Modigliani was correct in depicting her as an arrogant woman.

Juan Gris was an important Spanish Cubist painter. In *Portrait of Juan Gris* (fig. 10-4) it is easy to see how Modigliani sometimes saw the body as a precarious assemblage of parts. In this piece, the subject seems in fragile balance on the brink of disaster.

There is a separation of the face from the body. You get the impression that he is a puppet or a doll. Gris resembles a ventriloquist's dummy. His head is tilted at an impossible angle. His nose sits awkwardly on the face and the lips seem pasted on. The wavy hair looks like it is detachable. Yet, there is individuality here. This is Gris. It has his dark complexion, full lips, thick eyebrows, dark eyes and black hair. There is no mistaking the portrait for someone else.

Portrait of Jean Cocteau (fig. 10-5) has a very different look from Juan Gris. This portrait shows his social class to the point of caricature. There is his haughty demeanor and dandified attire. Look at the neat bow tie that is perched on the pristine white shirt. There is a decorative white handkerchief in his breast pocket. The suit with padded shoulders has a buttoned-up stiffness to it. The man is erect, self-controlled and tailored to perfection. He looks

by adding such simple details like a turn of the head, hunch of the shoulder, clasp of the hands, tilt of the eyebrow or the color of the eyes.

Woman in a Yellow Jacket (fig. 10-3) distinguishes itself from most of Modigliani's other portraits because it was his first commissioned work. It came from Baroness Marguirite de Hasse de Villers. As was usually the case, Modigliani was able to capture the sitter's personality and mood. Today, the piece is also known as *The Amazon*.

10-5. *Portrait of Jean Cocteau* by Modigliani, 1916, oil on canvas, Art Museum of Princeton University, Princeton, New Jersey.

so vain that you cannot help asking yourself could he really be that vain.

In these portraits, you get to see what Modigliani was about. It certainly was not sameness despite the long necks, sharp oval shaped faces, puckered mouths and long noses. Yet, with all the distortions, there is no mistaking who the individual is.

Where did these distorted, elongated heads and bodies come from? In other words, what were the important influences on Modigliani's art? Given his Italian ancestry and training, he was deeply rooted in Renaissance art and the periods near the Renaissance. Look back at the Mannerist painting, *Madonna with the Long Neck* (see fig. 4-2). Notice the elongated, distorted figure of Mary and her sorrowful gaze.

Many of Modigliani's portraits bare a resemblance to the lines of the old masters – his use of sorrowful gazes, titled heads, elongated figures and a sense of melancholy.

In effect, Modigliani was a Mannerist 350 years removed. This is a style of art that developed roughly from 1520 to 1580. It rejected the gracefulness and balance of the Renaissance in favor of a more distorted point of view. Figures were elongated and exaggerated. There were unusual poses. All of that sounds a lot like Modigliani.

The Mannerist art reflected the upheaval and dislocations of the time. Perhaps Modigliani gravitated toward it because of the upheavals and dislocations in his own life. But it would probably be a stretch to assume something like that.

It is possible to go even further back than the 16th century to trace the origins of Modigliani's distortions. For example, prior to the Renaissance, Simone Martini (1284-1344) who was a student of Giotto painted *The Annunciation* (fig. 10-6) in 1333. In this piece Mary's distortions look very similar to those of the Mannerists 200 years later. Modigliani would have been exposed to the art from both periods.

10-6. *The Annunciation* by Martini, 1333, tempera on panel, Galleria degli Uffizi, Florence.

10-7. *Madam Pompadour* by Modigliani, 1915, oil on canvas, Art Institute of Chicago, Chicago.

10-8. Photo of Beatrice Hastings.

Beatrice Hastings was an eccentric English writer born in South Africa. She was ahead of her time as an outspoken socialist and supporter of woman's rights, particularly abortion. She met Modigliani in 1914 and became one of his most important love interests and models. They had a two-year affair. Beatrice loved the bohemian lifestyle and, therefore, would have contributed to Modigliani's addiction to drugs and alcohol.

She was known to be a promiscuous and haughty woman. It is said she kept count of her lovers by carving notches in the headboard of her bed. She once attended an artist's ball clad only in a painting Modigliani had done on her naked body. Here are some notes that Beatrice wrote about her first two meetings with Modigliani. They are revealing because they show the variations in his personality, moods and behavior.

"A complex character. A swine and a pearl. Met him in 1914. I sat opposite him. Hashish and brandy. Not at all impressed. Didn't know who he was. He looked ugly, ferocious and greedy. Met him again at Café Rotonde. He was shaven and charming. Raised his cap with a pretty gesture, blushed and asked me to come see his work. And I

went. He always had a book in his pocket. He had no respect for anyone except Picasso and Max Jacob. Detested Cocteau. Never completed anything good under the influence of hashish."

The comment on how Modigliani felt about Cocteau is revealing. Maybe that is why he painted him as such a pompous individual. Also interesting is her observation that the use of drugs did nothing to foster his creative talents and probably inhibited them.

Due to Beatrice's haughtiness, Modigliani nicknamed her "Madam" and painted her as the legendary aristocrat in a piece named *Madam Pompadour* (fig. 10-7). She was the mistress of King Louis XV. Perhaps there is a subtle reference here to their relationship and her role as Modigliani's mistress.

She seems visibly weighted down by the large feathered hat, probably a sign of her showy femininity. Given the photograph of Beatrice in figure 10-8 it is no wonder Modigliani depicted her in this manner. The showy hat is the feature of the photo. Note the writing on the left of the portrait where Modigliani converts the official name from Madame de Pompadour to Madam Pompadour (dropping the e from Madame and omitting the de). There can only be speculation over why he did this. But remember she is British. In effect, he is anglicizing her name. Perhaps it ends there. Or, perhaps he is pointing out that his model is not French but she is parading as a sophisticated Parisian.

In *Nude Beatrice* (fig. 10-9) we see an entirely different depiction of Beatrice Hastings. It is another painting that refutes the charge of "sameness" in Modigliani's works. It is not even remotely close to *Madam Pompadour*. Modigliani shows her as a partial nude.

She looks almost shy as she partially covers herself with a sheet in a moment of contrived modesty. Given her reputation, this is not the Beatrice we would expect. Hastings likened the image of herself here to "the Virgin Mary without worldly accessories."

Little Girl in Blue (fig. 10-10) shows a different mood and influence on Modigliani's art. The sorrowful gazes in his works led one writer to say, "They all look like hurt children." The writer, who had known Modigliani in Paris, went on to say, "I believe the world seemed to Modigliani like an enormous kindergarten run by unkind adults." Perhaps so!

The "unkind adult" theme seems to be picked up in this painting. It shows a vulnerable looking child wringing her hands as if she has just been scolded. Perhaps that actually occurred. According to the stories that circulate about Modigliani's life, he had sent her out for a bottle of wine and she returned with lemonade. If that was so, no wonder she looks as if she has been scolded.

Beside sculpture and portraits, there was a third subject matter in Modigliani's body of work. It was nudes. Female nudes have been a staple of art since the begin-

10-9. *Nude Beatrice Hastings* by Modigliani. 1915, oil on canvas.

10-10. *Little Girl in Blue* by Modigliani, 1918, oil on canvas, private collection.

ning of time. Modigliani was certainly aware of that. He had seen the nudes painted by Italian Renaissance masters in the 16th century like Giorgione and Titian and by French painters like Cabanel in the 19th century. But often the subjects were mythological women like Venus. They always represented the idealized female figure and none were painted provocatively. They usually had a romantic aura about them.

Things began to change with Manet's *Olympia* (see fig. 6-14). Modigliani was responsible for extending this approach of painting nudes differently. His nudes are not rooted in Greek mythology. There is no Venus and even no extraneous props in the portraits to distract you as is the case with *Olympia*. Modigliani provides only the barest suggestion of a setting, perhaps a cushion or an expanse of cloth. His nudes are not romantic and are clearly provocative.

The figures are displayed boldly and the realistic body details emphasize the eroticism of the subject. These are "in your face nudes" and that is what made them so con-

troversial. Yet, the eroticism is tempered by the mask like features of the face and the blank stares that tend to remove any personal connection.

Modigliani had the ability to beautify his nudes and, at the same time, eroticize them. All of this shocked contemporary viewers. His females became individual yet distant, voluptuous yet generalized, sensuous yet with a sense of grace and innocence. In the final analysis, there is a fine balance between the erotic and the artistic beauty in Modigliani's nudes and that is what makes them so special and different.

Seated Nude (fig. 10-11) may have been his first nude. It is a much more complex painting than it looks to be at first glance. There are a number of contrasts that may even look like they are inconsistencies. For example, the model appears to be asleep. Her head rests on one slightly uplifted shoulder and her eyes are closed. But can the model be asleep and still be sitting upright? Maybe she is just resting.

The figure is close to the viewer and almost seems to be slipping toward us. Her resting head leads our attention down to the long line of the unbent arm on which she rests. Her body divides the canvas into two zones of contrasting colors.

The right side of the canvas is a deep mixture of browns and reds into which the flowing brunette hair dissolves. In complete contrast, the left side of the canvas is painted in cool, pale blue that flows around the top of her tilted head. The upper body has a lighter tone that is in keeping with the lighter background to the left. The lower body darkens in tone to match the darker hues of the red/brown chair against which she leans. Her face is darker so that it contrasts with the light blues around it.

Admittedly, most art observers will either miss such subtle changes in shades of color in the piece or may not even care about them. But the artist cared and, in the process of adding them, made the work more interesting even if we as viewers don't know why.

It was nudes like this that were part of the only one-man show that Modigliani had in Paris in 1917. Unfortunately, the gallery was located near a police station. The show was temporarily closed down because the paintings were considered obscene and offensive.

Reclining Nude (fig.10-12) is at the Guggenheim Museum in New York. Paris was not the only place that Modigliani's nudes generated controversy. Even as late as the 1950s, the Guggenheim was pressed by some of the outraged public to withdraw from sale in its bookstore the picture postcard of this piece. Perhaps what made it so controversial are the upraised arms of the woman. It adds a sense of invitation to the piece.

Picasso used African mask like features in the creation of his masterpiece *Les Demoiselles d'Avignon* in 1907 (see fig. 11-6). That painting will be discussed in the next chapter. Although Mo-

10-11. *Seated Nude* by Modigliani, 1916, oil on canvas, Courtauld Institute Galleries, London.

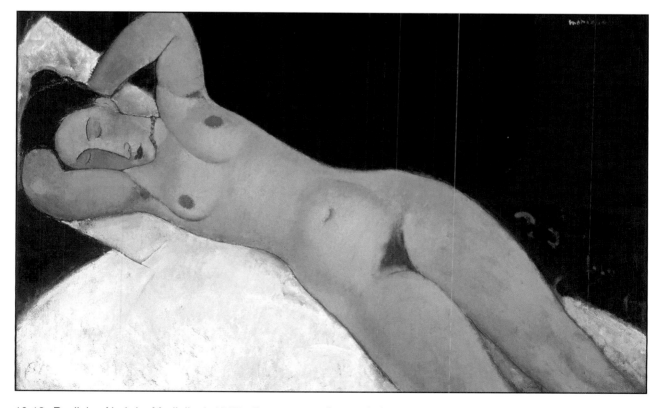

10-12. *Reclining Nude* by Modigliani, 1917, oil on canvas, Guggenheim Museum, New York.

10-13. *Nude With Coral Necklace* by Modigliani, 1917, oil on canvas, Allen Memorial Art Museum, Oberlin, Ohio.

10-14. *Reclining Nude* by Modigliani, 1919, oil on canvas, Museum of Modern Art, New York.

digliani's art never approached Cubism, he also discovered the spellbinding power of African art. Remember the comment by Beatrice Hastings regarding how much respect he had for Picasso. Modigliani's nudes may stare back at us but they show no emotion. There is a sense of stoicism about them. In fact, they are similar to the African mask like faces painted by Picasso. *Reclining Nude* shows the contrast between the model's lithe body and stony face.

Between 1916 and 1919 Modigliani did more than two dozen paintings of female nudes. His nudes are seen close up and often from above. Sometimes they appear asleep or resting as is the case with *Reclining Nude*. Most often they face the viewer. Either their hands or feet or perhaps both remain outside the picture frame.

In *Nude With Coral Necklace* (fig. 10-13), as is usually the case, the figure is displayed boldly with the absence of props or a setting. In this case she wears a single accessory, a coral necklace. The realistic details of her body, her nipples and pubic hair, add to the eroticism of the piece. But like artists before him (see the discussion of Manet and *Olympia* in chapter 6) Modigliani borrowed from other artists in *Nude With Coral Necklace*. For example, the diagonal lie of the figure and the placement of her hand in a show of modesty recall Titian's splendid *Venus of Urbino* (see fig. 3-25).

Nevertheless, Modigliani's nude is different. There is no reference to mythology. Here the figure is presented in a straightforward manner, listlessly outstretched. She is completely detached. Any contact she might have with the viewer is blunted by her mask like face and blank eyes. They are rendered pupil-less. Yet, Modigliani maintains a fine balance. She is sensual but not indecent, pleasing but not overly erotic.

The Titian piece is less provocative because the nude is not alone. There are a number of distractions such as the rose petals in her hand, the dog on the bed and the maids in the background that present a domestic setting to the painting.

A similar comparison can be made between Modigliani's later *Reclining Nude* (fig. 10-14) and Cabanel's *Birth of Venus* (fig. 10-15). The poses of the two are close including the turn of the hips directly toward the viewer and the placement of the arms. But the Cabanel piece is a perfect example of the popular artistic taste of the period. It represents an episode from classical mythology where Venus is born of sea-foam and carried ashore. Because themes like this were so popular they provided some artists with the opportunity to introduce eroticism into their paintings without offending public morality.

Consider that this painting was shown the same year as Manet's *Olympia* which caused such a scandal. Even though the subject of the two paintings was similar with reclining nudes, Manet's nude stares back at the viewer with no sense of modesty or shame. Modigliani's reclining nudes were considered so indecent 54 years later that they forced a temporary closing of his only one-man show in his lifetime.

Contrast these reactions with what occurred when *The Birth of Venus* was introduced in the 1863 Salon. It was

10-15. *Birth of Venus* by Cabanel, 1863, oil on canvas, Musee d'Orsay, Paris.

10-16. *Portrait of Jacques and Berthe Lipchitz* by Modigliani, 1916, oil on canvas, Art Institute of Chicago, Chicago.

10-17. Photo of Jeanne Hebuterne.

that about *Reclining Nude or Seated Nude*. In the Lipchitz portrait, the woman has a haughty air about her. There is the egg-shaped face perched on top of her long neck. Her dainty collar becomes more noticeable because her elongated nose leads down to it.

The man above her has his hand suavely tucked into his pocket. Does he stand there protectively or is he showing his dominance? Who are these people and what is their relationship? They are the prominent sculptor Jacques Lipchitz and his wife Berthe.

In many respects, Jeanne Hebuterne was the exact opposite of Modigliani's previous love interest Beatrice Hastings. She was a shy, quite, delicate 19-year old art student when she met Modigliani in 1917. Those characteristics come across in the photo of her (fig. 10-17). She became his final muse.

Their relationship was immediately all-consuming for Jeanne. But her association with Modigliani outraged her strict Catholic parents because he was a wild living penniless artist 14-years her senior. The fact that he was a Jew did not help matters. Jeanne was not fond of the café scene as was Beatrice. Instead, she preferred to stay

one of the art scene's great successes and was bought by Napoleon III for his private collection.

In this writers view, there is a difference between Modigliani's nudes and his portraits and not just in their naked versus clothed bodies. Although his nudes are an integral part of his painted work, they seem separate from his portraits. His nudes are closer to reality. His portraits are more subject to his emotional whims. Yet, his nudes seem less personal. When I look at one, I do not care to know her name. That is not the case with his portraits. I tend to ask who is this person.

Portrait of Jacques and Berthe Lipchitz (fig. 10-16) is an example of what I mean. I find myself asking: who are these people? But I do not find myself asking

10-18. *Jeanne Hebuterne With Hair In Point* by Modigliani, 1918, oil on canvas, Barnes Foundation, Philadelphia.

10-19. *Portrait of Jeanne Hebuterne*, 1918, oil on canvas, Yale University Art Gallery, New Haven, Connecticut.

at home and sketch, paint or sew and, later, tend to their baby. Modigliani painted her more than two dozen times but never naked.

Jeanne Hebuterne With Hair In Point (fig. 10-18) shows her pregnant for the first time. A daughter also named Jeanne was born late in 1918. It recalls the Egyptian influence on his early art with her hair worn in an early Egyptian style. The same year he painted *Portrait of Jeanne Hebuterne* (fig. 10-19). It is my favorite portrait of her. It shows her chestnut color hair with reddish highlights. It contrasts with her pale complexion which led her friends to nickname her "Coconut."

What is striking is the tranquility in her portraits that is in total contrast with the constant chaos in Modigliani's life. You cannot help wondering how such a modest looking woman could be painted by an artist with the reputation of Modigliani. In *Hair In Point* her hands are folded and placed neatly in her lap. She has a sort of dreamy look. There is a tenderness in both pieces that could not be further from the vibrant sexuality of his nudes.

Probably aware of his imminent demise, Modigliani painted a self-portrait in late 1919 (fig. 10-20). He presents himself as a caricature as he had done with so many others in his portraits. He wears his signature corduroy jacket. It is as if he wanted to challenge the image he had of a bohemian philanderer and a bitter, failed artist. Instead, he paints himself as noble and elegant, poised in his lofty artistic profession.

Modigliani died in January 1920 at the age of 35 from tuberculosis exacerbated by drugs and alcohol. He died penniless and destitute, managing only one solo exhibition in his life and giving away his art in exchange for meals and drinks. A neighbor found him in a bed strewn with open cans of sardines with Jeanne holding onto him.

His last words were "cara Italia" or "beloved Italy" thus passing on to the Italian public his deathbed allegiance to his homeland. His funeral was attended by a number of prominent artists such as Picasso, Lipchitz, Derain, Soutine, Leger and Susan Valadon indicating he

10-20. *Modigliani Self-Portrait* by Modigliani, 1919, oil on canvas, Museu de Arte Contemporanea da Universidade, Sao Paulo, Brazil.

was another artist's artist. Those in the artistic community respected his work before the critics and public.

How good was Modigliani? Good enough today to be regarded as one of the leading artists of the 20th century. During his short career, Modigliani's contemporaries were two of the masters that dominated the 20th century, Picasso and Matisse. His artistic accomplishments did not match either of them. But Matisse lived 50 years longer and Picasso 57 years longer. The material covered in this book spans just 12 years, yet it included sculpture, portraits and nudes all in a style never seen before. One has to wonder what he could have accomplished if he had lived decades longer. He died too soon.

Two days after Modigliani's death, a second lightening bolt struck. Jeanne Hebuterne, nine months pregnant with their second child, committed suicide by tumbling out of the fifth story window of her parent's apartment in Paris.

Her brief time with Modigliani was hardly like living the fairy tale she hoped for. The contradictions of her life continued in death. She was strong enough to handle Modigliani's excesses, the depravation and turmoil that came with living with him. But she was not strong enough to live without him.

Their orphaned daughter Jeanne, who was 15 months old at the time of her parent's death, was adopted by Modigliani's sister in Florence. In 1958 she would write a biography of her father, *Modigliani: Man and Myth*.

Jeanne's family blamed Modigliani for her death. They would not allow her to be buried with him. But five years later, Modigliani's brother persuaded them to be placed together. They finally allowed her remains to be buried beside her lover. A single tombstone marks the grave of both. His epitaph reads: "Struck down by death in the moment of glory." Hers reads: "Devoted companion to the extreme sacrifice."

IMAGES

10-1. Photo of Modigliani.

10-2. *Tete* by Modigliani. A limestone sculpture sold at auction in 2010.

10-3. *Woman in a Yellow Jacket* by Modigliani, 1909, oil on canvas, private collection.

10-4. *Portrait of Juan Gris* by Modigliani, 1915, oil on canvas, Metropolitan Museum of Art, New York.

10-5. *Portrait of Jean Cocteau* by Modigliani, 1916, oil on canvas, Art Museum of Princeton University, Princeton, New Jersey.

10-6. *The Annunciation* by Martini, 1333, tempera on panel, Galleria degli Uffizi, Florence.

10-7. *Madam Pompadour* by Modigliani, 1915, oil on canvas, Art Institute of Chicago, Chicago.

10-8. Photo of Beatrice Hastings.

10-9. *Nude Beatrice Hastings* by Modigliani. 1915, oil on canvas.

10-10. *Little Girl in Blue* by Modigliani, 1918, oil on canvas, private collection.

10-11. *Seated Nude* by Modigliani, 1916, oil on canvas, Courtauld Institute Galleries, London.

10-12. *Reclining Nude* by Modigliani, 1917, oil on canvas, Guggenheim Museum, New York.

10-13. *Nude With Coral Necklace* by Modigliani, 1917, oil on canvas, Allen Memorial Art Museum, Oberlin, Ohio.

10-14. *Reclining Nude* by Modigliani, 1919, oil on canvas, Museum of Modern Art, New York.

10-15. *Birth of Venus* by Cabanel, 1863, oil on canvas, Musee d'Orsay, Paris.

10-16. *Portrait of Jacques and Berthe Lipchitz* by Modigliani, 1916, oil on canvas, Art Institute of Chicago, Chicago.

10-17. Photo of Jeanne Hebuterne.

10-18. *Jeanne Hebuterne With Hair In Point* by Modigliani, 1918, oil on canvas, Barnes Foundation, Philadelphia.

10-19. *Portrait of Jeanne Hebuterne*, 1918, oil on canvas, Yale University Art Gallery, New Haven, Connecticut.

10-20. *Modigliani Self-Portrait* by Modigliani, 1919, oil on canvas, Museu de Arte Contemporanea da Universidade, Sao Paulo, Brazil.

PICASSO:

His Art and His Women

11

Pablo Picasso (1881-1973) was more than a Cubist. He painted some of the most extraordinary portraits of the 20th century. His style varied between Cubism, Neoclassicism and Surrealism. But one thing was consistent with Picasso. Whatever style he chose when he painted his female portraits, most often they were inspired by a woman in his life. His career as a portraitist followed the women he knew. Each inspired him in a different way. In this chapter we will see how.

Picasso's grandson Oliver Widmaier Picasso could not have put it more succinctly and accurately in his book *Picasso: The Real Family Story* when he wrote, "Women were to Picasso what paint is to the brush: inseparable, essential, fatal." Female relationships never lasted with Picasso. By the count of this writer, he had seven significant women in his life that influenced his art. They are laid out chronologically in the text headed: "The Cast of Picasso's Muses in Order of Their Appearance." I will introduce you to each one of them.

There was Fernande who accompanied Picasso during his move into Cubism. Eva, who was there when he introduced collage and his art approached abstraction. Olga was the focus of his neoclassical portrait painting. Marie-Therese became the inspiration for some Surrealistic works in the 1930s. Dora was there during the war years and for Guernica. Francoise was his muse in the post-war years. Finally, Jacqueline was at Picasso's side in his old age.

Picasso had two wives and numerous lovers. He had one child Paulo with his first wife Olga and three illegitimate children, Maya with Marie-Therese, Claude and Paloma with Francoise.

Even though Picasso's mother adored her son she knew of his weaknesses. She warned, "My son lives only for himself. No woman could be safe and happy with him." She could not have been more accurate. He would abandon woman after woman. What he gained from the process was inspiration for his art. What they gained was the immortality of being in his art. Given the eventual impact on the lives of most of the women in his life, it could hardly be considered a fair tradeoff.

He had intense relationships with all seven of the women covered in this chapter. But basically he was incapable of love. For Picasso it was all about total devotion and submissiveness to him. Those were the preconditions for a relationship with him. He would start out as charming but turn out to be overbearing, dominating and demanding.

Artistically, a pattern would emerge for Picasso. He had a compulsion to rearrange the faces and bodies of his women on canvas. At first, when the relationship was going well, he would deify them on canvas. However, inevitably the relationship would deteriorate. Then he would debase them in his art.

Picasso was a great artist because of his monumental creativity and exceptional capacity for invention. He was an explorer and a great risk taker who pulled the familiar apart and put it back together again in a way that no one had seen before. While doing that, he created a new tradition in art, that is, a new way of seeing art. When you do that, art history puts its stamp of greatness on you and it occurred with Picasso fairly early in his long career. He became so famous in his lifetime (an achievement that escapes many

THE CAST OF PICASSO'S MUSES IN ORDER OF THEIR APPEARANCE

Fernande Olivier (1881-1966) Met in 1904 and separated in 1912.

Eva Gouel (1885-1915) Met in 1909 or 1912. Died in 1915.

Olga Khokhlova (1891-1955) Met in 1917. Married 1918 and separated in 1935.

Marie-Therese Walter (1909-1977) Met in 1927. Separated in 1943. Committed suicide in 1977.

Dora Maar (1907-1997) Met in 1935. Separated in 1944.

Francoise Gilot (1921) Met in 1943. Separated in 1953.

Jacqueline Roque (1926-1986) Met in 1954. Married in 1961. Committed suicide in 1986.

great artists) that American soldiers in Paris at the end of WWII rated him with the Eiffel Tower among the sights they most wanted to see. The American Red Cross had to arrange tours of his studio.

Yet, Picasso is a challenge. A lot of people don't like his art because it is intimidating. He represents the incomprehensible. He distorts things so people don't understand him. You can get bogged down trying to study his art. Viewers don't like that. They like art that is easy to look at and understand.

Navigating Picasso's career can be a disorienting experience. Picasso was always changing and, in the process, moving into new art spaces and challenging us. He adopted and discarded styles over and over again. He said, "If one knows what one is going to do, what is the sense in doing it. Better do something else." As an example of how his art changed, he quipped when attending an exhibition of some of his earlier works that those are "paintings by an artist who has the same name as me."

He was truly a child prodigy. His mother said he could draw before he could talk. She said his first word was "lapiz" which is Spanish for pencil which he was always asking for so he could draw. Picasso said that when he was a child his mother told him, "If you become a soldier you'll be a general. If you become a monk, you'll end up as the Pope." He said, "Instead, I became a painter and wound up Picasso."

By the time he was a young teenager he could paint like some of the masters. But that wasn't good enough for Picasso so he spent the rest of his life learning how not to paint like that. The result was that 20th century art belonged to him. Picasso is modern art.

With all the women in his life you might think that it is a wonder he found time to paint. But it didn't work like that with Picasso. As noted above, women to him were like paint to his brush. He needed them to inspire him. He had difficulty functioning without a woman around. Whenever a new woman comes into his life, everything changes. His personal life and the women in it represent a large part of answering the mystery of his creative process.

11-1. *First Communion* by Picasso, 1895-1896, oil on canvas, Museo Picasso, Barcelona, Spain.

Perhaps one should not be surprised by his continuous attraction to different women given his definition of a Spaniard's perfect Sunday: "Mass in the morning, bullfight in the afternoon, whore house in the evening." A study by two British psychologists may help to explain his behavior. They found that artists and poets were more promiscuous than others and the frequency of promiscuity increased with the artist's success. Mathematicians, on the other hand, were extremely monogamous.

Unfortunately, Picasso's life was not just about revolutionary art. He was also the center of great tragedy. Late in his life Picasso said, "When I die it will be a shipwreck. When a large ship goes down many people in the vicinity are swept into the whirlpool." It was a very prophetic statement. Marie-Therese, his long time mistress, committed suicide by hanging herself in her garage in 1977, four years after he died. His second wife, Jacqueline, committed suicide by shooting herself in the temple in 1986.

Before Picasso's funeral was over, his grandson Pablito committed suicide by drinking bleach. Two years after Pablito's death, the boy's father and Picasso's only legitimate child, Paulo died of liver cancer from excessive drinking.

First Communion (fig. 11-1) was painted when Picasso was just 14 or 15. It shows his sister Lola at her first communion. Look at the details he could paint even at this early age. There is a clumsy acolyte who looks like he is about to upset the flowers. There are rose petals on the altar steps. He includes symbolism with the two lit candles and two that have burned out. They refer to two children that are alive and the two early deaths of a brother Jose and sister Conchita.

Picasso was an artist driven by his emotions and not all of them were associated with women. He said, "Anyone can paint things the way they are. I paint them the way I feel." *Self Portrait* (fig. 11-2) was painted in 1901 when he begins his blue period. He was 21.

He often painted the outcasts of Paris in weary poses and with a coldly expressive blue color. He was surrounded by the underclass when he lived in poverty during his early years in the Montmartre district of Paris. There was often a sense of melancholy in the paintings. Picasso was always sensitive to those he considered as victims of society. It was one reason why he eventually joined the Communist Party.

A lot of influences have been suggested as catalysts to his blue period. He was very poor and disappointed with his lack of success as an artist even at that early age. Perhaps there were other influences. It has even been suggested as part of the Picasso legend that he was so poor that he painted in blue because it was the least expensive color. That is untrue.

The real reason was that his friend and fellow painter, Carlos Casagemas, committed suicide in 1901 over a failed love affair with his model Germaine. Picasso was devastated by the event and later admitted it triggered his blue period. In this portrait he has a melancholy look. His face is pale almost death like, all influenced by the suicide of Casagemas.

Images of manual labor abound in the 19th and early 20th century French art. For example, there was Courbet's *The Stone Breakers* (see fig. 6-8), Millet's *The Gleaners* (see fig. 6-12) and Degas' *Two Laundresses* (see

fig. 7-25) just to mention a few. But there are none more moving than Picasso's *Woman Ironing* (fig. 11-3). It even surpasses Degas' seminal work on the same subject matter in pure pathos.

Picasso was able to focus on the underclass from 1901 to 1904 because he lived among them. Gloomy themes and a melancholy palette that featured blue tones characterized his art. He depicted his subjects with great sensitivity and pity. Woman Ironing, with its bleak color scheme, may be one of the quintessential works on physical exhaustion.

In painting her elongated form he was influenced by El Greco. He depicts her as a skeletal woman. Her eyes are hollow and her cheeks are sunken. She presses down on the iron with whatever strength she has left.

When Picasso exits his blue period after meeting Fernande Olivier in 1904 his paintings become more joyful. They are colorful and he often paints clowns. An example of his transition to this new artistic style is *At the Lapin Agile* (fig. 11-4). The melancholy blues have been replaced by orange. Picasso appears as a harlequin and stands next

11-2. *Self-Portrait* by Picasso, 1901, oil on canvas, Musee Picasso, Paris.

11-3. *Woman Ironing* by Picasso, 1904, oil on canvas, Guggenheim Museum, New York.

But by 1905 when *At the Lapin Agile* was executed he had emerged from his blue period.

Picasso had a brief affair with Germaine after his friend's death. In *At the Lapin Agile* Germaine is decked out in a hat with a feather, a gaudy orange dress, bead choker and boa. She has heavy make-up and pouty lips. Picasso wears a vivid diamond patterned shirt and a three-cornered hat. He looks melancholy and gaunt. Even though they are dressed for a night on the town, there is no joy in their faces. Both appear grim and do not even look at each other. You get the sense they are haunted by the ghost of Casagemas.

The Lapin Agile (The Lively Rabbit) was a Montmarte cabaret that was a favorite watering hole for struggling artists like Picasso and Modigliani. The painting has come a long way in value. Originally it was executed to embellish the wall of the dark, dingy tavern. It was done in exchange for credit at the bar for Picasso. The seated guitarist at the rear of the painting is Frede Gerard the café's owner. Eventually, the piece was purchased by Walter Annenberg in 1989 for $40.7 million. At that time it was the third highest amount paid at auction for an artwork.

An interesting sidelight to all these details about the painting is that the Lapin Agile is the setting for a hilarious play written by actor/comedian Steve Martin called *Picasso at Lapin Agile*. It takes place in 1904 and is a fictional account of a meeting between Picasso and Albert Einstein at the café. Both Fernande Oliver and Germaine are depicted in the play. In actuality, both were regulars at Lapin Agile.

Fortunately, the misery did not last. When Picasso meets the first love of his life Fernande Olivier they move in together. A happier Picasso exits his blue period, enters his rose period and begins to paint clowns and acrobats. The period of sadness and despair was over. It is an example of an artist driven by his emotions. Later he would begin his investigation of space and perspective that would lead to Cubism.

Interestingly, Picasso's works from his blue and rose periods have become as highly valued as many of his later pieces. Perhaps that is because during these periods he was at his most human and poignantly expressive point of his career. When he chose to, no one depicted the plight of the underclass with greater poignancy than Picasso. He rarely painted things just as they were. He made these people a

to model and femme fatale Germaine Pichot who his friend Carlos Casagemas committed suicide over.

Picasso met Casagemas in a tavern in Barcelona. They shared a studio for a short time in Paris and then returned to Spain. But Casagemas soon left for Paris again. He was still tormented by Germaine because their affair was ending. While with her and some friends in a Montmartre café, he shot himself in the temple.

Even though he did not actually witness the suicide, Picasso was deeply troubled by his friends violent end. He said that when he realized Casagemas was dead he began to paint in blue. He drew portraits of Carlos lying dead.

11-4. *At the Lapin Agile* by Picasso, 1905, oil on canvas, Metropolitan Museum of Art, New York.

beside it on a pine table. In another corner, a trunk painted black provided rather uncomfortable seating. A wicker chair, an easel, pictures of all sizes, tubes of paint scattered all over the floor, brushes, containers, no curtains. In a table drawer there was a tame white mouse that Picasso looked after tenderly and showed to everyone."

Cubism did not happen overnight. It is something that evolved. Picasso said that, "When we (he and Braque) invented Cubism we had no intention of inventing it." Most important about Fernande is her association with his move into Cubism. In the summer of 1906, Picasso and Fernande spent time in the small town of Gosol in the Spanish Pyrenees. It is in the Basque region in northern Spain near the French border. They were isolated in the mountains. Picasso wanted to temporarily return to a stark more primitive life. This started his Iberian period.

metaphor for the working poor. Another appeal of his early pieces is that they provide a road map to Cubism. He begins the process of distorting and deconstructing the human figure.

For a short time, Picasso lived with Casagemas and a third artist in a studio that they shared with three women. A quote from Picasso describing the life of the three couples reveals how he considered women and the role that they played. "We will dedicate ourselves to our paintings and they will do women's work – sew, clean up, kiss us and let themselves be fondled. This is a kind of Eden."

Fernande provided a snapshot of Picasso's lifestyle in his early years. She wrote in her memoirs about the studio they lived in.

"Large unfinished pictures stood in the studio, where everything spoke of work. But what untidiness to work in . . . my God! A mattress on four-legs in one corner. A small cast-iron stove with a yellow earthenware basin on it that served as a wash bowl; a towel and a piece of soap lay

While in Gosol, Picasso became fascinated with the figure of a 90-year old Iberian named Josep Fontdevila with whom he became friends. He made numerous sketches of him, eventually reducing his face to mask-like features. Fernande described him as "a fearsome old man of a strange and savage beauty." Apparently, Picasso felt the same way. When he returned to Paris, the experience was reflected in his art. He completed portraits of Fernande and himself where the faces had a sort of primitivism about them.

The Americans, Gertrude Stein and her brother Leo were big early supporters of Picasso. Their purchases of his work virtually pulled him out of poverty and began to establish his career. Gertrude was a writer who spent most of her life in France. She developed relationships with young avant-garde artists like Matisse and Picasso and writers like Hemingway.

Gertrude persuaded Picasso to do her portrait. There were numerous sittings over a period of months. That was unusual for Picasso because he did not have that type of patience. One day, a frustrated Picasso suddenly painted out her whole head saying, "I can't see you anymore."

When Picasso returned to Paris from Gosol, he quickly repainted Stein's face. This final version of *Portrait of Gertrude Stein* (fig. 11-5) reflected the primitivism he adopted in Gosol and his efforts to reduce the face to a kind of mask. Stein liked the outcome and a number of years later she wrote, "for me, it is I, and it is the only reproduction of me which is always I, for me." But when some people told Picasso that Gertrude did not resemble her portrait he replied, "She will."

Picasso's Iberian period and the mask-like features in his works culminated in the painting *Les Demoiselles d'Avignon* in 1907 (fig. 11-6). It is a scene of five ferocious nudes in a brothel. Avignon is not the picturesque French town; it is a street in the red light district of Barcelona. The influences for the work come from Iberian sculpture, African art and Cezanne. It demonstrates Picasso's exceptional capacity for invention. It seems likely that the piece was partly in response to the challenge of Matisse's *Le Bonheur de Vivre* (see fig.12- 2) that was painted the year before.

Les Demoiselles is the centerpiece of the Museum of Modern Art's collection and is arguably the most important painting of the 20th century. It is a large piece, 8 x 8 feet. It is important because it made all other paintings that were thought to be radical seem unadventurous in comparison. It is one of the most shocking paintings of all time. It is important because it opened the floodgates to modern art. Some art historians say that the day *Les Demoiselles* was painted was the day the modern art movement began.

Most of all, it is important because it was Picasso's lead-in to Cubism and Cubism is important because it is the most fundamental break in art perspective since the Renaissance. With Cubism, Picasso takes the familiar and pulls it apart then puts it back together in ways never seen before. But when Picasso painted the piece he was not consciously trying to challenge historical pictorial tradition. He was using the distorted forms to represent his view of women. In the process, he started a revolution in perspective that

11-5. *Portrait of Gertrude Stein* by Picasso, 1906, oil on canvas, Metropolitan Museum of Art, New York.

secured him his place at the forefront of avant-garde art. *Les Demoiselles* sharpened his interest in altered forms that led him to Cubism.

The viewer becomes a participant in the painting in that the figures look directly at us. The three women on the left have wild almond shaped eyes that show the Iberian influence. The faces of the two figures on the right have a much different style and were inspired by another primitive source, African masks. All in all, Picasso is changing our perspective. That is something he learned from Cezanne.

Picasso was always attacking traditional art. The female nude has usually been presented with some combination of beauty, sensuality and tenderness. But all of that changed with *Les Demoiselles* . The painting is an attack on everything that went before. Picasso was out to shock and, if need be, appall. There is a savagery in the women's faces that surpasses anything before.

11-6. *Les Demoiselles d'Avignon* by Picasso, 1907, oil on canvas, Museum of Modern Art, New York.

Even at this early stage of his career, he is painting women that contradict the image laid down since the Renaissance of gentile, passive creatures that are appealing to men. Two of the women have their arms raised above their heads in a gesture that they are available. But that image of accessibility is countered by their fierce, staring eyes. The fruit shown in the foreground, which generally might be considered a symbol of female sexuality and appeal, looks hard and uninviting.

One has to wonder what Picasso was thinking when he was painting these nearly 7 foot tall ferocious women who towered above the 5'3" painter. At some point he must have begun to wonder if he had gone too far in creating such monsters. Did he think about turning back to something less shocking and less extreme?

Whatever his thoughts were, we know that Picasso chose not to turn back. In fact, he decided to take more risks as the project progressed and pushed the composition into an even more extreme presentation. Originally, the heads on the two figures on the right were painted in the relatively tamer style of the other three. But then Picasso changed and did something unheard of giving them the heads of African masks. It was this revision that furnished *Les Demoiselles* with a savageness not seen before in modern art.

The squatting woman on the right probably has the greatest impact on the viewer. Here, Picasso destroys the traditional approach to representing anatomy and perspective. He shows her simultaneously from the front and the back. In the process, we are seeing the dawn of Cubism.

The figure's hips and torso are presented from the back. But her African mask-like face is shown from the front and looks directly at us. But her blue-striped nose is not facing us, it is shown in profile. She rests her chin on her left arm or, with all the distortions, does it now become her right arm? It takes the shape of a boomerang.

The woman behind her has green stripes on her nose that are repeated on what is probably the first square breast in the

11-7. *Ma Jolie* by Picasso, 1912, oil on canvas, Museum of Modern Art, New York.

history of art. The figure on the far left stands in profile but she has one eye facing front. There is drapery behind the two figures standing with their arms raised over their heads. But the placement of the drapery gives the impression that they could be lying down adding to their accessibility. The bottom line on all of this distortion is that the viewer is getting different perspectives and that is what Cubism is all about.

The two figures to the right are disturbing but they are indispensable to the shock value of the painting. Try to cover them with your hand and you will see how relatively mild the painting becomes without them. *Les Demoiselles* is shocking but also mesmerizing. The spellbinding appeal of the painting is that it is so different from anything else, it is beyond strange. The longer you look at it the more there is to discover. It is so radical that it is ageless. More than 100 years later it is still a tough painting to understand and the figures still look brutal and dangerous.

The painting was so shocking that nobody wanted to buy it. The response from Picasso's friends was underwhelming. One asked, "What would you say if your mother met you with a face like that?" It stayed in his studio for four years and was not exhibited until 1916.

Picasso walked out on Fernande in May 1912 and never saw her again. Their relationship had been deteriorating for years. But the final blow came when Picasso learned she had an affair with an Italian painter. He set-up with Eva Gouel the same month. She also went under the name of Marcelle Humbert and was Fernande's friend. Years later he would finally give a penniless Fernande a substantial amount of money but on the understanding she would not publish her account of their eight years together.

Ma Jolie (fig. 11-7) is the nearly indecipherable image of Eva playing a stringed instrument. Ma Jolie means "my pretty one." It was the title of a popular song of the day. Picasso proclaimed he loved Eva so much he would write it on his painting. It shows how he incorporated his private life into painting. He said, "My painting is a diary."

This is far from the traditional portrait of an artist's beloved one. The only clear reference to Eva is the boldly stenciled letters "Ma Jolie" at the bottom of the painting. But there are other clues to her presence in the painting. To the left of the letters is a treble clef sign. In the lower center you can see four fingers on some vertical lines that represent strings. There is an elbow jutting to the right. If you look very closely, slightly above that configuration, a floating smile is barely discernable. But everything tends to disappear into an abstract network of flat planes.

This is one of the most complex, abstract images of its day. Although it has a traditional theme (i.e. a woman holding a musical instrument) it is an example of high Analytic Cubism where planes interact and colors are muted. Works like this brought Picasso to the brink of abstraction but he never got there because he always favored representational subjects such as a figure or still-life. But when you see a painting like this you realize Cubism was influential in the development of abstract art. One wonders if there would have been Abstract Expressionism without Cubism first.

11-8. *Portrait of Olga in the Armchair* by Picasso, 1917, oil on canvas, Musee Picasso, Paris.

11-11. *Bather With a Beach Ball* by Picasso, 1932, oil on canvas, Museum of Modern Art, New York.

11-10. *Seated Bather* by Picasso, 1930, oil on canvas, Museum of Modern Art, New York.

Picasso's short time with Eva was a happy period for him. It leads him into Synthetic Cubism. In this phase, Picasso begins to incorporate materials into his paintings so he is inventing collage. What is so important about collage? Art had taken the representation of reality as far as it could. So the concept of actually presenting materials on a canvas rather than depicting them was revolutionary. Collage also enhances the 3-D appearance of a Cubist painting.

In addition to the use of collage, in Synthetic Cubism figures and objects rather than just planes interact. The pictures become more recognizable and the colors become more vibrant. The desire to dismember gives way to the joy of being decorative. Not coincidently, all of this coincides with the entrance of Eva into his life. Now Cubism becomes joyous and radiant just like Picasso over his new love.

11-9. Photograph of Picasso and Olga 1919.

Unfortunately, Eva died in December 1915 of cancer or perhaps tuberculosis. At that time, Picasso was painting a portrait of her. But he left it unfinished for the rest of his life.

After that tragedy, Picasso was not interested in another affair. He was 35 and wanted a wife. As head of his Spanish family he was under pressure to live up to his position and produce a son and heir. Olga Khokhlova, a Russian ballerina, entered his life in 1917.

Portrait of Olga In An Armchair (fig. 11-8) is considered to be his greatest painting of his future wife. It was controversial because his supporters accused him of abandoning Cubism and thus, modernism. But it shows what an accomplished neoclassical portrait painter he could be. He did not have to distort.

Olga was a proper woman. She wanted to recognize herself in his paintings. So Picasso initially painted her with all the respect she demanded. He cleaned up his art and, for a while, he cleaned up his life. At this point, Olga appears only in representational portraits. He even tried to give up his bohemian life and become comfortable with the drawing rooms of Paris to please Olga.

The photograph of Picasso and Olga in 1919 (fig. 11-9) is not the image of Picasso we imagine. This was part of his "classical period" which was represented by his trend toward more conservatism in his art. Olga tried to de-bohemianize him. For a while he abandoned his bohemian life and tried to be comfortable with the drawing rooms of Paris to please Olga. He found himself involved in fancy dress balls often in the company of people like Scott and Zelda Fitzgerald. But Picasso could not change. Later he would admit, "Olga likes tea, caviar and pastries. I like sausage and beans."

As noted previously, Picasso had an obsession with rearranging the faces and bodies of the women in his life on canvas. For a time, he would love passionately and possessively. Later, he would love to hate. He said that there were two types of women – goddesses and doormats. Unfortunately, you entered Picasso's life as a goddess and exited as a doormat.

By the late 1920s, a new woman had entered his life, Marie-Therese Walter although he was still living with Olga. A decade earlier, Picasso had treated Olga like a goddess in his art. Now he was debasing her. In *Seated Bather* (fig. 11-10) Picasso evokes the type of violent psychological themes often shown in the works of the Surrealists. She is depicted as a repulsive figure with an impenetrable tortoise like back and a steel-trapped mouth. She is the image of a preying mantis that devours its mate during sex.

Contrast that painting with the new love of his life, Marie-Therese Walter. In *Bather With a Beach Ball* (fig. 11-11) Picasso celebrates her rounded form and blond hair. She is a weightless figure playing joyfully with a beach ball. This is hardly the Surrealistic monster that Olga had become.

Picasso met Marie-Therese shopping on Boulevard Haussmann at Galeries Lafayette in 1927. He was 46 and married. She was 17. It is said his introductory line was, "Mademoiselle you have an interesting face. I would like to paint your portrait. I have a feeling we will accomplish great things together. I am Picasso."

In her memoirs, Marie-Therese wrote that she had never heard of Picasso so he took her to a bookstore to show her a book about him. She agreed to meet him because he had a kind smile and her mother had a great romance with a painter. That started a 16-year relationship. She was shopping for a peter pan collar that she would keep until her suicide in 1977.

11-12. *Le Reve or The Dream* by Picasso, 1932, oil on canvas, private collection.

11-13. *Marie-Therese Seated* by Picasso, 1937, oil on canvas, Musee Picasso, Paris.

11-14. *Dora Maar Au Chat* by Picasso, 1941, oil on canvas, private collection.

The Marie-Therese portraits of the 1930s represented a sea change in Picasso's art. His curvilinear Cubism became known as the "Marie-Therese style." The portrait *Le Reve* or *The Dream* (fig. 11-12) is most representative of that style and it is one of his most important works of that era. It is owned by Steve Wynn and it was the initial working name for his $2.7 billion casino in Las Vegas.

The painting got a lot of notoriety when he agreed to sell it to the art collector and hedge-fund mogul, Steven Cohen for a record price of $139 million. When showing it to friends at his casino, he backed up close to it and with his gesticulations punched a hole in her left forearm with his elbow. The incident became known as the $40 million elbow. The sale was cancelled but the painting has been restored. Wynn still owns it.

It is one of the most coloristically lush of all Picasso's works. There is a range of rainbow colors that reflect his joy over his new relationship. The contrasted colors resemble early Fauvism. Then there is Marie-Therese's heart shaped face that is split in two by a phallus. The implication being that sex is on her mind even in her dreams. So the painting is about love or, perhaps more accurately, lust. It is considered one of the most erotic paintings of

the 20th century. Over and over again, particularly with Marie-Therese and later with Dora Maar, Picasso would use color, line and distortion to convey his emotional state.

By 1937, Picasso was involved with the fifth major female influence on his art, Dora Maar. Marie-Therese and their daughter Maya had been removed from Paris and sent to rural seclusion near Versailles. In *Marie-Therese Seated* (fig. 11-13) she is shown with her head gripped between the door handle and the wall. She sits in the imprisoning frame of the wooden chair. The vivid colors in "Le Reve" had become more subdued. Her hands and fingers are locked together with nothing to do.

Marie-Therese looks like a lonely woman who may be walled up in the country forever. Picasso once remarked to his biographer with no sign of guilt, "It must be painful for a girl to see in a painting she is on the way out."

Dora Maar was different from Marie-Therese. She was aggressive, intellectual and creative. He fell in love with the 29-year old when he was 55. In *Dora Maar au Chat* (fig. 11-14) she appears with distinctive features and long nails, a reflection of her rebellious personality. Dora is regally posed with an amusing black cat perched behind

11-15. *Guernica by Picasso, 1937, oil on canvas, Museo Reina Sofia, Madrid.*

her. The brilliant color from some of the Marie-Therese years reappears.

Dora was an accomplished photographer. One of her achievements is that she is linked to the development of Picasso's masterpiece *Guernica* (fig. 11-15) through her extensive photographs of him when he was creating the painting.

The small Basque town of Guernica was destroyed by German planes during the Spanish Civil War in 1937. The hamlet was pounded for hours. The result was that thousands died or were wounded, most of them women, children and older people. The bombing of the defenseless civilians was meant to demoralize Franco's enemy.

Guernica is a mural-sized canvas 11 x 25½ feet and one of Picasso's masterpieces. It is modern art's most powerful antiwar statement and may be the most terrifying statement on the horrors of war ever produced by an artist. Its starkness is symbolic of the epic battle between the helpless good and evil. *Guernica* is painted in black and white to represent the photos of the massacre in the newspapers. The details and their symbolism are incredible.

On the left side of the canvas, a wide-eyed bull stands over a mother grieving hysterically carrying her dead child. Her tongue is shaped like a dagger pointing at heaven. This is a symbol of the innocent, mortally wounded victims. In the center there is a horse pierced by a lance. Daggers that suggest screaming replace the tongues of the bull, a grieving woman and the horse. The bull and the horse are important in Spanish culture. The dying horse is emblematic of the suffering of all victims.

Under the horse is a dead, dismembered soldier. His hand on a severed arm still grasps a shattered sword from which a flower grows. The broken sword symbolizes the defeat of the people at the hand of the evil tormentors. On the open palm of the hand is a stigma. It is a symbol of martyrdom derived from Christ's stigmata.

On the right are three women. One falls screaming from a burning house,

11-16. *Weeping Woman* by Picasso, 1937, oil on canvas, Tate Gallery, London.

her clothes aflame. A second horror struck woman seems to float into the scene thrusting forth a lamp into the gloom to survey the calamity. It only serves to illuminate the carnage. A third awe-struck woman in mindless flight staggers ahead starring blankly at the blazing light bulb that looks like the bare bulb of a torturer's cell. But it also is in the shape of an all-seeing eye or, perhaps, it represents the sun. There can be many interpretations of its presence.

Picasso shows us the misery close up and where it had its terrible impact, in the shelter of the home. The figures can be interpreted to represent a peasant household. There are women, children and animals. *Guernica* laments their merciless destruction.

Rather than paint the war, Picasso chose to paint the cry of the war thus depicting, not only the carnage in Guernica but a universal image of suffering. You can almost feel the pain, distress and agony in the crying faces. Human grief had never before or perhaps since been depicted in such a stark manner.

It is not clear where the threat comes from. But that very anonymity of the source of the devastation makes the painting a protest against all wars. Picasso uses newspaper print in the painting to show how the world heard of the massacre. There is a story about how German soldiers often ransacked Picasso's studio during the occupation of Paris. One day they discovered a photo of *Guernica*. A soldier asked, "Did you do that?" Picasso replied, "No, you did."

From WWII to 1981, *Guernica* was housed in the MOMA in New York because Picasso refused to allow it to travel to Spain until public liberties were restored. In 1981, on the 100th anniversary of his birth and after the death of Franco, it finally goes to Spain.

Picasso's vivid condemnation of the Luftwaffe's bombing of *Guernica* during the Spanish Civil War and with the evils of war in general did not end with his monumental painting Guernica which was completed just weeks after the bombing. There were postscripts. Throughout the rest of 1937, he was seemingly obsessed with the subject.

Picasso painted and drew dozens of weeping women images. They represent an extension of the tortured figures in *Guernica*. It is as if the mourning continued without end.

11-17. *The Yellow Sweater* by Picasso, 1939, oil on canvas, Museum Mountain-Green, Berlin.

They cry and cry with their faces twisted beyond recognition. One has to wonder where they came from because Picasso never before portrayed faces so intense in their emotion. Even today, more than 75 years later, his weeping women portraits are unequaled in their expression of grief and anguish.

Weeping Woman (fig. 11-16) is just one of the numerous images of grief over Guernica that Picasso painted but it may well be the best and most elaborate one of the series. It is a study in just how much pain can be expressed in a human face. In effect, it becomes the universal face of pain over the effects of war.

Immediately you are drawn to the center of the face where the flesh seems to be peeling away from the corrosive action of the tears. They cut deep into the face revealing the hard white bone. The handkerchief she stuffs into her mouth looks like a piece of glass. The eyes are black openings. There is an intensity of expression in them as they seem to pop out of their sockets. It is a symbol of the deep pain. They stare in disbelief at the horrors they have witnessed. The painting is done in brilliant colors of red, blue, yellow and green. Normally one would not associate such colors with sorrow and grief. But here they create a disturbing tension.

The model for this painting and for the entire series was Dora Maar who was working as a professional photographer when Picasso met her in 1936. She was his mistress from 1936 to 1944. Often these unsettling emotional works are interpreted only as descriptions of Dora's fiery temperament and her volatile relationship with Picasso. After all, Picasso once willingly admitted:

> *"I couldn't make a portrait of her laughing. For me she's the weeping woman. For years I've painted her in tortured forms, not through sadism, and not with pleasure, either, just obeying a vision that forced itself on me. It was the deep reality, not the superficial one."*

But to read the works as only descriptions of Dora would be much too simplistic. They are far more complex in that they explore the linkages between the tragedy of the war, the artist and his model. They are por-

traits of each. In the case of Picasso, they represent a man tormented by the horrific images of the massacres taking place during the Spanish Civil War. As far as Dora is concerned, she was more than a model. As a committed leftist, she was Picasso's impassioned accomplice because of her outrage over Fascism. Dora willingly allowed her features to be so brutally distorted in the paintings because she was so deeply committed to conveying such powerful messages condemning the war. Thus, she allowed Picasso to turn her beauty into such harsh ugliness in an attempt to arouse others to respond to the anguish and despair of the situation.

Picasso was never a card carrying Surrealist but here he ventures into that artistic space. Every detail in the painting has been skillfully treated to convey a sense of emotional intensity that realism could never do. Thus the method of depiction goes far beyond realism.

11-19. *Woman Flower* by Picasso, 1946, oil on canvas, private collection.

11-18. Photo of Francoise Gilot with Picasso on the French Riveria.

By 1939, Picasso's relationship with Dora Maar was already on an inevitable downward path. In *The Yellow Sweater* (fig.11-17), instead of the fine hands and lacquered nails we saw in an earlier portrait, two paws emerge. Dora has been banished to the animal kingdom. This piece also reflects her personality. She is shown as a determined, not a tender person. Her face shows beauty and anguish. Her sweater looks like a protective coat of armor.

Picasso met his sixth love, Francoise Gilot in 1943 when he was 62 and she was a 22-year old emerging painter. In this early photo (fig. 11-18) taken on the beach near Antibes on the French Riviera where they spent a lot of time, he playfully shields her from the sun. When Picasso was in a mood like this it would be hard not to love him. But there were many other times when Picasso was not nearly as playful and loveable. Too many violent arguments and too many affairs ensued. Later, Francoise said she knew she was heading for a catastrophe but "it was a catastrophe I didn't want to avoid."

11-20. *Francoise, Claude and Paloma* by Picasso, 1954, oil on canvas, Musee Picasso, Paris.

When Picasso painted *Woman Flower* (fig. 11-19) he had just persuaded Francoise to leave her family and move in with him. This latest conquest inspired Picasso to paint a number of portraits. Picasso visited Matisse with Francoise in early 1946. Matisse responded by telling him how he would like to paint her portrait. Picasso reacted to what he apparently considered as a challenge from Matisse by painting the very decorative *Woman Flower*.

Because of her youth and energy Picasso told her, "I don't see you seated. You are not at all the passive type. I see you standing." In this portrait he sees her as a flowering reed. This becomes his signature portrait of Francoise. He told her, "You are like a growing plant. I've never felt compelled to paint anyone else this way."

Picasso had two children with her, Claude in 1947 and Paloma in 1949. With their births, Picasso's portraits become increasingly devoted to his children with Francoise. *Francoise, Claude and Paloma* (fig. 11-20) painted in 1954 is a demonstration of his more compassionate side and the variations in his temperament.

Few of his works show his family relationships so beautifully and lovingly as this one. It is an example of what could have been. But that was not to be the case. There are no paintings of any of his children past an early age. For example, portraits of his son Paulo disappear when he turns four. When their mothers disappear from his life, so do the children.

With *Bull's Head* (fig. 11-21), Picasso steps outside the boundary of what, at least until then, had been considered artistic endeavor. It was 1943 and this was probably the bleakest period of his life. The world was in flames and France was occupied by the Nazis. Then suddenly out of the blue comes this moment of wit and whimsy in the form of the assemblage *Bull's Head*.

Picasso turned an old bicycle seat and a rusty pair of handlebars into a bull's head. What pleased him was that the piece was reversible. He said, "Everybody who looks at it says, 'Well there's a bull,' until a cyclist comes along and says, 'Well there's a bicycle seat.'" The assemblage is truly a tribute to Picasso's power of imagination. It is so simple and childlike yet so sophisticated.

Given that Picasso was always acutely aware of what was occurring around him in the art world, it is hard not to imagine that his assemblage was a response to Duchamp's readymades and his *Bicycle Wheel* in 1913. Readymades are anti-art objects. They were found objects that were simply labeled as art. They were not a product of the artist's hand of skill. Essentially, they eliminated the role of the artist.

Duchamp's combination of the bicycle wheel and stool may seem the same as Picasso's *Bull's Head* but there is an important difference. Those pieces are joined together precisely because they have nothing in common. Together they suggest nothing beyond themselves: a wheel and a stool. But that is not the case with Picasso's piece. His individual elements, the seat and handlebars, become something else. We are never in doubt that we are looking at the image of a bull's head.

The sculpture *Baboon and Young* (fig.11-22) is still another example of Picasso's creative genius. As was the case with *Bull's Head* he again shows anything he touched could be turned into a work of art even his son's toy. In works like these Picasso is extending the principle of collage. He is introducing the revolutionary technique of assemblage providing sculptors with the option of not only molding or carving the pieces but also constructing the works out of found objects and materials.

The baboon's face is formed from two toy cars, one upright and the other turned upside down. Picasso had borrowed the cars from his four-year old son Claude. The whiskers come from a car's grill. Her tail was an automobile spring. The baboon's ears were made from cup handles. Her round belly was a large jug whose handles form the shape of her shoulders. Then the entire assemblage was cast in bronze.

Back to Francoise. She was a challenge for Picasso. For the first time it was a woman's independence not her dependence that bothered him. By 1950, they were drifting apart and their relationship ended in 1953. She was only 28 when they separated.

At the end, one thing had changed. Partly because of her independence, Picasso never depicts her in anguish like he had done with Dora. She remains impassive and independent to the end in her portraits. Perhaps that was because she was the only woman who actually chose to leave Picasso. When she told Picasso she was considering leaving him he laughed and said, "Nobody leaves a man like me."

Picasso was horrified that Francoise was too far gone to care when he was attracted to other women. He told her,

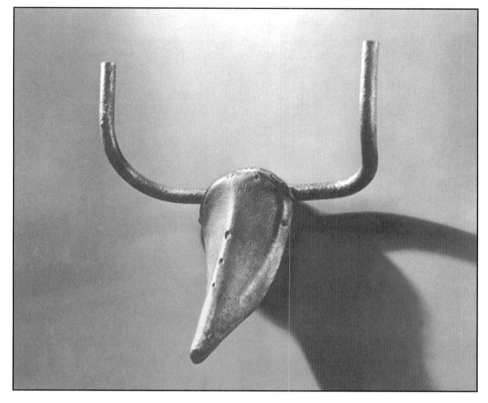

11-21. *Bull's Head* by Picasso, 1943, bronze, Musee Picasso, Paris.

11-22. *Baboon and Young* by Picasso, 1951, bronze, Museum of Modern Art, New York.

11-23. *Jacqueline With Flowers* by Picasso, 1954, oil on canvas, private collection.

"If you knew how Marie-Therese suffered when I began making portraits of Dora Maar but you are a monster of indifference."

All along Francoise was different. She was a strong-willed, self-confident woman who, despite her fascination with Picasso's personality and achievements, could never surrender her free will. She was the only woman to remove herself from his overpowering influence and create a life for herself as a successful artist. In 1970, she married Jonas Salk of polio vaccine fame. Their marriage lasted for 25 years until Salk died in 1995.

Picasso met the seventh and final female influence Jacqueline Roque in 1954 when she was 28. They married in 1961 when she was 35 and he was 80. The marriage was possible because Picasso's first wife Olga had died in 1955.

Jacqueline With Flowers (fig. 11-23) is an example of his "tender period." He painted more than 400 portraits of her, more than any of his other loves. This is a Matisse inspired portrait with flowers, decorative colors and designs. His paintings of her, on a whole, were probably less interesting than those of Fernande, Olga, Marie-Therese, Dora and Francoise. But that is because of the relative tranquility of their relationship.

What set Jacqueline apart from the previous women in Picasso's life was that they assumed his love for them would give them primacy in his life. But that was never possible. For Picasso, art was always given preeminence. Remember that quote from his mother, "My son lives only for himself. No woman could be safe and happy with him." Jacqueline never tried to force Picasso to choose between her and his art. She was completely committed to him.

Her gentile personality was in sharp contrast with her two predecessors, Dora and Francoise. That gentleness is reflected in this portrait. It summarizes the theme of the years with Jacqueline. The turbulence, violence, tears and anguish that characterized his previous relationships with women is missing. Because she was Picasso's last love, she was never debased in his art like her predecessors.

Picasso died on April 8, 1973 of a heart attack. As part of the tragedy surrounding his life, Jacqueline prevented his children Claude and Paloma by Francoise from attending his funeral. She said she was following Picasso's instructions. When Francoise published her tell-all best selling book *Life With Picasso* in 1965, he reacted by disinheriting their children.

Unfortunately, that is not the end of the story of Picasso's influence on women. There was one final tragic event to occur. Jacqueline's commitment to Picasso was so great that, after he died, she was unable to reconstruct a life for herself. She oversaw the opening of the Picasso Museum in Paris. She then organized a large exhibition of her collection in Madrid under the patronage of the Spanish royal family. After that, she felt she had no more reason to live. She committed suicide by shooting herself in the temple near Picasso's grave site.

IMAGES

11-1. *First Communion* by Picasso, 1895-1896, oil on canvas, Museo Picasso, Barcelona, Spain.

11-2. *Self-Portrait* by Picasso, 1901, oil on canvas, Musee Picasso, Paris.

11-3. *Woman Ironing* by Picasso, 1904, oil on canvas, Guggenheim Museum, New York.

11-4. *At the Lapin Agile* by Picasso, 1905, oil on canvas, Metropolitan Museum of Art, New York.

11-5. *Portrait of Gertrude Stein* by Picasso, 1906, oil on canvas, Metropolitan Museum of Art, New York.

11-6. *Les Demoiselles d'Avignon* by Picasso, 1907, oil on canvas, Museum of Modern Art, New York.

11-7. *Ma Jolie* by Picasso, 1912, oil on canvas, Museum of Modern Art, New York.

11-8. *Portrait of Olga in the Armchair* by Picasso, 1917, oil on canvas, Musee Picasso, Paris.

11-9. Photograph of Picasso and Olga 1919.

11-10. *Seated Bather* by Picasso, 1930, oil on canvas, Museum of Modern Art, New York.

11-11. *Bather With a Beach Ball* by Picasso, 1932, oil on canvas, Museum of Modern Art, New York.

11-12. *Le Reve or The Dream* by Picasso, 1932, oil on canvas, private collection.

11-13. *Marie-Therese Seated* by Picasso, 1937, oil on canvas, Musee Picasso, Paris.

11-14. *Dora Maar Au Chat* by Picasso, 1941, oil on canvas, private collection.

11-15. *Guernica* by Picasso, 1937, oil on canvas, Museo Reina Sofia, Madrid.

11-16. *Weeping Woman* by Picasso, 1937, oil on canvas, Tate Gallery, London.

11-17. *The Yellow Sweater* by Picasso, 1939, oil on canvas, Museum Mountain-Green, Berlin.

11-18. Photo of Francoise Gilot with Picasso on the French Riveria.

11-19. *Woman Flower* by Picasso, 1946, oil on canvas, private collection.

11-20. *Francoise, Claude and Paloma* by Picasso, 1954, oil on canvas, Musee Picasso, Paris.

11-21. *Bull's Head* by Picasso, 1943, bronze, Musee Picasso, Paris.

11-22. *Baboon and Young* by Picasso, 1951, bronze, Museum of Modern Art, New York.

11-23. *Jacqueline With Flowers* by Picasso, 1954, oil on canvas, private collection.

20TH CENTURY MODERNISM

This book is about art history and how it progresses. One description of the progression of art history was provided earlier but it is worth repeating. "The avant-garde artists are surrounded by the art of the day. They see it, want to challenge it, change it and create something new. That is how art history progresses."

This final chapter of the book surveys some of the artistic developments from the start to the middle of the 20th century. It is a period when modern art or modernism bursts into full bloom. But what is modernism? The term modernism is often associated with art where the spirit of experimentation results in works that are in sharp contrast with the artistic traditions of the past.

Modernism is characterized by tremendous artistic diversity. In the 20th century, innovation in the art world accelerated at a dizzying pace. Artistic movements or "isms" such as Fauvism, Cubism, Dadaism, Surrealism and Abstract Expressionism followed each other in quick succession. Some were short-lived but each, in their own way, had an impact on the movements that followed.

A detailed review of all modern movements is beyond the scope of this book. So this chapter will be limited to discussions of some of the highlights of a number of movements during roughly the first half of the 20th century. The first question to ask is when did modernism begin? The foundations for 20th century modernism were laid well before the start of the century. They can be traced back as far as 1863 when Manet painted what some have called the first modern works of art *Le Dejeuner sur l'Herbe* and *Olympia* (see figures 6-13 and 6-14).

After Manet and the Impressionists that followed him, fresh ideas about seeing art and presenting it began to pick-up momentum. It was the Post-Impressionists like Cezanne, Gauguin, Van Gogh and Seurat that set the stage for the development of modern art.

The baton of color passed from artists like Gauguin and Van Gogh to Matisse in the first decade of the 20th century. Matisse along with several other artists shocked the Paris art world with their multi-colored, highly expressive paintings of figures and landscapes. Their approach was so shocking to the critics that they were labeled as Fauves in France or "wild beasts."

Next it was Picasso and Braque that pushed art perspective even further away from the traditions of the past with their Cubist paintings inspired, in part, by Cezanne's use of

solid geometric shapes like cones, cubes and spheres. Cezanne's works already represented a sharp departure from the artistic tendencies of the day. The Cubist inventions resulted in radically new approaches to perspective.

Although Matisse and Picasso were the initiators of the completely new artistic beginnings in the 20th century, other approaches quickly followed building on one another and resulting in a wave of new movements. After Fauvism and Cubism came the anti-art movement of Dada which led to Surrealism. After WWII, the center of art moved from France to the U.S. and New York in particular where Abstract Expressionism emerged as the principal art style in the 1950s.

Each of the artistic styles mentioned can legitimately be characterized as a "movement." That is because they all had the support of a number of active participants and because they were all adopted internationally.

MATISSE
Color Above All Else

Henri Matisse (1869-1954) was one of the most influential artists of the 20th century. Along with Picasso, he fundamentally altered the course of modern art. His career can be divided into several periods where his artistic approach changed stylistically. But one thing always remained a constant with Matisse. Decorative color was the crucial element of his paintings.

By 1905, Matisse had established himself as the leader of the first modern movement of the 20th century, Fauvism. Another important member was Andre Derain. They were the artists of pure color. Fauvism is the first modern art movement where color rules supreme even more so than Impressionism.

The art of this group was derived from the color of painters like Van Gogh and the primitivism of Gauguin's works in Tahiti. There was an emphasis on strong raw color, roughness of execution and flat surfaces. The Fauves became the most controversial artists in Paris.

Matisse and other artists who would become known as Fauves exhibited their works in 1905 at the Salon d'Automne. One critic's response was "Donatello au milieu des fauves." The translation is "Donatello among the wild beasts." He was referring to the placement of the paintings in the same room with the Renaissance sculptor Donatello.

The result of the critique was that the name Fauves or wild beasts was born.

The movement grew out of a loosely knit group of painters who, at least initially, shared common interests which is usually the case for most movements. They emphasized the use of intense color as a vehicle for describing the subject matter and for conveying the artist's emotions. They applied pure, unmixed colors and sometimes increased the intensity by applying the paint in thick dabs or smearing it on the canvas. But Fauvism never developed into a coherent movement in the manner of Impressionism or, later, Surrealism.

Because the Fauves were preoccupied with color and the emotion it could convey, they were not particularly concerned with the nature of their subject matter. This was different from the Impressionists who focused on painting scenes from modern French life. The Fauves wanted to paint whatever they saw and depict it in the most emotional and spontaneous manner. For example, that meant a face could be any combination of clashing colors. A sky could be red or a tree orange. Color was the single most important subject of the painting.

Fauvism was about spontaneity, impulsive brushwork and the liberal application of saturated and explosive colors. They were advancing the tradition of the colorist painters that dated back to Delacroix and continued with the Impressionists and Post-Impressionists like Gauguin and Van Gogh. The Fauves painted what their artistic energy generated. The result was the deliberate creation of disharmonies of clashing colors that reflected their emotional reaction to the subject rather than its realistic appearance.

Matisse's career as a Fauve was short-lived. For that matter, Fauvism as a movement died out by late in the first decade of the 20th century. Nevertheless, Matisse's fame and success continued to grow throughout his career. His chief competitor was Picasso. Both artists had long and varied careers and by WWI many considered them to be the two greatest living artists. They dominated the 20th century.

In different ways, both artists distanced themselves from the detailed, highly finished painting styles taught in French art schools. But the only thing they really had in common was that their favorite subject matters were women and still-lifes. Other than that, there was a mega difference between the styles of the two artists. When Cubism entered the scene, it brought with it an analytical and cerebral quality to modern art. Fauvism and Matisse, on the other hand, aimed at achieving sensual pleasure through the use of color. He transmitted his message with a strong direct impact.

Both the Fauves and the Cubists were crucial in the development of abstract painting. The Cubists liberated form. Their work suggests an illusion of four-dimensional space in which the subject matter is seen simultaneously from several perspectives. This was different from the traditional three-dimensional view of the world. The Fauves, in turn, departed from the traditional use of color. Although neither the Fauves nor the Cubists were interested in depicting abstraction, their striking departure in the way they viewed form and color was important in the development of abstract painting in the 20th century.

Matisse painted what he saw while Picasso tended to work from his imagination. Matisse emphasized color and serenity while Picasso embraced form and anguish aggressively. In his masterpiece *Les Demoiselles d'Avignon* (see fig. 11-6) Picasso painted five monstrous primeval female nudes. He contorted his figures in ways that Matisse would never do. Matisse favored painting decorative, sensuous nudes.

Picasso violently rejected the past in many of his paintings. But Matisse's work refutes the notion that the great discoveries in modernism are made by such an extreme departure from the past. Nowhere during his 60 plus year career do you find a trace of alienation and conflict in Matisse's work. He gravitated to the beautiful. To him, art should be a respite from the pressures of life. In his world, art should be "soothing, calming… like a good armchair that provides relaxation from physical fatigue." But it was not always like that with the critics, particularly when, in 1905, he showed the shocking *The Woman with the Hat* (fig. 12-1).

The reaction of the critics to avant-garde art in that day was to be expected. The model, who was Matisse's wife Amelie, was described as a "victim." The critics thought there was a disregard to the details one would expect in traditional portraiture. Of course, what they missed is that there is nothing traditional in the piece because it was done in a completely uninhibited and spontaneous manner.

The controversy was sparked not because of the subject. After all, a portrait of a woman in a hat was conventional. It was because of the way the subject was depicted with crude drawing, sketchy brushwork and clashing colors that create a harsh effect at least in terms of what was expected at that time.

On critic went so far as to proclaim, "A pot of paint has been flung in the face of the public." The use of what was considered disagreeable color on the familiar form of a salon portrait was considered scandalous. For example, they criticized the strokes of color that made up her nose, mouth and jaw or the dab of purple underneath her chin. But the script for this type of vehement criticism had been written 30 years before with the Impressionists as the target.

This piece, with its celebration of color, became one of the most iconic works of Fauvism. There are the haphazard brushstrokes. Her face is blotched with arbitrary combinations of vivid colors. There is mauve, yellow and stripes of blue and green. Although the painting was signaled out for condemnation, it was bought by the great collectors Gertrude and Leo Stein and hung in their Paris apartment where they hosted informal gatherings of many leading literary and artistic figures.

12-1. The Woman with the Hat by Matisse, 1905, oil on canvas, San Francisco Museum of Modern Art, San Francisco

The woodland nymphs are engaged in a celebration of life. The juxtaposed complimentary colors of red/green, blue/orange and yellow/violet generate a rare amount of energy in the painting. With the use of the complimentary colors and the flowing curves of the trees, parts of the painting take you to the verge of abstract expressionism that would not become a fixture in the art scene for another 40 years.

In 1908 Matisse wrote, "I dream of art devoid of troubling or depressing subject matter." *In The Joy of Life* he achieves that dream. It is a colorful, rhythmic presentation of the joy of love, music, dance and communing with nature. It is about serenity and it represents a complete relief from the stress of modern life.

Today it is considered a masterpiece of color. But then the critics and public were shocked by how he used color. Rather than subtly blending them together, the colors seemed to crash into one another contributing to what was considered to be a tasteless, gaudy scene. Using vivid yellows and fiery reds to depict a pastoral landscape seems incomprehensible.

Also disorienting to the critics was that a scene of supposed pastoral harmony could have such sudden shifts in scale. There is a tiny flute player immediately above the two large figures embracing in the foreground on the right. The ring of dancers in the center of the painting is out of scale with the large reclining females immediately in front of them. But this was the 20th century and such apparent inconsistencies were about to become inconsequential in the era of modernism.

Like Picasso's *Les Demoiselles* this is a painting that initiates 20th century modernism. It challenges everything that came before. There are many stylistic references here. Some of the lines recall prehistoric cave drawings. As already noted, the sweeping curves in the upper part of the painting and the complimentary colors take you to the verge of Abstract Expressionism that was still decades away.

Matisse followed in 1906 with *Le Bonheur de Vivre* or *The Joy of Life* (fig. 12-2). Although still in his Fauvist period, there is a change to greater serenity here. The brushwork is softer and laid down more broadly. There is less nervous excitement in the piece.

He creates a mythical earthly paradise occupied by nymphs in an idyllic field dressed in lively color with sensual outlines. Two women are reclining in the sunlight while two others are on the edge of the forest. One crouches to pick flowers while the other weaves them into her hair. A couple embrace while a group engages in a round-dance in the distance. There is an individual playing a double flute in the foreground.

12-2. *The Joy of Life* by Matisse, 1906, oil on canvas, Barnes Foundation, Philadelphia.

12-3. *The Dance II* by Matisse, 1910, oil on canvas, The Hermitage Museum, St. Petersburg, Russia.

Maybe it is only part of the made-up legend about Matisse and Picasso but it has been speculated that *The Joy of Life* was important to the development of Picasso's *Les Demoiselles*. Picasso painted *Les Demoiselles* in the spirit of competition with Matisse. After all, their intense rivalry through much of the 20th century resulted in some of the most important art of the era.

What we do know is that Picasso saw *The Joy of Life* when it hung in Leo and Gertrude Stein's apartment for all to see after they bought it in 1906. It was there when the two artists came face to face with each other for the first time. That meeting resulted in one of the most fruitful rivalries in art history.

With his creation of *Les Demoiselles*, Picasso seems to be determined to outdo Matisse. In 1907, he deconstructs *The Joy* in almost every way. *The Joy* is curvilinear, exuberant and colorful. *Les Demoiselles* is angular, harsh and monochromatic. *The Joy* is innocent. It is a celebration of life in a country setting. Picasso depicts the harsh realities of an urban brothel.

Notice the pose of the nude figure to the far left in *The Joy* with her arms raised behind her head. It is almost identical to the stance of the figure at the center of *Les Demoiselles* (see fig. 11-6). Did Picasso copy it? He knew that the critics attacked Matisse for having gone too far with his painting. It was as if Picasso was saying with his creation of *Les Demoiselles*, Matisse you have not gone far enough. I am going to take art to the next level of creativity.

The Joy of Life is part of the collection at the Barnes Foundation in Philadelphia where there are 59 Matisse's. It is one of the largest collections of his works in the world. But for years the Barnes never permitted color reproductions of its works and the pieces have never been allowed to travel to other museum shows. For those reasons it is probably one of the least familiar modern masterpieces. But its familiarity is likely to grow with the opening of the new Barnes in downtown Philadelphia and the placement of *The Joy of Life* in its own gallery area on the second floor where it stands alone as a monument to modernism.

Matisse was always fascinated with the subject of the dance. Notice the group of nude dancers in the central background of the painting. You will see that repeated with *The Dance II* which is discussed next.

There is simplicity in *The Dance II* (fig. 12-3). Yet there is also boundless energy. There are few more convincing images of physical ecstasy in art. The piece extends the dance theme of *The Joy* painted four years earlier. In that piece there are six naked figures dancing. In The *Dance II* the number is reduced to five. But that simplification is countered by the strident color.

The Dance II is the second of a two painting series commissioned by the Russian art collector Sergi Shchukin. There is also a study made for the painting. It is in the MOMA in New York. The painting is a simplistic design of five dancing figures. But the subject matter becomes the raw and daring color scheme that captures the viewer's attention like nothing else in that era.

There are five glowing bright red figures clutching each other's hand to form a circle. They have red hair and are depicted in wild dancing poses. The grass below is leaf green, the complimentary color to red. That combination heightens the intensity

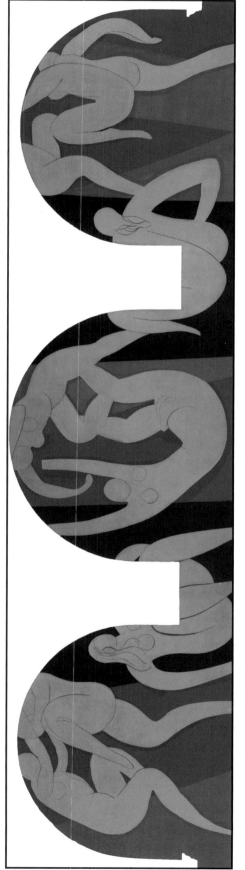

12-4. *The Dance* by Matisse, 1932-1933, oil on canvas, Barnes Foundation, Philadelphia.

of the colors and adds even more energy to the composition. The sky is navy blue. The goal of Matisse's art was always to portray the joy of living. One gets the sense in this piece that the figures are accomplishing that in their pleasurable pursuit of dance.

There is a flattened perspective. The figures are all the same size rather than the ones further away being smaller as would occur normally with perspective that provides depth (i.e. foreshortening). But this approach heightens the in-your-face aspect of the coloring. Notice the line between the green and the blue is curved, thus echoing the circle of the figures.

Twenty-two years later, Matisse would create the colossal *Dance* mural (fig. 12-4) for Dr. Albert Barnes. It hangs above the main gallery at the Barnes Foundation. The scene is marked by turbulence as tumblers leap and prance across three canvases. Rhythm dominates the composition. There is the absence of a single focal point. Although the piece was created 80 years ago, because of the

modern dance element, it does not even approach looking dated.

There is a contrast between the curved pairs of leaping and diving figures that dominate the canvases and the perpendicular panels of pink, blue and black. The curved bodies of the figures reflect the rounded lines of the lunettes above them. The two sets of reclining figures under the pendentives (i.e. the downward thrusting architectural elements) link the three canvases together. Their forms echo those of the reclining women in the foreground of the *Joy of Life* which is placed in a special viewing space directly across from *The Dance* so it is easy to compare the two works from the balcony that overlooks the main gallery.

Rather than working on site, the usual approach for such a large piece, Matisse painted the canvases in his studio in Nice. Eventually, he traveled to The Barnes to oversee their installation. But before that, there was one major glitch. About one year into the project it was discovered that Matisse had the wrong measurements. A new

12-5. *Chapel of the Rosary* by Matisse, 1947-1951, Vence, France.

version was started in 1932 and completed in 1933. The earlier painting hangs at the Musee d'Art moderrne de la Ville de Paris.

In developing this piece, Matisse used color cutouts and pinned them to the canvases. When he achieved the effect he wanted, the cutouts could be lifted and the images could be painted on the canvases below. The colors of pale blue and gray are less intense than you would normally associate with Matisse. The gray is designed to echo the gray sandstone exterior of the original Barnes building while the blue reflects the sky that can be seen through the large windows below. Matisse decided on the dance theme because that was at the center of *The Joy of Life* that Barnes had owned since 1922.

As evidenced by the project at the Barnes, the decline of the Fauvist movement early in the century did nothing to affect the rising importance of Matisse. In 1917, he traveled to Nice in the south of France to experience the color and light of that area. Eventually, he settled there permanently. His oriental odalisque paintings with lavish decorative patterns characterized the 1920s. In the 1930s there was a bold simplification of his work as evidenced by *The Dance* mural at the Barnes.

As his health deteriorated and he could no longer stand at the easel, he became permanently wheelchair-bound. But this did not deter his enthusiasm or his endless creativity. He focused on creating stylized cutouts from gouache-stained paper. As already noted, he first began to experiment with them early in the 1930s while executing the mural *The Dance* at the Barnes Foundation. Matisse called it "painting with scissors" and he thought of it as creating colorful paper sculpture. From 1940 on, cutouts became his favorite medium of artistic expression. An excellent example is *The Thousand and One Nights* crafted in 1950.

The crowning achievement of his career and a final testament to his creative genius was his design for the Chapel of the Rosary (fig. 12-5) in Vence just north of Nice. He created all the wall decorations including the Stations of the Cross, the stained glass windows, the altar and even the vestments and altar cloths. It was a four-year project that stretched from 1947 to 1951 that resulted from his close relationship with the Dominican nun Sister Jacques-Marie. She had helped to nurse him back to health from serious surgery. Matisse was 81 when the project was completed.

There are three sets of semi-abstract stained-glass windows with intense yellow for the sun, green with cactus forms for the vegetation in the area and vivid blue for the Mediterranean Sea, the Riviera sky and to represent the Madonna because that was her color since Renaissance times. On a sunny day the colors from the windows dance across the white marble floor and the tiled walls.

The altar is warm brown to resemble the color of the bread at the communion. Behind the altar is the image of St. Dominic, founder of the Order of Dominicans and the practice of the Rosary. This is the origin of the name, Chapel of the Rosary.

When the project was finished, Matisse said, "Despite all of its imperfections, I consider it to be my masterpiece." Indeed it was. It is a must see experience if you are in the area of Nice. As you exit the chapel there is a photo of Matisse with Sister Jacques-Marie. Below it there is a quote from Matisse that defines his entire career in seven words, "Color, color, color. Color above all else."

DERAIN
Intense Raw Color To Convey Feeling

Andre Derain's (1880-1954) career, when looking over its entire span, is hard to categorize. Early on, along with Matisse, he was an important leader of the Fauve style. But after 1908, he abandoned Fauvism and bounced from one style to another. Unfortunately, he came to believe that Fauvism was too remote from reality and put excessive emphasis on the artist's own feelings. He never again created the type of bold works displayed here and that is a shame.

Later, Derain temporarily came under the influence of Cezanne which led him to use quieter colors. He dabbled in Cubist-influenced works. Eventually, the spontaneity and impulsiveness that characterized his earlier works disappeared. He concentrated on painting nudes, still-lifes and portraits in a more conservative style. He created a great variety of sets and costumes for the Ballet Russe. Given all of these changes he went through it is difficult for the critics to evaluate him.

Most of Derain's paintings during his early years were landscapes, seascapes and cityscapes. They have the typical Fauvist characteristics of raw color that he often squeezed onto the canvas directly from the tube. There would be choppy brushstrokes, frenzied composition and a lack of concern for the reality of the scene. Derain once said, "I used color as a means of expressing my emotion and not as a transcription of nature."

On Matisse's invitation, Derain joined him to paint landscapes in the Mediterranean fishing port of Collioure in the south of France in the summer of 1905. It was there that he painted *Mountains of Collioure* (fig. 12-6). This piece has all the characteristics of Derain's work outlined above. It was one of the first major Fauvist works. There are short almost frenzied looking strokes of pure color that are reminiscent of Van Gogh. The curvilinear planes of flat color are inspired by Gauguin and the Art Nouveau decorative style.

Derain called this type of coloring his "sticks of dynamite." He enjoyed squeezing tubes of bright color onto the canvas particularly pink, blue and violet. Obviously he was not recording what he actually saw in the landscape. He created what he said were "deliberate disharmonies"

12-6. *Mountains at Collioure* by Derain, 1905, oil on canvas, National Gallery of Art, Washington, D.C.

12-7. *Boats in the Port of Collioure* by Derain, 1905, oil on canvas, private collection.

with broken brushstrokes that emphasize the spontaneous nature of the composition.

The robust use of complimentary colors adds energy to the piece. There are green leaves next to red tree trunks and red/orange mountainsides against blue slopes. It is the same approach that Matisse used with color in *The Joy of Life* (see fig. 12-2). The mountains are shown as flat areas of bright color and the sky is painted in jade and turquoise. There are strokes of pink and mauve throughout the painting. All in all, the piece is alive with color. It reflects what Matisse once said, "Fauve art isn't everything but it is the foundation of everything."

Distinguishing between right and wrong is one way to describe Fauve art. Although the subject matter in Fauve paintings is usually traditional (i.e. a portrait or a landscape) the colors are not traditional. They are unusual as is the fragmented way they are applied. To the average viewer, the form looks right but the color looks wrong.

In traditional art, both form and color look right or representational. The artist starts with form and that, in turn, determines color. But the Fauves like Matisse and Derain liberated color so that it no longer is determined by form. The color becomes unnatural or non-representational. It is not used to convey likeness. Rather, it is used to convey sensation. For the Fauves it is not a matter of whether color is right or wrong because color reflects only their own subjective vision driven by their emotions at the time.

That is the case with *Boats in the Port of Collioure* (fig. 12-7). The color jumps out at you. It is one of Derain's most vibrant works. The scene is clearly recognizable but the color is blatantly extreme. The beach in the foreground is saturated red. The mountains in the distance are bright pink. The sky has swirls of yellow with dots or specks of green. The boats, sailors and fisherman are outlined with strokes of blue and sometimes red. This allows each one to stand out even more sharply from its surroundings.

The Impressionistic brushstrokes have become sketchier and even broken. The dots and dabs of color of Seurat's Pointalism have been thickened and made coarse almost to the point of ridicule of that artistic style. All of these techniques appear to be a fundamental declaration against the idea that the number one goal of a painter is to represent a scene naturally.

Derain painted the images not as they are supposed to look but as they felt to him. Everyone knows that a sandy beach is not red. But perhaps on that summer day under the bright sun the beach felt scorching hot under the artist's bare feet. The sky is shown in rainbow colors instead of blue because it may have seemed to have that radiance to Derain on that particular day. Or, perhaps those are the colors he thought it should be. In Boats in the Port of Collioure he departed far from the literal truth to convey his own perceptions and feelings about the landscape before him.

DADA
Anti-Everything

Like Fauvism, Dadaism was a short-lived movement that lasted from roughly 1915 to 1923. A group of artists, writers and intellectuals, largely of French and German nationality, took refuge in neutral Switzerland where they could protest the brutality of the war in Europe. Their protests were based on the belief that conditions in society had gotten so bad that destruction of traditional values and beliefs was desirable for their own sake independent of any constructive efforts to change the situation. Dada's purpose was to ridicule the meaninglessness of the modern world.

Dada had only one rule, never follow the rules. Its philosophy was deliberately negative. It was anti just about everything: anti-establishment, anti-technological progress, anti-religion, anti-existing moral values and anti-social in that it criticized society that it thought had sponsored the barbaric violence of WWI.

It is hard to classify Dada as an artistic movement because many of its participants were not artists and its so-called art was not art. Then why is it discussed in this book? The reason is primarily because it laid the foundation for other art movements such as Surrealism, Pop-Art, Conceptual art and installations. One of the main influences on Dada was Expressionism. Cubism also had an impact because it was so different and it released a revolutionary spirit into the art world.

The name Dada, probably deliberately, was selected because it is a nonsense word. It means yes-yes in Russian, there-there in German and hobbyhorse in French. Some felt it was just baby talk. It became a catch-word that made no sense, as did Dada the movement.

After seeing what men were capable of doing to each other, the Dadaists thought that nothing mankind had achieved was worthwhile. With society going in the wrong direction, the Dadaists wanted no part of its traditions including artistic traditions. They would create non-art since art, and everything else for that matter, had no meaning. So they created art that was anti-art. Whatever art stood for their creations represented the opposite. For example, if art was to have some sort of message, Dada strove to have no meaning. If art is appealing to the senses, Dada offends.

One interesting twist on this movement is that, although Dadaism was based on serious underlying principles such as the horrors of war, its protest art became whimsical and sometimes downright silly. The irony of Dada is that the art, which supposedly meant nothing and was against everything, had such an important influence on other movements. Its biggest impact was on Surrealism.

When Dada spread to the U.S., it became an international movement. It centered in New York at Alfred Stieglitz's 291 Gallery. Two of the leaders were Marcel Duchamp and Man Ray. New York Dada lacked the total

12-8. *Nude Descending a Staircase, No. 2* by Duchamp, 1912, oil on canvas, Philadelphia useum of Art.

There is nothing here that resembles an actual human body. There are lines that suggest successive positions that create a sense of motion. But the elements of a nude in motion occur only in the mind of the viewer. Duchamp tries to create a figure that is in a state of perpetual motion. This is very different from the effects that Braque and Picasso created in Analytic Cubism where figures were held tightly in place.

Duchamp shows the descending nude in a series of some twenty different static positions to convey movement. He even goes so far as to adopt the somber palette of early Cubist works. The movement seems to rotate counter-clockwise from the upper left to the lower right of the canvas. At the edge of the painting, the steps are shown in darker colors.

The piece made its first appearance at the Parisian Salon des Independents in 1912. But the Cubists rejected the painting on the tongue-in-cheek grounds that, "A nude never descents the stairs – a nude reclines." The jury felt that Duchamp was poking fun at Cubist art. They especially objected to the title. Duchamp had painted it along the bottom of the piece like a caption. That reinforced their impression of the artist's comic intent.

The work was then exhibited at the 1913 Armory show in New York where it created a huge stir. Many critics thought the painting was utterly unintelligible. Nevertheless, Duchamp was delighted with the widespread notoriety the painting received. It encouraged him to move to New York two years later.

Whatever Duchamp's intent, *Nude Descending the Staircase, No. 2* was a seminal work for him in establishing his reputation for witty ridicule of traditional approaches to art. He would build on it with his first readymade *Bicycle Wheel* in 1913 where he proposed that an object could become a work of art simply because the artist designated it as such. In his Fountain in 1917 he tested the limits of public taste and once again the boundaries of what might be called art.

Duchamp continually criticized the work of his fellow artists as designed only to please the eye. His intent he said was, "to put art back in the service of the mind." Perhaps the painter Willem de Kooning was right when he described Duchamp as a one-man movement. But in this case, he was a movement against the art of the day.

disillusionment of European Dada. Instead, it was driven by humor and tended to be more whimsical.

In 1912 **Marcel Duchamp** (1887-1968) painted the Cubist inspired work for depicting motion, *Nude Descending a Staircase, No. 2* (fig. 12-8) showing a human figure in motion. It uses the Cubist ideas related to deconstructing forms. As such, it counteracts Cubism's greatest weakness in that those paintings were static. Here, rather than portraying the subject from multiple views at one moment, Duchamp portrays it at multiple moments.

After arriving from France, Duchamp was at the center of the radical anti-art activities in the U.S. The philosophy of absolute artistic freedom allowed Duchamp to "create" readymade sculptures. He exhibited the *Bicycle Wheel* which was an ordinary bicycle wheel mounted on a wooden stool and the *Bottle Rack*, a bottle drying rack signed by Duchamp. The idea of these readymades was to challenge the very notion of art and press the public to consider how they felt about the definition of art by showing them how far the definition could be stretched.

Later, Duchamp made a parody of the *Mona Lisa* by adding a mustache and goatee to a cheap reproduction of the painting. That was not done as an attack on the *Mona Lisa*. Rather it expressed the Dadaist scorn of the past.

Duchamp performed his most notable outrage by proudly trying to display his "sculpture" entitled *Fountain* (fig. 12-9). It was actually a porcelain urinal without plumbing turned 90 degrees. He dated it 1917 and added a fake signature R. Mutt. He submitted his readymade to a major Parisian exhibit. It was promptly rejected. Nevertheless, the *Fountain* has been almost canonized by some as representative of the essence of the Dada movement.

His readymade demonstrated a profound contempt for the bourgeois concept of art.

Duchamp's philosophy of the readymade was succinctly expressed in an editorial in a journal that he helped found.

> *"Whether Mr. Mutt with his own hands made the fountain or not has no importance. He CHOSE it. He took an ordinary article of life, placed it so that its useful significance disappeared under its new life and point of view – created a new thought for that object."*

As outrageous as the Dada view seems to be that art could be made from anything and found objects could be represented as art, this point of view was used in some form by the Pop-artists that came along later. It also essentially represents the view of the modern Conceptual artists that the idea behind the work of art is more important than the creative effort itself. In fact, Duchamp has been called the father of Conceptual art.

Dada was a liberating movement that inspired rebellion. But it was born in protest against the war. So its thrust became more absurd and extreme after WWI ended. In short, Dada lost its relevance. Having pushed its negativity to the limit, new ideas were needed to inspire artists and Dada floundered at the start of the 1920s and ceased to exist. The immediate successor was Surrealism. In fact, some of Dada's important supporters like Max Ernst and Man Ray became leading Surrealists.

SURREALISM
Tapping Into the Subconscious

Surrealism sprung out of the Dada movement after WWI. Initially, it was centered in Paris but it spread throughout the world. The Dadaists protested against everything because they believed the bourgeois society and the failure of reason were responsible for the war in Europe. The Surrealists wanted to free people from false reasoning and its effects on their behavior.

Whereas Dada was a negative movement that deliberately defied reason, Surrealism was not based on negation. It did not rail against artistic traditions as did Dada which wanted no part of any traditions. It aimed at

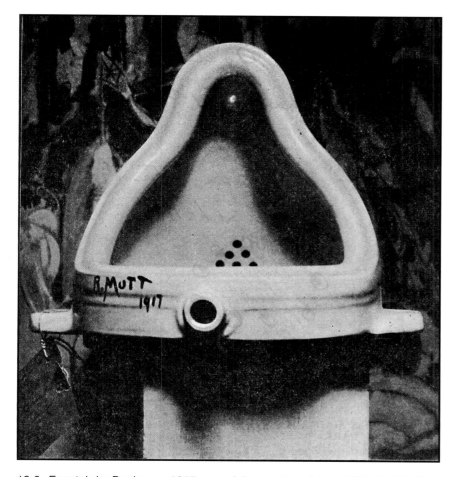

12-9. *Fountain* by Duchamp, 1917, porcelain plumbing fixture, Philadelphia Museum of Art, Philadelphia.

liberating the mind and focused on positive expression. If the Surrealist movement was anti, it was in its reaction to the type of reason that resulted in the horrors of WWI.

One of Surrealism's founding fathers was Andre Breton who had been a participant in the Paris Dada movement. But when the war ended, he became frustrated by Dada's emphasis on nonsense activities. He wanted to form something that was more orderly and constructive out of Dada's desire to free human behavior from the influences of the past.

Surrealism had its basis in psychology, notably the works of Sigmund Freud and Carl Jung. Breton was trained in psychiatry and served in a hospital where he was exposed to Freud's psychoanalytic methods. He and a group of other artists and writers began experimental work with automatic writing, where they would write spontaneously allowing the mind to release subconscious thoughts and images. They believed that following this course was a better approach to generating social change than Dada's attack on almost everything.

In 1924, Breton published his "Manifesto of Surrealism" after he broke with the Dada group in 1922. He saw the human psyche as a battleground where the rational aspects of the conscious mind are in conflict with the irrational spontaneous urges that occur in the subconscious. His premise was that one can achieve happiness if they can liberate the unconscious mind and thereby help to discover a larger reality or a "surreality" that lies beyond the traditional narrow notion of what is real. That is, to attempt to reach beyond the limits of what is considered real. Breton believed that the only way to improve the world was to expose the unconscious demon that lives within each one of us and to battle the demon so it can never escape your mind.

Freud's work with dream analysis, free association and tapping into the subconscious formed the basis for the Surrealist's attempts to develop methods to liberate the imagination. By so doing, they aimed to improve all aspects of human experiences.

The result of all this as far as artistic works go was fantastic imagery, unexpected juxtapositions and startling overall effects. Often, the imagery that resulted had little or no resemblance to actual people, objects or places seen in the real world.

Given that Freud's and Jung's theories were so important to the Surrealists, many within the community split into two groups. The Jungians favored the view that we should accept unconscious images without judgment. Another group preferred Freudian analysis. They sought to analyze the meaning behind the images created.

By way of comparing artistic approaches, Salvador Dali appeared to embrace the Freudian approach of studying and analyzing the subconscious images he produced. Picasso, on the other hand, who was not committed to Surrealism but produced a number of paintings that could be characterized as Surrealistic, did not believe in analyzing his images. Rather, he focused on spontaneously painting them.

Marc Chagall (1887-1985) has been called the quintessential Jewish artist and the greatest Jewish artist of the 20th century. They are certainly deserving accolades but he was much more than both of those. He lived a long and exceptionally productive life dying at age 98 in France. He lived and painted in Russia, France and the U.S. But Chagall is almost impossible to classify because he worked in so many artistic mediums and large parts of his output fall within the style of a wide range of art movements.

For the purpose of this book, I have classified him with the Surrealists because the painting discussed here has Surrealistic qualities as do many other of his works. But that is too narrow a categorization for Chagall. He flirted with several modern styles throughout his career including Fauvism, Cubism, Symbolism and Surrealism. His mediums included painting in oil, gouache and watercolor, prints, murals, drawing, etching, book illustration, stained glass, tapestries, ceramics, stage sets and costume design. He undertook large-scale projects such as painting part of the ceiling of the Paris opera.

Most of all Chagall was committed to figurative and narrative art that had a lyrical poetic style to it. Throughout his long career he remained emphatically a Jewish artist whose work often reverted back to dreamy memories of life in his native town of Vitebsk in Russia.

He was also a committed colorist. In fact Picasso remarked during the 1950s, "When Matisse dies Chagall will be the only painter left who understands what color really is." Whatever style Chagall pursued you always got the sense that he was constantly in search of the meaning of life in his art. He admitted as much when he commented on his search for his life's work:

> *"My hands are too soft. I had to find some special occupation, some kind of work that would not force me to turn away from the sky and the stars, that would allow me to discover the meaning of life."*

What is unique about Chagall is that he never completely aligned himself with any single movement. His artistic style is entirely his own, built upon a rich mixture of different modern art disciplines all woven in a dreamlike fashion into Jewish folklore. Perhaps if you want to compare him to a single artist he was much like Picasso in being a modern artist who mastered so many styles and artistic techniques.

Whatever stage of Chagall's career you focus on, it is always his color that captures your attention. They are not naturalistic colors. They do not imitate nature but they are always vibrant. In terms of presenting subjects, one thing that is constant in his art is a sense of happiness. In that regard, musicians are present during all stages of his work.

12-10. *The Green Violinist* by Chagall, 1923-1924, oil on canvas, Guggenheim Museum, New York.

The magic of Chagall's art is in the dream-like fantasies that float from the images of his childhood memories of his home town of Vitebsk. Chagall stated in his autobiography, "The soil that nourished the roots of my art was Vitebsk."

In the 1920s, Chagall was claimed by the Surrealists and, indeed, he borrowed from them in the almost supernatural nature of his work. All of what has been said here is a good lead into *The Green Violinist* (fig. 12-10) because the painting represents so many of the influences on Chagall's art including the fact that as a youth he learned the violin. There is a huge amount of symbolism in the painting but then we should expect that from Chagall.

After moving to Paris in 1922 he seemed to experience a period of profound homesickness. He painted *The Green Violinist* the next year. We can see his longing for home in that the violinist plays while standing above a home and synagogue. The piece is about change and tradition. Imagine the changes that had taken place in Vitebsk over a period of just decades, not centuries. When Chagall was born, the town was under Tsarist rule. Then the Communist revolution brought huge political change. Next the Nazis took over the area for three years and 150,000 Jews died. After WWII, the Soviet Union was in control and ruled until 1991. Now the city is part of the nation of Belarus. The painting asks the question how one can move forward into the future and still maintain the essential nature of who they are and where they came from even amidst profound change?

In the Jewish villages like Vitebsk, a fiddler would come out and play at birthdays, weddings and deaths. These are all transforming events that cause people to reflect on the past, present and future. It was part of the tradition of these villages. Because of tradition, everyone knows who they are and what God expects them to do. In effect, the fiddler is a modern Moses who commands the people to remember the past even though they are experiencing incredible changes in the present and they are questioning what the future holds. In Deuteronomy 6:10-12 Moses said:

Chagall does not attempt to provide a representation of reality. Rather, he creates an atmosphere of fantasy. But the objects, places and people he presents are from his own life. In trying to explain his paintings he said, "I don't understand them at all. They are not literature. They are only pictorial arrangements of images that obsess me."

"When the Lord your God brings you into the land he swore to your fathers, to Abraham, Isaac and Jacob to give you a land with large, flourish-

ing cities you did not build, houses filled with all kinds of good things you did not provide, wells you did not dig, and vineyards and olive groves you did not plant, then when you eat and are satisfied, be careful that you do not forget the Lord, who brought you out of Egypt, out of the land of slavery."

The fiddler reminds us of our tradition. He is playing even to people leaving the village as symbolized by the horse and cart at the top right of the painting and those that are finding freedom elsewhere as suggested by the man floating at the top. The dog is there to remind us of fidelity to the past. The ladder is at once both bound by the ground it stands on and free with one end up in the air. The tree that it leans against is barren but there is a bird on a branch. Chagall used birds in other paintings as a symbol of freedom. The barren tree tells us that change does not always deliver what we want. Trees do not always bloom, friends leave and the promise of the future is not always realized.

The exuberant fiddler is part of a joyful tradition. He is bigger than life and stands on the bedrock institutions of the village home and synagogue. He is joyful even in the midst of all the changes that are going on around him. He is green because it is the color that is the symbol of life like grass, leaves and plants.

The rich color of the violinist is in striking contrast to the stark background of the painting. The fiddler is dressed in vibrant secondary colors of purple, orange and green. He is set against a background of gray, brown and black. He remains exuberant, free from all the drabness around him.

The rich purple jacket is particularly striking. It speaks of the passion and emotion of the fiddler. He is excited about the future even while he remembers the past. But not all fiddlers show joy in what they try to celebrate about tradition and change. Thus, there is the small man on the left that is shown as of lesser importance and lesser quality of character. He is using his fiddle as a club instead as an instrument.

The Green Violinist was the inspiration for the hit Broadway show and movie *Fiddler on the Roof*. In both productions Vitebsk has been replaced by Anatevka as the home town.

Among the opening lines Tevye the milkman says:

"A fiddler on the roof. Sounds crazy, no? In our little village of Anatevka you might say everyone of us is a fiddler on a roof trying to scratch out a pleasant simple tune without breaking his neck. It isn't easy. You might ask, why do we stay up here if it is so dangerous? We stay because Anatevka is our home. And how do we keep our balance? That I can tell you in one word. Tradition!"

Giorgio de Chirico (1888-1978) is considered a very influential forerunner to Surrealism which began to flourish in the 1920s. De Chirico is best known for his paintings he produced in the period from roughly 1909 to 1919 which were memorable for their haunting and often brooding moods. He had a powerful impact on the Surrealist paintings of Salvador Dali and Max Ernst. Because de Chirico opts for a frank, realistic manner in which he depicts objects with simplicity his style is closest to Rene Magritte's in the mystery it conjures up despite the straightforward nature of the depiction. In fact, when Magritte first saw one of his paintings he was so deeply affected that he said, "De Chirico is the first painter to have thought of making a painting speak about something other than the painting itself."

The course of de Chirico's career is one of the most curious in art history. He started out as a fabricator of images that spoke of frustration, tension and loneliness. At the time he had no equal in this approach and the Surrealists adored his early work. In his metaphysical works reality and a dream world mingle. He paints fantastic architecture, empty squares and faceless statutes. Strange objects are placed in mysterious ways.

His cityscapes have a strange artificiality. They are far from the conventional paintings of cities with normal everyday activities. They are more like haunted streets that we might encounter in a dream. Sometimes there is a collection of objects that take on the form of city-like still-lifes. They can suggest sorrow, even disorientation.

Then he changed and moved toward classical representations. He imagined himself as a heir to Titian or Raphael. His style began to embrace Renaissance and Baroque art. This move drew criticism from his old Surrealist supporters and the critics. De Chirico, in turn, became antagonistic toward modern art.

De Chirico's reputation became soiled by his later habit of creating new versions of his metaphysical paintings and backdating them as if they had been created back in the 1910s. Why did he do it? Because his work of that period had attracted more interest and that bothered de Chirico because he was convinced he had gotten better as he got older. But the critics and collectors did not agree. He knew that early de Chirico's fetched many times the price of late ones so, as a matter of revenge, he decided why not let them buy fake ones. After all, the worst insult you can give to an artist is to tell him how good he used to be. By producing back dated self-forgeries he could profit from his earlier success and, at the same time, gain some retribution for the preference for his early work.

Although his career spanned 70 years his early metaphysical works are his best. In that period he was happy to be accepted and courted by the Surrealists. But as they turned against him he turned against them. At one point he referred to them as "the leaders of modernistic imbecility."

When you look at *Ariadne* (fig. 12-11) the scene seems to be beyond the real world. But that is exactly what de Chirico is trying to convey to us. It has dream like qualities. There is a sense of loneliness and melancholy. There are elements of everyday life like the train and ship in the far distance. There is a smokestack and archways that cast a long shadow. But then there are other elements that seem out of place. Why is there a lonely reclining statue in an otherwise deserted square that casts a mysterious sweeping shadow? It all comes off as a mysterious unresolved puzzle. But that is a common aspect of de Chirico's metaphysical paintings.

The figure of Ariadne had great symbolic meaning to de Chirico partly because it was tied to the classical works that he was exposed to during his childhood. He was born in Greece. He would have been very familiar with the story of the princess of Greek mythology.

According to the legend, Ariadne saved the life of Theseus by giving him a length of silk thread which he used to navigate the labyrinth in which the man-eating Minotaur lived. Ariadne fell in love with Theseus and he promised to marry her during their journey to Athens. But instead be betrayed her, abandoning her on the deserted island of Naxos. She was later rescued by the god Dionysus.

The story appealed to classical artists and Ariadne was often shown slumbering on empty shores. She became a symbol of exile and loss. In this painting she is portrayed as a statue based on the marble piece in the Vatican.

The melancholy story of Ariadne and the image of the abandoned princess sleeping were particularly attractive to de Chirico during his early years in Paris because it was a period of extreme loneliness for him. So much so that he completed a series of seven paintings on the subject from 1912 to 1913.

The reclining statue of Ariadne is in a sunlit area of the square surrounded by shadows. De Chirico uses the shadows and dark colors around the statue to heighten the sense of loneliness and depression. The ship in the far distance on the right is related to the myth of Ariadne. In the story she is waiting for a ship to come and save her. Dionysus comes by ship and rescues her and they go on to be married.

12-11. *Ariadne* by de Chirico, 1913, oil and graphite on canvas, Metropolitan Museum of Art, New York.

The train in the distance could serve several purposes. It could be a modern version of the ship that is coming to save her. More likely, it is a tribute to de Chirico's father who was a railroad engineer. Trains appear in many of his works. The smoke stack tower highlights the fact that the classical figure of Ariadne has been brought into the industrial modern world. The fact that she is placed away from everything else in the painting shows once again the loneliness that both Ariadne and de Chirico feel.

Salvador Dali (1904-89) became the best known and the most flamboyant Surrealist artist. He joined the movement in the late 1920s after reading Freud's writings on the significance of subconscious imagery. Using bright colors he was able to execute his bizarre images in an extremely precise manner. If Surrealism was, in part, about stripping ordinary objects of their normal significance in order to create compelling images that were beyond ordinary, Dali was a master at it.

The Surrealistic dilemma was how to change the world without politically conquering it. Dali believed he had found the solution in his "paranoiac-critical method."

He felt his own vision could be improved in such a way as to color the world to his liking. Then it would be unnecessary to change the world directly. Specifically, it meant Dali had trained himself to develop hallucinatory power to look at one object and "see" another. His premise was that if an irrational person misreads ordinary appearances, then a sane person should be able to cultivate the same ability and, in the process, liberate himself from the constraints of conventional thought.

Dali's paintings depict a dream world in which common objects, painted in meticulous realistic style are juxtaposed and strikingly altered in appearance in bizarre ways. His most celebrated and recognized work, *The Persistence of Memory* (fig. 12-12) is an example.

This piece qualifies as what Dali called his "hand painted dream photographs." Typical of Dali, there are bright colors applied to small objects set off against large areas of dull color. There are three soft melting pocket watches. The orange clock at the bottom left of the painting is covered in ants. The amoeba-like creature in the center has one closed eye with eyelashes suggesting it is in a dream state. In the background, there is a bleak landscape.

12-12. *The Persistence of Memory* by Dali, 1931, oil on canvas, Museum of Modern Art, New York.

One interpretation of the fish-like monster that looks like it has been washed ashore and is draped across the painting's center is that it resembles Dali's face in profile. In that regard, the abstract form becomes something of a self-portrait. It was not unusual for Dali to represent himself in some form in his works. It was the year before this piece was painted that Dali developed his "paranoiac-critical method" where he cultivated self-induced hallucinations to create art.

The Persistence of Memory is appropriately named because it is supremely memorable. But what does it mean? One cannot look to Dali for explanations because he often provided none or gave incorrect interpretations of his works in order to confuse the critics and art lovers. In the process, he encouraged multiple interpretations of the same work. For example, Dali said the soft watches were inspired by camembert cheese melting in the sun. Perhaps so but maybe not!

One interpretation of the many perspectives on this painting is that Dali may have been referring to a dream he had himself and the watches symbolize the irrelevance of time during sleep as one experiences a dream. That is, when one is asleep, time does not persist, only memories do. The ants attacking the clock could signify the anxiety often associated with the passage of time. The cliffs in the distance represent the coast of Catalonia, Dali's home. Or, alternatively, none of these explanations may apply.

The painting seems full of psychological undertones. Or, perhaps Dali is simply trying to fool us and there is no meaning to the images. One thing is certain; the painting encourages analysis and explanation while baffling viewers. The MOMA wrote that the watches are, "irrational, fantastic, paradoxical, disquieting, baffling, alarming, hypnotic, nonsensical and mad – but to the surrealist these adjectives are the highest praise." That says it all.

Dali doesn't go over the edge in his paintings. He successfully walks a fine line. He doesn't try to shock or disgust the viewer. Rather, he arouses your curiosity or he may bewilder the viewer.

Max Ernst (1891-1976) studied abnormal psychology at Bonn University from 1910 to 1914. Consequently, like so many of the Surrealists he had the background to easily fit in with the movement. Although he never received formal artistic training he took a deep interest in painting early on. The horrors of WWI had a lasting impact on his art. He referred to his time in the army in this way: "On the first day of August 1914 Max Ernst died. He was resurrected on the eleventh of November 1918." That was the date he was demobilized.

His overwhelming imagination produced a body of work that was subject to constant experimentation and often included fantastic creatures. Breton described him as "the most magnificently tormented mind that could possibly exist."

Ernst became a part of the Dada movement in Germany in 1919. In 1922 he settled in Paris and was among the founders of Surrealism. His romantic life was colorful to say the least. He was married four times. His third wife was Peggy Guggenheim, the American art dealer and collector.

In 1925, as part of his experimentation process to enhance his imagination, he introduced his new technique called frottage. He placed sheets of paper on floorboards, tiles, bricks or any other material he could find. Then he rubbed them with graphite to produce strange, bizarre effects. This approach fitted in with the Surrealist's experiments with automatic writing to spontaneously release subconscious thoughts and images. The resulting imprints from his frottage efforts stimulated his imagination. The images were then applied by Ernst to his paintings.

He also created another technique called grattage in which paint is scraped from a canvas laid over a textured surface to reveal the imprints of the objects placed beneath. He would then create representational forms by over painting.

Forest and Dove (fig. 12-13) is an example of the grattage technique. It is a forest scene with bizarre, nearly abstract trees. In the midst of the forest (lower center) is a child-like drawing of a dove. The forest is near Ernst's childhood home. According to the Tate Gallery in London where the painting is hung, the forest inspired a sense of "enchantment and terror" in the artist as a youth. The painting is heavily textured with a three-dimensional appearance resulting from the grattage technique.

It is easy to see from this painting why Ernst had an influence on the Abstract Expressionism movement, particularly Jackson Pollock. But it is more than just the appearance of paintings like this that influenced the group. It was the manifestation of his and, for that matter, other Surrealist's state of mind that impacted them. Creativity came from the subconscious in an immediate fashion.

Rene Magritte (1898-1967) approached Surrealism differently. His approach and because he was a precursor to Pop Art are what make him important. His artistic staple was the presentation of bizarre images in a realistic manner. That, of course, was also the style of Ernst and Dali. But often Magritte chose ordinary things to depict in his works – people, shoes, landscapes, trees, etc. He would then present them in very unusual ways and often in a witty manner. For example, a number of his paintings showed a dignified well dressed man in a bowler hat but with his face obscured in strange ways. He once praised "that pictorial experience that puts the real world on trial." His body of work bears out that he followed such an approach.

Magritte's art can be described as representational Surrealism. There was usually something in it that the viewer could identify with. He never adhered to the "automatic" style of other Surrealists like Ernst and Dali that tried to release impulses from their subconscious in order to create art. He turned his back on the world of dreams. He did not purposely seek to be obscure. Rather, he relied on shock and surprise to liberate our conventional visions of things. To Magritte, the world as it exists had more than an adequate source of subjects to reveal in his art. He did not draw on hallucinations or dreams as a source for his paintings.

Nevertheless, with Magritte the viewer must relinquish their usual expectations of art, particularly Surrealistic art. There is a great deal of ambiguity in his themes. He pointed out that no matter how closely an artist comes to depicting something realistically, they can never capture the item itself. For example, he painted a realistic image of a pipe and wrote below it "This is not a pipe." That seems like a contradiction but it isn't. It is only an image of a pipe. When Magritte was asked about this he pointed out that it was not a pipe and added that if you think it is then just try to fill it with tobacco.

Magritte's use of simple, everyday images makes him a forerunner to Pop Art. The content of his art had a great appeal to the public and was widely used in commercial advertising in the 1960s and 1970s. The Pop artists, in turn, used the commercial products themselves as a focus of their art.

The Son of Man (fig. 12-14) was painted as a self-portrait. The man's face is largely hidden by a green apple. However, his eyes can barely be seen peeking over the edge of the apple.

Surrealist paintings typically offer the viewer a confused reality. Magritte demonstrates this in *The Son of Man*. His aim was to encourage others to consider more closely the reality that surrounds them and not to simply accept things as they seem to be. He explained this when he talked about the painting.

> *"At least it hides his face partly . . . Everything we see hides another thing, we always want to see what is hidden by what we see. There is an interest in that which is hidden and which the visible does not show us. This interest can take the form of a quite intense feeling, a sort of conflict, one might say, between the visible that is hidden and the visible that is present."*

The painting was very prominent in the 1999 remake of the film *The Thomas Crown Affair* starring Pierce Bronsan and Rene Russo. Numerous bowler-hatted men carrying briefcases filled with copies of *The Son of Man* flood the museum where an art heist is taking place.

12-13. *Forest and Dove* by Ernst, 1927, oil on canvas, Tate Gallery, London.

ABSTRACT EXPRESSIONISM
All About Emotion in Painting Style

Abstraction comes in many forms. In its basic form, it represents a departure from accurately depicting the subject matter. The departure can be partial or complete. It can be in the use of color or in form. Total abstraction occurs when there is no trace of anything recognizable in the work of art. For example, one cannot refer to a work of art that has some figurative content as totally abstract regardless of how deliberately altered it has been relative to reality. But figurative or representational art can be partially abstract.

The work of the Post-Impressionist artists like Gauguin, Seurat, Van Gogh and Cezanne led, in differing ways, to the development of modern art and to the advent of abstraction. Many of the works of the modern art movements incorporated partial abstraction.

Fauvism, as practiced by Matisse, Derain and Dufy deliberately altered color relative to reality. Cubists altered the forms in which objects and people are presented. The Surrealists provided even more ways to alter reality and, in the process, tapped into the subconscious through methods

12-14. The Son of Man by Magritte, 1964, oil on canvas, private collection.

The most important predecessor was Surrealism with its ideas about dream imagery and subconscious creativity. Spontaneity, or at least the appearance of spontaneity, was considered an important part of Abstract Expressionist art. The movement emphasized freedom of emotional expression, technique and execution in implementation. But even though the final effect may appear to be achieved by accident or chance, often the paintings were carefully planned. This was particularly the case for those that were large in scale.

Although the artists had quite different styles, Abstract Expressionism can be broadly divided into two groups: Action Painting and Color Field. The term "Action Painting" was first used by art critic Harold Rosenberg in 1952 to describe the works of painters like Jackson Pollock, Franz Kline and Willem de Kooning. These were artists that would drip, spatter, throw or pour paint onto the canvas using various tools like sticks, brushes or palette knives.

To some observers, the canvas was seen as an arena and the process of painting became an epic struggle between the artist, the canvas and the material. According to Harold Rosenberg, "What was to go on the canvas was not a picture but an event." Nevertheless, the artistic impression provided by each painter was quite different. For example, Pollock's "action paintings" expressed his energy and had an incredibly busy feel to them. De Kooning's figure paintings in his "Woman" series appeared violent and grotesque.

Not all the artists associated with Abstract Expressionism produced purely abstract work. They would sometimes delve into somewhat more realistic portrayals of objects and people. One was Willem de Kooning. While Pollock's work was pure abstraction, de Kooning alternated between abstract work and powerful figurative images.

Nevertheless, the Abstract Expressionist paintings share certain characteristics. These included the use of large canvases and an "all over" approach in which the entire canvas is treated with equal importance. This is in contrast with other artistic approaches where the painter starts at the center of the canvas and that area continues to hold more interest than the edges.

like automatism. By the 1940s, American artists painting in diverse styles began to unite into a unified style that became known as Abstract Expressionism. It held prominence until the 1960s and the emergence of Pop Art.

This art form embraced the Surrealist's idea that the instantaneous human act was the source of creativity. That idea was heavily influenced by European artists like Andre Breton and Max Ernst who fled Europe with the rise of fascism and the outbreak of WWII and came to New York. The new approach was brought about by a loose affiliation of artists in Greenwich Village. It became known as the New York School and it was the first American art movement that achieved worldwide influence. It established New York as the center of the art world replacing Paris.

Color Field painters like Mark Rothko, Helen Frankenthaler, Barnett Newman and Robert Motherwell took more of an intellectual route. Their focus was on large areas of pure color. These artists eliminated all recognizable imagery. They were seeking to achieve intense, emotional effects from color. There is no attempt at representation of anything but color. The subject is pure color.

The political climate and the McCarthy era after WWII, while negative for many artists, actually helped to spur the development of the Abstract Expressionist movement. It was a time of suspicions about the political motives of artists and there were even efforts aimed at censorship. But if the subject matter of a painting was totally abstract then it could be seen as apolitical and, therefore, safe. It became a safe strategy for artists to pursue this style. Even if there was a political message in the abstract art, it could be concealed for insiders only.

By the 1960s, **Jackson Pollock** (1912-1956) was recognized as the most important figure in the most important American art movement in the 20th century, Abstract Expressionism. With its emphasis on spontaneous, subconscious creation, Pollock's painting technique had its roots in Surrealism. He can be considered the quintessential Abstract Expressionist. Abstract because most of his art showed no traces of visible reality and Expressionist because his paintings appeared to have been created through uncontrolled painterly gestures.

For Pollock, the journey toward making a work of art became almost as important as the finished product. He redefined the way of producing art. In 1947 he created his first "drip" painting giving up the easel and adopting his drip technique of walking around and through the canvas. This spontaneous method of work inspired the terms "action painting" and "gesturalism." By laying his canvases on the floor where they could be attacked from all sides and even walking on them pouring paint or flinging it, he challenged the tradition of using an easel and a brush. He used brushes, sticks and pieces of cloth to apply the paint. Sometimes he would create a thickness to the painted surface by adding foreign matter like sand, broken glass or even cigarette butts.

He moved away from using only the hand or wrist, as was the case with almost all artists, since he used his entire body to paint. He also moved away from traditional artist materials. Pollock preferred the liquidity of commercial enamel house paint to the sticky texture of traditional oils. This allowed him to weave more intricate webs of lines using the drip technique. In the process he blasted art making beyond its previous boundaries and provided a liberating signal to future artists regarding the way they could create new works of art.

Pollock put it this way when he wrote:

"My painting does not come from the easel. I prefer to tack the unstretched canvas to the hard wall or the floor. I need the resistance of a hard surface. On the floor I am more at ease. I feel nearer, more part of the painting, since this way I can walk around it, work from the four sides and literally be in the painting . . . When I am in my painting, I'm not aware of what I'm doing . . . there is pure harmony."

Pollock took line and freed it from its function of representing objects or figures. The result was huge areas covered with dynamic linear patterns that virtually engulf the vision of the viewer. The quality of Jackson's line is unique. His draftsmanship is amazing. At times his lines seem to accelerate across the canvas. He had the ability to quicken a line by thinning it. The color may change as it twists across the surface generating an intricate, colorful web.

His drip painting technique also added a new element to Surrealistic thought. Surrealism had previously sought to produce images by tapping into the subconscious. But the drip technique allowed Pollock to spontaneously release all of his physical energies and "let go" in creating a work of art. As he circled the canvas and let the paint run off, it flowed from the motion of his body.

No pre-painting sketches were made. In fact, the design of his paintings had no relation to the shape and size of the canvases. The final work was sometimes trimmed to fit the image created. Nor were they totally spontaneous. Pollock would often retouch the drip with a brush. But the final result was so intricate that it is very difficult to make a forgery. He did what imitators could not do. That speaks to the authenticity of him as an artist.

Pollock's most famous paintings were made during the "drip period" between 1947 and 1950. It was when he was at the height of his powers. He poured, dripped, flicked, spattered and spread the pigment with his fingers. Eventually, he abandoned titles in his works and began numbering them. He did this to discourage viewers from looking for a subject matter in the painting. His wife Lee Krasner explained, "Numbers are neutral. They make people look at the picture for what it is — pure painting."

An excellent example of Pollock's art and technique is *No. 5, 1948* (fig. 12-15). It is one of the most defiantly abstract works ever made. It is a densely tangled composition with an intricate web of lines in reds, yellows, blues and grays. It is a large piece measuring about 4 x 8 feet painted on fiberboard. Although the work has been described as somewhat resembling a dense bird's nest, there is a lyrical harmony to the lines.

It was reported in 2006 that *No. 5, 1948* was sold to a private collector for the astronomical amount of $140 million. If that is correct, it would make it the highest amount ever paid for a painting at that time, exceeding the $135 million paid earlier in that year for Gustav Klimt's *Adele Bloch-Bauer I*.

Most critics believe that Pollock's technique was avant-garde and brilliant but there are still a few that see his paintings as childish and lacking talent. Among the public there are doubters. Sometimes when going to an exhibition of Pollock's works you will here comments like, "Anyone can do that even my little sister. It's just paint thrown on the canvas." Do not be deceived. These are works by a near genius. He purposely tried to stay away from creating any image that could be recognized. Rather than painting a picture of something, he tried to capture his movements along with his feelings and mood.

There is a structure to his work that may go unnoticed. Unlike most paintings, there is no central point of focus and this is done on purpose. Also, there is no hierarchy of the parts of the composition. Every bit of the surface is equally important. Yet, you get the sense of a physical choreography in applying the paint that shows up in the rhythms of the graceful, arcing, swirling, buoyant lines of color. Yet, with all the spontaneity Pollock remained in control. He said, "I can control the flow of paint: there is no accident." Whatever your particular viewpoint, one thing is sure, when discussing the Abstract Expressionist movement the first name to come to mind is Jackson Pollock and there is a reason why that is the case.

Willem de Kooning (1904-1997) was part of the group of painters that came to be known as the New York School and can be considered Jackson Pollock's chief rival for supremacy within the group. His career went through a number of phases of abstraction but the female figure often was an integral part of his painting.

De Kooning's best known works came during the 1950s when the Abstract Expressionist movement reached international scope and its highest level of influence. Until the start of the 1950s there had only been somewhat obscure references to figures in his works. But in 1950 he began to explore the subject of women exclusively and in 1953 he unveiled his "Woman" series of paintings. These images were shocking and charged with the type of explosive energy one might expect from Abstract Expressionist works.

Jackson Pollock is easy to categorize as a drip painter, but de Kooning is more difficult to brand. He painted rich abstractions and figurative pieces of large, coarse dames that are hard to classify. Also, he was not the impulsive "action painter" that described Pollock. Although his paintings may look spontaneous, he could be very deliberate. For de Kooning, each painting could be something to experiment with and to rework.

Typically, he would begin with a sketch. Then he would add paint and draw on top of that. Next he would scrape the surface down and do more drawing and painting, building up the images. This process was at the opposite end of the painting spectrum from Pollock.

He began his first series of "Woman" paintings in 1950. It took him nearly two years to complete the first painting *Woman I* (fig. 12-16). According to his wife, the

12-15. *No. 5, 1948* by Pollock, 1948, oil on fiberboard, private collection.

artist Elaine de Kooning, he scraped it and repainted it at least a dozen times. The startling ferocity in this painting and, in the whole series for that matter, brought him a great deal of notoriety.

De Kooning was not always completely happy with the results of his artistic efforts. Part of his dissatisfaction with this and other works in the series was because, although inspired by attractive women in advertisements that he saw, what emerged in his paintings was a shockingly brutal depiction of the female. The critics questioned his feeling about women and de Kooning defended himself by

12-16. *Woman I* by de Kooning, 1950-52, oil on canvas, Museum of Modern Art, New York.

viewer with a glare and a grin. All in all, the wide eyed toothy snarl makes her look even more menacing than Picasso's monsters in *Les Demoiselles d'Avignon* (see fig. 11-6). Even the paint is applied in an aggressive manner. It is slashed, scraped and dragged across the canvas. But this could be considered the ultimate Abstract Expressionist style.

The "Woman" paintings II through VI are all variants on the theme of *Woman I*. Their appeal to collectors has been enormous. *Woman III* sold for $137.5 million in 2006. Thus, at that time, the two costliest paintings of all time were by Abstract Expressionist artists.

After completing the "Woman" series in 1953, de Kooning abandoned the female figure in favor of purer abstraction. But, evidently, he was not totally comfortable with that style. In the 1960s he returned to the female figure and painted a second "Woman" series.

Mark Rothko (1903-1970) offered an alternative to the "action painting" of other Abstract Expressionists. He moved through several artistic styles before he reached his recurring theme in the 1950s of soft, rectangular forms floating on a field of color. Early in his career, Rothko concentrated on figurative work that had a heavy Surrealistic content. But over time and influenced by his association with artist Clyfford Still and his abstract fields of color, his work became increasingly abstract shifting away from Surrealism.

In 1946, he began to create what came to be known as his "multiform" paintings. These were blocks of color that were completely devoid of reference to the symbols, figures or landscapes that dominated his earlier works. He described them as providing a "breath of life" lacking in the figurative painting of the time. Rothko never abandoned this form of painting.

With the total absence of figures, the drama that comes from Rothko's paintings as his style matures is found in the contrast of colors that radiate against one another. It is color alone that provides the energy and emotion in his paintings.

saying, "I like beautiful women, in the flesh and even the models in the magazines. Women irritate me sometimes. I painted that irritation in the 'Woman' series." Nevertheless, accusations of misogyny continued.

De Kooning once observed that "flesh was the reason why oil paint was invented." It is obvious from *Woman I* he was not thinking about the flawless flesh painted by the Renaissance masters like Titian. Instead, the flesh in this painting looks ugly and thick. The colors look chaotic with streaks of red and yellow jabbing out at us. Everything about this painting looks frenzied. The energy level in it appears as if it has reached a crescendo.

The figure is executed in a tortured manner with a face that suggests the presence of a demon. It is as if she mocks the

Early on, the colors are bright and vibrant, particularly reds and yellows. Later, he would emphasize darker colors.

Rothko painted large-scale canvases. His aim was to make the viewer feel "enveloped." He said, "The reason I paint them . . . is precisely because I want to be very intimate and human." He recommended that the viewers stand as little as 18 inches from the canvas so that they might experience a sense of intimacy and awe. He said, "I paint big to be intimate."

For Rothko, it was more than just about painting colorful canvases. Color was an instrument. It was all about generating an emotional experience through the use of color. Regarding his color field paintings he said, "If you are only moved by color relationships, you are missing the point. I am interested in expressing the big emotions – tragedy, ecstasy, doom."

During his lifetime, Rothko was never satisfied with the degree of attention his art received. His reputation as a tortured artist was assured when, in 1970, in poor health and separated from his wife he slashed his arms and bled to death. Over the years his art gained enormous value in the auction market. In 2005, his *Homage to Matisse* (fig. 12-18) sold at auction for $22.4 million. But that was only the beginning. In 2007, his color field painting *White Center* sold for a record for the artist of $72.8 million.

Rothko painted *Homage to Matisse* in 1954, the year Matisse died. The uneven sized patches of color have soft, blurry edges. As is the case with all of Rothko's mature works, the canvas is displayed without a confining frame.

Rothko honored Matisse with the painting because he credited him with heightening his appreciation of color. In 1949, he became fascinated with Matisse's *Red Studio* (fig. 12-17). Matisse presents his own studio saturated with a single color that floods the canvas: bold red. It is a color that can be violent or scary. But not here!

12-17. *Red Studio* by Matisse, 1911, oil on canvas, Museum of Modern Art, New York.

This painting presents a small retrospective of Matisse's recent works, sculpture and ceramics displayed like they are floating against a sea of red. The walls and floor of the studio are red. Even the table at the lower left with objects on it is submerged in red. Rothko said, "When you look at the painting you become color, you become totally saturated with it, as if it were music."

Matisse was using color to get an intense emotional response. He certainly got that from Rothko who said he was moved to tears when viewing the painting in the Museum of Modern Art in New York. Rothko said he spent hours studying the painting and credited it with being the determining factor that allowed him to break through into his mature style of color field works with floating rectangles of luminous color. No wonder it brought him to tears because it is, in effect, the basis for color works and the first true color field painting that Rothko would become famous for years later.

Rothko rarely titled his works once he painted in his mature style. But *Homage to Matisse* was an exception for him. Like most artists in the New York School he wanted to be seen as an independent painter and an originator of his own style. Therefore, it would be unusual for him to allow his work to be seen, in any way, as being tied to the French art tradition. But this was different because Matisse gave Rothko the courage to once and for all break away from representational forms and symbols and concentrate on painting rectangles and blocks of pure color.

AMERICAN REALISM
Artists Portraying the World Around Them As They See It

In its most basic form, Realism is an approach to art in which subjects are portrayed in as straightforward manner as possible without idealizing them in any way. This approach has been around for much of art history. It has come in many styles and a countless number of subject matters. As far back as at the end of the 16th century, the artistic innovator Caravaggio introduced a new style of Realism (see his work in chapter 5). He came upon the scene when Realism was not in fashion and figures were painted in a manner that satisfied a taste for gracefulness. But by introducing strong contrasts of light and dark and avoiding prettiness in color, Caravaggio added never before seen drama to realistic subject matters.

Fast forward to the 19th century French art world and you can identify an increasing number of artists that felt paintings should faithfully record real life. The work produced by these independent minded painters of figures and landscapes can be labeled as Realism although the more common term was naturalism.

The Realistic art movement emerged in France in the aftermath of the Revolution of 1848 that overturned the monarchy of Louis-Phillippe as the people fought for democratic reforms. The Realists contributed to this by depict-

12-18. *Homage to Matisse* by Rothko, 1954, oil on canvas, private collection.

ing modern subjects drawn from the working class. They based their paintings on a direct observation of what was going on in the modern world around them with no attempt at idealization. Often they concentrated on recording in gritty detail the daily existence of humble people.

Gustave Courbet painted poor and ordinary people in *The Stone Breakers* (see fig. 6-8) and *A Burial at Ornans* (see fig. 6-9). Jean-Francois Millet painted a scene of extreme rural poverty in *The Gleaners* (see fig. 6-12).

In the second half of the 19th century Realism traveled to the U.S. Winslow Homer painted rural scenes like *Snap the Whip* which showed boys playing outside a one-room schoolhouse in the Adirondack Mountains. It provides an image of the innocence of childhood in rural America. Later he would paint more dramatic themes showing heroism such as *The Life Line*.

Another noted Realist of the era was Thomas Eakins who specialized in painting straight forward scenes of everyday life. His most famous work was *The Gross Clinic* which shows Dr. Gross performing an operation in vivid detail with young medical students observing.

At the start of the 20th century the American Realist tradition firmly established itself with the emergence of the Ashcan school. This was a group of artists that sought to capture the feel of life at the turn-of-the century in New York City. It was not a formal organization but a group of urban Realists who focused on capturing the more dismal aspects of city existence in New York's poorer neighborhoods. The group was referred to in many ways such as the New York Realists and the far from complimentary "apostles of ugliness."

In effect, their art was everything that American Impressionism was not. Their works were dark and portrayed subjects like tenements, drunks and prostitutes. Rather than focusing on beauty they realistically captured the harsher moments of life. Among the prominent names associated with this style were Robert Henri who took on the role as the unofficial leader of the group. Others in the group included William Glackens, George Luks, John Sloan and Everett Shinn. A number of the painters had a common background in that they were once illustrators for local newspapers in the Philadelphia area.

In this section I will discuss three American Realists who came along later, each with their own unique style. One painted rural America, another idealized America and a third urban America. All three had some exposure to commercial illustration. Perhaps that is one reason why their accomplishments have not always received widespread critical acclaim. But this writer has always been fascinated by their work and feels they need to be included in a discussion of 20th century modernism.

Andrew Wyeth (1917-2009) embraced Realism as a style and landscapes and people as his subjects. When using the term landscapes it is appropriate to include both indoor and outdoor scenes when discussing Wyeth. His landscapes have a calming effect. When an individual appears there is usually a union. The person is not just placed in the landscape but seems to become fused within it. The figures rarely appear to be part of a story or dramatic event.

The people and land that he painted came from nearby, family or friends in his hometown of Chadds Ford, Pennsylvania and his summer home in Cushing, Maine. His artistic training came from his father N.C. Wyeth, a distinguished illustrator famed for his vivid magazine illus-

trations for classics like "Treasure Island," "Robin Hood," "The Last of the Mohicans" and "Robinson Crusoe." They sold in the millions.

Andrew's skills as a draughtsman came from the training he received from his demanding father. But he resisted the goal his father set for him of becoming an illustrator. It turned out that Andrew's artistic style was the antithesis of his father's swashbuckling art. The quiet and sometimes leanness of his art with a sense of nostalgia seems almost like a reaction against his father's blood-and-thunder approach.

Rather than showing action and drama, Andrew's work often had no people in it. He painted images that were silent and sometimes dissolute like a barn door ajar, tracks in the mud or snow, an abandoned weathered house and quiet snowy landscapes. He painted these subjects in watercolor or in a medium abandoned by most artist's centuries ago, egg tempera on panel. For the most part, modern day artists use oil on canvas that long ago replaced tempera.

It seemed as if Wyeth swam against the current of the art world most of his career. He was a Realist when abstract art and other movements dominated the art scene and captured the attention of critics. Yet he was never confused about how he wanted to paint. There were never any dramatic turns in his style or subject matter.

The public has always loved his works. An indication of this is that he was given a large retrospective in 1976 at the Metropolitan Museum of Art in New York, the first time a living American artist had received such an honor. To many his paintings are accessible because they bring them in touch with some imaginary rural past they can relate to. Or perhaps it is because Wyeth's art came to represent middle-class values and ideals that modernism seems to reject.

His reputation with the critics was less secure possibly because his style and subject matter were never even close to what was generally accepted as avant-garde art. Wyeth completely refused to become modern. The critics never thought it was fashionable to practice his type of unyielding Realism. But as the critics usually heaped abuse on his work, the people jammed his exhibitions. The critics think he was a hopelessly sentimental painter of rural scenes. But it is because of that characteristic that he has so many supporters.

Through all the controversy over the quality and originality of his art he was on the cover of Time magazine in 1963 and President Johnson awarded him the Presidential Medal of Freedom. Until the other Andy came along – Andy Warhol – Wyeth and Norman Rockwell were the two most recognized names in American art. One art historian was asked in 1977 to identify the most overrated and underrated artists of the 20th century. He provided one name for both categories: Andrew Wyeth.

Wyeth's most famous painting is *Christina's World* (fig. 12-19). It shows what appears to be a young woman in the midst of a vast expanse of grassland looking at her

12-19. *Christina's World* by Wyeth, 1948, tempera on panel, Museum of Modern Art, New York.

home in the distance. But if you look closely you can see that the girl's arms are thin and deformed. Wyeth was inspired to create the work when he saw Christina crawling across a field while watching from a window in the house. The scene is in Maine. Wyeth had a summer home in the area and was friends with Christina Olson and her younger brother whom he had used as subjects in other paintings.

It is impossible to tell her age in the painting or what she looks like. But that adds to the mystery of the piece. In turns out that Christina was 55 at the time and she suffered from a degenerative muscular disorder for the past 20 years, perhaps polio, which made it impossible for her to walk. Although Christina was the inspiration for the painting, she was not the primary model. Her head and torso were modeled after Wyeth's wife Betsy.

This is an example of the type of realism where we do not always at first see the true identity of what is in the picture. But beyond the surface there can be facts that are not clearly visible.

The scene evokes a sense of sorrow as the woman drags herself through the field toward her home in the distance. The house is isolated against a cloudless sky. Its shingles are warped and the paint dulled by age. It is a somber and remote scene. Yet the public was fascinated by it. Maybe it is because they saw a dignity in Christina's struggle up

the hill. This was a woman who was fiercely independent. In real life she refused a wheelchair and struggled to be on her own rather than to be dependent on anyone. Perhaps the viewers sense that.

Another appeal of the piece is how Wyeth painted each blade of grass and individual stands of her hair remarkably realistically. That is partly because it was painted in egg tempera, a medium that allows for great control and lends itself to that type of realistic detail. This makes the piece particularly distinctive because it was done at a time when Abstract Expressionism was taking over the American art scene with its thick, oil paint and swirling nonrepresentational brushstrokes.

Whatever the reason, the painting has always been beloved by the public even as it has been loathed by the critics. It has been a source of personal inspiration to many, so much so that the farmland in the scene has been named a National Historical Landmark.

Wyeth's paintings have been criticized because he did not move on with his style and subject matter. He just presents "the facts" as he sees them. He was a good technician and drew well but his subject matter is thought by some to be repetitive. The critics will ask, how many farms do you want to look at? But Wyeth disagreed. He felt his work was steeped in subject matter. In fact he said, "I think the great weakness in most of my work is subject matter. There's too much of it." When this writer looks at *Christina's World* he has to agree with Wyeth. It is easy to see that the painting is steeped in subject matter.

The painting has become an iconic image in American art, more so than many of the most heralded paintings. In addition to the beauty of the piece it has an emotional appeal to millions of Americans. Obviously it had that same type of appeal to Wyeth. A short distance from Christina's house in Maine is a cemetery where she, her brother and Andrew Wyeth are buried. In an interview with his granddaughter Victoria, she said he wanted to be buried near Christina and the spot where he painted *Christina's World.*

Norman Rockwell (1894-1978) was the consummate American illustrator. He painted his first cover for *The Saturday Evening Post* in 1916 and went on to publish a total of 321 original covers over 47 years. He then painted illustrations for *Look* magazine for ten years. Portraits of presi-

WHAT IS EGG TEMPERA?

Andrew Wyeth was a modern practitioner of the medium of egg tempera. It was the primary method of painting until the 16th century. Given that many of those ancient paintings are still in very good condition, it is obviously an extremely long lasting paint. Many of the Renaissance masterpieces such as Botticello's Birth of Venus were executed in egg tempera. But it was gradually replaced by more versatile oil paint at the start of the 1500s.

Egg tempera is composed of egg yolk, powdered pigment and distilled water. The egg yoke serves as a binder that holds the pigment together. It can only be used for a single painting session because it thickens and becomes difficult to paint with. It is not a flexible paint and must be used on panel. If applied to canvas it can crack and pieces of the paint will fall off. It is applied thinly in layers and is fast drying so it has to be applied in a very precise manner. It is not suitable for thick application like impasto painting. Regarding tempera, Wyeth said:

"There is something incredibly lasting about the material, like an Egyptian Mummy...I love the quality of the color...They aren't artificial. I like to pick the colors up and hold them in my fingers. Tempera is something with which I build – like building in great layers the way the earth itself built. Tempera is not the medium for swiftness."

dents were another one of his specialties painting Presidents Eisenhower, Kennedy, Johnson and Nixon. Rockwell received the Presidential Medal of Freedom in 1977, the United State's highest civilian honor.

His success can be tied to how he could tap into the nostalgia of people during times that seemed kinder and simpler. He was able to demonstrate a careful appreciation for everyday American scenes and the warmth of small-town life in particular. He filled his canvases with the details and nuances of people in everyday life.

Rockwell knew that the world around him was not a perfect place so he consciously chose to paint only the ideal aspects of it. His was a cheerful America. The filmmaker Steven Spielberg who is a major collector of his works said, "Rockwell painted the American dream better than anyone."

He painted America as he saw it in his day. It was an America painted in the ideal. For some, it is a time they would like to return to. There are doctors who make house calls, students who remember their teacher's birthdays and citizens who stand up at town meetings and speak their mind without getting booed down. He painted the qualities one would like to see society return to like compassion, decency, integrity and fair play and he did it with a sense of whimsy. His niche was visual storytelling about decent people.

Rockwell was part of the healing process for Americans during and coming out of the Great Depression and in the war years of the 1940s. His subjects were imaginary so he composed fictions about everyday life. Although his art was beloved by the public it suffered at the hands of the critics. They were more interested in the new art movements like Surrealism, Abstract Expressionism and Pop Art.

He was accused of painting an artificial and idealistic view of America. True, he omitted reference to ugliness and social hardship. But hadn't that been part of art tradition going back to the Renaissance. The masters of the 15th and 16th century often painted religious figures in an idealized way and attractive scenes from Greek mythology. Is Rockwell's work any more unrealistic than some of the highly regarded images painted hundreds of years earlier?

Rockwell's status among the critics has improved over the years. There have been important exhibitions since his death. His painting *Breaking Home Ties* sold for a record $15.4 million in 2006. Nevertheless, quite a few critics still see his subject matter as overly sentimentalized portrayals of American life. The word "tacky" can sometimes appear and there are those that dismiss him as a serious painter because, as an illustrator, his work was dominated by commercial interests. If the word "Rockwellesque" is applied to a contemporary artist that is not usually meant as a compliment.

It is difficult to select a single painting out of Rockwell's oeuvre to show and comment on. His most famous scenes dealt with the *Four Freedoms: Freedom of Speech, Freedom of Worship, Freedom from Fear* and *Freedom from Want*. They were painted in 1943. He translated abstract concepts of freedom into four scenes of everyday American life. The paintings went on tour and became an integral part of the massive U.S. bond drive during WWII.

In the 1960s Rockwell's work turned more serious and he began to address some of the country's concerns in his illustrations for *Look* magazine. So another artistic piece to consider presenting in this book is *The Problem We All Live With*. It addresses the issue of school racial integration and shows a little African-American schoolgirl escorted by white federal marshals walking past a wall smeared with the juice of a thrown tomato.

However, these paintings represent departures from the style that Rockwell pursued through most of his career. Consequently, I selected *Doctor and Doll* (fig. 12-20) because it is more representative of his career-long style. Rockwell said, "I guess I am a storyteller and, although this may not be the highest form of art, it is what I love to do." It shows in this painting.

Doctor and Doll is an example of how the artist celebrated goodness and innocence. Also, it demonstrates how he found his subjects among the ordinary and wholesome people in the community where he lived. There is a feeling of warmth and a sense of humor in the piece and even a gush of sentimentality that is vintage Rockwell.

The models are Dr. Donald Campbell and his granddaughter. Dr. Campbell posed for Rockwell a number of times. He was the town doctor in Stockbridge, Massachusetts where Rockwell lived. The piece has been reproduced more than any other in a variety of Rockwell collectables.

The little girl has brought her doll to the doctor's office perhaps for a check-up. Her expression is one of concern. She may be worried that something isn't right. She has braved the wet and cold to bring her "baby" in for the doctor's care. She has long stockings and wears a wool skirt, a jacket, scarf, mittens and a red beret. It must be wet outside because she has rubber shoes. Rockwell has spared no details in constructing the scene.

The anxious little girl knows the ritual of an office examination because she has been there with her mother. She has removed the doll's dress tuck-

ing it under her arm. The image is one of perfect trust. She trusts the doctor because she has been through such a medical ritual. He accepts her trust and willingly becomes part of the child's play by listening intently to a heart that isn't there. This is a frozen moment that was intended to remind the viewer of simple and innocent goodness. Today, it reminds some of us of a past era of American medicine.

There are a lot of other details in this little drama. The doctor sits in a somewhat battered Windsor chair with a worn armrest. There is a roll-top desk with medical books and candle sticks on top of it. The doctor's large black bag sits by his feet suggesting he makes house calls. He has shinny black shoes and wears a white shirt with cuffs and gold cuff links and a cravat. He has a signet ring on the

12-20. *Doctor and Doll* by Rockwell, 1929, oil on canvas, Norman Rockwell Museum, Stockbridge, Massachusetts.

little figure of his right hand. His eyes almost twinkle as he plays out his role. This is a good man. It is the image of a country doctor long in practice of comfortable but modest means.

Renoir once said, "I believe a painting should be joyful and pretty, yes pretty. There are enough unpleasant things in life without the need to manufacture more." Matisse expressed the same viewpoint when he wrote, "I dream of art devoid of troubling or depressing subject matter." Essentially, Rockwell is saying the same thing as those masters. He once stated his artistic goal, "The view of life I communicate in my pictures excludes the sordid and ugly. I paint life as I would like it to be." Can there be any doubt that he did this in *Doctor and Doll*.

Edward Hopper (1882-1967) had an artistic style that evokes feelings of loneliness and solitude whether he was painting urban scenes or New England landscapes and seascapes. Even when he painted places where there should be people like hotels, restaurants, theaters and offices they were usually semi-deserted. His cityscapes often showed deserted streets at night.

Hopper studied under Robert Henri from 1900 to 1906, one of the fathers of American Realism and a leader of the Ashcan school. He described him as, "the most influential teacher I had." Hopper exhibited at the famous Armory Show in New York in 1913 but his work received little attention. He turned to commercial illustration for the next ten years to support himself. But he came to detest illustration.

He was quiet and introverted. Perhaps the loneliness, melancholy and sense of isolation embodied in his art came from his distant personality and his reclusive life style. His wife of 44 years Jo commented, "Sometimes talking to Edward is just like dropping a stone in the well except that it doesn't thump when it hits bottom."

Robert Henri told his students, "It isn't the subject that counts but what you feel about it." Apparently, Hopper took his advice and expressed his feelings in his paintings. When asked about the profound loneliness and lack of communication in his works he responded, "It's probably a reflection of my own, if I may say, loneliness. I don't know. It could the whole human condition."

His works rarely show action. He relies on bold contrasts of light and shadow to create a mood in his paintings. They seem to combine incompatible qualities. They look very modern because of their bleakness and simplicity. Yet, they are full of nostalgia as they evoke memories of America in the past. It is this nostalgic aspect of his work that has resulted in comparisons being made with his contemporary Norman Rockwell.

Hopper rejected the comparison because he considered his works to be less illustrative, more obscure in their meaning and definitely not sentimental. Also, he regretted that, for a period, he had to support himself as a commercial illustrator while Rockwell thrived in the profession. In fact, other than their nostalgic aspects, the artists could hardly be more far apart in their styles. Hopper's somewhat bleak view of life is in strong contrast to Rockwell's optimistic, wholesome and good natured images of daily life.

His art was already a success when he painted his best known work *Nighthawks* (fig. 12-21). It is another one of

12-21. *Nighthawks* by Hopper, 1942, oil on canvas, Art Institute of Chicago, Chicago.

12-22. *House* by the Railroad Tracks by Hopper, 1925, oil on canvas, Museum of Modern Art, New York.

those iconic images of 20th century American art. The painting shows three customers sitting at the counter of an all-night diner and a waiter inside the counter. The location is probably Greenwich Village in New York where Hopper lived most of his life. On the surface, this would seem to be a rather mundane subject matter to paint but not the way Hopper presents it.

The viewpoint is something you would expect in the cinema. We view the scene from the sidewalk as if we are approaching the diner. Hopper eliminates any reference to an entrance. By doing this he heightens the sense of isolation of those inside. It is as if he has imprisoned them. The harsh light in the diner isolates it from the dark outside. It also calls attention to the fact that there is no interaction among any of the people. There is a sense of eerie stillness.

The mood is the real subject of the painting. It is one of solitude and all-embracing loneliness. Hopper denied that he purposely tried to create scenes of isolation and emptiness. But he did acknowledge that with *Nighthawks*, "unconsciously, probably, I was painting the loneliness of a large city."

Hopper's interests lay more in the play of light than in human subjects. The bright light of the diner has the yellowish cast of fluorescent bulbs. Fluorescent lighting had just come

into use in the early 1940s. The moody contrast of light that spills out of the large plate-glass windows contrasts with the darkness outside. It creates an air of menace in the big city linking the scene to film noir, an American film movement that featured stories of urban crime and moral corruption.

The light from the diner spills out onto the sidewalk and there is even enough of it to partially illuminate the brownstones on the other side of the street. An unseen street lamp allows us to see the image of a lonely cash register in a shop window. The sign above the diner advertises Phillies cigars. The seamless glass of the diner window forms a wedge with the horizontal lines of the diner that give the illusion of the bow of a ship moving toward the solid row of buildings.

Inside the diner, the woman's red blouse and lipstick make her stand out. The model is Jo, Hopper's wife. She plays the role of all the female characters in his paintings. Hopper models for the two male characters in fedora hats at the counter. They all seem as cold as the fluorescent light that bathes them. We see all the specifics you would expect in a diner: coffee mugs, napkin holders and salt and pepper shakers. There are cherry wood counter tops and surrounding stools. We can imagine that the tops probably spin.

There is a lot of mystery surrounding the painting. The anonymous and uncommunicative night owls seem as remote from the viewer as they are from one another. We sense there is a story here or maybe it is just that we would like there to be one. We want to know who they are and why they are there so late at night. Is the diner a scene out of a gangster movie or is it a safe haven in the big city?

Even the title is mysterious. It evokes something menacing and carries tension with it. Most likely it simply refers to someone who habitually is out late at night like a night owl. But Jo, Hopper's wife, named the piece. In her notes about it she made a reference to the beak-shaped nose of the man at the counter. Hopper himself added mystery when he said, "*Nighthawks* has more to do with the possibility of predators in the night than loneliness."

There have been comparisons made between the work of Hopper and de Chirico. It is true that loneliness and melancholy are common themes with the two. But the difference is that de Chirico tries to make the unreal seem real while Hopper's scenes are concrete and familiar to us. What about the artist's legacy? The interest in his works has grown over the years and Hopper's approach of simplified pictorial form did have an impact on the Pop Art movement.

The artist did not just create moods of loneliness and isolation when he painted scenes with people in them like *Nighthawks*. He did it with vacant landscapes and homes such as *House by the Railroad Tracks* (fig. 12-22.). This piece may look like just a portrait of a house but it is much more than that. Hopper always insisted that he never purposely painted emotionally expressive scenes. They were just factual representations. But in his hands supposedly factual representations can generate a lot of feeling.

It is a bright cloudless day. The sunlight illuminates the old Victorian mansion casting deep shadows on it. On a day like this you would think there would be some activity but there is none. There is an eerie sense of stillness that is heightened by the train tracks where there is a total lack of movement. The once grand Victorian mansion appears deserted. It looks like an emblem of the past.

Perhaps that is all Hopper intended to paint. Perhaps historians have gone too far in searching for meaning in the painting when there really is none. But there seems to be something going on beneath the portrait of a house. The railroad in the 1920s was a sign of progress and an important agent of rapid change in modern life. Yet, this scene is remarkably still and silent even with the railroad present.

It appears in this painting that Hopper has found little to celebrate in the urbanization of America. Industrialization brought with it mass migration of the rural population to the cities. Hopper is using the railroad as a metaphor for the change to an industrialized society. For many this meant progress but for others it meant abandonment and decline. The forsaken once grand structure shown in the painting stands for that decline.

The tone is one of melancholy and sadness because we see that the splendor of the building has disintegrated and it will soon be in ruins. Some parts of the small towns will be lost forever. But we as the viewer are separated from this. Hopper uses a pictorial design of a straight horizontal railroad track to separate us from the picture space.

The canvas was acquired in 1930 by the fledgling Museum of Modern Art. It was the first painting in the museum's collection. In 1960, Alfred Hitchcock chose Hopper's house as the model for the dwelling of Norman Bates and his mother in the movie *Psycho*.

POP ART
Witty Celebrations of Commercialism and the Consumer Society

In part, Pop Art was a reaction against Abstract Expressionism. Its emergence was linked to the prosperity of the post WWII era and the emphasis on a consumer society. Pop Art focused on producing images of everyday objects like Campbell Soup cans, flags, advertisements, comic strips and even famous people.

The artists reacted against the psychology of Abstract Expressionism and its emphasis on the instantaneous human response as being the source of creativity. They saw this as being over-intense and pretentious. In some regards, it had similarities with Dada given its emphasis on common objects and images. But it was also divorced from Dada in that it did not have destructive and satirical impulses. It was certainly not "anti-everything" as was Dada.

The artists wanted to bring art back to the popular material realities of the everyday life of modern culture (hence the use of "pop" in the movement's name). Thus, the name Pop Art refers not so much to the type of art itself but to the culture it represents.

Since ordinary people derived so much pleasure from advertising, mass-produced products, comics and movie stars, these were the types of things the Pop artists focused on. They celebrated materialism and consumerism. The movement put art into terms of everyday contemporary life. In the process, it eliminated the distinction between the commercial arts and fine arts.

The Pop Art movement began in Britain in the early 1950s and spread to the U.S. in the late 1950s. It occurred during the consumer boom and coincided with the spread of pop music globally and the growing importance of the youth culture. Hence, it could be considered brash, fun and a movement that was contrary to the artistic establishment.

Jasper Johns (b1930) features immediately recognizable images in his art. Technically, he is not a Pop artist per se. His art is distinct from the classic Pop Art movement of the 1960s. What he and Robert Rauschenberg did was to form a bridge between Abstract Expressionism and Pop Art.

Johns was influenced by the ideas of the Dadaists. In particular, he was interested in the "readymades" of Duch-

12-23. *Three Flags* by Johns, 1958, encaustic on canvas, Whitney Museum of American Art, New York.

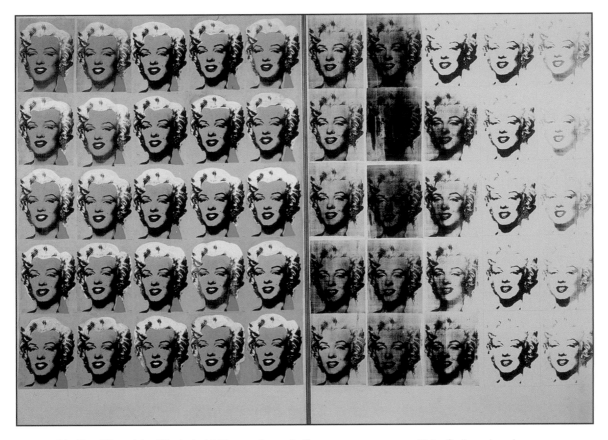

12-24. *Marilyn Diptych* by Warhol, 1962, acrylic and silk screen on canvas, Tate Gallery, London.

amp like his bottle racks, bicycle wheels and urinals that challenged the idea of what was art. But Johns differs in one important respect, he did not use "found objects" as the subject for his paintings. Instead, he sought out "found images" like the American flag, numbers and targets. It was his representation of such familiar images that inspired Pop artists.

Johns' familiar images provided a contrast to the obscurity of the Abstract Expressionist works that had no images. His subjects were ordinary but they were immediately recognizable. In terms of brushstrokes, his approach was far removed from the emotional gestures of the Abstract Expressionists.

The American flag is typical of Johns' use of everyday imagery in his early works in the mid-to late 1950s. As he explained, they are "things the mind already knows." His choice of subjects was, in part, a reaction to Abstract Expressionism where paintings had no recognizable content. He started with *Flags* in 1954-55 which he said he painted after having a dream of the American flag. He followed with *White Flag* in 1955 and eventually *Three Flags* (fig. 12-23) in 1958.

His single flag images did not show depth. They are not patriotic works. He did not paint a wavy, windblown banner on a flagpole. Instead, he eliminated its conventional patriotic meaning. The flag was simply the start of the widespread subject matter that Johns would pursue in later paintings of targets, letters, numbers and even beer cans.

In *Three Flags*, each American flag is displayed flat, lying one on top of another. Each of the tiered flags is diminished in scale by about 25% from the one behind. Thus, they project outward, directly opposite standard perspective. Note there are only 48 stars on the smallest flag that is closest to the viewer and the only one you can see entirely. But remember, Johns painted it in 1958, before Alaska and Hawaii became states.

Johns combined the unique subject matter of his works with serious concern for the craft of the painting process. He did not work with oil paint. Instead, he used encaustic, also called hot wax painting. It is a technique where the artist mixes beeswax with color pigments. The result is a thick surface on the canvas that is clearly visible.

In *Three Flags*, the smallest painting stretches five inches above the largest painting beneath it. The final result is that it almost seems like a sculpture piece mounted on the wall. It makes the viewer consider the question, "what is a painting?"

Johns' art has continued to evolve throughout his career making him one of the defining artists of the 20th century. He continued to paint popular and simple subjects claiming there was no hidden symbolic meaning in his work. He has tried to highlight the difference and the similarities between a real object and its painted image.

In the 1960s, while continuing to paint objects, he introduced sculptural elements into his work by attaching ordinary things like beer cans and light bulbs to the canvases. He cast sculptures of commonplace things like two Ballantine Ale cans called *Painted Bronze*. In the 1970s, he produced near monochrome paintings composed of parallel lines that he called "crosshatchings." His paintings in the 1980s had figurative and autobiographical elements. His artwork continues to evolve.

Andy Warhol (1928-1987) was an artist who personified Pop Art. He had a successful ten year career in New York in magazine illustration and advertising. The experience served him well as he became a leader in the Pop Art movement. He was so successful that he became known as the "Pope of Pop." In the 1960s, he began to make paintings of brand named products such as Campbell Soup cans and leading celebrities such as Marilyn Monroe and Elizabeth Taylor. He used the silkscreen printing technique in producing images.

His silkscreen process was a perfect means for Warhol to call attention to commercialism and the mass production society. His earliest images were hand drawn but he soon progressed to photographically derived silkscreen images. This was his defining niche. In a departure from tradition, he removed all traces of the artist's "hand" in his works with his photo-realistic mass production printmaking technique. In the process, he could mimic advertising overload and mass consumerism.

In a society where there was a glut of information on mass produced products and people were bombarded over and over by banal images of products on TV or in print, Warhol believed there was a role for what some believed to be tasteless art. In this way, he was making his own commentary on contemporary society and culture.

His approach was totally different from earlier artists like Monet who painted the same subject in a series over and over (e.g. haystacks) in order to show slight shifts in light and color over time. But Warhol's reproductions of Liz or Jackie and 32 Campbell Soup cans were nothing like that. They are about sameness, not change. There would be the same product or same face produced over and over again in the same size. In that way, they imitate mass advertising. His artwork is a spoof about image overload in a culture saturated by the media.

Warhol took his silkscreen mass production process one step further in mimicking culture. He purposely avoided cleaning up the imperfections in the print process. The blotches of ink and general graininess of the finished product were there to call attention to the pervasiveness of the mass marketing culture and its tastelessness.

Warhol's studio was appropriately named "The Factory." He mass produced vast numbers of printed works there. He could reproduce images endlessly. In the process, he was overturning the historical approach to art where uniqueness was highly valued.

His *Marilyn Diptych* (fig. 12-24) exemplifies everything he was trying to accomplish. It was the first work in which Warhol used the assembly-line technique of silk-screening photographic images onto a canvas. The work was completed just after Marilyn Monroe's death in August, 1962. The photograph used was a publicity photo from the movie *Niagara*.

There are fifty images of the actress in five rows that resemble a filmstrip acknowledging her movie star status. The repetition also signals the mass production of images of stars. The diptych style is taken from medieval paintings of Christian saints. Thus, Warhol is pointing to the saint-like status that society attaches to famous people and movie stars in particular. The contrast of brightly colored images and those in black and white that become blurred and faded as the printing ink runs out symbolizes Marilyn's life and death and, perhaps, the ephemeral nature of fame.

12-25. *Drowning Girl* by Lichtenstein, 1963, oil on canvas, Museum of Modern Art, New York. Credit to the estate of Roy Lichtenstein.

Roy Lichtenstein (1923-1997) was a master of parody and became a breath of fresh air in the art world. In the 1950s, he fluctuated between Cubism and Abstract Expressionism. In the early 1960s, he began to paint his first Pop Art images focusing on comic-strip subjects and painted them in the same style only on a much larger scale. He enjoyed quick success. Lichtenstein had his first show at the Leo Castelli gallery in New York in 1962 and it sold out before the show opened.

His format was fixed with black outlines, bold colors, thought bubbles and sometimes including boxed words such as "WHAAM." All of these techniques were copied from comic books. The use of Benday dots to represent certain colors was a Lichtenstein trademark. Benday dots are a printing process which combines two or more different small, colored dots to create another color. In the 1950s and 1960s, comic books used the process to inexpensively create secondary colors such as flesh tones. He made them by applying paint with a toothbrush through a perforated screen.

Although Lichtenstein's format remained fixed, what changes is his subject matter. It evolved in comic strip im-

agery to an exploration of different subjects like interpreting modern art styles. Nevertheless, his mode of expression remained that of the comic book.

All along, Lichtenstein's approach was one of parody. He never took himself seriously. Although his work was quickly and enthusiastically accepted by galleries and collectors, Lichtenstein remarked, "It was hard to get a painting that is despicable enough so that no one would hang it. . . Everybody was hanging everything. It was almost acceptable to hang a dripping paint rag, everybody was accustomed to this. The one thing everyone hated was commercial art; apparently they didn't hate that enough, either."

Lichtenstein's comic strip style paintings continue to meet heavy demand in the auction market. In May 2012, his *Sleeping Girl* sold at Sotheby's in New York for $45 million, a record for the artist.

Two of his favorite topics that he loved to parody came from war and romance comic books. One of his most celebrated transcribed sounds from a war theme was "WHAAM!" It showed a fighter pilot exalting in the destruction of a rival combatant. A favorite from the brokenhearted lover theme portrayed in romance comics was *Drowning Girl* (fig. 12-25).

Drowning Girl is one of the most beloved works identified with Pop Art partly because it makes a humorous statement about drama in the culture of the day. The situation presented is ridiculous with someone preferring death by drowning because of feelings of spite. Yet, it is not too far removed from what one might expect to find in the romantic dramatic presentations at the time.

Lichtenstein lifted the piece from *Run for Love* published by DC Comics in 1962. But he made alterations to the original version. In the original illustration, the drowning girl's boyfriend appears in the background, clinging to a capsized boat. But Lichtenstein shows the girl alone surrounded by a stormy wave. He also slightly changed the words in her thought bubble and the boyfriend's name from Mel to Brad.

By making such adjustments, Lichtenstein was able to tighten and strengthen the final image. Yet, his painting retained the sense of the cartoon plot it drew upon. Also, by blowing up the image to a huge size and focusing entirely on the drowning girl, he was able to place all the emphasis on the ridiculousness of the melodrama. All of this was in total contrast to the emotion of the "action paintings" of the Abstract Expressionists. It is another example of how art history progresses and the final one offered in this book.

IMAGES

12-1. *The Woman with the Hat* by Matisse, 1905, oil on canvas, San Francisco Museum of Modern Art, San Francisco

12-2. *The Joy of Life* by Matisse, 1906, oil on canvas, Barnes Foundation, Philadelphia.

12-3. *The Dance II* by Matisse, 1910, oil on canvas, The Hermitage Museum, St. Petersburg, Russia.

12-4. *The Dance* by Matisse, 1932-1933, oil on canvas, Barnes Foundation, Philadelphia.

12-5. *Chapel of the Rosary* by Matisse, 1947-1951, Vence, France.

12-6. *Mountains at Collioure* by Derain, 1905, oil on canvas, National Gallery of Art, Washington, D.C.

12-7. *Boats in the Port of Collioure* by Derain, 1905, oil on canvas, private collection.

12-8. *Nude Descending a Staircase, No. 2* by Duchamp, 1912, oil on canvas, Philadelphia Museum of Art.

12-9. *Fountain* by Duchamp, 1917, porcelain plumbing fixture, Philadelphia Museum of Art, Philadelphia.

12-10. *The Green Violinist* by Chagall, 1923-1924, oil on canvas, Guggenheim Museum, New York.

12-11. *Ariadne* by de Chirico, 1913, oil and graphite on canvas, Metropolitan Museum of Art, New York.

12-12. *The Persistence of Memory* by Dali, 1931, oil on canvas, Museum of Modern Art, New York.

12-13. *Forest and Dove* by Ernst, 1927, oil on canvas, Tate Gallery, London.

12-14. *The Son of Man* by Magritte, 1964, oil on canvas, private collection.

12-15. *No. 5, 1948* by Pollock, 1948, oil on fiberboard, private collection.

12-16. *Woman I* by de Kooning, 1950-52, oil on canvas, Museum of Modern Art, New York.

12-17. *Red Studio* by Matisse, 1911, oil on canvas, Museum of Modern Art, New York.

12-18. *Homage to Matisse* by Rothko, 1954, oil on canvas, private collection.

12-19. *Christina's World* by Wyeth, 1948, tempera on panel, Museum of Modern Art, New York.

12-20. *Doctor and Doll* by Rockwell, 1929, oil on canvas, Norman Rockwell Museum, Stockbridge, Massachusetts.

12-21. *Nighthawks* by Hopper, 1942, oil on canvas, Art Institute of Chicago, Chicago.

12-22. *House by the Railroad Tracks* by Hopper, 1925, oil on canvas, Museum of Modern Art, New York.

12-23. *Three Flags* by Johns, 1958, encaustic on canvas, Whitney Museum of American Art, New York.

12-24. *Marilyn Diptych* by Warhol, 1962, acrylic and silk screen on canvas, Tate Gallery, London.

12-25. *Drowning Girl* by Lichtenstein, 1963, oil on canvas, Museum of Modern Art, New York. Credit to the estate of Roy Lichtenstein.